ABOUT THE AUTHOR

Nick Redfern is the author of thirty books on UFOs, Bigfoot, lake monsters, the Abominable Snowman, and Hollywood scandals, including *Monster Files*; *Monster Diary*; *Memoirs of a Monster Hunter*; *Celebrity Secrets*; *There's Something in the Woods*; *Contactees*; *Final Events*; *The Real Men in Black*; *The NASA Conspiracies*; *Science Fiction Secrets*; *On the Trail of the Saucer Spies*; *Strange Secrets*; and, with fellow Texas-based researcher and author Ken Gerhard, *Monsters of Texas*. He has appeared on more than seventy TV shows, including *Fox News*; the BBC's *Out of This World*; the SyFy Channel's *Proof Positive*; the Space Channel's *Fields of Fear*; the History Channel's *Monster Quest*, *America's Book of Secrets*, *Ancient Aliens*, and *UFO Hunters*; Science's *The Unexplained Files*; the National Geographic Channel's *Paranatural*; and MSNBC's *Countdown with Keith Olbermann*. Originally from the UK, Nick lives on the fringes of Dallas, Texas.

ALSO FROM VISIBLE INK PRESS

Alien Mysteries, Conspiracies, and Cover-Ups
by Kevin D. Randle
ISBN: 978-1-57859-418-4

Angels A to Z, 2nd edition by Evelyn Dorothy Oliver and James R Lewis
ISBN: 978-1-57859-212-8

Armageddon Now: The End of the World A to Z
by Jim Willis and Barbara Willis
ISBN: 978-1-57859-168-8

The Astrology Book: The Encyclopedia of Heavenly Influences, 2nd edition by James R Lewis
ISBN: 978-1-57859-144-2

Conspiracies and Secret Societies: The Complete Dossier, 2nd edition
by Brad Steiger and Sherry Hansen Steiger
ISBN: 978-1-57859-368-2

The Dream Encyclopedia, 2nd edition
by James R Lewis and Evelyn Dorothy Oliver
ISBN: 978-1-57859-216-6

The Encyclopedia of Religious Phenomena
by J. Gordon Melton
ISBN: 978-1-57859-209-8

The Fortune-Telling Book: The Encyclopedia of Divination and Soothsaying
by Raymond Buckland
ISBN: 978-1-57859-147-3

Hidden Realms, Lost Civilizations, and Beings from Other Worlds
by Jerome Clark
ISBN: 978-1-57859-175-6

Real Aliens, Space Beings, and Creatures from Other Worlds,
by Brad Steiger and Sherry Hansen Steiger
ISBN: 978-1-57859-333-0

Real Encounters, Different Dimensions, and Otherworldly Beings
by Brad Steiger with Sherry Hansen Steiger
ISBN: 978-1-57859-455-9

Real Ghosts, Restless Spirits, and Haunted Places, 2nd edition
by Brad Steiger
ISBN: 978-1-57859-401-6

Real Miracles, Divine Intervention, and Feats of Incredible Survival
by Brad Steiger and Sherry Hansen Steiger
ISBN: 978-1-57859-214-2

Real Monsters, Gruesome Critters, and Beasts from the Darkside
by Brad Steiger and Sherry Hansen Steiger
ISBN: 978-1-57859-220-3

Real Vampires, Night Stalkers, and Creatures from the Darkside
by Brad Steiger
ISBN: 978-1-57859-255-5

Real Zombies, the Living Dead, and Creatures of the Apocalypse,
by Brad Steiger
ISBN: 978-1-57859-296-8

The Religion Book: Places, Prophets, Saints, and Seers
by Jim Willis
ISBN: 978-1-57859-151-0

The Spirit Book: The Encyclopedia of Clairvoyance, Channeling, and Spirit Communication
by Raymond Buckland
ISBN: 978-1-57859-172-5

Unexplained! Strange Sightings, Incredible Occurrences, and Puzzling Physical Phenomena, 3rd edition
by Jerome Clark
ISBN: 978-1-57859-344-6

The Vampire Book: The Encyclopedia of the Undead, 3rd edition
by J. Gordon Melton
ISBN: 978-1-57859-281-4

The Werewolf Book: The Encyclopedia of Shape-Shifting Beings, 2nd edition
by Brad Steiger
ISBN: 978-1-57859-367-5

The Witch Book: The Encyclopedia of Witchcraft, Wicca, and Neo-paganism
by Raymond Buckland
ISBN: 978-1-57859-114-5

"Real Nightmares" E-Books by Brad Steiger

Book 1: True and Truly Scary Unexplained Phenomenon

Book 2: The Unexplained Phenomena and Tales of the Unknown

Book 3: Things That Go Bump in the Night

Book 4: Things That Prowl and Growl in the Night

Book 5: Fiends That Want Your Blood

Book 6: Unexpected Visitors and Unwanted Guests

Book 7: Dark and Deadly Demons

Book 8: Phantoms, Apparitions, and Ghosts

Please visit us at visibleinkpress.com.

THE BIGFOOT BOOK
THE ENCYCLOPEDIA OF SASQUATCH, YETI, AND CRYPID PRIMATES

THE BIGFOOT BOOK

Visible Ink Press®
43311 Joy Rd., #414
Canton, MI 48187-2075
Visible Ink Press is a registered trademark of Visible Ink Press LLC.

Most Visible Ink Press books are available at special quantity discounts when purchased in bulk by corporations, organizations, or groups. Customized printings, special imprints, messages, and excerpts can be produced to meet your needs. For more information, contact Special Markets Director, Visible Ink Press, www.visibleink.com, or 734-667-3211.

Managing Editor: Kevin S. Hile
Art Director: Mary Claire Krzewinski
Typesetting: Marco DiVita
Proofreaders: Larry Baker and Aarti Stephens
Indexer: Shoshana Hurwitz
Cover images: Shutterstock.

Library of Congress Cataloging-in-Publication Data

Redfern, Nicholas, 1964-
  The Bigfoot book : the encyclopedia of Sasquatch, yeti, and cryptid primates / by Nick Redfern.
    pages cm
  ISBN 978-1-57859-561-7 (pbk. : alk. paper)
  1. Sasquatch—Encyclopedias. 2. Yeti—Encyclopedias. 3. Monsters—Encyclopedias. 4. Primates—Encyclopedias. I. Title.
  QL89.2.S2R43 2015
  001.944--dc23   2015012595

Printed in the United States of America

10 9 8 7 6 5 4 3 2

THE BIGFOOT BOOK

THE ENCYCLOPEDIA OF SASQUATCH, YETI, AND CRYPTID PRIMATES

Nick Redfern

VISIBLE INK PRESS

Detroit

CONTENTS

PHOTO CREDITS

ACKNOWLEDGMENTS

I would like to offer my sincere thanks to all of the following: my agent, Lisa Hagan, for her fine and much appreciated work; Roger Jänecke, Kevin Hile, and everyone else at Visible Ink Press for being a great company to work for; and Stan Gordon, Richard Freeman, Jonathan Downes, Liz Randall, and Neil Arnold for their contributions.

INTRODUCTION

Bigfoot: it's a controversy-filled word that is instantly recognizable to just about one and all. And, regardless of whether one is a true believer, an open-minded skeptic, a definitive non-believer, or a semi-interested observer of the controversy, pretty much everyone knows what the word implies and describes: a large, hair-covered, ape-style animal that is said to roam and lurk within the mysterious, forested wilds of the United States.

The number of people who claim to have seen a Bigfoot is now in the thousands. The beast has been the subject of big-budget hit movies. Today's world of reality television loves the legendary monster—audience viewing figures make that abundantly clear. It occupies the minds and weekends of monster hunters and creature seekers everywhere, each and every one of them hoping to be the person who finally bags a Bigfoot and, as a result, goes down in history.

But, there's more to Bigfoot than that. In fact, there's far more.

The term "Bigfoot" was created in 1958, when huge, apelike footprints were found in Del Norte County, California. We have a journalist named Andrew Genzoli of the *Humboldt Times* to thank for coming up with the famous, monstrous moniker. It's a fact, however, that giant, lumbering, hair-covered, upright creatures have been encountered in the United States for centuries, and long before "the B word" was even a dim blip on anyone's radar.

Ancient Native American lore tells of the legendary, and sometimes savage, beasts that were as feared as they were revered. Encounters with violent, so-called "wild men" from the deep woods and ice-cold, frozen mountains were regularly reported in the pages of nineteenth century-era American newspapers.

Photographs and film footage—of varying degrees of credibility and clarity—purport to show the elusive animals in action, so to speak. Audio recordings exist of the creature's eerie chatter and bone-chilling screams. Startling witness accounts abound. There are whispers that elements of the U.S. government have the bodies of several Bigfoot on ice, hidden at some Area 51-style, secret installation.

There are claims of a UFO link to Bigfoot. Theorists suggest the reason why we lack a body of a Bigfoot—and the reason for their near-mystifying, overwhelming elusiveness—is because the creatures are the denizens of a vast underworld; animals that spend most of their time living in dark caves and deep caverns, unknown to man, and which extend and spread out for miles underground.

Then there is the matter of the other Bigfoot-like creatures. That's right: while Bigfoot—also known as Sasquatch—is certainly America's most famous unknown ape, it's far from being a solitary monster. Florida is home to the Skunk Ape, for example. Southern Arkansas has the Beast of Boggy Creek. Texas is the domain of the Lake Worth Monster. In fact, the creature has been seen in every single U.S. state (aside from Hawaii, which is not surprising, given that it is not connected to the mainland).

Bigfoot and somewhat similar creatures extend widely, and wildly, outside of the United States, too. Australia can boast of its own equivalent to Bigfoot. Its name is the Yowie. And, just like Bigfoot, the Yowie is a towering, hairy, man-like animal, one best avoided at all costs. In China there are reports of a similar creature: the Yeren. The Abominable Snowman—also known as the Yeti—forages on, and around, the vast Himalayas of Tibet. The cold, harsh landscape of Russia is the territory of the Almasty. Even the people of England and Scotland claim to have such legendary beasts in their midst. The names of the animals of the U.K. include the Big Grey Man, the Beast of Bolam, and the Man-Monkey.

Moving on—and demonstrating that there are very few places on the planet that do not appear to be home to cryptid apes and monkeys of very strange kinds—there is the Orang-pendek of Sumatra, India's Mandeburung, the Kikomba of the Congo, Pakistan's Bar-manu, the Hibagon of Japan, Cuba's Guije, and the Mumulou of the Solomon Islands. And that's just barely touching upon what amounts to a vast, monstrous menagerie of Bigfoot-like creatures seen across pretty much the entirety of the globe.

With all that said, it's now time for you to join me on a strange, wild, and sometimes terrifying journey into Bigfoot's A to Z world. It's a world dominated by the man-monster in reality, in history, in folklore, in movies and entertainment, in the domain of conspiracy theory, in the world of the supernatural, and, quite possibly, in the wild, dark woods of just about here, there, and everywhere....

The Abominable Snowman (1957 movie)

From the mid-1950s to the early 1970s, the U.K.'s Hammer Film Productions ruled the roost in the field of cinematic horror. Hammer's movies were in sharp contrast to the fairly tame black-and-white monster productions of the 1930s and 1940s, which starred the likes of Boris Karloff, Bela Lugosi, and Lon Chaney Jr. *The Curse of Frankenstein* (1957), *Dracula* (1958), *The Plague of the Zombies* (1966) and *Quatermass and the Pit* (1967) are just four of dozens of productions from Hammer that became firm favorites with horror fans.

There was one movie from Hammer that, although highly acclaimed, was in sharp contrast to what viewers generally expected of Hammer. Its title was *The Abominable Snowman* (which was released in the United States as *The Abominable Snowman of the Himalayas*).

Made in 1957, *The Abominable Snowman* is very different from just about everything else ever put out by Hammer at its height. First, it was shot in moody black and white—at a time when Hammer was known for its spectacular full-color horrors. Second, there is not a single, heaving breast in sight (never mind a pair of them). Third, the movie relies far more on atmosphere than it does on-screen horror and blood. Nevertheless, it does contain one key, Hammer ingredient: its star, actor Peter Cushing, who, along with Christopher Lee, helped to steer the movie company to massive success.

The movie was based upon a story called "The Creature" which was penned in 1955 by screenwriter Nigel Kneale and that was turned into a show for the BBC in the same year. Unfortunately, there are no surviving copies of "The Creature"; they were destroyed or lost decades ago. Kneale was also the brains behind Hammer's *Quatermass and the Pit*—a movie that focused on stories of spectral ape-men manifesting in and around the London Underground rail system. One might be forgiven for assuming that a Hammer movie that dealt with the legendary Yeti of the Himalayas would be filled with crazed creatures, severed bodies, and blood-soaked mountains. Not so. In fact, the exact opposite is what Hammer chose to deliver to its fans in the 1961 BBC television series *Quatermass and the Pit*.

The Abominable Snowman primarily focuses on the character of Dr. John Rollason, played by Cushing—a role that he had portrayed in the BBC's 1955 version of Kneale's story. Rollason is on an expedition to the Himalayas with his wife, Helen, and a colleague, Peter Fox. Although the reason for the expedition is chiefly to study the area's plant life, Rollason has a secret fascination for the tales of the Abominable Snowman—something that is increased when the trio visits the monastery of a Tibetan lama (played by Arnold Marlé, who appeared in a number of horror movies in that era, including *The Snake Woman* and *The Man Who Could Cheat Death*) and meets

Forrest Tucker (right) and Robert Brown manage to capture a huge, hairy creature in the 1957 Hammer film, *The Abominable Snowman.*

with a certain Tom Friend—an American monster-hunter who is determined to catch or kill a Yeti and present it to the world, for one and all to see.

Although most cinema-goers of the day were not aware of it, the character of Tom Friend (played by Forrest Tucker, who, one year later, starred in another creature-feature: *The Strange World of Planet* X) was clearly based upon a real-life Yeti seeker named Tom Slick. A somewhat enigmatic character, Slick could be accurately described as a combination of Indiana Jones and James Bond: born into big money in San Antonio, Texas, Slick traveled the world in hot pursuit of strange creatures and did secret contract work for the CIA, using his Yeti-hunting expeditions as a convenient way to spy on the Chinese (see "Slick, Tom, and the Yeti").

In *The Abominable Snowman*, Friend and Rollason join forces and head off in search of the beast—much to the concern of Helen (actress Maureen Connell). The duo is not alone: also along for the adventure is a guide named Kusang; Ed Shelley, who is an expert animal-tracker; and a photographer, Andrew McNee. They head up to the Himalayas, determined to solve the mystery of the Abominable Snowman, once and for all. They get far more than they ever could have bargained for.

As the movie progresses we see disaster upon disaster and calamity upon calamity beset the team. McNee is badly injured when he steps on one of Shelley's steel-traps. It gets even worse when Kusang flees the area, McNee falls to his death, and Shelley dies, too—but not before Friend actually manages to shoot and kill a Yeti. It quickly becomes clear to the viewer that there is something deeply mysterious about the dead creature. It's clearly not just a dumb, brutish animal; in fact, quite the opposite. Hammer demonstrates a great deal of careful and thoughtful restraint by not showing us any up-close and personal images of the slain beast, instead allowing our imaginations to ponder on what it really looks like.

The comrades of the dead animal are understandably enraged and they set out to ensure that the group—or, rather, Friend, specifically—kills no more of their kind. Being a Hammer movie, one might be forgiven for thinking the Yetis systematically tear the adventurers apart, one by one, limb by limb. No so: the creatures are actually highly evolved beings and possess the ability to manipulate the human mind. Voices in the head on the part of Rollason and Friend are put down to a lack of sufficient oxygen at such high altitudes, when they are actually due to something much stranger: the Yetis. A radio that is broken, but which still broadcasts, at least in the mind of Rollason, tells them to leave the area and return to civilization—as in immediately. And the howling cries of dead Shelley plague Friend and, ultimately, lure him to his death in a massive avalanche. Eventually, there is only Rollason left.

As the movie closes, and in a particularly eerie scene, we see two immense Yetis reclaim the body of their dead comrade, one of which looms over petrified Rollason. Finally, we get to see its face: far from looking like a giant, brutish ape, the beast has an uncanny human-like appearance, its staring eyes exuding an ancient wisdom and intelligence. They are creatures that are determined to stay hidden, at least until the time comes when the human race exterminates itself—after which they can reclaim the world that, perhaps thousands of years ago, was once theirs. Rollason is allowed to go free, is reunited with Helen and Peter, and decides to hide the truth of what really occurred on the fierce mountain.

It's unfortunate that, despite its intelligent and thought-provoking storyline, *The Abominable Snowman* was not a big hit. It is filled with subtlety, restraint, and monsters that aren't actually monstrous, after all. That's not, unfortunately, what the viewers wanted. Hammer got the message: in 1958, *The Revenge of Frankenstein* surfaced. In 1959, *The Mummy* followed. And, as the 1960s began, *The Curse of the Werewolf* was unleashed. All three were filled with color, blood, and babes. Restraint was nowhere to be seen.

Alabama's Ape-Man

The origins of Anniston, Alabama, date back to the height of the American Civil War. It's a city, in Calhoun County, of around 23,000 and it is dominated by the huge, picturesque Blue Ridge Mountains. In 1938, however, it was something else that was dominating the people of Anniston: a strange and distinctly out-of-place ape. It was in April 1938 that sightings began, in the Choccolocco Valley, of what was quickly referred to by the local press as "a hairy wild man."

Rather notably, the beast—which apparently had a hatred for dogs—would walk on two legs, but then drop down onto all fours when it wanted to run, which was usually when it was being pursued by frightened and enraged gun-toting locals. Most fascinating of all, the beast was not always spotted alone. On several occasions witnesses reported seeing it with a female and "a child," both displaying thick coats of hair and both having the ability to move around in bipedal and quadruped mode, as the mood took them.

Interestingly, one of the main reasons why the Alabama wild things were not killed was because those hunting them backed off from taking definitive shots because of the eerie human-like appearances of the mysterious beasts. One of those was Rex Biddle, a farmer, who told Sheriff W. P. Cotton that the beast "was about five feet tall and had hair all over his body. He was unclothed. Despite his beastlike appearance, his nose and other features indicated he was human."

> In the 1960s, the Choccolocco Valley was once again the site of mysterious activity. It was May 1969 when sightings of the "Choccolocco Monster" began.

Rather tellingly, Biddle admitted that the human qualities the beast possessed had a major bearing on his decision not to kill it, despite the fact that he could have done exactly that, if he had wanted to. He said to the press: "I didn't know whether that would be legal." It's an interesting question!

In the 1960s, the Choccolocco Valley was once again the site of mysterious activity. It was May 1969 when sightings of the "Choccolocco Monster" began. It was a strange beast, to be sure: upright, white, and with what looked like a cow's head on its shoulders! It turns out that is exactly what it was: on Halloween 2001, a local man, Neal Williamson, admitted that he—just fifteen years old at the time—was the monster. He roamed around the area late at night, sometimes wearing a bed sheet and on other occasions a long coat. And he would top it all off by holding a cow's skull above his head! He was fortunate enough not to get his head blown off his shoulders by frightened locals.

"Back then, you didn't have nothing to do, really. You didn't have computers. You just had to create your own fun," said Williamson.

Alexander the Great and Hairy, Wild Men

For evidence that people have reported seeing large, hairy hominids not just in relatively recent years, but in the distant past, too, we have to turn our attention to the writings of a Greek historian by the name of Arrian, who was born in 86 C.E., and whose origins were in the ancient Turkish city of Nicomedia. As well as being a noted military figure and philosopher, he was also the author of *Anabasis Alexandri* (in English, *The Anabis of Alexander*), an insightful and lengthy piece of work that chronicles the life, career, and military campaigns of Alexander the Great.

The mighty, ancient tome was translated into English in the 1930s by E. Iliff Robson, who, in 1929, wrote a book titled *Alexander the Great* and who was fluent in many languages. One particular section of *The Anabis of Alexander* tells of an astonishing confrontation between Alexander the Great's army and what can best be described as a weapon-wielding Sasquatch! Chapter 23 of Book VIII describes the adventures and exploits of Admiral Nearchus on the Indus River. Robson's translation on this aspect of the story states, in part:

> Leaving the outlets of the Arabis they coasted along the territory of the Oretians, and anchored at Pagala, after a voyage of two hundred states, near a breaking sea; but they were able all the same to cast anchor. The crews rode out the seas in their vessels, though a few went in search of water, and procured it. Next day they sailed to dawn, and after making four hundred and thirty stades [a Greek measure of length that is about 150 to 200 feet long] they put in towards evening at Cabana, and moored on a desert shore.

It wasn't long before a violent confrontation occurred between Nearchus's soldiers and native people who, it later transpired, didn't sound like people, after all. Robson's translation continues:

The Macedonian king Alexander the Great (356–323 B.C.E.) is said to have encountered an armed Sasquatch during his military conquests.

Thence they set sail and progressed with a favoring wind; and after a passage of five hundred stades they anchored by a torrent, which was called Tomerus. There was a lagoon at the mouths of the river, and the depressions near the bank were inhabited by natives in stifling cabins. These seeing the convoy sailing along the shore stood ready to repel any who should attempt a landing.

Robson writes of the "natives":

They carried thick spears, about six cubits long; these had no iron tip, but the same result was obtained by hardening the point with fire. They were in number about six hundred. Nearchus observed these evidently standing firm and drawn up in order, and ordered the ships to hold back within range, so that their missiles might reach the shore; for the natives' spears, which looked stalwart, were good for close fighting, but had no terrors against a volley.

The translation expands on what happened next:

Then Nearchus took the lightest and lightest-armed troops, such as were also the best swimmers, and bade the swim off as soon as the word was given. Their orders were that, as soon as any swimmer found bottom, he should await his mate, and not attack the natives till they had their formation three deep; but then they were to raise their battle cry and charge at the double.

Was there once an army of spear-wielding Sasquatch-like beasts that Alexander the Great encountered? According to accounts of the time, that was exactly what the Macedonians saw.

On the word, those detailed for this service dived from the ships into the sea, and swam smartly, and took up their formation in orderly manner, and having made a phalanx, charged, raising, for their part, their battle cry to the God of War, and those on shipboard raised the cry along with them; and arrows and missiles from the engines were hurled against the natives.

The account suggests the battle was a particularly violent one:

They, astounded at the flash of the armor, and the swiftness of the charge, and attacked by showers of arrows and missiles, half naked as they were, never stopped to resist but gave way. Some were killed in flight; others were captured; but some escaped into the hills.

Now, we come to the most significant part of the translation:

Those captured were hairy, not only their heads but the rest of their bodies; their nails were rather like beasts' claws; they used their nails as if they were iron tools; with these they tore asunder their fishes, and even the less solid kinds of wood; everything else they cleft with sharp stones; for iron they did not possess. For clothing they wore skins of animals, some even the thick skins of the larger fishes.

To this day, the origin and identity of these hairy, spear-using man-beasts remain unknown. To be sure, the idea of an army of Sasquatch-style beasts, ready and willing to fight off the invading hordes sounds bizarre and unlikely in the extreme. And, yet, that appears to have been exactly what happened. If the story was not a fabrication or a distortion of the facts—and there is nothing to suggest it was either—then clearly these beasts were far more intelligent than so many cryptid apes, such as the Almasty of Russia. Remember that as well as using spears to combat Nearchus's forces, the creatures also lived in huts.

Monster-soldiers in ancient India? Just maybe, yes.

Almasty Expedition

In the summer of 2008, a team from the British-based Centre for Fortean Zoology (CFZ)—which investigates reports of unknown animals on a full-time basis—headed off to Russia in search of its equivalent of Bigfoot, the Almasty. Just a couple of weeks after the investigation was over, I had the opportunity to speak with one of the team-members, Adam Davies, the author of the book *Extreme Expeditions* and someone with a fascination for the Almasty. It was an interview that went as follows:

Nick Redfern [NR]: Adam, what was it that got you involved in the Almasty expedition?

Adam Davies [AD]: In the first instance, I went down to the CFZ's *Weird Weekend* conference last year. Jon Downes [the director of the CFZ] invited me to do a talk on the Congo. I had been there looking for the Mokèlé-mbèmbé [a long-necked, lake monster-type, creature]. While I was [at the *Weird Weekend*], I saw [sic] a talk by Grigoriy Panchenko on the Almasty. I was really impressed by his depth of knowledge and research. So, I considered the idea of going. I then found out that Richard Freeman, [the zoological director] from the CFZ, was also planning on going. So, Richard said: "Why don't we join forces and go?" It made sense, so that's what we did.

NR: And, for you, what were the big revelations and developments?

AD: As far as what we achieved, my view has always been that anything you find in field-research has to be independently, scientifically analyzed. That's the ultimate test for all of these things. Now, in terms of evidence, what we got first was eyewitness reports—some more credible than others. Some of it was anecdotes from old guys—such as an old guy telling us over his cognac how his dad saw an Almasty. But that's not much in the way of evidential value.

The Centre for Fortean Zoology in England holds an annual "Weird Weekend," which is touted as the largest gathering of English-speaking cryptozoologists, parapsychologists, ufologists, and folklorists. In this 2005 photo, speakers for the conference are shown, including CFZ director Jon Downes (back row with beard, long hair, and glasses).

We spoke with a direct eyewitness, a guy called Tahir, who had seen an Almasty in 2005. His sheep were being disturbed, and he had seen this large Almasty watching him. So, we got a lot of good eyewitnesses of that sort. Interestingly, many of them described the Almasty as having this conical-shaped head, rather like the Yeti.

We also found some evidence that can be analyzed properly: skull fragments and some strange bones found in caves. But what really excited me was in a place where there had been Almasty activity Dave Archer [one of the team-members] found a nest—what looked like a nest, and it didn't appear to have been made by any animal that I could recognize that was indigenous to the area. And we found around twenty hairs there which can be analyzed. And we can get the DNA extracted from them, too.

But even if the evidence isn't conclusive, I've still learned a lot more about the Almasty, and about its numbers: there's probably between 100 and 300 of them in the area we were investigating. And if we went back again, we'd have a better opportunity. There's nothing wrong with armchair research, but my job is as a field researcher. That's what I'm into; and finding any evidence that can be analyzed scientifically. And I think the scientific community is starting to listen to us more now. There's a huge upswing in interest in cryptozoology.

There was also a case we investigated of an Almasty seen at a barn in the area—which happened to be the scene of a triple-murder. You could hear the jackals howling, and it was well spooky. In 2005, a couple of shepherds had been sleeping in the barn. One had come outside, and there was an Almasty going for their food. It didn't attack the shepherd, but physically moved him from one place to another.

On the first night when I was doing the stake-out with Dave, one of the Russians, Anatoly, claimed to have heard an Almasty calling; but I didn't hear that. But on the second night, me and Richard were doing a stake-out. On this occasion, both of us heard movement across the front of the barn, and we saw a large shape. You can imagine the adrenalin rush: we both rushed out, but the thing had gone. So, I can't say I saw an Almasty; and it's important to stress that. But there was a lot of interest and evidence around that barn—which was in the mountains.

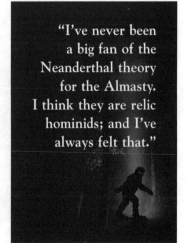

"I've never been a big fan of the Neanderthal theory for the Almasty. I think they are relic hominids; and I've always felt that."

NR: And based on the investigation, have you reached a personal conclusion as to what you think the Almasty is or isn't?

AD: I'd say I have a tentative conclusion; but that's partly going to be decided by what we get back from the analysis. I'd say there are certainly more of them than in, say, Mongolia. But it's a different sort of hominid. If there are pockets of something that were related to *Homo erectus*, and that got pushed into remote areas and isolated geographically, then I don't see anything inconsistent with having pockets in different places that might mutate differently.

I really don't think it's Neanderthal in any way though. I've never been a big fan of the Neanderthal theory for the Almasty. I think they are relic hominids; and I've always felt that. For example, I've never seen any evidence of them using tools or fire. And even if there was cultural recession, it wouldn't be to the extent where there would be no use of fire or tools at all, if these were Neanderthals. And if they were using fire, particularly at night, you'd see it in the mountains. But there's no evidence of that.

NR: Any final words on the expedition?

AD: It was definitely worth going. But, of course, it's always going to be difficult to prove anything in just two or three weeks. But the team as a whole, I think, would say we have learned a lot about the Almasty and its movements. And I would like to go back at some point.

Unfortunately, the DNA samples collected by the Centre for Fortean Zoology did not prove the existence of the Almasty. Nevertheless, the CFZ's quest to resolve the matter of the Almasty continues unabated, with further expeditions in the planning stage.

Almasty of Russia

It should not come as a surprise to learn that the vast wildernesses, thick forests, and massive mountain ranges of Russia are home to Bigfoot-type beasts. They are known to the local folk as Almasty. For some researchers, the creatures are unknown apes. For others, they are nothing less than still-surviving pockets of Neanderthals. Both scenarios are amazing, in terms of their potential implications. But, whatever the true identity of the Almasty, there's very little doubt that it exists. The sheer number of witness reports makes that very clear. The Almasty is a creature that has a long history attached to it, something that also adds to the likelihood of it being a genuine animal of very ancient proportions.

What is very possibly the earliest report on record of the hairy, giant Almasty came from one Hans Schiltberger. In the 1400s, Schiltberger was taken prisoner by Turkish forces and was, as David Hatcher Childress noted, placed "in the retinue of a Mongol prince named Egidi."

In the fifteenth century, traveler Hans Schiltberger learned of savage creatures which lived in the Tien Shan Mountains, shown here, between Mongolia and Russia.

It transpires that upon his return to Europe in 1427, Schiltberger began writing a book about his experiences with the Turks. It was a book that surfaced in 1430 and which is made highly notable by its reference to strange and savage creatures that he was told of, and which were said to live high in the Tien Shan Mountains of Mongolia, which border upon Russia. Schiltberger's translated words state:

The inhabitants say that beyond the mountains is the beginning of a wasteland which lies at the edge of the earth. No one can survive there because the desert is populated by so many snakes and tigers. In the mountains themselves live wild people, who have nothing in common with other human beings. A pelt covers the entire body of these creatures. Only the hands and face are free of hair. They run around in the hills like animals and eat foliage and grass and whatever else they can find. The lord of the territory made Egidi a present of a couple of forest people, a man and a woman. They had been caught in the wilderness, together with three untamed horses the size of asses and all sorts of other animals which are not found in German lands and which I cannot put a name to.

Evidently, the creatures still exist: in August 2005, a Ukranian newspaper, *Situation*, described a then-recent encounter with no less than an entire group of Almasty on the Demedzhi Plateau, in the Crimea. The newspaper reported that "Ivan S., 21, and his group of 12 tourists were spending their second day camped on the plateau. The kids went to sleep early, while the adults stayed up a while. 'The night was very bright with a full moon,' reported Crimean ufologist Anton A. Anfalov."

Anfalov continued: "Ivan's assistant, Sasha, and several of the men left the campsite to use the bathroom and when they returned, they looked terrified and trembled with fear. It was then everyone heard a frightful growl near the camp."

Suddenly, the group was confronted by a pack of huge, approximately eight feet tall, "naked, hairy men."

According to Sasha:

There were three creatures. And they were about six meters away from us. The hair humanoids were 2 to 2.5 meters in height. Their true height was hard to estimate because they were all crouched down and balancing themselves on their fists, like large apes. All three were growling at us. Their faces were very hairy, almost without wrinkles, and their eyes were not shiny at all. Their heads were set or positioned very low, as if they had no necks. On their backs they had something like humps on their spine. The creatures were very aggressive. Everyone was scared and the beasts' growls awoke the children who became hysterical.

Situation had more to say:

The standoff lasted for about 45 minutes. Finally the creatures turned and bounded away with strange ape-like bouncing leaps. The campers spent a sleepless night around their fire. In the morning Ivan and the others searched the ground around their camp, but due to a dense layer of fallen leaves the creatures didn't leave any distinct prints.

Kosmopoisk founder Vadim Chernobrov is a ufologist and researcher who has asserted that evidence for the Yeti has been discovered in the Kirov region of Russia.

Moving on to 2009, in April of that year the Russian newspaper, *Pravda*, revealed—in an article titled "Russian Scientists Use Google Maps to Find Yeti" that there had been more than twenty sightings of Almasty by hunters in the forests of Kemerovo. Not only that, there were reports of strange, large footprints having been discovered in the depths of nearby caves: "Scientists found two identical Yeti footprints. One of them was left on the rock and it dates back 5,000 years ago, and the other footprint which was left not long ago was found at the bottom of the cave."

Pravda spoke with one of the unnamed scientists, who said:

They are absolutely identical. Five thousand years ago Yetis settled down in this cave and now their descendants are still living here. The conditions in the cave are suitable for Yeti. The cave defends them from rains, snow and wind. There is also a lake in the middle of the cave where Yetis can find clean water.

The newspaper added:

Unfortunately, the scientists did not manage to see Yetis that time. They say their snowmobiles were too noisy and Yetis had to hide somewhere in the forests. However, the scientists say they managed to reach their main goal—they got the proof that Yetis are living there. A new expedition to the site will be arranged this summer.

But that was not all, as *Pravda* made very clear:

Members of the Kosmopoisk association have returned from an expedition to Russia's Kirov Region where they searched for a Bigfoot that allegedly lived in that region. Kosmopoisk leader Vadim Chernobrov says the expedition has discovered a den occupied by a mysterious giant and an underground passage dug obviously not by a human.

Ivan Konovalov was a forest warden who, for thirty years, worked in the Kirov region. He told of his 1985 encounter with an Almasty:

It was snowing on the day when I was walking along the fir wood and suddenly heard snap of twigs. I turned around and saw an awesome creature covered with dark hair that was much taller than me. It smelt strongly. The beast leant against a pine tree and started bending it down to the ground.

The tree was rather thick, but it cracked under the creature's burden. Then the creature started breaking the tree against the knee. Its hands were as thick and long as its legs. Quite [all] of a sudden, the creature felt something and turned its "face" to me. I saw two black eyes and the impression at the bottom of the eyes deeply impressed me. I still remember the look of the eyes. Then the creature flung the tree and quickly left. But I stood thunderstruck and could not move a finger. (*See also* "Zana and the Half-Human Controversy.")

Altered States (1980 movie)

A 1980 movie based on Paddy Chayefsky's novel of the same name, *Altered States* brought to the fore the acting skills of William Hurt, who took on the lead role of Dr. Edward Jessup. Hurt's solid, believable performance is added to by the fact that not only was he the star, but it was also his very first cinematic appearance. The film also stars Blair Brown (who appeared in, among many other titles, a 1973 television version of Bram Stoker's *Dracula*) and Bob Balaban, who had a leading role in 1977's *Close Encounters of the Third Kind*. And, in one of those "blink and you'll miss it" roles, a very young Drew Barrymore pops up.

The storyline of *Altered States* is an engaging and strange one. Hurt's character—the aforementioned Dr. Jessup—is a university professor who, although his primary area of expertise is schizophrenia, has a fascination for the subject of altered states of mind, hence the title of the movie. And we are talking about extremely altered states of mind.

As well as starting a relationship with, and ultimately marrying, Brown's character of Emily, Jessup begins to spend more and more time addressing the ways and means by which so-called isolation tanks—sensory-deprivation environments, for wont of a different term—can open the human mind to profoundly unusual experiences.

During the course of his research, Jessup and a colleague travel to Mexico, where, having gained the trust of a local tribe in the mountains, he takes part in a ritual involving the ingestion of *Amanita muscaria*, a psychoactive mushroom that can have radical effects on the human mind, and which has been a staple part of ancient ceremonies since time immemorial, particularly those of a shamanic nature.

After having ingested a spoonful of a soup-like cocktail derived from the mushroom, Jessup experiences a series of spectacular and traumatic visions that radically alter his mindset and lead him to believe that the answers to the origins of life can be found by placing the mind into a profoundly skewed state. Despite warnings from Emily, and also from his friends and colleagues, Jessup decides to take things a step further. As well as taking his mushroom-derived trips, he spends more and more time in the university's isolation tank. And that's where things go very wrong.

At first, Jessup has incredible visions of the earliest humans—proto-apes—roaming the ancient landscape of the earth an untold number of millions of years ago. As Jessup ups the ante even further, something terrifying happens: not only does his mind regress to the distant past, but his body does likewise.

Jessup's body spontaneously mutates: his throat transforms into the throat of something akin to a gorilla—which temporarily prevents him from speaking. His hands and feet take on ape-like appearances. His forehead becomes prominent and primitive-looking. Fortunately, the mutations do not last and Jessup returns to his original self; at least, for a while. As Jessup continues to go where no one has gone before—and, arguably, never should go—he transforms into nothing less than an approximately five-foot-tall ape-man. In his savage state, Jessup breaks out of the tank and races wildly around the university late at night, attacking two staff members, and finally ending his violent spree in a local zoo.

Altered States continues with Jessup struggling to retain his humanity (both mentally and physically) and keep the ape-man at bay, and it does so in a fashion that leads to a satisfying conclusion. It is a cautionary movie about what can happen when the mind takes a trip down avenues that can be as amazing as they are dark, disturbing, and terror-filled.

Amomongo

See: Philippines' Hairy Dwarfs

Ancestral Memories of Giant Apes

"What I saw at Bolam in January 2003 was a very real phenomenon. But whether it had any objective reality outside of my own experience, I'm not sure. But there were several of us who saw this thing at once. I'm fairly convinced that what I saw was a para-psychological phenomenon, rather than a flesh-and-blood one," says Jonathan Downes (*see* "Bolam Lake").

Downes explains his experience:

What I believe is a theory that Richard Freeman [the zoological director of the Centre for Fortean Zoology] and I came up with years ago. Actually, he came up with it first. Richard noticed that wherever he went on an expedition, the same types of mystery animal were being reported.

As just one of many examples, he was in Thailand in 2000 and came back telling me that, as well as the Naga—this giant snake he was looking for, and which is analogous to the western dragon, and perhaps lake-monsters as well—there were sightings of a Bigfoot-type of hairy beast, a large and mysterious golden cat, and a large winged thing [author's note: the Garuda, a bird-man from Indo-Chinese legend that is akin to the Japanese Tengu], very much like the Mothman of Point Pleasant, West Virginia. Everywhere you go, there is what Richard calls a "global template" for monsters.

And, me and Richard have looked into this very deeply, and you basically have got the same types of paranormal mystery animals reported all over the world, and in nearly each and every culture. There are the big, hairy, ape-like creatures. You have the little, hairy, ape-like creatures. You have phantom black dogs, phantom big cats, dragons and lake-monsters, and you have the large, flying things. So, we were looking for a unifying theory behind all this.

And it's now that we come to the heart of that unifying theory:

Richard and me have concluded that you have to go back to when the human race was a bunch of a couple of thousand, small, hairy creatures walking around on the plains of East Africa. And every man, woman and child on the planet is descended from these same, little, hairy creatures. And, at that time, there would have been a lot of things that would have scared the hell out of them, and which they would have been in mortal danger from, such as large, wild hunting dogs, and big cats of that era.

They may even have been in dire danger from their own relatives, such as the smaller, stronger, hairy men, and the larger, and now-extinct, primitive, giant apes. They would have also been in danger from crocodiles and possibly very large birds, too, which the fossil record shows did exist—*very* large. All of these things would have provoked a "fight or flight" response in our ancestors. And all of these types of creatures are present in today's world as mystery animals.

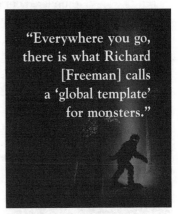

"Everywhere you go, there is what Richard [Freeman] calls a 'global template' for monsters."

Richard and I believe the memories of these creatures, and our ancestors' experiences with them, and fear of them, have become hardwired into our subconscious as a kind of fossil memory. And when I say "our," I mean everyone. It's in all of us, whether we know it or not. And that, under certain circumstances, something can make your brain reboot to that primitive state, and perhaps create images of those primitive creatures our ancestors lived in fear of.

This is, we believe, in much the same way as when your computer reboots it first goes back to its most primitive state, no matter how many programs you might be running when it crashes and needs to reboot. And, we think that when this happens to the human brain, you can experience one of those archetypal, primal fears, in the form of a dragon, a big cat, a black dog, and even the large hairy man-beast, Bigfoot.

A fascinating theory, certainly, but what might make the human brain reboot in the fashion that Downes describes? Once again, he has some specific theories and ideas with which Freeman accords:

The human brain is, basically, an incredibly sophisticated computer. And one of the things that make computers reboot from time to time is an electrical power surge. I think it's very interesting that in places where the British Bigfoot has been seen, such as at Bolam Lake, we had an enormous amount of electrical equipment fail on us. This was equipment that was tested in Devon before we left, and even on the day before I had my encounter, and it all worked perfectly—until we got to the lake. The idea of power-failures in Fortean situations goes back to John Keel, et al., and is very well known.

We also found there were strange magnetic anomalies at the lake, too. And when we got back to Devon we found there were veins of magnetic iron-ore underneath that very part of the country. And we're wondering if these weird magnetic anomalies, caused by perfectly natural phenomena, can affect, or interfere with, the human brain, and cause it to reboot to that most primitive stage, and those very primitive, fossil memories—as me and Richard call them—of all these various types of archetypal creatures in cryptozoology, and you can experience one of these great primal fears. In my case, at Bolam, it was in the form of a large ape-like animal.

But, what of the so-called Bigfoot teepees found at Bolam? Some might say that these are evidence of the presence of a tangible, living entity, rather than one that thundered out of the depths of some form of inherited memory. Downes feels that this issue is a definitive red-herring that actually has only served to muddy the waters:

I've always found the whole "Bigfoot Teepee" thing dodgy as hell. I'll give you an example. Just recently, we bought a chainsaw, as there are places in the garden—the trees—that haven't been pruned in years. And there are bits and places where the branches have grown together in what look like quite a complicated way. This is in my little garden in Woolsery. You've got trees and branches doing odd things. And, it is things like this that mean I've never been impressed by the Bigfoot Teepees. I think they are purely natural phenomena and nothing to do with Bigfoot—in Britain or anywhere.

"And we're wondering if these weird magnetic anomalies, caused by perfectly natural phenomena, can affect, or interfere with, the human brain, and cause it to reboot to that most primitive stage...."

Getting back to the issue of rebooting Bigfoot, Downes is careful to point out the following:

Now, we admit it's not a theory that can explain everything, because some of the world's man-beasts, such as the Yeti and Orang-Pendek, are flesh and blood. Some of the Bigfoot sightings are; some aren't. But, for the ones in Britain, they aren't flesh and blood; so, both Richard and I feel that this theory is a very viable one to explain why people might see Bigfoot in Britain.

And what I can also tell you is that what I saw at Bolam had a great effect on my cerebral cortex. Endorphins are the pleasure chemicals released during sex. There are two substances which mimic the production of endorphins. They are chocolate and opiates, both of which I have abused in my time. And I know the effect that drugs can have on the central nervous system. And, after whatever it was I saw in Bolam in 2003, my body was immediately flooded with endorphins. That is a sign, to me, that something was playing around with my cerebral cortex.

As for the other people at Bolam who saw the same thing I saw, well, maybe, we can externalize these images—like a Tulpa. Or, quite possibly, the expectation of us all potentially seeing a British Bigfoot at Bolam made us all hardwire the very same image when we were all rebooted.

Antelope Mountains' Hairy Man

Demonstrating that beasts such as Sasquatch are not the creations of twentieth-century moveimakers and hoaxers are the surprisingly large number of newspaper accounts on the subject that date from the 1800s. A classic, and perfect, example, is a fascinating feature that appeared in the pages of the Sacramento, California-based *Daily Union* newspaper on November 1, 1879. It was titled, very appropriately, "A STRANGE CREATURE: Two Hunters Chased by a Wild Man in the Antelope Mountains"

> William Shegan, who came in from Antelope Valley last evening with a load of produce, tells a *Leader* reporter a very strange and startling story of the experience of two men who were hunting in Antelope Valley last week. He says that Peter Simons and John Gore had been out all day hunting ducks and such other game as they came in their way, and as evening came on they took a short cut across the mountains on their way back to the ranch. The mountain over which the trail led them was a very rugged one—in fact, the wildest place in the Antelope range of mountains—and a few years ago used to be infested with the larger species of wild animals.

The story continued that as the pair made their careful way around what was described as a "large chasm," they heard a strange, animalistic noise coming from the vicinity of a nearby cliff face. As they looked to see the source of the chatter, both men were shocked by the sight of a large, hairy, manlike animal that sprung from behind the cliff face and headed towards the mountains with "the speed of the wind."

Realizing that the beast was something distinctly out of the ordinary, and being hunters, Simons and Gore did what hunters do best of all: they opened fire on the animal. Gore managed to clip the creature on one of its arms, which was more than evident when the beast came to a sudden, screaming halt and grabbed its arm, clearly in severe pain. The wild-eyed creature wasn't just in agony, however; it was also enraged to the max: in seconds it charged both men in violent fashion.

Hardly surprising, Simons and Gore didn't try and get a better shot; instead, they dropped their rifles and fled for their lives. It was only due to their ability to outrun the animal that they didn't finish up as the hunted, rather than as the hunters.

The *Daily Union* noted, of this almost-fatal affair, that it did not stand alone. There were additional reports of the creature, and perhaps of others of its savage kind, roaming around:

> Mr. Shegan's story revives a long forgotten but now distinctly-recalled yarn, to the effect that many years ago a lunatic, then a young man, escaped from his keepers in California and gained

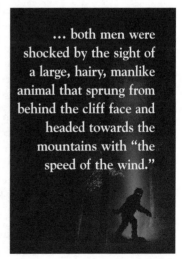

... both men were shocked by the sight of a large, hairy, manlike animal that sprung from behind the cliff face and headed towards the mountains with "the speed of the wind."

the fastness of the Sierra Nevada, where he evaded pursuit, and, it is thought, subsisted on the flesh of small animals killed through some means best known to himself.

Shegan had more to say, too, about additional encounters with the hairy wild things of the woods, as the newspaper noted:

> Several months ago, says Shegan, a strange creature answering the description of the being recently seen, with the exception of the grizzle beard, was discovered by a party of men who were hunting on the mountain some fifteen miles from Antelope, and it is thought that this may be the same. The hunters say they are positive it was no optical illusion, but a genuine wild man, and a very fierce one at that.

It seems to have been much different to a person who had simply descended into a wild lifestyle in the forests, however. That much is evident from the physical description presented in the newspaper: "The creature's arms, they say, were long and hairy, and it looked very much like a full-grown gorilla. They aver that it ran with remarkable swiftness, all the time uttering loud cries, as though in pain and enraged."

Despite assertions that "there is talk of organizing an armed force in Antelope Valley to go in search of this creature," the wild man that came close to taking the lives of a pair of petrified hunters back in 1879 was never identified or caught.

The Ape (1940 movie)

Quite possibly, *The Ape*, a 1940 movie starring horror legend Boris Karloff, is the most bizarre of all the many movies dealing with what could be termed something half-human and half-animal. We're not, however, talking about anything along the lines of ape-men or werewolf-style shape-shifting, however. No: *The Ape* takes a decidedly alternative approach to the matter of monstrous transformation.

Produced by Monogram Pictures, *The Ape* was co-written by Curt Siodmak, who also wrote *The Wolf Man* (1941) and *Frankenstein Meets the Wolf Man* (1943) and penned the screenplay for *I Walked with a Zombie* (1943), among many other horror-themed movies.

Although the plotline is utterly ludicrous, Karloff does his absolute best to make the most out of what is, admittedly, a distinctly odd affair. Karloff's character is the creepy Dr. Bernard Adrian, whose home the local kids throw stones at and who the townsfolk view as being downright sinister. He's a man doing his absolute utmost to cure what is seemingly his one and only patient, a young woman named Frances Clifford (played by Maris Wrixon). She has been wheelchair-bound and paralyzed for years.

Adrian believes he can cure Frances, and restore her to normal health, by injecting her with human spinal fluid. Obtaining large amounts of such fluid, one scarcely needs telling, is hardly the easiest thing to achieve at the best of times, and certainly not in a small-town environment. Fortunately for Adrian, fate sometimes works in a very strange fashion.

A marauding gorilla escapes from a local circus that burns down and soon makes its way to—where else?—the doctor's home. When the beast comes crashing through the window of Adrian's lab, he quickly kills it. Dr. Adrian does not dispose of the body, however. At least, not all of it. What he does do, is to remove the entire hide of the creature, effectively turning it into a "monkey suit" that he can wear, from head to foot that completely camouflages his real identity—although this is not made fully clear to the viewer until the very end of the movie. Adrian is quite clearly a doctor of the "mad scientist" variety, but that doesn't prevent there being a degree of method to his nuttiness.

In his deranged state, and decked out in his gorilla outfit, the doctor prowls around town attacking whoever he can, with the intent of stealing their spinal fluid and curing Frances. Since the whole

Acting legend Boris Karloff starred in the 1940 horror film *The Ape.*

town was plunged into fear when the gorilla escaped from the circus, by adopting the role of the animal, Karloff's character is confident the gorilla will be blamed, and his real identity will remain a secret and all will be well—aside, of course, for those unfortunate souls drained of their spinal fluids.

At the time of filming, Karloff was fifty-two years of age and was in no mood to go gallivanting around the studio in a hot, stifling, ape costume for hours on end. So, while in ape mode, Karloff handed over the reins to Ray "Crash" Corrigan, a muscular stunt man who was quite the regular expert when it came to playing marauding, wild apes. For example, he donned gorilla suits in *Tarzan and His Mate (1934)*, *Captive Wild Woman* (1943), *Nabonga* (1944), *White Pongo* (1945), and *The Monster and the Ape* (also 1945). As an interesting aside, *White Pongo* also starred Maris Wrixon, the unfortunately paralyzed Frances Clifford of *The Ape.*

Inevitably, things don't work out well in the end: at the height of his final attack, the doctor is fatally stabbed. And, mirroring the closing scenes of a typical episode of *Scooby Doo*, he is unmasked and shown not to be a violent, killer gorilla, after all, but the dastardly and certifiably insane Dr. Adrian. There is one bit of good news in this strange story: the doctor's work has ensured that Frances can finally walk again, something that he sees her do just before taking his last breath. Just over an hour of deranged, horror-hokum comes to an end. (*See also* "*White Pongo* [movie, 1945]".)

Ape Canyon

ypically, Bigfoot is not known as a violent creature. There are, however, exceptions to the rule. One classic and disturbing example occurred back in the summer of 1924, in a canyon in the vicinity of Kelso, Washington. As evidence that tales of Bigfoot are not solely limited to the last few decades, the story was reported, at the time, in the pages of the *Oregonian* newspaper. An extract of the salient points reads thus:

> The strangest story to come from the Cascade Mountains was brought to Kelso today by Marion Smith, his son Roy Smith, Fred Beck, Gabe Lefever and John Peterson, who encountered the fabled "mountain devils" or mountain gorillas of Mt. St. Helens this week, shooting one of them and being attacked throughout the night by rock bombardments of the beasts.

The reference to "mountain gorillas" is notable, given that this was decades before Bigfoot—both the name and the beast—became part of popular culture. It demonstrates that a lore and tradition of the hairy giants were already firmly in place. The *Oregonian* continued:

> The men had been prospecting a claim on the Muddy, a branch of the Lewis River about eight miles from Spirit Lake, 46 miles from Castle Rock. They declared that they saw four of the huge animals, which were about 400 pounds and walked erect. Smith and his companions declared that they had seen the tracks of the animals several times in the last six years and Indians have told of the "mountain devils" for 60 years, but none of the animals ever has been seen before.

The night's events were decidedly traumatic, as the newspaper noted:

> Smith met with one of the animals and fired at it with a revolver, he said. Thursday, Fred Beck, it is said, shot one, the body falling over a precipice. That night the animals bombarded the cabin where the men were stopping with showers of rocks, many of them large ones knocking chunks out of the log cabin, according to the prospectors.

Forty-two years later, Bigfoot enthusiast Roger Patterson (*see* "Patterson, Roger, Film of Bigfoot") conducted a question-and-answer session with the by-then elderly Fred Beck, who was happy to talk about his memories of that tumultuous night when Bigfoot went wild. Beck told Patterson:

Ape Canyon, just east of Mount St. Helens in Oregon, is the home of the "mountain devils" or mountain gorillas, according to several witnesses.

I wanna tell you, pretty near all night long they were on that house, try-ing to get in, you know. We kept a shooting. Get up on the house, we'd shoot up through the ceiling at them. Couldn't see them up there; you could hear them up there. My God, they made a noise: sounded like a bunch of horses were running around there.

Beck then turned his attention to a description of the beasts, something that makes it very clear that Beck and company were not dealing with anything so down-to-earth as bears or mountain lions:

They was tall, they looked to me like they was eight feet tall, maybe taller, and they were built like a man, little in the waist, and big shoulders on, and chest, and their necks was kinda what they call bull necks.

Beck, one year later, in 1967, expanded upon the battle of what became known in the Bigfoot research community as "Ape Canyon." He said:

The only time we shot our guns that night was when the crea-tures were attacking our cabin. When they would quiet down for a few minutes, we would quit shooting. I told the rest of the party, that maybe if they saw we were only shooting when they attacked, they might realize we were only defending ourselves.

Ape Canyon, just east of Mount St. Helens in Oregon, is the home of the "mountain devils" or mountain gorillas, according to several witnesses.

We could have had clear shots at them through the opening left by the chinking had we chosen to shoot. We did shoot, howev-er, when they climbed up on our roof. We shot round after round through the roof. We had to brace the hewed-logged door with a long pole taken from the bunk bed. The creatures were pushing against it and the whole door vibrated from the impact. We responded by firing many more rounds through the door.

They pushed against the walls of the cabin as if trying to push the cabin over, but this was pretty much an impossibility, as pre-viously stated the cabin was a sturdy made building. Hank and I did most of the shooting—the rest of the party crowded to the far end of the cabin, guns in their hands. One had a pistol, which still is in my fam-ily's possession, the others clutched their rifles. They seemed stunned and incredulous.

As for how the events came to their close, Beck said:

The attack ended just before daylight. Just as soon as we were sure it was light enough to see, we came cautiously out of the cabin. It was not long before I saw one of the apelike creatures, standing about eighty yards away near the edge of Ape Canyon. I shot three times, and it toppled over the cliff, down into the gorge, some four hundred feet below.

Then Hank said that we should get out of there as soon as possible; and not bother to pack our supplies or equipment out; "After all," he said, "it's better to lose them, than our lives." We were all only too glad to agree. We brought out only that which we could get in our packsacks. We left about two hundred dollars in supplies, powder, and drilling equipment behind.

Today, the violent and almost fatal battle of Ape Canyon remains a classic within Bigfoot lore.

The Ape Man (1943 movie)

Bela Lugosi was a Hungarian-born actor who famously made his name in the world of Hollywood horror in the likes of such movies as *Dracula* (1931), *The Black Cat* (1934), and *Son of Frankenstein* (1939). While Lugosi's performance as Dracula was, and still is, seen as a defining aspect of big-screen, gothic terror, the same cannot be said for all of Lugosi's performances. One of his best-left-forgotten movies is one that has deep relevance to the nature of Bigfoot, and for that reason, and that reason alone, it deserves a mention.

In many respects, the plotline of *The Ape Man*, made in 1943, was a cheap rip-off of *The Ape*, a movie that surfaced three years earlier. And, it must be said, *The Ape* was not a movie that any self-respecting movie-maker should ever want to emulate. Apparently, however, and for unfathomable reasons, that appears to have been exactly what director William Beaudine and producers Sam Katzman and Jack Dietz had in mind. Unfortunately, all that the trio succeeded in doing was creating an inferior version of something else that was inferior to begin with.

In *The Ape Man*, Lugosi's character, Dr. James Brewster, spends most of his time hunkered down in his mad-scientist-style lab, which is hidden in the basement of his creepy, old mansion. In no time, we find that Brewster, an expert in the field of human glands, has transformed himself into something that is half-ape and half-human. His only friend is a large, caged gorilla, for whom the basement is also home. The only time the hairy duo are not in the basement is when (distinct shades of *The Ape*) they are roaming around town at night, slaughtering people for their spinal fluid—the only thing that allows Brewster to return to human form.

Everything inevitably turns to disaster: the doctor is violently killed by the gorilla, as the latter defends the movie's leading lady, Billie Mason (played by Louise Currie), from Lugosi's evil clutches, as his ice-cold character seeks out yet more spinal fluid to help him retain his humanity.

The Ape Man is worth watching from the "so-bad-it-is-good" perspective—but only just barely.

Australian Upright Ape

Those of a skeptical nature very often maintain that unknown hairy hominids are never seen by credible, respectable sources. In reality, however, that is far from the case. A perfect example is the December 1, 1882, affair of Australian naturalist H. J. McCooey. So impressed, and also disturbed, was McCooey by the encounter in his home country that he quickly contacted the *Australian Town and Country Journal*, which published his account the following week. It read:

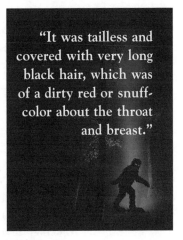

"It was tailless and covered with very long black hair, which was of a dirty red or snuff-color about the throat and breast."

> My attention was attracted by the cries of a number of birds which were pursuing and darting at it…. [It was] partly upright, looking up at the birds above it in the bushes, blinking its eyes and distorting its visage and making a low chattering kind of noise. Being above the animal on a slight elevation and distant from it less than a chain, I had ample opportunity of noting its size and general appearance. I should think that if it were standing perfectly upright it would be nearly 5 ft high.

> It was tailless and covered with very long black hair, which was of a dirty red or snuff-color about the throat and breast. Its eyes, which were small and restless, were partly hidden by matted hair that covered its head. The length of the fore legs and arms seemed to be strikingly out of proportion with the rest of its body, but in all other respects its build seemed to be fairly proportional. It would probably weigh about 8 st [approximately 112 pounds].

> On the whole it was a most uncouth and repulsive looking creature, evidently possessed of prodigious strength, and one which I should not care to come to close quarters with.

Notably, McCooey was not the only person who saw the creature: six workers in nearby Bateman Bay caught sight of it. Of greater significance, there was talk of the skeletal remains of a four-foot-tall ape having been found in the depths of a dark cave, somewhere in the region of Ulladulla, around fourteen miles from where McCooey had his encounter. What became of the remains of the dead beast is unknown to this day—somewhat frustratingly.

Nearly twenty years later, the New South Wales region of Australia was plunged into terror by the presence of an unknown, hairy beast of manlike proportions. The *Mudgee Guardian* recorded the facts:

> During the past few weeks the residents of the "Bar" have been disturbed from their slumbers by noises, resembling at times a person choking, and at others a woman screaming and then crying. These strange cries remained a mystery till Thursday last, when at about 5 pm they were again heard, and shortly afterwards several persons residing in the locality were astonished to see a peculiar animal, five feet high, standing on his two legs, and at the same time brushing away with his claw like hands the long, unkempt looking hair from his eyes.

Notably, the creature was described as having "long white hair," which is similar to a significant number of Bigfoot sightings in the United States (*see* "White Bigfoot") Like so many anomalous apes, this one's reign of terror and torment ended as quickly and as mysteriously as it had begun.

Whatever both this creature and the beast seen in 1882 by H. J. McCooey were, they clearly were not examples of Australia's most famous equivalent of Bigfoot, namely, the huge, hulking Yowie (*see* "Yowie Sightings in Australia"). With that in mind, we are faced with the controversial and amazing prospect of Australia being the home of several kinds of mysterious apes.

Australia's Beast-Men

There is no doubt that Australia's most famous cryptid ape is the Yowie (*see* "Yowie Sightings in Australia"). It resembles Bigfoot in both size and appearance to an incredibly close degree. It stands around seven to ten feet tall and is covered in a thick coat of hair. Far less famous, though no less fascinating than the Yowie, is Australia's Wakki, also known as the Njmbin, the Junjudee, the Waladherahra, as well as many other names, depending on the relevant Aborigine tribe that tells of its existence. Like the giant Yowie, the Wakki is covered in hair and walks upright. It rarely, if ever, however, exceeds five feet in height.

One of the most fascinating accounts of an encounter with a Wakki was reported in the pages of a Sydney, Australia-based newspaper, *The Empire*. The date was April 17, 1871, and the story revolved around the encounter of George Osborne, an employee of the Illawarra Hotel, in Dapto, New South Wales. Osborne's experience was related in the newspaper by himself, in his own, unaltered or edited words:

> On my way from Mr. Matthew Reen's, coming down a range of about a half a mile behind Mr. John Graham's residence, at Avondale, after sunset, my horse was startled at seeing an animal coming down a tree, which I thought at the moment to be an Aboriginal, and when it got to within eight feet of the ground it lost its grip and fell.

> My feelings at that moment were anything but happy, but although my horse was restless I endeavored to get a good glimpse of the animal by following it as it retreated until it disappeared into a gully. It somewhat resembled the shape of a man, according to the following description.

Osborne said of the animal:

> Height, about five feet, slender proportioned, arms long, legs like a human being, only the feet being about eighteen inches long, and shaped like an iguana, with long toes, the muscles of the arms and chest being very well developed, back of the head straight, with the neck and body, but the front face projected forward, with monkey features, every particle of the body except the feet and face was covered with black hair, with a tan colored streak from the neck to the abdomen. While looking at me its eyes and mouth were in motion, after the fashion of a monkey.

> It walked quadruped fashion, but every few paces, it would turn around and look at me following it, supporting the body with two legs and one arm, while the other was placed across the hip. I also noticed that it had no tail.

Osborne concluded with a tantalizing statement that alluded to additional sightings of the creature:

> It appears that two children named Summers saw the same animal or a similar one in the same locality about two years ago, but they say it was then only the size of a boy about thirteen or fourteen years old. Perhaps this was the same animal that Mr. B. Rixton saw at the Cordeaux River about five or six years ago.

Bald Peter Bigfoot

In 1885, what sounds very much like a Bigfoot was stumbled upon in the wilds of Oregon. It fired up the local press, who reported the following:

> Much excitement has been created in the neighborhood of Lebanon, Oregon, recently over the discovery of a wild man in the mountains above that place, who is supposed to be the long lost John Mackentire.

> About four years ago Mackentire, of Lebanon, while out hunting in the mountains east of Albany with another man, mysteriously disappeared and no definite trace of him has ever yet been found. A few days ago a Mr. Fitzgerald and others, while hunting in the vicinity of the butte known as Bald Peter, situated in the Cascades, several miles above any settlement saw a man resembling the long-lost man, entirely destitute of clothing, who had grown as hairy as an animal, and was a complete wild man.

> He was eating the raw flesh of a deer when first seen, and they approached within a few yards before he saw them and fled. Isaac Banty saw this man in the same locality about two years ago. It is believed by many that the unfortunate man who was lost became deranged and has managed to find means of subsistence while wandering about in the mountains, probably finding shelter in some cave. A party of men is being organized to go in search of the man.

The report is notable, since it implies a direct connection between the hair-covered creature and the strange disappearance of a pair of hunters. Of course, it's absurd to imagine that either the vanished John Mackentire, or his colleague, could have sprouted a body of thick hair as a result of living wild in the woods for just a few years. Such a scenario is not just unlikely; it's downright impossible.

This aspect of the story does, however, provoke a very important question: might the hairy animal—and, quite possibly, others of its kind—have been directly responsible for the disappearance of the two men? It might seem an outlandish scenario to suggest, but, let's look at the facts: when the creature was seen, it was "eating the raw flesh of a deer." If the beast had a taste for the meat of animals, it may be the case that it also had a voracious appetite for human meat, too. Mackentire and his friend may not have vanished, after all. They just might have been … devoured and digested.

Basingstoke Ghostly Baboon

In 1913, Elliott O'Donnell—the author of more than fifty acclaimed titles on spooks, spectres, and supernatural mysteries—penned the classic title *Animal Ghosts*, which included in its pages the decades-old story of a phantom baboon-like animal seen in a large, old, imposing country house-style abode near the English town of Basingstoke, Hampshire.

In O'Donnell's own words:

A sister of a well-known author tells me there used to be a house called *The Swallows*, standing in two acres of land, close to a village near Basingstoke. In 1840 a Mr. Bishop of Tring bought the house, which had long stood empty, and we went to live there in 1841. After being there a fortnight two servants gave notice to leave, stating that the place was haunted by a large cat and a big baboon, which they constantly saw stealing down the staircases and passages.

They also testified to hearing sounds as of somebody being strangled, proceeding from an empty attic near where they slept, and of the screams and groans of a number of people being horribly tortured in the cellars just underneath the dairy. On going to see what was the cause of the disturbances, nothing was ever visible. By and by other members of the household began to be harassed by similar manifestations. The news spread through the village, and crowds of people came to the house with lights and sticks, to see if they could witness anything.

One night, at about twelve o'clock, when several of the watchers were stationed on guard in the empty courtyard, they all saw the forms of a huge cat and a baboon rise from the closed grating of the large cellar under the old dairy, rush past them, and disappear in a dark angle of the walls. The same figures were repeatedly seen afterwards by many other persons. Early in

> After being there a fortnight two servants gave notice to leave, stating that the place was haunted by a large cat and a big baboon....

December 1841, Mr. Bishop, hearing fearful screams, accompanied by deep and hoarse jabberings, apparently coming from the top of the house, rushed upstairs, whereupon all was instantly silent, and he could discover nothing.

After that, Mr. Bishop set to work to get rid of the house, and was fortunate enough to find as a purchaser a retired colonel, who was soon, however, scared out of it. This was in 1842; it was soon after pulled down. The ground was used for the erection of cottages; but the hauntings being transferred to them, they were speedily vacated, and no one ever daring to inhabit them, they were eventually demolished, the site on which they stood being converted into allotments.

There were many theories as to the history of "The Swallows"; one being that a highwayman, known as Steeplechase Jock, the son of a Scottish chieftain, had once plied his trade there and murdered many people, whose bodies were supposed to be buried somewhere on or near the premises. He was said to have had a terrible though decidedly unorthodox ending—falling into a vat of boiling tar, a raving madman.

> "... they all saw the forms of a huge cat and a baboon rise from the closed grating of the large cellar under the old dairy, rush past them, and disappear in a dark angle of the walls."

In closing, O'Donnell asked the important questions: "But what were the phantasms of the ape and cat? Were they the earth-bound spirits of the highwayman and his horse, or simply the spirits of two animals? Though either theory is possible, I am inclined to favour the former."

There ends the story. Interestingly, however—and directly connected to O'Donnell's questions about earth-bound spirits returning to our plane of existence in animal form—there existed a deep belief in the English counties of Staffordshire and Shropshire in the nineteenth century that sightings of a creature that became known as the Man-Monkey of the Shropshire Union Canal were linked to the death of a man who had drowned in the waters of the canal shortly before the sightings began, in January 1879 (*see* "Man-Monkey of the Shropshire Union Canal").

Are restless human spirits really returning from the depths of the grave and manifesting in the form of marauding, ghostly monkeys and apes? Just perhaps, they are.

Batutut of Borneo

From Borneo, situated east of Sumatra, home of the cryptid ape known as Orang-Pendek (*see* "Orang-pendek of Sumatra") come stories of an approximately four-and-a-half-foot-tall ape-man referred to as the Batutut. Like so many other man-beasts, this one is covered in hair. There is, however, one intriguing difference: the Batutut sports a noticeable, thick mane of hair that runs down the back of its head, not unlike that of a horse. Somewhat ominously the creature is said to have a particular liking of human meat—and an even greater liking of human livers.

A fascinating, and very credible, account that may have a direct bearing upon the story of the Batutut is that of zoologist John MacKinnon. In 1970, while on Borneo, he stumbled upon a series of unusual, small, human-like footprints. He said:

I stopped dead. My skin crept and I felt a strong desire to head home … farther ahead I saw tracks and went to examine them. I found two dozen footprints in all. I was uneasy when I found them, and I didn't want to follow them and find out what was at the end of the trail. I knew that no animal we know about could make those tracks. Without deliberately avoiding the area I realize I never went back to that place in the following months of my studies.

BBC and Bigfoot

In 2003, specifically following the publication of, and the publicity given to, a series of then-recent Bigfoot encounters in central England's Cannock Chase woods, Ian McCaskill, BBC Television personality, weatherman, and star of *The Morning Show*, became embroiled in the mystery. Along with cryptozoologists and Centre for Fortean Zoology stalwarts Jon Downes and Richard Freeman, McCaskill headed to the area in search of the mysterious creature. The BBC was full of good humor as it reported on McCaskill's adventurous romps on and around the Cannock Chase with Downes and Freeman:

Apparently he's hairy, giant and ape-like. And not at all the sort of person you want to bump into in a deserted place, on a dark night. Unfortunately, "Bigfoot," or the "Yeti" as it's become known, is out and about, on the prowl, and could be coming to a place near you. Never fear, for *The Morning Show*'s gallant Ian McCaskill was here. In the first week of February, he went off to Cannock Chase in Staffordshire to hunt down the eight-foot Yeti spotted recently in the area.

Ian joined monster hunters Jon Downes and Richard Freeman, from the Centre for Fortean Zoology based in Exeter. Richard, a qualified zoo keeper and center founder Jon describe themselves as "Britain's foremost professional monster hunters."

They were following up the recent sighting on the side of the road near Stafford. It was only

Jon Downes is the director of the Centre for Fortean Zoology.

miles from another "Bigfoot" appearance four years earlier. Although they have been mocked, a U.K. website devoted to Bigfoot research contains many reports, including yet another Staffordshire sighting. Lots of sightings occur near telecom towers, and one of the theories is that apparitions are caused by radiation surges from these towers.

Granted, the segment of the show that focused on the Cannock creature was presented in the light-hearted, mystery-soaked fashion that was always intended, but it did at least ensure that stories of the British Bigfoot reached a prime-time, and fairly large, daytime audience.

Beaman Monster

See: Zoo Escapees

The Beast of Boggy Creek (1972 movie)

For many people with an interest in the Bigfoot phenomenon, any mention of the Boggy Creek beast inevitably conjures up imagery and memories of Charles B. Pierce's 1972 production *The Legend of Boggy Creek*. It's a film that more than a few cryptozoologists cite as having had a major influence on them, in terms of prompting them to seek out the truth behind some of the monstrous mysteries of our world (*see* "The Legend of Boggy Creek [1972 movie]"). In 2012, Anomalist Books published Lyle Blackburn's book *The Beast of Boggy Creek*, a nonfiction title that revealed the truth behind Pierce's fiction.

From the opening chapter, Blackburn skillfully, and in an eerie, atmospheric style, takes us into the very heart of a time long gone—the early 1970s—and places as mysterious and eerie as they are captivating and picturesque: southern Arkansas, the huge Sulphur River Bottoms, the town of Fouke, and, of course (where else?), Boggy Creek. Then there's the matter of that legendary monster.

As Blackburn makes clear to the reader, it was May 1971 when all hell broke loose and the creature of the creek was born (although, as will be demonstrated shortly, the mystery—Blackburn's investigative digging shows—actually appears to date back much, much further).

We are treated to a fine and captivating story filled with tales of frightened Fouke folk, of what almost turned into a home-invasion by a hairy horror, of people running around the darkened woods in search of the diabolical thing, of the police trying valiantly to keep things under control and preventing gun-toting citizens from mistakenly blowing the heads off each other, and of a local media enormously pleased with the sensational story in its very midst.

And with the genie out of the bottle, so to speak, the monster, and its attendant controversies, was not going to go away anytime soon.

Blackburn details the many and varied additional sightings and discoveries that sprung up in and around Fouke in the days, weeks, and months that followed—namely, a large, hairy beast seen lumbering across the roads late at night, curious three-toed footprints found, strange howls and screams coming from the wooded shadows, and much more.

And, of course, we are exposed to the fascinating story of how the monster of Fouke came to make its way to the big screen, courtesy of the aforementioned Charles B. Pierce. This section of the book, alone, makes for essential reading, as Blackburn regales us with the ups and downs that dominated the funding, development, production, and distribution of the film.

But, more importantly, *The Beast of Boggy Creek* makes it acutely clear that without the people of Fouke itself, there would have been no movie—period. If you're a fan of Pierce's movie, you won't want to miss what Blackburn has to say about it and what he has uncovered.

Very significantly, Blackburn sets the record straight and reveals that, contrary to what many have assumed, (a) the presence of the beast, or beasts, was actually

A display of the Boggy Creek monster is showcased at Peavy's Monter Mart in Fouke, Arkansas.

reported long before 1971—albeit certainly not on the scale that occurred during the 1970s; and (b) sightings of the hairy thing have continued up until pretty much the present day. In other words, while Boggy Creek monster hysteria was certainly at its height during the '70s, the encounters of that period only tell a part of the story.

Blackburn doesn't shy away from controversy either—particularly so when it comes to those curious (some have said highly suspicious) three-toed footprints and a certain, intriguing skeleton that play major roles in the story and the development of its attendant legend. Blackburn also addresses the nature of the beast itself at length and the theories posited to explain what it might really be: Bigfoot, circus-escapee, legend gone wild, and more are all part of the beastly mix as answers are diligently sought.

Packed with fine artwork and a wealth of black and white photos that undeniably capture the eerie essence of the area in which the beast has for so long lurked, Lyle Blackburn's *The Beast of Boggy Creek* is a book that one and all with an interest in Bigfoot should read and own.

Big Gray Man

See: Scottish Bigfoot

Big Thicket Sasquatch

For many people, any mention of the words *Texas* and *The Lone Star State* provoke imagery of vast plains, cactus, tumbleweeds, and scalding hot deserts. In reality, however, the traditional image of Texas is very wide of the mark. Yes, much of west Texas is noted for its massive amounts of cotton fields. However, the desert environment that often springs to mind is far more applicable to New Mexico and Arizona. On top of that, most of east Texas is very heavily forested. Indeed, one only has to drive east out of the city of Dallas to be in the heart of dense forest land. All of which brings us to a place called the Big Thicket, an undeniable magnet for mysterious apes and savage wild men.

To demonstrate just how heavily wooded Texas is, the Big Thicket alone—which is situated not far from the city of Houston—is more than 80,000 acres in size. It's dominated by near-endless numbers of oak trees, beech trees, pines, and swamps and rivers. By day, the Big Thicket looks like pretty much any other large, sprawling mass of forestland. It's after the sun has set, however, and darkness has fallen on the Big Thicket that things begin to change—and to a significant and creepy degree.

Much of the high-strangeness of the Bigfoot variety is focused in the vicinity of a six-mile-long stretch of the fairly primitive Bragg Road that runs through the woods. While that's the road's official title, it also has an unofficial name, too: Ghost Light Road. It takes its curious name from the fact that, for centuries, people have reported seeing strange, eerie, floating balls of light flitting around the woods—balls of light

U.S. Forest Service employees canoe through the lush and biologically diverse Big Thicket National Preserve in southeast Texas. The forest is dense here, a good place for a Sasquatch to hide from humans.

that vary from the size of a tennis ball to a soccer ball. And, it's against this weird background that the Big Thicket Bigfoot dwells.

No one had done more research into the strange creatures of the Big Thicket than Rob Riggs, the author of a 2001 book appropriately titled *In the Big Thicket*. Riggs, a journalist and the former publisher of a series of award-winning newspapers in Texas, has uncovered a massive amount of data and witness testimony demonstrating that wild, monstrous things inhabit the darkest regions of the Big Thicket. As with so many other encounters across the United States, the phenomenon of the Big Thicket man-beast existed before the term "Bigfoot" was coined. Riggs, himself, has confirmed this:

> The first I heard of the Big Thicket's Wild Man was in the mid-1950s as a ten-year-old boy growing up in Sour Lake. My grandpa had been planning for weeks to take me and my older brother, Mickey, on an overnight camping and fishing trip. Just days before we were to leave, rumors began flying around Hardin County that a wild man, wearing no clothes, but covered with hair, had been seen in the northern part of the county in the dense bottom land forests along village creek—[the] very place we intended to go.

Riggs's research dates back to 1979. He says: "I have been investigating the Bigfoot phenomenon for over 30 years. I'm reluctant to use the word 'Bigfoot' because I can't say for sure that what we're investigating here is the same animal that's seen in the Pacific Northwest."

Rob Riggs (right), author of *In the Big Thicket,* with Nick Redfern.

Riggs has uncovered data on encounters with huge, ape-like animals from the 1960s to the present day, as well as highly controversial—but deeply intriguing—accounts suggesting a connection between the wild men and the Big Thicket's resident ghostly lights, and even stories of isolated pockets of Native Americans living deep in the most dense parts of the woods.

The *Houstonia* noted:

When Riggs ran a notice in the paper calling for stories of unusual sightings in the woods, he was deluged with letters. A teenage girl claimed that a giant ape had chased her away from a cemetery. A couple in a car on Ghost Road—the local lovers' lane—reported that Bigfoot jumped on their hood, forcing the man, who fortunately had his shotgun handy, to scare the creature away by firing at it through the front windshield.

At the time of writing, Riggs's research into the Big Thicket Bigfoot continues at a steady pace.

Bolam Lake

In the period from late 2002 to early 2003, the United Kingdom was gripped by a series of strange but intriguing reports of Bigfoot-style beasts, all across the nation.

Jon Downes, of the Centre for Fortean Zoology, well recalls the events, more than a decade down the line:

There occurred a huge "flap" of Big Hairy Men (BHM) sightings throughout the British Isles that we could not afford to ignore and that required our immediate attention. Indeed, such was the scale of this extraordinary wave of encounters that, even as we made firm plans for an expedition in March, a handful of new sightings of large, man-beasts from the Bolam Lake area of Northumberland, England, arrived in our e-mail In-Box in January that prompted us to undertake an immediate study of the evidence.

It was a bitterly cold, winter's morning when Downes's Centre for Fortean Zoology hit the road. The trip turned out to be a fortuitous one, however. There was distinct high-strangeness afoot, too, as Downes recalled:

> "Together with two companions he had been making his way back to the car-park when they encountered a huge, dark, man-shaped object about seven to eight feet in height with what he described as sparkling eyes."

After arriving on-site, a veritable wave of paranormal chaos erupted in the direct vicinity of Bolam Lake. Although we had tested all of our electronic equipment the night before, had charged up batteries where necessary, and had even put new batteries in all of our equipment that needed them, practically without exception all of our new equipment failed. The laptop, for example, has a battery, which usually lasts between 20 and 35 minutes. It lasted just three minutes before failing. Admittedly, we received an enormous number of telephone calls during our stay at the lake, but not anywhere near enough to justify the fact that we had to change handsets four times in as many hours. The batteries in our tape-recorders also failed. It seems certain that there was some strange electromagnetic phenomenon at work here.

We met with a witness, named Neil, who had been fishing at Bolam Lake one night four or five years previously. Together with two companions he had been making his way back to the car-park when they encountered a huge, dark, man-shaped object about seven to eight feet in height with what he described as sparkling eyes. The three fishermen did not stop to investigate but ran back to the car.

However, this was by no means the only encounter that Neil had reported to us. Together with one of his companions from the first adventure, he had again been night fishing at Bolam Lake during the summer of 2002. They had been camped out on this occasion, and had heard noises, which they assumed were from an enormous animal moving around in the bushes outside of their camp. Deciding that discretion was most definitely the better part of valor, they decided not to investigate any further; but when they broke camp the next morning they found that the fish they had stored in a bait-tin had been taken, and there were distinct signs that something very large had been lumbering around in the immediate vicinity.

As the investigation came to its close, and as the dark skies of winter closed in, something extraordinary and menacing occurred at Bolam Lake, as Downes revealed:

At about half-past-four, one of the members of Twilight Worlds [a research group that accompanied Downes to the area] reported seeing something large, human-shaped and amorphous in the woods directly in front of the car-park. As the dusk gathered at about 5 o'clock, we again heard the raucous noise of the crows that he had reported just before dawn. Suddenly, once again, they fell silent and one of the Twilight Worlds members shouted that she could hear something large moving around among the undergrowth. All of the car-drivers present were ordered to switch on their headlights and to put them on full-beam. We did not hear any noise in the undergrowth; although other people present did. Eight people were watching the woods and five of us saw an enormous man-shaped object run from right to left, disappear, and then a few moments later run back again.

The most amazing aspect of the encounter, however, was that the hulking, racing thing was one-dimensional; shadow-like, and utterly lacking in any sort of 3-D substance. But, even so, it was still some form of mystifying entity in its very own right. The bizarre event was over in an instant. And Jon Downes found his life forever changed.

Brassknocker Hill Monster

The strange saga all began in July 1979, amid wild rumors that a terrifying monster was haunting the dark woods of Brassknocker Hill, situated near the old English city of Bath. Described variously, and in both excited and hysterical tones, as a long-fanged, four-foot-tall creature resembling a baboon, chimpanzee, spider-monkey, gibbon, or lemur, the creature was of far more concern to some than it was to others.

Locals Ron and Betty Harper were hardly in good moods when they discovered that the mysterious creature had stripped whole sections of their old, mighty oak tree bare of its bark. To the kids of Brassknocker Hill, however, the hunt for the beast provided them all the excitement they needed for a jolly adventure of *Hardy Boys* proportions—particularly so when, only one month later, the number of trees targeted had reached an astonishing fifty, and the woods were plunged into an eerie silence after almost all the local birds summarily fled the area, presumably for far safer and beast-free pastures.

Meanwhile, eighty-one-year-old Brassknocker Hill resident Frank Green, clearly hyped up to the max and desperately trying to live out his *Dirty Harry* fantasies, took a far more grave and serious view of the strange situation. He took up nothing less than a night-and-day shotgun vigil and told the media in loud and worried tones: "I am very fond of some animals, but I reckon this creature could be dangerous and I am taking no chances."

Fortunately, or unfortunately—depending on one's personal perspective on the monstrous matter—Green did not have the opportunity to blast the baboon-like beast to kingdom come, or, indeed, to *anywhere*. It skillfully avoided all of his attempts to

The Brassknocker Hill area near Bath, England, is reportedly the home of some kind of long-fanged, four-foot-tall primate creature.

track it down, much to the relief of the police, who were hardly enamored by the idea of a grouchy, old-age pensioner roaming around Brassknocker Hill with a loaded shotgun in search of a marauding, unknown creature.

Nearby Monkton Combe became the next locale terrorized by the beast of Brassknocker Hill. As for the creature, it was seen by a man who was driving through the area late one night, and who offered the anonymous description to the press that the animal he crossed paths with was of a significant size, seemed somewhat bear-like in appearance, briefly stood on its thick and substantial hind legs, and possessed a pair of large eyes that were surrounded by great white circles of fur or hair.

Getting in on the growing sensationalism, a Dutch newspaper—*Het Binnenhof*—ran a story that, translated into English, practically suggested an assault on Brassknocker Hill of the type of proportions one would expect to see in a Tokyo-shattering on-screen attack by Godzilla! The sensationalized title of *Het Binnenhof*'s eye-catching article, which provided an entertaining summary of the affair, was: "Beast of Bath Destroys British Wood!" Far more cataclysmic than the real picture, the story and its attendant title guaranteed not just local and countrywide interest, but now international coverage, too.

By the time the following summer arrived, the mystery seemed to have been solved. Police inspector Michael Price caught sight in the woods of what he thought was a large chimpanzee running around, although the identification of the animal was never fully confirmed, thus leaving the cage-door open to the possibility it had been a baboon, after all. The local press quickly sought out comments from the police. And they got them, too:

"We were sure this mystery creature would turn out to be a monkey of some sort," said Inspector Price, clearly and happily wallowing in a brief wave of very odd publicity. "After all, men from Mars aren't hairy, are they?" But rumors of strange and savage activities at Brassknocker Hill persisted, much to the glee of the local media.

Two years later, the stories returned, only this time—rather curiously—the tales of a baboon, or some other type of monkey, on the loose were replaced by sightings of something very different. A stag, polecat, or even a Japanese deer were among the many and varied candidates for the new beast of the hill. Then, one morning in the summer of 1984, reports started coming in to the news-desk of the *Bath Chronicle* newspaper of a strange-looking creature holding up traffic on Brassknocker Hill. Once again, for the press, the game was afoot, to reference a certain famous and fictional detective.

> A stag, polecat, or even a Japanese deer were among the many and varied candidates for the new beast of the hill.

"I grabbed my notebook," said reporter Roger Green, who later became the editor of the *Littlehampton Gazette*. "Colin [Shepherd] the photographer grabbed his camera, and we rushed out to the hill. The reports were pretty credible, so we were convinced that there was something there," Green recalled. "It was with slight trepidation that we entered the woods. After several minutes of stalking, we came across the 'beast,' by then calmly grazing in a field. It was an Alpacca, a type of llama, and had escaped from a paddock. It was later reunited with its owner by the police."

But, quite obviously, this did not explain the earlier sightings of a baboon-like animal, which—under no circumstances, at all—could have been confused with a llama! Needless to say, the mystery was never resolved, and the baboon, if that is what it really was, vanished, died, or moved on to new pastures and tree-bark. Its place of origin, obviously, was forever a mystery.

Bridge-based Encounters

Traditionally, and for centuries, within the folklore, mythology, and legends of countless cultures, bridges have been associated with a wide array of paranormal phenomena, including strange beasts, UFOs, and spectral entities. Of course, the big question is: Why? The answers are as strange as they are intriguing.

One of the most macabre bridge encounters of a paranormal kind occurred in Shropshire, England, in January 1879. It was a cold and moonlit night when a work-

Montford Bridge in Shropshire, England, has been the site where a number of simian creatures have been spotted. Reports usually describe them as appearing like chimpanzees.

man was traveling home, his tiring day finally over. As he reached a halfway-point on Bridge 39, which spans the Shropshire Union Canal, a diabolical, hairy man-beast leaped out of the trees and jumped atop the cart, which, not surprisingly, sent his horse into a frenzy.

The beast, said the man, resembled a large, hairy monkey and sported a pair of glowing eyes. In other words, it wasn't a local. Incredibly, as the witness attempted to strike the beast with his whip, it passed through its body, suggesting that whatever the nature of the monstrous form, it was hardly flesh and blood. Seconds later, the "animal" bounded off into the darkness and was gone. Thus was born the legend of the Man-Monkey—a creature that still haunts Bridge 39 to this day. (*see* "Man-Monkey of the Shropshire Union Canal")

Nearly a century later, strange things were afoot at England's Montford Bridge—a bridge constructed in the early 1790s, and which is located in a village of the same name. Declassified British Ministry of Defense files reveal that, in both 1964 and 1966, a young woman named Diane Foulkes had undergone a series of traumatic UFO encounters at the bridge—encounters that adversely affected the engine and headlights of her car, made her feel "very ill" and "extremely frightened," and gave every indication that alien entities were secretly lurking around the old bridge.

Notably, one extract from the Ministry of Defense's official report on the affair says:

> Miss Foulkes further stated that she believed that the objects could be associated with a Mr. Griffin who lived in the area and who is reputed to have made contact with these objects and actually entered one and met one of the occupants. He is also alleged to make his contacts with them at Montford Bridge.

Very intriguing is the fact that Montford Bridge has been the site of several large creatures resembling chimpanzees, the first in 1921 and the latest in 1978. In each case the beasts possessed fiery, blazing red eyes that struck terror into the unfortunate eyewitnesses.

Meanwhile, on the other side of the Atlantic....

There can be very few people who have not heard of Mothman—a creature that haunted the town of Point Pleasant, West Virginia, between November 1966 and December 1967. A winged monster Mothman came hurtling out of nowhere. And, some say, its presence culminated in high tragedy. On December 15, 1967, Point Pleasant's Silver Bridge, which spanned the Ohio River and connected Point Pleasant to Gallipolis, Ohio, collapsed into the river, claiming forty-six lives.

After the disaster at the bridge, encounters with Mothman largely came to a halt. While a down-to-earth explanation for the bridge circulated—that a flaw in a single eye-bar in a suspension chain was the culprit—many saw the cause of the disaster as being connected to the dark presence of Mothman. It may not come as a surprise to learn that when Mothman was prowling around Point Pleasant, so was Bigfoot.

Moving on to Texas, there is the tale of the diabolical Goat-Man that haunts the Old Alton Bridge in the town of Denton. One legend says that many years ago, wannabe devil-worshipers in the area inadvertently opened up a portal to some hellish realm that allowed the vile beast access to our world. And now, today, and as a direct result of this reckless action, the Goat-Man has no intention of returning to the twilight zone from which he surfaced; hence his deep desire to forever haunt Denton's steel-and-wood bridge. Notably, there is also a local legend suggesting the pale-haired Goat-Man is actually a white-colored Bigfoot (*see* "White Bigfoot").

So, what's going on? Is it merely down to chance and coincidence that bridges seem to play integral roles in encounters that involve Bigfoot and anomalous apes? Almost certainly not. It's at this point we have to turn our attention to what have become known as Liminal Zones. In her 2006 book *Mystery Big Cats*, author Merrily Harpur writes of these mysterious locales: "These are the transitional zones between one area and another—the kind of no-man's-land traditionally regarded as magical."

Harpur notes that such zones include streams, gates, churchyards, and … bridges.

Are some of the ancient, historical bridges that pepper our world really acting as portals and doorways, through which a collective multitude of paranormal phenomena such as Bigfoot enter our realm of existence? It's a question you would be wise to keep in mind the next time you find yourself crossing a darkened old bridge, late one stormy night.

British Beast

See: Snowdonia, Wales

Bullets and Bigfoot

On the night of November 28, 2014, on the hugely popular radio show *Coast to Coast AM*, author and Sasquatch expert Stan Gordon spoke about his Bigfoot research and writing. Gordon's Bigfoot studies demonstrate a connection between the strange beasts and multiple, weird phenomena—including matters of a psychic nature and also UFOs. One of the issues that Gordon discussed on the show was Bigfoot's seeming ability to remain unaffected when blasted with bullets. This was made clear in the summary of Gordon's interview, which appeared at the *Coast to Coast AM* website the very next day:

> [Gordon] explained that, in October of 1973, witnesses spotted a slow-moving, bright red UFO apparently land in the pasture of a farm. On the way out to investigate the craft, the group heard a high-pitched whining sound that got louder as they got closer as well as an eerie sound which resembled a baby crying. As they reached the top of the pasture, they were stunned to see the UFO now resembled a white dome which illuminated the entire area. Suddenly, they noticed two Bigfoot creeping along a barbed wire fence about 75-feet away from the UFO and making those strange sounds. When a witness shot a tracer bullet at the creatures, one of the Bigfoot reached up as if to grab it and, suddenly, the UFO disappeared into thin air. The man then tried shooting the Bigfoot with live ammunition, but the bullets had no effect and the creatures wandered off into the woods.

This was not a one-off event, however: it's just the tip of the iceberg.

Philip Rife, Bigfoot investigator, says: "In 1959, a policeman had a scary encounter with a Bigfoot on a rural road in Carroll County. The officer watched in amazement as the creature crossed directly in front of his patrol car and stepped effortlessly over a barbed wire fence.

> He stopped the vehicle and got out, shouting at the creature to stop. The officer had immediate second thoughts about the wisdom of his action when the creature turned around and began to walk toward him. The policeman then withdrew his service revolver and fired at the Bigfoot. When the bullets appeared to have no effect, the officer sprinted to his car and sped from the scene.

Tom Black tells of a bizarre Bigfoot encounter in the town of Rising Sun, Indiana, in 1977. In this case, one of the witnesses, Tom Courter, attempted to shoot and kill the creature. No surprises here: the beast was utterly impervious to bullets. There may well have been a very good reason for this, as Black notes:

Tom Courter … attempted to shoot and kill the creature. No surprises here: the beast was utterly impervious to bullets.

> Tom shot the creature but appeared to miss. He fired more shots but he either missed or the bullets had no effect on the 12 foot tall beast. Then, strangely, the Rising Sun Bigfoot appeared to dive into the ground and disappear. I've never heard of a disappearing Bigfoot before, but if you think about it, a phantom creature may make more sense than a physical 12 foot tall monster.

Robert Lindsay has performed the arduous task of collecting just about every single "Bigfoot and bullets" case on record. They run, literally into the dozens and dozens. Two, perfect examples from Lindsay's files follow:

Summer 1966: Near Richland, Washington: Several boys—Greg Pointer, Roger True, Tom Thompson, Carl and Jim Franklin, John McKnight, Alvin Anderson, Selby Green,

Roger Howard, Bob McDonald and Ron Blackburn—saw an 8 foot whitish-gray Bigfoot and shot at it several times with no effect.

August 2000: Fort Mitchell, Alabama. A man and his friend were camping at Rood Creek Park Campground and Boat Landing on the Chattahoochee River, Georgia. One of the men's dogs started whimpering, and the man went to check on it. Then he saw a Bigfoot coming out of the woods and approaching the camp. The man fired two shots from his pistol at the Bigfoot, but they didn't seem to faze it. The Bigfoot then grabbed the man's dog and tore it to shreds.

Trying to come to some form of conclusion for these cases that suggest Bigfoot is impervious to the effects of bullets is a difficult task. Those who believe Bigfoot to be an unknown ape, but one of regular flesh and blood proportions, would likely say those who shot at Bigfoot either missed their target—perhaps as a result of hand-shaking fear and a dark night—or the sheer bulk and mass of the creatures meant the bullets had little effect.

On the other hand, however, there is the story from Stan Gordon, of a bullet-proof Bigfoot seen in the same time-frame and location as a UFO, and that of Tom Black, in which a creature—after being shot at—dived at the ground and mysteriously disappeared.

Whether bullet-proof or just lucky 100 percent of the time, the fact is that, so far, no one who has attempted to shoot and kill a Bigfoot has ever succeeded in doing so. And, of the handful of people who have claimed to have done precisely that, not one of them has been able to present the corpse for study and autopsy.

Burntwood Bigfoot Sighting

On September 2, 2008, the Birmingham, England-based *Sunday Mercury* newspaper published a lengthy letter from a resident of the nearby town of Cannock that told an extraordinary tale. The fact that the newspaper chose to withhold the name of the writer doesn't help when it comes to trying to validate the encounter, but given that the story is a fascinating one—and deeply relevant to the subject of this book—I include it without edit. And here it is:

Last year around June time, me and two other friends were supposed to go to a 24-hour basketball event for charity. Us being lads we decided to skive and go and sit down the lane in my car, and do what typical teenage lads do.

Anyway, so me and two others were parked up in a little pull-in, down a lane in Gentleshaw not too far from Burntwood, Cannock. We were parked in this pull-in facing the road, with trees either side of us, and a gated-field behind. It was around two o'clock in the morning and we had the interior light on in the car, when my friend in the front passenger seat said he could see something moving outside, on the right side of the car.

"It was too dark to see whether it was staring at us, but I'm guessing it was! As soon as it realized we had seen it, it stood up straight, hesitated and ran towards us."

We turned off the interior light to get a better look and could definitely see something moving in the trees in the distance. Our first thoughts were a person or an animal, all we could see was something large moving around. This thing must have been about 10–15m away. (I didn't exactly have time to measure!) I turned the car headlights and hazard lights on, to see if I could see anymore. This thing was the shape of a human, but stood about 7–8ft, it was hard to tell with it being dark and such a distance away.

At first sight it was crouching, not completely to the floor, but approx half way and facing directly at the car. It was too dark to see whether it was staring at us, but I'm guessing it was! As soon as it realized we had seen it, it stood up straight, hesitated and ran towards us. Well as you can imagine I wasn't sticking around. This thing was definitely not human, it was huge! It wasn't just tall, but broad and stocky too. I haven't got a clue what its face was like, or its skin or fur, or whatever it had. It wasn't light enough.

My back passenger darted to the other side of the car, and nobody said a word. As it came towards us it was rustling big bushes, shaking pretty big trees, it was just like in a horror movie. I drove out of the pull-in and turned left down the lane, this thing was keeping up with the car, but in the trees. I was trying so hard not to look in my mirrors, but I could see it in the corner of my eyes, I don't know whether it was flying or jumping or what.

Its strength and quickness was unbelievable. Obviously I wasn't thinking that at the time, I just wanted to get the hell out of there! I drove to the bottom of the lane doing about 80mph, and it just vanished as soon as I came up to a pub at the bottom of the lane. I didn't stop until I entered a residential area.

The fear was unreal, I have never been so scared, and didn't think I would ever experience anything that would scare me so much. I felt physically sick, cold and shaky. I just didn't want to believe what I had seen. None of us discussed it, I think we were all in denial! I completely blanked it from my mind after that, and didn't discuss it again until 3 days ago, when the front seat passenger brought it up in conversation, and now I can't forget about it.

I hate re-living it, but I thought I would let others know of my experience. I'm not asking you to believe me, because to everyone else it probably seems so far-fetched, but I know what I saw and so do the other two lads. I'm not at all saying I saw "bigfoot" but I know 100% this thing was not human. I know other stories say the thing they saw had red eyes, but I didn't see red eyes, I wasn't close enough to see. Glad I wasn't too.

What haunts me now, is…. What would its face have looked like? Where is it? It must have been watching us, and what would it have done if we didn't get away?

Caddo Critter

See: Texas Sasquatch

Canada's Cryptid Ape-Men

Sightings of Bigfoot-style creatures are widespread across Canada, and particularly so the west coast. This is hardly surprising, given that pretty much the entire Pacific northwest of the United States is home to the legendary man-beast. It's possible that the legends of the savage and infamous Wendigo of Canada may have developed out of near-fatal, and even deadly, encounters with violent, murderous Bigfoot (*see* "Wendigo")

There are, however, several kinds of unknown ape-men in Canada that are far removed from the likes of Sasquatch and the Wendigo. One of these is the tongue-tying Geow-lud-mo-sis-eg. It's a diminutive, goblin-like creature that is covered in black hair and prefers to live in caves and which lurks and feeds in deep woods, surrounded by dense marshland. Rather like the fairies of Middle Ages-era Europe, the Geow-lud-mo-sis-eg enjoy playing pranks on people—pranks that sometimes turn malevolent if the creatures feel they have been slighted or disrespected. Also like the elementals of fairy lore, the Geow-lud-mo-sis-eg have an obsession with braiding the manes of horses (*see* "Horse-braiding and Bigfoot"). Rather notably, this tradition extends all the way to Russia, where the Almasty is said to do exactly likewise (*see* "Almasty Expedition").

Then there are the Memegwesi, primitive ape-like humans that are a major part of the lore of the Ojibwe, Cree, Innu, Metis, Algonquin, and Menominee Indians. They are hairy things, around four feet tall at adulthood, and, according to legend,

A 1917 illustration from the Mabel Powers book *Little People,* contains this illustration of Iroquois little people, or Geow-lud-mo-sis-eg, diminuitive creatures who enjoy playing pranks.

have had a good relationship with the Indians for many centuries. Like a number of unknown ape-men they have a particular liking for tobacco. They are significantly developed too, having a language and also the ability to construct sturdy canoes, in which they hunt for fish.

Of potential (although, admittedly, not proven) connection to the stories of the Memegwe-si and the Geow-lud-mo-sis-eg is the strange 1635 story of Arctic explorer Captain Luke Foxe. In his journal for that year, Captain Foxe wrote of an extraordinary discovery of a huge number of small coffins in the region of Baffin Island, Canada. Foxe recorded, after speaking with the locals about the strange find:

The news from the land was that this island was a Sepulchre, for that the Savages had laid their dead (I cannot say interred), for it is all stone, as they cannot dig therein, but lay the corpses upon the stones, and well them about with the same, confining them also by laying the sides of old sleddes above, which have been artificially made. The boards are some 9 or 10 ft long, 4 inches thicke [sic].

In what manner the tree they have bin [sic] made out of was cloven or sawen [sic], it was so smooth as we could not discerne [sic], the burials had been so old. And, as in other places of these countries, they bury all their utensils, as bowes [sic], arrows [sic], strings, darts, lances, and other implements carved in bone.

Demonstrating a potential connection to the Memegwesi and the Geow-lud-mo-sis-eg, Captain Foxe said: "The longest corpse was not above 4 foot long, with their heads laid to the West. Their corpses were wrapped in Deare [sic] skinnes [sic]. They seem to be people of small stature."

Canal Creature of Alaska

One of the most fascinating of all Bigfoot reports dates from July 1969. It was made public by the witness, himself, J. W. Huff, who worked in the field of mining, and who shared the details with the Bigfoot research community shortly after it occurred. The location, said Huff, was on land near the Bradfield Canal, Wrangell, Alaska.

Huff began:

I have been working for another mining company during this past season and one of my camps was in the Bradfield Canal general area. We were flown in by helicopter later in the afternoon and as soon as the 'copter was unloaded it immediately departed for Ketchikan. We started to get our camp up and prepare for the coming operations. While working on the camp shortly after the departure of the 'copter I happened to look up on a ridge about 300 feet higher than we were and about 500 yards distant. I saw a man standing there watching us....

Huff's initial thought was that this was just a regular person, that the land had already been claimed, and that—as a consequence—he and his colleague would have to leave the area. It turns out that this was no regular person, after all. It wasn't a person, at all. Huff continued with his story:

> Huff's initial thought was that this was just a regular person.... It turns out that this was no regular person, after all. It wasn't a person, at all.

My partner and I watched this man for ten or fifteen minutes expecting him to come down to our camp and visit with us and inform us this was his area and, of course, we were prepared to tell him we would leave the next day. He stood absolutely motionless and we had a good look at him and he appeared to be extremely large.

That was not the only odd characteristic of the man:

As we kept watching him he seemed to have no hat of any kind and looked very dark and we had the impression he had no clothing on. After watching him, I resumed my work in getting the tent up while my partner continued to watch. He then yelled to this man and waved to him whereupon this man took off with a lumbering gait rather rapidly and soon disappeared over the ridge from our sight.

We looked several more times expecting him to appear somewhere else coming down to our camp but no further sighting was made. We did not have our radio antenna up yet, or I would have recalled the 'copter to investigate further.

Although nothing dramatic occurred during the night, the story was not quite over. Come the next morning, Huff and his colleague decided to do a bit of exploring and see if they could track down the giant man—if he *was* a man:

We had to decide where we were going to start our prospecting so we decided we might as well start where we had seen this huge man. It took us some time to get there as we had to take a roundabout route and were prospecting all the way. It was very warm and rainy so the rocks were pretty slick and we were taking our time. When we got to the place where this man had been standing, there were no tracks, of course, as it was bare rock. Nearby was a snowfield and we searched this area but could not find anything we could definitely pin down as tracks. There had been goats up on that same ridge the day before but we could not find their tracks either due to the melting condition of the snow.

We did find some depressions in the snow that would require quite a bit of imagination to definitely call them tracks. This snowfield was rather small and once across it bare rocks were once again encountered. What this thing was that we saw I do not know except that it was no known animal that I have ever encountered and all I can say is that I have never seen anything even approaching this thing. We were in that camp for about three weeks and never again saw a trace of him.

Huff signed off:

I am writing this letter in answer to your request for information and have related these experiences to you just as I saw them and whether or not they are believed I personally could [not] care less as I know what I saw or at least what I appeared to see. I am fully positive that there is no reason that these Sasquatch could not exist as there have been too many reported sightings of similar man-like creatures.

Car-chasing Sasquatch

In January 2003, Peter Rhodes, of England's *Express and Star* newspaper, wrote an article on an extraordinary encounter on the Cannock Chase—a large area of woodland in the county of Staffordshire. Rhodes reported, under the graphic and memorable headline of "Night Terror with a British Bigfoot": "Whatever it was, it scared the living daylights out of Craig Blackmore. His mother Val says: 'I have never seen Craig like that before. He came home shaking, absolutely petrified and white, as though he'd seen a ghost.'"

What Blackmore—and a friend named Jo—had actually seen was not a ghost but a "huge, ape-like creature at the side of the road on Levedale Lane between Stafford and Penkridge." Blackmore told Rhodes:

> **"I have never seen Craig like that before. He came home shaking, absolutely petrified and white, as though he'd seen a ghost."**

I was driving my [Ford] Fiesta [car] down the road towards Penkridge and as we approached a house, the security light came on. I saw something in the corner of my eye. It was coming towards the car, running very fast. It wasn't a dog or a deer. It was running like a human would run, but it was really hairy and dark. It came level and jumped at the car but just missed. My friend turned round and said it was huge and had run through the hedge and across the field. I turned the car around but there was no sign of it.

Blackmore's mother added: "I thought maybe Craig had been drinking, or perhaps someone had spiked a drink. But that hadn't happened. He is a very truthful boy. He would not say something had happened if it hadn't. And anyway, his friend was in the same state of shock."

Rhodes noted: "Although the event had been terrifying, Craig, a 19-year-old HGV mechanic, did not report it to the police. He told a few friends ('they all laughed') and tried to forget the experience."

Rhodes also spoke with British-based Bigfoot investigator Geoff Lincoln, who told the *Express and Star*: "Bigfoot in Britain is an odd subject and very often the target of ridicule. But sightings are taking place and I am currently looking into two other reports in 2002, one in Northumberland and another in Lancashire."

To Craig Blackmore, Lincoln offered a simple message (and one that Rhodes said was "worthy of *The X-Files*"): "You are not alone."

Interestingly, this particular case closely echoes one from 1994 that occurred in Scotland and which was investigated by a researcher named Mark Fraser. The location was the area around Torphins, near Aberdeen, and involved three young men who had actually undergone an earlier encounter with a Bigfoot-like entity in the area, and who, while driving, encountered a large, dark-colored, hairy man-beast at the side of the road, which proceeded to pursue them at an incredibly fast rate of knots. As with Craig Blackmore and his friend, the outcome was fortunately not disastrous for the three terrified souls: after a brief chase, the beast simply gave up and came to a halt in the road.

Central Park, New York, Creature

For the most part, the overwhelming majority of all reports, stories, accounts, and tales I receive of strange beasts roaming the United States tend to be relatively down-to-earth—or at least as down-to-earth as it's possible to be when dealing with accounts relative to Bigfoot, lake-monsters, werewolves, and a truly wide and varied assortment of other creepy critters. Sasquatch, for example, is generally reported from within the deep woods and eerie forests of the Pacific northwest; lake-monsters generally surface from within the murky depths of some of the United States' larger bodies of water; and as for werewolves: well, for some reason, there are a huge number of reports from the dense woodland and plains of rural Wisconsin.

In other words, in those places that are very much dominated by long stretches of wilderness, forests, and deep lakes, strange creatures absolutely proliferate. But, what do you do when someone earnestly tells you that they have seen a distinctly weird creature roaming around the fringes of New York's Central Park?

Of all the places one would *least* expect to see a cryptid creature of any sort, New York's Central Park has to top the list, yet reports have been made.

Well, you try and listen very carefully to what the witness has to say, and you do your best to try and come to some meaningful conclusion—which is what I attempted to do when I was on the receiving end of an email from a man named Barry, who claimed to have seen a very strange beast in the park, itself, back in 1997.

Of course, the date of the case meant that the trail had long since gone cold—and I do mean that quite literally, too. But, that didn't stop me from at least taking the time to sit down with the witness while he was on a managerial training-course in Waco, Texas (which is only a relatively short drive from my Arlington, Texas, home).

Barry's story was certainly one of the weirdest I have ever heard; however, I learned a long time ago that the world of cryptozoology and monster-hunting can be a very strange and surreal one. And, for that reason, I always try and give everyone a fair hearing—which is precisely what I did with Barry.

An assistant manager at a certain, prestigious hotel that overlooks the park, Barry told me that on the day in question—which was a sunny weekday in either June or July 1997—he was strolling through the park, while on his lunch break from his then-job as a store worker. All was utterly normal until, as he approached one particularly tree- and bush-shrouded area, he was shocked to the core when, out of nowhere, an unknown animal burst wildly through the foliage.

> Barry claimed to me that the creature was man-like in shape and covered in hair of a distinctly rusty color—but, unlike the towering Bigfoot of the west coast, was little more than three feet in height.

Barry claimed to me that the creature was man-like in shape and covered in hair of a distinctly rusty color—but, unlike the towering Bigfoot of the west coast, was little more than three feet in height. Little-Foot might have been a far better term to use, I mused, as I listened to the very odd tale.

He could only watch with a mixture of shock and awe as the diminutive man-beast charged across the path in front of him at a distance of no more than about twenty feet, came to a screeching halt for a couple of seconds to stare intently into his eyes, and then headed off at high speed again, before finally vanishing: beneath a small bridge inside the perimeter of the park, no less.

Barry was clearly very embarrassed about discussing his sighting—even twelve years later. And, as a person who was clearly intelligent, coherent, and presentable, he acutely realized how strange his story sounded, too. I had to agree; however, I also had to realize that Barry had absolutely nothing to gain at all by relating the details of his experience of the highly unusual kind. I asked Barry to relate the details for me again.

He did so, and I carefully took notes, ensuring that we finally had every aspect of the story accounted for. He admitted that the facts were scant; aside from his unswerving position that for a few, brief moments in the summer of 1997 he saw a small, hairy, man-like beast scurrying across the grass of Central Park.

As I admitted to Barry, there was really very little that I could do; aside from carefully logging the details of the tale in my database, and seeing if anything else of a similar nature ever surfaced. Unsurprisingly, it most assuredly has not, so far. Barry's was just one of those very odd, fringe cases that seem to perplex from time to time those of us who dare to dig into the world of Bigfoot and its smaller compatriots.

Chichiricu

See: Cuba's Very Own Bigfoot

Chimpanzee vs. Humanzee

Within the domains of Bigfoot and additional, cryptid ape lore, there are numerous stories of alleged crossbreeding between the creatures and humans—something that, it is claimed, has occasionally resulted in the birth of freakish creatures that are half-human and half-something else. The tales are many. The hard proof is 100 percent lacking. Nevertheless, the stories endure—chiefly because of the high levels of controversy attached to them. And, in terms of such controversies, they don't come much bigger than the story that surrounded a chimpanzee named Oliver.

Born, it is estimated, in the late 1950s, Oliver really came to prominence in the mid-1970s, for several reasons, all of them notable and inflammatory. It was in the seventies that the media learned of how a man named Michael Miller, a New York-based attorney, had purchased, for a five-figure sum, a chimpanzee owned by a man named Frank Burger, who was noted for his animal acts that he regularly took on the road to entertain audiences. Burger had a good reason for selling Oliver. The hairy, horny animal was definitely hot for Burger's wife, Janet. For Janet, it was a case of: either he goes or I do. So, it was Oliver who went.

But there was far more to Oliver than his attraction to females of the human kind. He was shunned by the other chimpanzees that Burger used in his acts. Oliver was good at housecleaning, liked to sit cross-legged on his favorite chair, and—most amazing of all—walked upright.

Then, there was the matter of Oliver's physical appearance: he was bald, his cranium was smaller than normal, his jaws were far less prominent than what one would expect to see in the average chimpanzee, his face was noticeably freckled, and he had pointed, as opposed to rounded, ears. It's no wonder, then, that Oliver was rumored to be some kind of missing link. Darker tales suggested he just might have been the product of a mixed human-chimpanzee union—a "humanzee," as such theoretical creatures are known. On top of that, there were claims—that were never verified, it should be noted—that Oliver's chromosome count was off: he allegedly had forty-seven. Humans have forty-six and chimpanzees have forty-eight.

Artist Liza Phoenix sketched what she called a "chuman," or humanzee, a hybrid born of a chimpanzee and human.

Were the stories of deranged cross-breeding true? Might Oliver have been from a completely different species of chimpanzee, one completely unknown to the world of science? Inquiring minds—in the fields of zoology, cryptozoology, and Bigfoot-seeking—wanted answers. Unfortunately, the answers were a long time coming, as Oliver's next few years saw him languishing in obscurity and what were hardly good circumstances, as Dr. Karl Shuker, who has studied the saga of Oliver in-depth, notes: "During the late 1970s and through the 1980s, Oliver vanished from the headlines but was often exhibited as a freak or 'missing link' at various sideshows." Michael Miller sold the missing link to Ralph Helfer in 1977. Helfer exhibited Oliver at a theme park called Enchanted Village of which he was part owner, and, after it closed, he displayed it at another attraction called Gentle Jungle, which closed in 1982. Oliver was next seen at the Wild Animal Training Center in Riverside, California. Ken Decroo, who owned the facility, sold Oliver to Bill Rivers in 1985. Dr. Karl Shuker then notes:

Artist Liza Phoenix sketched what she called a "chuman," or humanzee, a hybrid born of a chimpanzee and human.

In 1989, Oliver was purchased by the Buckshire Corporation, a Pennsylvanian laboratory leasing out animals for scientific and cosmetic testing. Mercifully, he was never used in experiments, but for the next seven years his home was a 7 × 5 ft cage, whose restricted size resulted in his muscles becoming atrophied so much that his limbs trembled.

Fortunately, there was light at the end of the tunnel: in 1996, Oliver was transferred to the Primarily Primates sanctuary in Boerne, Texas. He lived there, contentedly, with a female chimpanzee named Raisin. Oliver died in June 2012. He was estimated to have been in his fifties. Although Oliver was cremated (his ashes were spread across the grounds of the sanctuary, meaning his corpse was not available for study), while he was still alive and vibrant he became the subject of a number of investigations to try and determine if he was just a regular chimpanzee, or if he was something more—or less.

It turned out that, contrary to the rumors, his chromosome count was absolutely normal for chimpanzees. Additional studies demonstrated that Oliver was not half-human, or indeed half-anything: he was all chimpanzee. As for his odd physical appearance, primatologists said that they saw nothing in Oliver that didn't fall within the parameters of what one might encounter in chimpanzees. On the matter of Oliver walking upright, this was put down to "conditioning" during his early years on the road in Frank Burger's traveling act—although this was disputed by Burger, who said that Oliver had always walked in such a fashion.

The mystery, mostly, was solved.

Choccolocco Monster

See: Alabama's Ape-Man

Cleadon Wild Beast

In August 2001, Mike Hallowell, a very well-respected researcher of numerous anomalies—mystery animal-based and otherwise—penned an article for the Centre for Fortean Zoology's (CFZ) in-house magazine, *Animals & Men*, on the subject of the sighting of a large cat of unknown origins in Cleadon, which is a village located in South Tyneside in the northeast of England. The origins of the village date back more than one thousand years, and it happens to be situated only a few short miles from where Mike and his wife reside. The sightings of the giant cat, which were never satisfactorily resolved, began in January 1999 and attracted Mike's attention for years.

Then, in December 2009, Mike commented on a new development in the saga; although it was a development that most observers and commentators of the mystery would probably never, ever have anticipated. As Mike began, regarding the latest strand in the curious saga: "Over a decade after the Cleadon Big Cat first strutted onto the cryptozoological stage, something has happened to resurrect it."

Or, he added: "Maybe not, as it's all a bit confusing." It certainly is that: the "something" was the emergence of a large, hairy, Bigfoot-like beast.

With the above said and outlined, let us address the story of Mike himself, who, on December 10, 2009, told of how several days earlier he spoke with a friend and research colleague, John Triplow, who informed Mike of a website that contained "an intriguing BHM [Big Hairy Man] story, not unlike that of the infamous Beast of Bolam Lake, which I actively investigated with a CFZ team in early 2003" (*see* "Bolam Lake").

What puzzled John—and also deeply flummoxed Mike—was that this particular sighting of a large, hairy man-beast allegedly occurred right in the heart of Cleadon Village, in the very same year that the large black cat was reportedly prowling, in sinister and similar fashion, around the neighborhood. As for why it so confounded Mike, let's take a closer look.

He noted, correctly, that the borough of South Tyneside is the smallest metropolitan borough in the United Kingdom and is comprised of only half a dozen villages and towns, a handful of farms, and, if one is brutally honest, not much else at all. Aside, that is, from one thing. And it's a very significant thing, too. The area, Mike revealed, "also happens to be one of the hottest spots around for paranormal research, and I've written a good few books, articles and columns dealing with the wacky stuff that seems to happen here more than anywhere else I know."

As for the story of the Cleadon man-beast, Mike said that the witness in question reported seeing in the darkness of the night in question (precise date unknown) what appeared to be a large, two-legged animal covered in a thick coat of fur, as well as a second individual—but this one undeniably human—apparently out walking their pet dog. Mike added that "it seemed more than a little odd to me that this BHM sighting should occur in the same village that had only a short while previously been

This mill is located in Cleadon Hills in South Tyneside, England, where one theory is that a woman walking her huge Burmese mountain dog had her pet mistaken for a Big Hairy Man.

the setting for the infamous Cleadon Big Cat incident. Two spectacular cryptids in the one village, only a few short years apart?"

It was a most puzzling question to be sure, and one that Mike dug into further, as he attempted to resolve the nature of what, exactly, was afoot:

My suspicions were further fuelled by the presence of someone walking a dog when the Cleadon BHM was allegedly seen. During my investigation into the Cleadon Big Cat case, the press (the *Shields Gazette*, January 14, 1999) reported that a woman who had been walking her huge Burmese mountain dog on Cleadon Hills believed that she—or rather her pet—may have been mistaken for the big cat. I was subsequently able to discount this, but the fact that both the Cleadon Big Cat story and the account of the Cleadon BHM included a dog-walker on Cleadon Hills at the time of each sighting again made me wonder if the two stories had been melded together.

And there was yet another similarity, too, as Mike came to realize:

One of the witnesses in the Cleadon Big Cat case claimed that he'd seen the animal running past his hedge, approximately fifty feet away. If one substitutes the words "tree line" for "hedge" and "fifty yards" for "fifty feet," the two accounts are unnervingly similar.

Had the two stories—one of a huge man-beast and the other of a large, exotic cat—somehow become confused and intertwined in a fashion that, to this day, is still not altogether clear? Just like the true nature of the beast, the answer to that question remains unknown.

Clothes-wearing Sasquatch

Without doubt, one of the most bizarre aspects of the Bigfoot phenomenon is the clothed Bigfoot! It's one thing to encounter such a creature. It's quite another to see it attired in pants and shirts. Incredibly, such controversial claims do exist.

Loren Coleman says:

In the 1960s and 1970s, reports from the American West would occasionally surface of hairy bipedal Bigfoot being seen with tattered plaid shirts and ragged shorts on their bodies. In some research, there were intriguing attempts to relate these to files of paranormal encounters with sightings of upright entities said to be wearing "checkered shirts." (Within parapsychology, there is a subfield of study regarding "checkered shirted ghosts.")

Investigators generally did not know what to make of these Sasquatch wearing plaid shirts, but dutifully catalogued and filed them away, nevertheless.

One of the most fascinating of all such encounters occurred in California at the turn of the 1950s. The story came from a woman who, at the time of the encounter, was a young girl. She told cryptozoologist and Bigfoot authority Ivan T. Sanderson the following, in the late fifties:

When: About 9 years ago, at about 10 o'clock in the morning. Where: Near the Eel River above Eureka, California. At the edge of a meadow near the river's edge. Under what circumstances: My family and I were fishing on the Eel River. We had been camped in the vicinity for about two weeks and had had poor luck when it came to fishing.

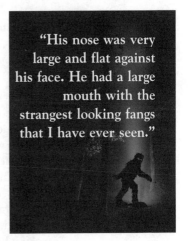

"His nose was very large and flat against his face. He had a large mouth with the strangest looking fangs that I have ever seen."

I used to go for a short walk before breakfast because there was a very pretty meadow about a mile or two from our camp and I used to love to see the mist rise off the grass. I was only about 10 years old at the time and the world of nature was something which both fascinated and enthralled me.

I entered the meadow and proceeded to cross it in order to reach a small knoll at the other side. When I approached the foot of the knoll I heard a sound. It was the sound of someone walking and I thought perhaps my little brother had followed me and was going to jump out and try to scare me. I hollered, "All right, stinker, I know you're there." Needless to say it was not my brother that appeared. Instead it was a creature that I will never forget as long as I live. He stepped out of the bushes and I froze like a statue. He or "it" was about 7 ½ to 8 feet tall. He was covered with brown stuff that looked more like a soft down than fur. He had small eyes set close together and had a red look about them. His nose was very large and flat against his face. He had a large mouth with the strangest looking fangs that I have ever seen. His form was that of a human and he had hands and feet of enormous size, but very human looking.

However, there was one thing that I have not mentioned, the strangest and most frightening thing of al. He had on clothes! Yes, that's right. They were tattered and torn and barely covered him but they were still there. He made a horrible growling sound that I don't think could be imitated by any living being. Believe me I turned and ran as fast as I could. I reached camp winded and stayed scared all while we were there.

Janet and Colin Bord, noted Bigfoot experts, say of this downright weird affair: "If Bigfoot—and the creature in this report really does sound like a Bigfoot—is as well adapted to living in the wild as most reports suggest, why does he need to don tattered clothes?"

It's a very good question, one for which the Bords have what may be a reasonable and viable answer: "The only explanation that occurs to us is that this was a 'freak' sighting: that the Bigfoot had found the old clothes somewhere and, having seen humans dressed in clothes, decided to copy them. The fact that the clothes 'barely covered him' does suggest that they once had a smaller, human, owner."

Coffee County Graveyard Dwarves

Given the fact that there are more than a few worldwide reports of hair-covered dwarfish, ape- and monkey-like animals on record, then the following account— from the *Anthropological Institute Journal* of 1876—may be of deep significance and relevance:

An ancient graveyard of vast proportions has been found in Coffee County. It is similar to those found in White County and other places in middle Tennessee, but is vastly more extensive, and shows that the race of pygmies who once inhabited this country were very numerous. The same peculiarities of position observed in the White County graves are found in these. The writer of the letter says: "Some considerable excitement and curiosity took place a few days since, near Hilsboro, Coffee County, on James Brown's farm. A man was ploughing in a field which had been cultivated many years, and ploughed up a man's skull and other bones. After making further examination they found that there were about six acres in the graveyard. They were buried in a sitting or standing position. The bones show that they were a dwarf tribe of people, about three feet high. It is estimated that there were about 75,000 to 100,000 buried there. This shows that this county was inhabited hundreds of years ago."

Cougar Lake Wild Men

In September 1957, Charles Flood of Westminster, British Columbia, prepared a fascinating statement, one that detailed a remarkable event that occurred more than forty years earlier, but which was still as fresh in Flood's mind as it was on the day that it occurred:

I, Charles Flood of New Westminster (formerly of Hope) declare the following story to be true: I am 75 years of age and spent most of my life prospecting in the local mountains to the south of Hope, toward the American boundary and in the Chilliwack Lake area.

In 1915, Donald McRae and Green Hicks of Agassiz, B. C. and myself, explored an area over an unknown divide, on the way back to Hope, near the Holy Cross Mountains. Green Hicks, a half-breed Indian, told McRae and me a story, he claimed he had seen alligators at what he called Alligator Lake, and wild humans at what he called Cougar Lake. Out of curiosity we went with him; he had been there a week previous looking for a fur trap line. Sure enough, we saw his alligators, but they were black, twice the size of lizards in a small mud lake.

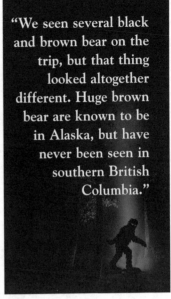

"We seen several black and brown bear on the trip, but that thing looked altogether different. Huge brown bear are known to be in Alaska, but have never been seen in southern British Columbia."

Awhile further up was Cougar Lake. Several years before a fire swept over many square miles of mountains which resulted in large areas of mountain huckleberry growth. Green Hicks suddenly stopped us and drew our attention to a large, light brown creature about 8 feet high, standing on its hind legs (standing upright) pulling the berry bushes with one hand or paw toward him and putting berries in his mouth with the other hand, or paw. I stood still wondering, and McRae and Green Hicks were arguing.

Hicks said, "It is a wild man" and McRae said, "It is a bear." As far as I am concerned the strange creature looked more like a human being. We seen several black and brown bear on the trip, but that thing looked altogether different. Huge brown bear are known to be in Alaska, but have never been seen in southern British Columbia.

Cuba's Very Own Bigfoot

It must be said, and it's hardly surprising, that the island of Cuba lacks any really credible reports of what one would accurately term Bigfoot. In times past, however, Cuba was said to be the home of a hairy creature of similar appearance but of far smaller proportions. Some researchers believe the creatures may still exist, living in deep stealth and out of harm's way. Very little is known of these legendary animals that are said to have lived in the eastern parts of the island and that became known as the Guije—also known in Cuba as the Jigue and the Chichiricu.

With a maximum height of around three feet, their appearance is part-human and part-monkey. Particularly noticeable about the Guije are their bulging stomachs and their long claws—the latter being most atypical of monkeys. Despite their small stature the Guije exhibited great strength. Few reports of the creatures being seen during daylight exist, something that strongly suggests they were nocturnal in nature.

One may surmise that the Guije, if they did exist, were some form of unknown monkey, or ape, despite the fact that such a discovery on Cuba would be phenomenal. It should be noted, however, that there are a number of legends that attribute supernatural powers to the Guije.

> **One may surmise that the Guije, if they did exist, were some form of unknown monkey, or ape, despite the fact that such a discovery on Cuba would be phenomenal.**

On this particular matter, *Cuban Headlines* notes: "Some identify him as a small old black man, others as a small boy of the same race and size with prominent eyes and even with great eyeteeth. Some people have seen him like a monster with goat legs and a caiman tail:

He behaves like an astute and evil goblin. It is said that he is faster than a horse and jump great fences better than a grasshopper. In addition, he becomes invisible like crossing a door.

Regarding his habitat, we can say that he lives in the pool of rivers whose water never ends; he uses to go out at any time.

Although it is said that he is able to do anything, he has never hurt anybody. In general, the stories about him explain that once he is discovered by a human being, he quickly run away at a supernatural speed.

Also on the paranormal path, there is a legend that the Guije have the ability to make themselves invisible—a occasionally controversial issue that crops up in Bigfoot lore.

Like some other man-beasts, male Guije lust after human women and, in rare cases, have supposedly impregnated them.

While the stories of human-Guije sexual relations, and the attendant supernatural themes, might seem dubious to many, it's not impossible that the more bizarre aspects of the lore developed from distorted reports of real encounters with an unknown kind of monkey—or even ape—that has long since succumbed to extinction in Cuba. There is also a very logical, though unlikely, explanation.

Cuba24h states:

Cuban historians claim that the myth was created to scare children and keep them away from rivers. Another version suggests the possibility of runaway slaves who create the legend to prevent white ranchers entering in mountains. In areas of America, where slave labor existed, there are similar versions of the myth. In Brazil is the Sacy, personage that shares the same characteristics with the Cuban, but with cap and smoking hookah instead. In Paraguay is the Yacy Yateré, this is blonde but lives in the rivers and makes the same antics as his African brothers. Colombia has the Ribiel, but this not only lives in rivers but also on the Caribbean coast of this great country. In Uruguay there is also the myth of the Black Water, the mixture of various traditions brought by slaves and used for the same purpose as in Cuba: prevent children from bathing in rivers.

Cypress Swamp Monster

See: Texas Sasquatch

De Loys' Faked Ape-Man

It is one of the most controversial stories within the domain of anomalous apes and cryptid monkeys. It has polarized the Bigfoot-seeking community into two camps: those who believe it and those who dismiss it as a fabrication. It's the strange saga of what has become known as de Loys' ape, named after Swiss geologist François de Loys. The story goes back to 1917, the year in which de Loys embarked upon an ambitious expedition to the wilds of Venezuela. The specific reason for de Loys' trek had nothing to do with unknown primates: it was focused solely on a quest to locate petroleum deposits in the vicinity of the Venezuela-Colombia border.

It was a hazard-filled, three-year expedition, in total, one that claimed the lives of <u>sixteen</u> of the nearly two-dozen members. Illness and violent attacks from local Indians were the two culprits that almost completely wiped out the team. In that sense, the expedition was a terrible failure. For years, however, entire swathes of the Bigfoot community believed that de Loys expedition had scored in a different way: by securing evidence of strange, unknown apes or monkeys in the jungles of Venezuela.

According to de Loys, it was when the straggling survivors reached an area near the Tarra River, and set up camp, that they were attacked by a pair of hair-covered, significantly sized animals that resembled apes that walked upright. As the beasts emerged wildly from the dense jungle, they made loud, threatening noises in the direction of the explorers, and even hurled their own feces at the group. The armed men wasted no time in opening fire on the animals, an action that reportedly killed the female, but not the male, which raced off into the thick, surrounding trees.

16 of 24 died

During a 1917 petroleum exploration project in South America, François de Loys reported that he killed this strange-looking primate creature in the jungles along the Colombia–Venezuela border.

With the male gone and the female dead, de Loys decided to take a close and careful look at the deceased animal. He noted that she had thirty-two teeth, like a human, whereas the majority of monkeys have thirty-six teeth. In addition, she lacked a tail. The next step was to photograph the animal, which was done by balancing the corpse on a crate and keeping it in place by propping a stick under its chin. Reportedly, a number of pictures were taken, and the creature was skinned. It was de Loys' intention to take the skull and hide back to civilization for analysis. Unfortunately, reportedly the hide, the skull, and all of the photos—aside from one—were lost when de Loys' boat capsized.

The story continues that one day in 1929, a friend of de Loys, an anthropologist named George Montandon, was digging through de Loys' old files, when he found the photo of the beast propped up on the crate. Montandon loudly declared that the beast in the picture was a new species, which he gave the title of *Ameranthropoides loysi*—Loys' American Ape. Since that day, the field of cryptozoology has been split on what the undeniably real photo shows. Attempts have been made to determine the size of the creature by comparing it to the size and make of the crate on which it was positioned. Researchers have carefully studied the physical nature of the creature. The acclaimed cryptozoologist Ivan T. Sanderson was sure the whole affair was a hoax of the bad-taste variety. He was right.

Even though there are still some within cryptozoology who continue to champion the de Loys photo, they are clearly losing the battle. A careful study of the picture shows a female spider monkey, almost certainly the white-fronted variety. Typical of white-fronted spider monkeys are characteristics seen in the picture, namely, nostrils pointing forwards, vestigial thumbs, and a large, external clitoris.

In other words, the whole affair was nothing but fakery. But it was fakery with a purpose, as monster-hunter Richard Freeman notes. The entire matter was designed to help boost and support the racist beliefs of de Loys' friend and colleague, George Montandon. Freeman explains:

> Montandon believed that White Europeans had evolved from Cro-Magnon man, but black Africans had descended from chimpanzees or gorillas, and Asians from orangutans. He needed a hypothetical South American ape to complete his story, an ancestor to modern Indians in the Americas.

Finally, we can lay to rest the matter of de Loys' ape. There is, however, an ironic postscript to this sorry saga. Although de Loys was an undeniable hoaxer, there are far more reliable and credible reports coming out of Venezuela concerning unknown man-beasts. Within certain portions of the nation, tribespeople tell of the Salvaje, an approximately five-foot-tall ape—or, possibly, a monkey—that has reddish hair and emits cries like a human. One such report came from a Venezuelan hunter named Fernando Nives, who encountered three Salvaje in 1980 while hunting along the Orinoco. A further sighting was made, five years later, by a construction worker who encountered a solitary beast around twenty miles from where Nives's confrontation occurred.

Despite the black cloud provoked by François de Loys and George Montandon, the anomalous apes and monkeys of Venezuela may not just be the stuff of conniving conmen, after all.

The Descent (2005 movie)

The Descent is a 2005 movie that deals with what happens when a group of women, all old friends, get together to do some caving in the wilds of North Carolina's Appalachian Mountains, and become the victims of cannibalistic humanoids that lurk deep underground. It's important to note that the movie is not specifically Bigfoot-themed. However, the fact that there are deep suspicions that Bigfoot's uncanny ability to elude us on almost every occasion is due to it being a creature that may spend most of its time living in caverns and caves makes *The Descent* a movie that Bigfoot enthusiasts should watch and think about carefully. There may be more truth in it than anyone might guess.

Although the movie is set in North Carolina, all of the filming occurred in the U.K.: the exterior wooded shots were filmed at Ashridge Park, Buckinghamshire (known locally as Ashridge Forest), while the caves were actually skillfully created fabrications, put together in Pinewood Studios, London.

The movie begins in traumatic and unforeseen fashion: Sarah (actress Shauna Macdonald) is the only survivor of a violent, head-on collision that killed her daughter and husband. About a year later, Sarah, still severely affected and traumatized by what happened, meets up in the Appalachians with her closest friends: Sam (MyAnna Buring), Beth (Alex Reid), Juno (Natalie Mendoza), and Rebecca (Saskia Mulder), as well as a friend of Juno's, Holly (Nora-Jane Noone).

The group is keen to explore a particular deep cave that has been discovered but which few people know about. Unfortunately, it doesn't quite work out like that. Unknown to the rest of the girls, Juno has decided to have them investigate a completely unknown cave system that—literally—no one knows about. That, in itself, would not be a problem, except for one thing: when there is a tunnel collapse, which leaves the six trapped, and Holly breaks a leg, they have no way to contact anyone in the outside world to tell them where, exactly, they are.

In mere moments, what should have been a fun, adventurous time in the ancient, shadowy caves and caverns that extend deep underground becomes a fight for survival. It's not just the rigors of Mother Nature that the six have to combat. In quick time, it becomes clear that the friends are not alone. They are being stalked and hunted by something terrifying. We are treated and tantalized by fleeting glimpses of vaguely human-looking creatures that are super-agile and charge around the tunnels in crazed fashion. The monsters have only one thing on their minds: turning the girls into their next meals.

Their danger becomes very apparent when all manner of bones—human and animal—are found piled high and wide in the tunnels. Terrible and savage screams and growls echo around the pitch black chambers. Finally, we get to see the monstrous things: they are humanlike, but clearly not of the *Homo sapiens* variety. The director of *The Descent*, Neil Marshall, said of the cave creatures: "They've evolved in this environment over thousands of years. They've adapted perfectly to thrive in the cave. They've lost their eyesight, they have acute hearing and smell and function perfectly in the pitch black. They're expert climbers, so they can go up any rock face and that is their world."

And they are very partial to human meat.

Thus, a battle begins between the friends—whose relationships fracture, splinter, and practically disintegrate as the fight for survival takes its unrelenting hold on one and all. Unlike so many of today's watered-down horror movies—which feel the need to provide some sense of hope for the characters and a degree of a happy ending—*The Descent* does nothing of the sort. It demonstrates that when we are far away from civilization and our technologies, we are not the superior beings we arrogantly assume ourselves to be. We're breakfast, lunch, and dinner, all rolled into one.

In some respects, the creatures are not unlike the Morlocks of H. G. Wells's acclaimed novel of 1895, *The Time Machine*. In Wells's story the chief character, rather surprisingly, is never named: he is simply referred to as the "time traveler." He constructs a machine, as the book's title suggests, to travel through time. He achieves this, finally ending up in England in the year 802,701. The world of the distant future is not a good one: nuclear war in the distant past—but in the future of the time traveler, who lives in Victorian England—has ravaged the planet. The human race has been reduced to two types of being: the Eloi, who look just like us, but who live passive, simple lives, lacking any kind of drive or ambition, and who inhabit a jungle environment. Then there are the Morlocks: large, muscular, hairy apes that live deep underground and who, essentially, breed the Eloi like cattle. The Eloi, then, are the Morlocks' food.

Both *The Descent* and *The Time Machine* are fiction. Bigfoot is not. Perhaps it really is a cave-dwelling creature, one that is rarely seen because, quite simply, it hardly ever surfaces from its massive network of underground lairs. If so, let's hope that if we one day stumble on the labyrinthine abodes of Bigfoot, they are not strewn with the bones of thousands of missing people.

Dev

See: Sleeping Soviet Sasquatch

Didi of Taushida, Guyana

Situated on the northern coast of South America, Guyana is a place that, like so many other locales dominated by thick jungles and high mountains, can boast of being the domain of a Bigfoot-style entity. It is known by the people of Guyana as the Didi. Interestingly, although the Didi resembles Bigfoot in the sense that it has a humanoid form and is covered in hair, there is one big difference: the monster of Guyana possesses razor-sharp claws, which is unlike all other apes. This has led to the theory that the Didi may actually be a creature known as Megatherium, a huge sloth that died out millennia ago—or, just perhaps, it didn't. On the other hand, many witnesses to the Didi have remarked on its eerie human-like qualities, despite its savage, primitive appearance.

In November 2007, an ambitious expedition was launched by the UK's Centre for Fortean Zoology (CFZ) to try, once and for all, to resolve the mystery of the Didi.

A Megatherium (fossil skeleton at the Museum of Natural History in Paris, France, shown here) was a giant sloth that was about twenty feet in length and lived during the late Pliocene period. If, somehow, these huge creatures still existed, they might be mistaken for a kind of Bigfoot, especially when standing on their hind feet.

Almost immediately upon arriving, the team was exposed to a number of accounts of Didi activity, many of which were downright hostile. For example, residents of the village of Taushida told of how, around 2003 or 2004, a Didi abducted a young girl from the area. According to the story, two pre-teens, a girl and a boy, were strolling across the plains when a huge, hair-covered hominid loomed out of a dense, treed area and charged in the direction of the terrified pair. In an instant, a huge arm grabbed the girl and the beast bounded for the camouflage of the surrounding woods. The boy, filled with fear, raced back to Taushida, to breathlessly report what had happened. Despite a quickly launched, intensive effort, the girl was never seen again.

Demonstrating the possibility that the Didis are not huge sloths, Damon Corrie, a local chief, discovered a cave in the mountains that contained what were described to the CFZ as clubs and shields, but which were clearly fashioned by, and for, something far bigger than a human. Since sloths do not create, or use, tools and weapons, a good argument can be made that their creator was a large, unknown humanoid.

A further report provided to the CFZ dealt with a 1950s-era encounter, in which a man—while traveling back to Taushida after a successful day of hunting in the mountains—almost literally stumbled upon a huge Didi sleeping in something akin to a hammock, but fashioned out of tree branches, vines, and leaves. Fortunately, the creature did not awaken, and the petrified man crept quietly out of the area and, when a significant distance away, fled for his life. The story, however, was not quite over.

Within hours of getting home, the man fell sick. For the superstitious people of Taushida—who perceived the Didi as a creature possessing supernatural powers—the man had become the victim of the equivalent of a witch's hex. Fortunately, this was not the case. While the possibility exists that the Didi could have supernatural origins and powers (as is believed to be the case with numerous Bigfoot-like animals), in this incident, the local witch-doctor deduced that the man had been plunged into a deep state of shock, rather than falling under a malevolent spell of the Didi.

Interestingly, the CFZ uncovered more than a few accounts suggesting the existence of a small, primitive humanoid that lived on the fringes of Taushida—at least, until around the dawning of the 1980s, when they either moved onto new pastures or became extinct. The creatures—known to the people of Taushida as the Bush People—were less than four feet in height, lived in teepee-like structures that were built around tree trunks, and had distinct, red faces. Somewhat amusingly, although the Bush People lived very private lives and did not overly mix with the villagers, they did share a passion for tobacco, which the village folk regularly left at the edges of the forest for their dwarfish neighbors.

Dogs and Bigfoot

T he Bigfoot Field Researchers Organization (BFRO) says: "Sasquatches are also known to kill dogs that chase or threaten them. Dogs often flee or cower in their presence, but some dogs are more aggressive and sometimes receive very brutal treatment as a result. Aggressive dogs have been found torn apart, with Sasquatch tracks around the remains."

The BFRO is right on target. There are many cases on record that demonstrate dogs seem to have innate hostility towards, and fear of, Bigfoot—and vice versa, too: Bigfoot seemingly has no love of dogs.

A particularly fascinating Bigfoot-dog case occurred in 1973, close to the 156-mile-long Big Muddy River, in southern Illinois. It involved a creature that, perhaps inevitably, became known as the Big Muddy Monster. This is hardly surprising, since local folk were reporting fear-filled encounters with an approximately seven-foot-tall Bigfoot, covered in white hair. One of the most significant reports surfaced from the town of Murphysboro, a report that provoked terror and even a response from the local police, who took the case very seriously—checking out the area, and following the tracks of the creature. When it came to the very close encounter of the Ray family, who saw a huge, lumbering, white beast, the police even prepared an official report on the affair. In part, the real-life *X-File*—which graphically details the dog's adverse reaction to the presence of the creature—noted:

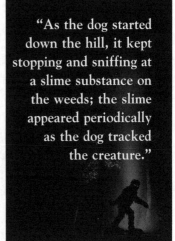

"As the dog started down the hill, it kept stopping and sniffing at a slime substance on the weeds; the slime appeared periodically as the dog tracked the creature."

> Officers inspected the area where the creature was seen and found weeds broken down and somewhat of a path where something had walked through. Jerry Nellis was notified to bring his dog to the area to see if the dog would track the creature. Upon arrival of Nellis and dog the dog was led to the area where the creature was last seen. The dog began tracking down the hill where the creature was reported to have gone.

> As the dog started down the hill, it kept stopping and sniffing at a slime substance on the weeds; the slime appeared periodically as the dog tracked the creature. Nellis put some of the slime between his fingers, rubbed it and left a black coloring on his fingers. Each time the dog found amounts of it, the dog would hesitate.

> The creature was tracked down the hill to a pond, around the pond to a wooded area south of the pond where the dog attempted to pull Nellis down a steep embankment. The area where the dog tracked the creature was too thick and bushy to walk through, so the dog was pulled off the trail and returned to the car. Officers then searched the area with flashlights. Officer Nash, Nellis, and the dog then proceeded to the area directly south of where the dog was pulled off the tracks. The area was at the end of the first road to the west past Westwood Hills turnoff. The area is approximately one-half mile south of the area of the pond behind 37 Westwood Lane.

> Nellis and the dog again began to search the area to see if the dog could again pick up the scent. Nellis and the dog approached the abandoned barn and Nellis called to Officer Nash to come to the area as the dog would not enter the barn. Nellis pushed the dog inside and the dog immediately ran out. Nash and Nellis searched the barn and found nothing

inside. Nellis stated that the dog was trained to search buildings and had never backed down from anything. Nellis could find no explanation as to why the dog became scared and would not go inside the barn. Officers continued to search the area and were unable to locate the creature.

In July 2012, the *Bigfoot Evidence* blog posted:

Just last month, we posted a photo by Jeff Y. of a German shepherd that was supposedly found buried under some logs over Memorial Day weekend. According to Jeff, the area had been a hotspot for Sasquatch activity and the most recent were some hand prints of a baby Sasquatch found the near campsite. "There were other signs that the campers had problems. We have 2 small hand prints from different times in this area that points to a baby Sasquatch in the area. The dog probably got too close to it," Jeff said.

Bigfoot Evidence continued:

In 2010, a North Carolina "Mountain Man" named Tim Peeler claimed he had an encounter near the South Mountains State Park with a 10-foot-tall Sasquatch with "beautiful hair" that was trying to attack his dog. Peeler said he probably lured the Sasquatch to him when he was using a game call to find coyote.

The High Shoals Falls in South Mountains State Park, North Carolina, are a beautiful sight to see; they are also situated in local Sasquatch territory.

Also in July 2012, the *Southern Missourian* newspaper published an article that told of events that had occurred in the summer of 1972 in the city of Louisiana, Missouri, a region of the country where the local Bigfoot is called a "Momo." It stated:

The Momo saga began on July 11, 1972. The Harrison family lived in a house along what was then known as Marzolf Hill. On a hot summer day, 8-year-old Terry Harrison and his 5-year-old brother, Wally, were chasing their dog through the woods.

Suddenly, 15-year-old Doris Harrison, who was inside, heard her brothers screaming, ran to the window and saw a creature she described as perhaps 7 feet tall with dark hair covering its face. It held a dead dog under its arm and blood—apparently from the dog—flecked the dark hair of the beast. And, ooh, that smell!

Another woman in the neighborhood reported hearing animal noises. A farmer said his dog disappeared. Maybe Momo took it! Soon, others were reporting smells, sightings of dark objects in the night, bizarre screams and cries.

The precise reason for the fraught relationship between dogs and Bigfoot remains unclear. Perhaps the massive creatures see dogs as sources of food, and the astute hounds recognize this. Maybe, it's the fact that Bigfoot represents something unknown, something terrifying, and monstrous that instills overwhelming fear in dogs. One thing is certain: If Bigfoot is roaming your neighborhood, keep your dogs locked up, inside.

Dokos

See: Kenya's Collection of Unknown Apes

Dreaded Wild Men in Canada

"**D**READED WILD MEN Strike Fear into Indian Children" was the eye-catching newspaper headline that jumped out of the pages of the March 3, 1934, edition of the *Lethbridge Herald,*which covered the Lethbridge area of Alberta, Canada. The story was a fascinating one, given that it focused on the often reported possibility that the Bigfoot creatures are able to remain out of harm's way and detection by living underground, such as in ancient caverns and incredibly deep cave systems.

The article began by stating that Native American children in the vicinity of Harrison Mills, British Columbia, had been warned to stay close to "their mothers' apron strings, for the fearsome 'Sasquatch' had returned to spread terror through peace-loving Chehalis tribes."

It was noted that although reports of the much-feared creatures were all the rage in the area some three decades earlier, this was the first time, since around 1914, that they had been seen "on the prowl" in the area. It appeared that news of the first of these new encounters came from a man named Frank Dan.

The *Lethbridge Herald* captivated its readers with the details of the uncanny event:

Investigating the persistent barking of his dog at night, Dan came face to face with a hairy giant who, according to Dan, was tall and muscular, prowling in the nude. He was covered in black hair from head to foot except for a small space around the eyes. Dan ran breathlessly into his house and secured the door. Peeking through the window, he saw the giant stride leisurely into the nearby bush and disappear.

The writer of the article noted something very interesting:

The Indians say the Sasquatch dwell in caves and subterranean caverns on the borders of lakes in the mountain vastnesses [sic]. Many strange tales are told of the appearances of the elusive people.

Despite the unsettling nature of the story, the newspaper finished on a humorous note, whether deliberate or not:

A Chehalis woman related that, when her husband was returning from the hunt with a score or more of ducks he had shot, a Sasquatch stepped out

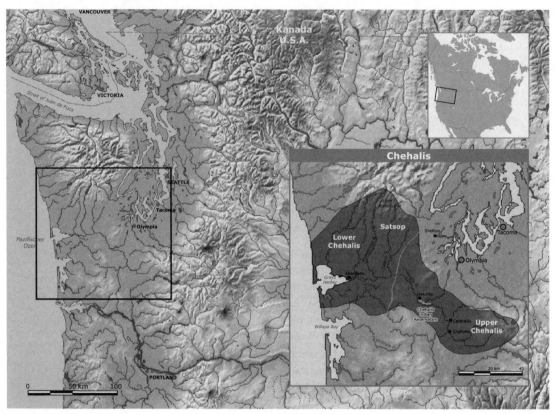

The Chehalis tribes live in territory southwest of Seattle, Washington, where there have been a number of Sasquatch sightings.

of the bush and took the ducks from him—except one, which the giant stuffed into the shirt of the frightened Indian.

Selfish, it would appear, Bigfoot is not!

Duende of Belize

In the Central American country of Belize exists an enigmatic and mysterious entity known as the Duende (also spelled Dwendi, depending on the particular region of Belize). A fascinating commentary on the Duende surfaced in 1961, from one of the world's most respected seekers of unknown animals, the late Ivan T. Sanderson. He said:

> Dozens told me of having seen them, and these were mostly men of substance who had worked for responsible organizations like the Forestry Department and who had, in several cases, been schooled or trained either

in Europe or the United States. One, a junior forestry officer born locally, described in great detail two of these little creatures that he had suddenly noticed quietly watching him on several occasions at the edge of the forestry reserve near the foot of the Maya Mountains.

These little folk were described as being between three foot six and four foot six, well- proportioned but with very heavy shoulders and rather long arms, clothed in thick, tight, close brown hair looking like that of a short-coated dog; having very flat yellowish faces but head-hair no longer than the body hair except down the back of the neck and midback.

In 2004, a good friend of mine, and a fellow mystery creature pursuer, Ken Gerhard, traveled to Belize to seek out the Duende for himself. It was a most profitable expedition. In Gerhard's own words:

We were quite fortunate to obtain as our guide Honorio Mai, whose great uncle discovered the famous ruins of Caracol in the jungle. Honorio is also one of only a few men who have crossed the notorious Rapaculo pass, armed only with a machete. Honorio immediately shocked me by telling me that his sister had, in fact, been kidnapped by a Dwendi at the age of two.

He claimed that she was playing near the forest when she began to point and shout, "Look at that boy!" Apparently, no one but the child was able to see the small, mysterious being. Soon afterwards, the young girl vanished, only to be found later sleeping next to a strange piece of cloth. When the material was taken as a bad omen and burned, Honorio's other infant sister died suddenly for no apparent reason.

It seems that the Dwendi (Spanish for "goblin") often take on supernatural characteristics in Belizean culture. They are often reputed to wear large hats or palm leaves on their heads and also to possess machetes or practice magic.

Gerhard also noted that, at a location called Mountain Pine Ridge,

I was most fortunate to come upon two separate sets of humanoid tracks in a remote region where the locals assured me they never went barefoot, due to scorpions and snakes. The first set was tiny (16½ cm x 7½ cm) and singly set in white gravel with a distinctly pointy heel. Two larger (23½ cm x 11½ cm) tracks were found twenty meters away in red clay. Later, another pair of tracks was discovered in a sandy creek bed nearby. I was able to make plaster casts of two of them, though there is not a great deal of definition in either one.

Gerhard concluded that "unexplored Belize with its dense jungles and numerous caves undoubtedly has the potential to harbor elusive man-beasts."

Ebu Gogo

See: Indonesia's Mysterious Ape

Ecuador's Hairy Horror

In the 1940s, a naturalist who spent time working in Ecuador as a dealer in live animals told cryptozoologist Ivan T. Sanderson:

> The so-called Shiru, I have heard of from the Indians and a few white hunters on both sides of the Andes but decidedly more so on the eastern slopes, where the vast mountains are still quite unexplored, and rarely, if ever visited. All reports describe the Shiru as a small (4–5 feet) creature decidedly hominid, but fully covered with short, dark brown fur. All agreed that the Shiru was very shy, with the exception of one Indian, who claimed having been charged after having missed with his one and only shot from a muzzle loading shotgun, a weapon still used by the majority of Indians along with the blowgun. These reports are rather sober and objective, and in no way tinged with the colorful imagination into which Latin-Americans are prone to lapse.

El Sisemite

See: Women Kidnapped by Unknown Animals

Eskimo Legends of Mighty Man-Beasts

W ithin the culture, legend, and lore of the Eskimos—people of Greenland, Canada, Alaska, and Siberia—there are stories of giant, marauding creatures with whom they had a highly fraught relationship. They were the Tunnit, a race of creatures that were human-like, but clearly not human in the way we understand the term today.

Certainly, no one did more to uncover the truth of the Tunnit than Ernest William Hawkes, as is demonstrated in his book *The Labrador Eskimo*, published in 1916. Hawkes was a noted anthropologist who spent a great deal of time in Canada and Alaska, along the Bering Strait, speaking with the indigenous people, gaining their trust and friendship, and securing a wealth of material on their lives, cultures, and beliefs.

It was during the course of his summer 1914 expedition to Hudson Bay, in northeastern Canada, that Hawkes learned of the terrifying Tunnit. He recorded the following, which demonstrates just how deeply, carefully, and extensively he listened to what his Eskimo informants had to tell him:

> Tunnit ("Tornit," in Baffin Island), according to tradition, were a gigantic race formerly inhabiting the northeastern coast of Labrador, Hudson strait, and southern Baffin island. Ruins of old stone houses and graves, which are ascribed to them by the present Eskimo, are found throughout this entire section, penetrating only slightly, however, into Ungava Bay. Briefly we may say that there is evidence, archaeological as well as traditional, that the Tunnit formerly inhabited both sides of Hudson strait. The oldest Eskimo of northern Labrador still point out these ruins, and relate traditions of their having lived together until the Tunnit were finally exterminated or driven out by the present Eskimo.

> According to the account given by an old Nachvak Eskimo, the Tunnit in ancient times had two villages in Nachvak bay. Their houses were built on an exposed shore (the present Eskimo always seek a sheltered beach for their villages, where they can land in their kayaks), showing that they had little knowledge of the use of boats. When they wanted boats, they stole them from the Eskimo. From this thieving of kayaks the original quarrel is said to have begun.

> For all their bigness and strength, the Tunnit were a stupid slow-going race (according to the Eskimo version), and fell an easy prey to the Eskimo, who used to stalk them and hunt them down like game. They did not dare to attack them openly, so cut them off, one by one, by following them, and attacking and killing them when asleep. Their favorite method was to bore holes in the foreheads of the Tunnit with an awl (a drill in the Greenland story in Rink).

Two brothers especially distinguished themselves in this warfare, and did not desist until the last of the Tunnit was exterminated. The Tunnit built their houses of heavy rocks, which no Eskimo could lift. They used the rocks for walls, and whale ribs and shoulder blades for the roof. At the entrance of the house two whale jaw-bones were placed. Ruins of these houses can still be seen, overgrown with grass, with the roof fallen in. They may be distinguished from old Eskimo iglus by the small, square space they occupy.

The Tunnit did not use the bow and arrow, but flint-headed lances and harpoons with bone or ivory heads. They were so strong that one of them could hold a walrus as easily as an Eskimo a seal.

They did not understand the dressing of sealskins, but left them in the sea, where the little sea-worms cleaned off the fat in a short time. The Tunnit dressed in winter in untanned deerskins. They were accustomed to carry pieces of meat around with them, between their clothing and body, until it was putrid, when they ate it. The Tunnit were very skillful with the lance, which they threw, sitting down and aiming at the object by resting the shaft on the boot. For throwing at a distance they used the throw-stick.

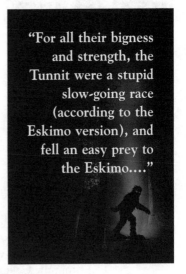

"For all their bigness and strength, the Tunnit were a stupid slow-going race (according to the Eskimo version), and fell an easy prey to the Eskimo...."

They did not hunt deer like the Eskimo, but erected long lines of stone "men" in a valley through which the deer passed. The deer would pass between the lines of stones, and the hunters hidden behind them would lance them. Remains of these lines of rocks may still be seen.

Their weapons were much larger, but not so well made as those of the Eskimo, as can be seen from the remains on their graves. The men used flint for the harpoon heads, and crystal for their drills. The women used a rounded piece of slate without a handle for a knife. They used a very small lamp for heating purposes, which they carried about them. For cooking they had a much larger lamp than the Eskimo. Until trouble arose between them, the Tunnit and the Eskimo used to intermarry, but after it was found that an alien wife would betray her husband to her people, no more were taken. A Tuneq woman, who betrayed the Eskimo of the village she lived in to the Tunnit, had her arms cut off. After that no women were taken on either side.

The Tunnit were gradually exterminated by the Eskimo, until only a scattered one remained here and there in their villages. How these were overcome by stratagems is handed down in the tales of the giant at Hebron, said to be the last of the Tunnit, and Adlasuq and the Giant. The giant allows himself to be bound in a snow-house, and is slain by the Eskimo hunters. This story has attained a mythological character in Baffin Island, but is ascribed by the Labrador Eskimo directly to the Tunnit. A story about the Tunnit, giving considerable circumstantial detail, was obtained from a Nachvak woman:

"At Nachvak the Tunnit were chasing a big whale (this was before the time of the present Eskimo). They were in two skin boats, about twenty men and women in each boat. They had the whale harpooned, and were being towed round and round the bay by him. Somehow the line got tangled in one of the boats and capsized. The other boat with the line still made fast to the whale, went to pick up the people in the water, and was capsized too. Another boat came off from the shore, and picked up some of the people in the water. Most of them were drowned.

"They were buried under a hill on a big bank near Nachvak. There are some thirty graves on this bank, with pots, harpoons, and knives buried by the graves. Even the remains of the boats are there. The knives and pots are of stone. The harpoon blades are of flint. The umiaks were much larger than the present boats."

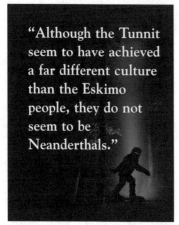

"Although the Tunnit seem to have achieved a far different culture than the Eskimo people, they do not seem to be Neanderthals."

On the specific matter of what, precisely, the Tunnit were, Jonathan Downes and Richard Freeman, of the Centre for Fortean Zoology, have made some noteworthy observations:

Although the Tunnit seem to have achieved a far different culture than the Eskimo people, they do not seem to be Neanderthals. They are too tall, for one thing, and also the level of cultural sophistication that they have reached seems to be beyond that ever achieved by Neanderthals. Our best guess is that they were a very primitive race of people, probably kin to the Mesolithic hunter-gatherers whom we suspect still live in the Transcaucasus, who keep their hairy skin and evolved a large size in order to cope with the climate of the frozen north.

In that sense, Downes and Freeman are of the opinion that the Tunnit may also be the Almasty of Russian lore—creatures that have been reported on a regular basis from the Caucasus Mountains (*see* "Almasty Expedition").

Exeter Watchman Publishes First Newspaper Article on Bigfoot

New York's *Exeter Watchman* might not be the most famous newspaper in the United States, but, in one major respect, it has gone down in the history books as the first newspaper to report on a creature resembling what we, today, refer to as Bigfoot, roaming around the countryside. Since this is a matter of profound significance, the article—titled "Another Wonder" and dated September 22, 1818, is reproduced below without interruption.

Reports say, that in the vicinity of Ellisburgh, was seen on the 30th Ult. by a gentleman of unquestionable veracity, an animal resembling the wild man of the woods. It is stated that he came from the woods within a few rods of this gentleman—that he stood and looked at him and then took his flight in a direction which gave a perfect view of him for some time. He is described as bending forward when running—hairy, and the heel of the foot narrow, spreading at the toes. Hundreds of persons have been in pursuit for several days, but nothing further is heard or seen of him.

The frequent and positive manner in which the story comes, induces us to believe it. We wish not to impeach the veracity of this highly favored gentleman—yet it is proper that such naturally improbable accounts should be established by the mouth of at least two direct eyewitnesses to entitle them to credit.

Fayette County, Pennsylvania, Bigfoot

Stan Gordon is one of the United States' leading researchers of the stranger side of the Bigfoot phenomenon. And it doesn't come much stranger than a case Gordon investigated in late 1973 in his home state of Pennsylvania. It's important to note that this case was one of dozens that Gordon received from 1972 to 1974, which, collectively, suggested the presence of unknown, hairy man-beasts all across Pennsylvania. Many of these cases, however, were dominated by phenomena that, for many Bigfoot investigators, fell far outside what one could call the norm—including an event that occurred in Fayette County in October 1973.

It was the dark night of October 25 when all hell broke loose in the heart of the county. The primary player in the story was Steve Palmer, who was both amazed and frightened to see a brightly illuminated UFO hovering over local farmland, around 9:00 P.M. But that wasn't all that Palmer encountered: a pair of immense, apelike animals with very long and muscular arms surfaced out of the shadows of the dark field and proceeded to walk right towards Palmer. He wasted no time and blasted them with a salvo of bullets.

Very weirdly, the bullets appeared to have no effect at all on either creature, and they retreated into the darkness. The UFO did likewise, vanishing in an instant. That was not the end of the affair, however. Approximately four hours later, things took on even stranger, and far more terrifying, proportions.

It was roughly 1:00 A.M. when Gordon arrived on the scene, having been alerted to the Palmer encounter by local police, who had been apprised of the facts. Along with Gordon were fellow investigators Dennis Smeltzer, Fred Pitt, David Smith, and George Lutz. They met with Palmer, who proceeded to tell them of his unearthly encounter with the two Bigfoot creatures and the UFO. Then, quite out of the blue, something horrifying occurred: Palmer's breathing changed, to the extent that he was literally panting heavily and deeply, and he broke into a deep, guttural growl and knocked both his own father and Lutz to the field floor. And that was only the start of things.

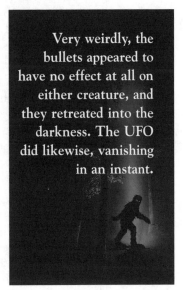

Very weirdly, the bullets appeared to have no effect at all on either creature, and they retreated into the darkness. The UFO did likewise, vanishing in an instant.

Pitt found himself unable to breathe properly, Smeltzer felt faint, and Palmer fell to the ground, having apparently passed out. A powerful, rotten odor of brimstone suddenly dominated the cold night air. The terrified group knew that it was vital they get out of the field—and quickly, too—before things got worse. Later, when Palmer regained consciousness, he told Gordon and his team that he, Palmer, while in his passed-out state, had seen before him a sickle-carrying, dark-robed figure that warned him the human race was on the verge of destroying itself—and would do exactly that unless it curbed its violent instincts.

Even stranger than that, a couple of weeks later, two Air Force officers, one in uniform and the other in plainclothes, visited Palmer at his home. It quickly became clear that the pair knew all about Palmer's weird encounter and the later experience. They even confided in him that they knew that both the UFO and the Sasquatches were genuine. There was a specific reason for the visit: first, they showed Palmer a number of photos of Bigfoot creatures and wanted to know if the beast he encountered resembled them. Second, they asked if Palmer would be willing to be placed into a hypnotic state, to ensure that the military secured all the relevant data. Palmer agreed. And with all the information in hand, the two men got up, thanked Palmer, and left. Despite telling Palmer they would keep him informed of any future developments, they failed to do so. He never saw them again. It was a fitting end to a case steeped in mystery.

Fish and Wildlife Service Document on Bigfoot

On December 21, 1977, the U.S. Department of the Interior's Fish and Wildlife Service (FWS) prepared a fascinating document that dealt with how, theoretically, the U.S. government might deal with the confirmation that Bigfoot—and other cryptids—really do exist. Its title was: *Are We Ready for "Bigfoot" or the Loch Ness Monster?* Since this is a document of some significance, it is presented below, in full. The FWS treated the entire matter in a serious fashion:

> What if they really did find the Loch Ness monster or the legendary Bigfoot of the Pacific Northwest? Most scientists doubt that these creatures exist, but thoughts of the discovery of a new species that might be the closest living relative to man, or the possibility of finding a leftover dinosaur, excite the imagination of scientist and nonscientist alike. It also poses another question: Would such a creature be subjected to the same kind of exploitation as the giant movie ape, King Kong?
>
> Scientists generally believe there are still many species of birds and mammals that have not been discovered because they live in remote areas and their populations are limited. After all, the gorilla and giant panda were only legends until the late 19th century when their actual existence was first confirmed by scientists. The komodo dragon, a 10-foot-long lizard, wasn't known to science until 1912. The coelacanth, a deep-water prehis-

The coelacanth is a fish that, most people thought, had gone extinct around the same time as the dinosaurs, but when one was discovered in 1938 the question arose: could other species believed extinct still exist today?

toric fish, was known only from 65 million-year-old fossils until 1938 when a specimen was caught alive off the Madagascar coast.

Just last year a Navy torpedo recovery vessel dropped a sea anchor into 500 feet of water off Hawaii. But instead of a torpedo, it hauled up a 15-foot representative of a new species of shark. The dead shark, named megamouth after its bathtub-shaped lower jaw, had an enormous, short-snouted head and 484 vestigial teeth.

To be sure, no remains of today's legendary "monsters" have ever been found. There are no living specimens in zoos or dead ones in museums. Most certainly, many "sightings" of these creatures are exaggerated or misinterpreted reports, and some are downright hoaxes.

But finding a Loch Ness monster or Bigfoot is still a possibility, and the discovery would be one of the most important in modern history. As items of scientific and public interest they would surely command more attention than the moon rocks. Millions of curiosity seekers and thousands of zoologists and anthropologists throughout the world would be eager to "get at" the creatures to examine, protect, capture, or just look at them.

What would the United States Government do?

"I doubt we'll ever have to do anything, because I don't believe there are any of the things around to be discovered in the first place," said Keith

Schreiner, Associate Director of the U.S. Fish and Wildlife Service. The Service is the Government agency with responsibility for protecting endangered and threatened species. "At least, we have the laws and regulations on the books to deal with newly discovered species."

Schreiner acknowledged, however, that a good deal of international cooperation would be needed if extremely rare species were found abroad. And finding one on U.S. soil would pose serious problems too, FWS officials agree.

Undisputed proof of a Bigfoot might cause an immediate, short-term problem no law could handle. Word of its discovery would be flashed around the world within hours. Hysteria, fear, or panic might accompany the news in the area where the creature was located. The throngs of curiosity seekers, would-be captors, and others wishing to find Bigfoot would not only create a serious threat to the animal itself, but to public safety as well. Some officials doubt whether any State or Federal action short of calling out the National Guard could keep order in the area within the first few hours or days of the creature's discovery. This could be essential until a team of scientists could do the necessary things to ensure the creature's survival.

> "The throngs of curiosity seekers, would-be captors, and others wishing to find Bigfoot would not only create a serious threat to the animal itself, but to public safety as well."

The key law in the preservation of a species is the Endangered Species Act, which pledges the United States to conserve species of plants and animals facing extinction. This broad, complex law protects endangered species from killing, harassment, and other forms of exploitation. The Act prohibits the import and export of, and interstate commerce in, endangered species. American citizens cannot engage in commercial traffic in endangered species between nations, even when the United States is not involved. Scientists wishing to study endangered species are required to have a permit issued by the U.S. Fish and Wildlife Service.

But before a creature can receive protection under the Endangered Species Act, a number of actions must occur that involve the public, scientists, and state and foreign governments where the species exists.

The first of these steps would be the creation of the species' formal description and naming in a recognized scientific publication. In addition, if it were a U.S. species, the Governor of the State where it was found would be contacted; in a case where the species was discovered outside the U.S., the officials of the foreign government would be contacted. Only after much information was collected could the Service make a formal determination as to whether the species should be afforded endangered or threatened status.

For the Loch Ness monster, the first step has already been taken. In 2014 a highly respected British journal published a description and proposed the name *Nessiteras rhombopteryx*, meaning "awesome monster of Loch Ness with a diamond-shaped fin."

"Nessie," as the creature is affectionately known by believers in its existence, has been periodically sighted in Loch Ness, Scotland, over the last 14 centuries. Loch Ness is a 2.5-mile-long, cold, deep lake whose peat-stained, murky waters make positive identification of almost anything from photographs next to impossible. But the most recent reports, based on sophisticated underwater cameras and electronic gear, identify a 30-foot-long creature with a massive, humped body bearing a small head and long slender neck with an immense set of flippers. Although no presently known aquatic organism answers this description, it would fit any of various species of prehistoric, carnivorous reptiles called plesiosaurs, which lived 100 million years ago.

In recent discussion in the British House of Commons, members of Parliament were assured that if "Nessie" were found it could theoretically receive immediate protection since it had already been described and named. If "Nessie" were taken out of Britain illegally, it would be a violation of the U.S. Lacey Act to bring it into the United States.

> The U.S. Army Corps of Engineers even lists Bigfoot as one of the native species in its "Environmental Atlas for Washington."

Bigfoot, also known as Sasquatch, is purported to be an 8-foot, 900-pound humanoid that roams the forest and wilderness areas of the Pacific Northwest. One "eyewitness" described an obviously female Sasquatch as a "tall, long-legged, gorilla-like animal covered with dark hair and endowed with a pendulous pair of breasts." It, too, has been described in publications and given a scientific name. In fact, so many people were stalking Bigfoot with high-powered rifles and cameras that Skamania County, Washington, is prepared to impose a fine of $10,000 and a 5-year jail term on anyone who kills a Bigfoot. The U.S. Army Corps of Engineers even lists Bigfoot as one of the native species in its "Environmental Atlas for Washington." In 2014 the Florida and Oregon legislatures also considered bills protecting "Bigfoot" type creatures. A Bureau of Indian Affairs policeman has 18-inch plaster cast footprints of the "McLaughlin monster," a Bigfoot-type creature he saw last month in South Dakota.

Under U.S. law the Secretary of the Interior is empowered to list a species as threatened or endangered for 120 days on an emergency basis. For endangered species in the United States, the Secretary can also designate habitat that is critical to their survival. No Federal agency could then authorize, fund, or carry out any activities which would adversely modify that habitat.

So long-term federal protection of Nessie or Bigfoot would basically be a matter of following the same regulatory mechanisms already used in protecting whooping cranes and tigers.

"Under normal situations," Schreiner said, "we must know a great deal about a species before we list it. How big is the population? Does it occur anywhere else? Is the population in danger of decline? Is its habitat secure?

"So long-term federal protection of Nessie or Bigfoot would basically be a matter of following the same regulatory mechanisms already used in protecting whooping cranes and tigers."

Is the species being exploited? What is its reproductive rate? Obviously, if a Bigfoot really were found we could use emergency provisions of the Act to protect it immediately. But for the record, I seriously doubt whether such a creature really does exist."

Along with the hundreds of requests received in 2014 to protect more well-known plants and animals, the U.S. Fish and Wildlife Service was queried about protection for Bigfoot and the "Lake Champlain sea serpent."

No requests have so far been received for the protection of the reputed foul-smelling Noxie monster, a 7-foot denizen of Oklahoma, or the skunk ape of the Everglades, or the infamous Mothman in West Virginia. But in time, they, too, might come. And when they do, they'll be treated accordingly.

While the FWS document does, admittedly, have its lighthearted moments, it's clear that a great deal of work and research went into creating the document—and particularly so in relation to the matter of how officialdom would respond to the discovery of Bigfoot, as well as matters relative to its safety and security. All of this begs two important questions. Is the lack of any subsequent, similar FWS document an indication that the matter is not considered important and serious enough to deal with? Or, has evidence for the existence of Bigfoot been found and, as a result, systematically and secretly hidden by the government?

Flying Saucers and Bigfoot

Many Bigfoot researchers are loath to investigate reports that appear to have connections to the UFO phenomenon. Likewise, numerous flying saucer investigators are highly reluctant to study accounts in which the witness claims to have seen not just UFOs or aliens, but large, hairy man-beasts, too—very often in the same time frame and location. One person who is not afraid to delve into such controversial areas is Stan Gordon, a longtime investigator of both phenomena in his native Pennsylvania.

Gordon shares, from his case files, a Bigfoot–UFO wave that hit Pennsylvania in 2010:

Sightings of Unidentified Flying Objects were frequently reported by residents of the Keystone State during 2010. Among the other odd events reported were encounters with strange creatures such as Bigfoot and giant birds, unexplained sounds, strange sky flashes and anomalous photographs. Reports of such mysterious events which crossed my desk during 2010, originated from 49 counties in Pennsylvania. In 1969 I established a hotline for the public to report UFO sightings. Today I still receive current reports concerning UFO sightings, Bigfoot, and any type of strange incidents from across Pennsylvania at 724-838-7768, or via email at paufo@comcast.net.

The information on cases which I receive are either reported to me directly, or originate from other sources, including various local and national researchers, many of which I have contact with. Also some reports are received from various local or national organizations. For example, The National UFO Reporting Center, www.nuforc.org and the Pennsylvania chapter of the Mutual UFO Network, www.mufonpa.com also receive UFO reports from this state. The Pennsylvania Bigfoot Society, (PBS) www.pabigfootsociety.com conducts field studies searching for evidence of Bigfoot in the state.

It is now approaching 52 years that I have been investigating and collecting information on these ongoing yearly strange accounts that originate from Pennsylvania. During that time period, I was involved with the investigations of thousands of very strange events. During the many on scene investigations that I was involved with, there were some cases

The Kecksburg, Pennsylvania, UFO, which was reported in 1965, supposedly looked like this acorn model. The sighting inspired the work of researcher Stan Gordon, who believes there may be a connection between UFOs and Bigfoot.

where some interesting physical evidence was observed at the scene. I personally, however, have never had a UFO sighting or had an encounter with Bigfoot.

I began my field investigations after the Kecksburg UFO incident in 1965. Since that time it has become clear that many UFO sightings, creature encounters, and various paranormal events when properly investigated are determined to originate from a natural or man-made source. There are some incidents of this nature that occur year after year, however, that are not easily explained away. Some of the UFO observations reported during 2010 could be explained as bright planets and stars, meteors, conventional aircraft, and Chinese lanterns or similar home-made hot air balloons.

Reported UFO sightings from across Pennsylvania started in January and continued throughout the 2010 year. Some of the UFO reports which came to my attention, can be found at: http://www.stangordon.info/sightings.htm.

A number of UFO sightings were reported from various statewide locations on May 26, 2010. I interviewed a woman, who along with her passenger was traveling on a busy roadway in the metro Pittsburgh area. On that morning, they observed a bright silver metallic disc shaped object rotating in circles as it moved steadily across the sky. An attempt to take a picture of it was unsuccessful.

On July 5th close to Jeannette in Westmoreland County, two people watched a bright yellow-orange light move across the sky that seemed to be pulsating or rotating. The object passed overhead, and 3 white lights positioned in a triangular pattern were attached to the underside of a darker silent object which moved towards the east. On July 17th, also near Jeannette, another witness reported a bright star-like object high in the sky that began to pulsate and grew larger in size. It pulsated 2–3 times, then the object became dim, and soon just vanished.

On the evening of July 18th, in Hempfield Township outside of Greensburg, several independent observers that I interviewed observed a bright orange-yellow glowing object moving slowly across the sky. One of the observers took several color photographs before the object seemed to accelerate as it moved off in the distance sky. One picture clearly shows three white lights in a triangular pattern. (Note: For several months there were numerous reports of luminous glowing objects being reported. It is quite likely that some of these reports can be attributed to someone launching Chinese lanterns or other similar home-made hot air balloon devices.)

Mini-UFOs: There were a number of reports of close range observations of small sized UFOs. Over the years I have received a number of similar types of reports.

Near Derry in July, a man who was taking a walk observed a pale white solid sphere that appeared to be about 2 inches in diameter. The slow moving object was observed about 15 feet above the ground, and approached the witness to a distance of about 15 feet. The witness watched as the object moved around some trees, then continued on in the distance. In August, near Norvelt, a witness reported observing a rectangular object about 8–9 feet long, rounded in the front, with a soft white glow to it. The object was observed as it moved about 3 feet above the ground, and was about 15 feet from the observer.

A wave of Bigfoot and UFO combined sightings occurred in Pennsylvania in 2010.

On November 24th, on the Youngstown side of the Chestnut Ridge, two witnesses observed a red spherical object about 60 yards away in a wooded area. One of the observers moved closer to the object to try to figure out what it was. The object, which was about 3–4 feet off the ground, was of an unusual configuration. The observer who approached to about 70 feet from the object said that it looked somewhat like, "a ball with the top quarter cut off."

The man explained that the top quarter was the "orb," which was flat on the bottom section. The entire object was estimated to be about 60–72 inches long, and about 30–36 inches high. The silent object was a solid red color, but non-glowing with a colored edge, and a bottom. While the object remained motionless, some sort of white spark was observed emitting from the bottom section. The object slowly moved off, made some direction changes, then with great speed moved over a hill and was lost from sight.

Strange Creatures: Bigfoot and Thunderbirds: Bigfoot sightings continue to be reported yearly from various locations across Pennsylvania. Westmoreland and Fayette Counties continue to be active areas where such reports have historically originated from. In June, two people say that they saw a 7–8 feet tall man-like creature covered with tan-brown hair at dusk in Derry Township. I also interviewed a fellow who had been a hunter for many years, but it wasn't until one early morning in July that he saw something he could not explain. The event occurred in Allegheny County, near a tree line. The witness observed a man-like creature covered with reddish-brown hair, that stood at least 7½ feet tall from a distance of about 50–60 feet. The creature was very broad shouldered, and had very long arms. The creature was observed for about 40 seconds.

The Pennsylvania Bigfoot Society (PBS) also received a number of reports of possible Bigfoot sightings from Fayette, Westmoreland and Cambria counties. One case they investigated occurred in April near Scottdale. A man was awakened by his dogs barking at something outside. He investigates and hears sounds like a woman screaming. He looks outside to see a large creature on all fours walking around the yard. The creature then stands up on two legs. It is described as about six feet tall, very thin, and covered with dark hair. The creature with arms swinging, walks off into the woods near the house. The PBS investigates and finds one possible track that measured 16 inches long.

There continue to be observations of giant birds with oversized wingspans reported from areas of Pennsylvania. There has been a long history of such observations from the Keystone State, as well as other parts of the United States. Many accounts refer to such observations as "Thunderbird sightings." Some of these sightings are likely misidentifications of known bird species observed from various distances and under various lighting conditions. Some reports however include close range observations with detailed accounts.

An Ojibwa pouch is decorated with two thunderbirds. Along with Bigfoot, there have been sightings in Pennsylvania of these giant avians from Native American mythology.

One such incident occurred on August 26th in South Greensburg in Westmoreland County. It was just getting dark when four people at a cookout heard a "swoosh" sound causing them to look to the sky. A tremendous bird was flying over a tree in the yard about 30–40 feet overhead. It was estimated that if the bird was on the ground, it would stand between 4½ and 5 feet tall. The entire body was either darkish brown or black in color. The body width was about 25–30 inches wide.

It was the size of the wingspan which was estimated to be 10 feet or more that impressed the observers. The observers watched as the huge bird flapped its wings as it moved down the road, taking about 20 seconds to go a distance of about ¼ mile as it moved off over some trees. It was just a short distance from this location where in September of 2001, another witness saw a huge dark bird with a massive wingspan flying over the traffic on Route 119.

Forbidden Bigfoot (2013 book)

On more than a few occasions in this book, I have noted the undeniable fact that many people within the Bigfoot research arena will simply not address the theory that the creature is far more than a mere unknown animal, and may possibly possess distinct, supernatural qualities. That is, aside from predictably attacking the theory.

Now, I have no problem with people concluding that the high-strangeness angle of Bigfoot has no validity if they actually do the research to prove their point. But, time and again, I come across researchers of the monstrous mystery who openly admit to refusing to even look at such cases, read books on the weirder side of Bigfoot, or engage the witnesses in debate. The reason? Their minds are already made up. And that's something I do have a problem with.

Unfortunately, a mind already made up (without even a single corpse or a living specimen available to support the flesh and blood angle, I might add!) is something else, too. Actually, it amounts to two things: biased and closed. Too bad. Like it or not, there are far more than a few reports out there that strongly suggest Bigfoot is not just an unknown primate that skillfully avoids capture, shooting, or killing with a 100 percent success rate, 100 percent of the time.

One person who knows this very well is Lisa Shiel. The author of a number of Bigfoot-themed books (including *Backyard Bigfoot*, for which I wrote the foreword), Shiel, in 2013, penned a book titled *Forbidden Bigfoot: Exposing the Controversial Truth about Sasquatch, Stick Signs, UFOs, Human Origins, and the Strange Phenomena in Our Own Backyards*.

In other words, we're dealing with territory, cases, and theories that most Bigfoot chasers wouldn't touch if you paid them to. Fortunately, Shiel takes the very wise approach that if the Bigfoot mystery exhibits evidence suggesting the creatures are significantly different from what they appear to be (and they certainly do exhibit such evidence), then the very least we can do is address the data.

But, Shiel does far more than her very least. She offers us her very best, which is a first-class study of the anomalous side of Bigfoot. And by that, we're talking about the telepathic aspect of Bigfoot, the creatures vanishing in puffs of smoke or flashes of light, the overwhelmingly elusive and "here one minute, gone the next" aspect of the puzzle, tracks that come to a sudden halt in the woods, associations between the beasts and strange aerial lights (such as "orbs"), and much more.

> "... Shiel takes the very wise approach that if the Bigfoot mystery exhibits evidence suggesting the creatures are significantly different from what they appear to be...."

And before the mainstream Bigfoot community starts on a tedious, tired rant, let us remember that Shiel's research is based on witness testimony. Time and again I hear that the witnesses are the most important people in the subject. And I agree fully: they most certainly are. Without the witnesses, we have nothing to go on. So show some respect—not rants, just because the words of the witnesses might not adhere to your personal "Bigfoot is an ape" theory.

Forbidden Bigfoot offers the reader a large amount of data of the type that the likes of John Keel, the author of *The Mothman Prophecies*, would have looked on approvingly, such as the trickster-like nature of the phenomenon, the "habituation" aspect of the mystery (which encompasses "repeater" witnesses), the links between Bigfoot and other anomalous entities (like elementals), multi-dimensions, and even cases where the witnesses experienced significant time-loss.

Shiel also provides the reader with something else: far more than a few choice words for the Bigfoot research community, those who engage in field investigations, and those whose minds are firmly stuck in the flesh-and-blood camp. And to her credit, Shiel pulls no punches when she notes the spectacular failure of the community to prove its point that the North American Bigfoot creatures are simply unidentified and unclassified apes—despite decades of research and countless sightings.

More importantly, Shiel is not just a commentator on the Bigfoot phenomenon. She has experienced it at very close quarters, too. And many of her experiences lead down a pathway that veers far from the mainstream. Good for Shiel, too, that she does not have to think twice about sharing such data with her readers. Whether you believe Bigfoot to be an unknown type of ape or something infinitely stranger, you should read *Forbidden Bigfoot*.

Of course, some seekers of Bigfoot will take the view that Shiel's words amount to near blasphemy and will likely deride and damn them. Shiel astutely knows this, as she herself points out: "Sometimes ignorance stems from laziness or lack of access to data; in other cases, however, ignorance is a choice. Avoid looking at the data and, voila, for you the data does not exist."

Keeping Shiel's words in mind, don't be lazy and don't be ignorant. Instead, pick up a copy of *Forbidden Bigfoot* and be prepared for a wild ride into the world of Bigfoot that so many steer clear of. Their loss can be your gain—if you are prepared to think, and look, outside of the Bigfoot box.

Geow-lud-mo-sis-eg

See: Canada's Cryptid Ape-Men

Gigantopithecus blacki

If the North American Bigfoot, the Yeti of the Himalayas, the Chinese Yeren, and the Russian Almasty are, indeed, giant apes, then the question needs to be asked: What is their precise identity? One candidate is *Gigantopithecus blacki*. It was a massive ape that lived in the distant past and which some Bigfoot researchers are convinced may explain sightings of large, anomalous apes in some of the wilder, desolate, and forested areas of our planet today. There is just one problem with this particular theory: mainstream science, biology, and zoology all assure us that *Gigantopithecus* became extinct thousands of years ago. Just maybe, however, it didn't.

In terms of what is known about *Gigantopithecus*, we have to travel back in time to a relatively recent period: the 1930s. The immense beast has the thorny problem of male impotence to thank for its discovery. For years, Chinese herbalists and doctors (some accredited and some not) have utilized fossilized teeth to create cocktails that they claim can cure this embarrassing ailment. Since the Chinese landscape is rich in fossilized bones, people have made significant profits from selling such items to apothecaries all across China.

It turns out that in 1936 a German man named Ralph von Koenigswald came across a huge fossilized tooth—specifically a molar—in a Hong Kong apothecary. It was highly fortuitous that von Koenigswald was the man who made the discovery, since he was a paleontologist and instantly recognized the significance of what had fallen into his lap. Not only was the molar giant-sized, but von Koenigswald was also able to determine it came from a very large primate. In the immediate years that followed, von Koenigswald found further such examples and coined the term *Gigantopithecus blacki*—the first word meaning "gigantic ape" and the second a reference to deceased friend Davidson Black.

Von Koenigswald was temporarily, and disastrously, interrupted at the height of the Second World War when he became a prisoner of war of the Japanese. Nevertheless, he was not deterred, and, when the hostilities were over, he continued his quest to understand the true nature and life of *Gigantopithecus*. As did several other people. One of them was an anatomist named Franz Weidenreich.

In his 1946 book *Apes, Giants, and Man*, Weidenreich made the controversial assertion that *Gigantopithecus* may have been far more human-like than ape-like. Chinese scientists also got hot on the trail of *Gigantopithecus* during this same time frame. Then, in 1956, a massive jawbone of the huge ape was unearthed at a cave in Liucheng, China. The result was that, in a relatively short time, a great deal was learned about this previously unheard-of hairy giant.

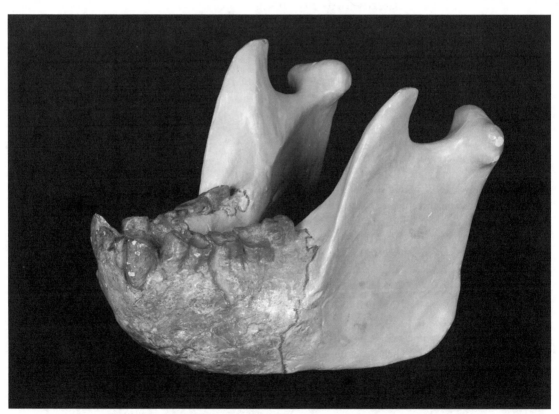

A reconstructed jawbone of the *Gigantopithecus blacki,* a large, supposedly extinct ape that, some speculate, might actually have survived into modern times to be mistaken for a Bigfoot.

Perhaps most amazing and impressive of all were *Gigantopithecus*'s statistics: estimates suggested that the height for an adult male would have been around ten feet, while it might have tipped the scales at 1,200 pounds in weight. As for when it lived, the estimates were intriguing.

Gigantopithecus authority (and biological anthropologist at the University of Iowa) Russell L. Ciochon said: "The next development came in 1965 with the discovery of twelve *Gigantopithecus* teeth at Wuming, a few hours' drive north of Nanning. These teeth were significantly larger than their counterparts from Liucheng, and the other animal fossils found with them suggested that the site was considerably younger (current estimates are that Liucheng is one million years old and that Wuming is between 300,000 and 400,000 years old)."

As for when *Gigantopithecus* is believed to have become extinct, Ciochon suggested around 200,000 years ago, but after having lived for roughly six million years. On the matter of why, exactly, the animal finally reached extinction, Erin Wayman, writing for the *Smithsonian*, said:

> … the rise of the Tibetan plateau 1.6 million to 800,000 years ago altered the climate of South Asia, ushering in a colder, drier period when forests shrank. Other factors could have exacerbated this crisis. *Gigantopithecus*'s neighbor, *Homo erectus*, may have over-hunted and/or outcompeted their larger ape cousin. And at least one dental study indicates *Giganto-*

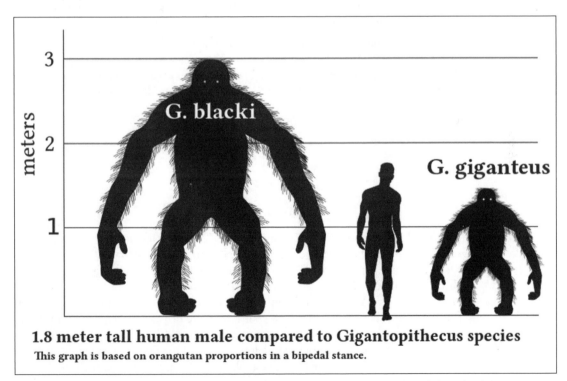

1.8 meter tall human male compared to Gigantopithecus species
This graph is based on orangutan proportions in a bipedal stance.

A graph comparing the height of *Gigantopithecus black* to an average human male and the related *G. giganteus.*

pithecus developed and matured very slowly—a sign they probably had low reproductive rates, which can elevate a species' risk of going extinct.

Of course, one could make an extremely valid argument that since people are still claiming to see giant apes in the very areas where we know *Gigantopithecus* roamed—such as Tibet, Vietnam, China, and India—this is evidence that the mighty, hairy giant is still amongst us, but now known by the far more famous names as Yeti, Bigfoot, Yowie, and Yeren.

The graph comparing the height of a 1.8 meter tall human male with the *Gigantopithecus* species shows a relative comparison against orangutan proportions in a bipedal stance. It is most likely that *Gigantopithecus* would have spent most of its time in a quadrupedal stance, on all fours.

There is, however, one problem: due to its massive size, there is a general consensus among primatologists that *Gigantopithecus* walked on its knuckles, in very much the same way that today's baboons move around. Bigfoot, the Yeti, and the rest of the monstrous pack are almost exclusively described as standing and walking in an upright fashion. Plus, many of the cryptid apes of our world are described as tall—generally about seven to eight feet in height. Encounters with man-beasts in excess of ten feet in height are far fewer in number. On top of that, there are even suggestions that *Gigantopithecus* may have reached—and possibly even surpassed—a height of thirteen feet. This is far in excess of what is generally reported in Bigfoot. Admittedly, however, there are reports from Tibet of a particular type of Yeti referred to as the Nyalmo which, incredibly, is reputed to reach stratospheric heights of twenty feet (*see* "Nyalmo")!

Is it possible that *Gigantopithecus* adapted over millions of years, to the extent that the original, huge, knuckle-walker became a generally smaller, upright beast? Perhaps, given the sheer number of sightings of anomalous apes in the precise areas where the immense creature lived, we should give some deep consideration to this particular theory.

Glamis Castle Ghoul

Situated just west of Forfar, Scotland, Glamis Castle is referenced by Shakespeare in *Macbeth*; it is where Macbeth killed Duncan in 1040. And it is also at the castle where assassins murdered King Malcolm II in 1034. In addition, Glamis Castle was the childhood home of both Queen Elizabeth II and the Queen Mother, and the birthplace of Princess Margaret. And then there is the castle's very own monster. Jonathan Downes notes that "the castle is, of course, the site of yet another, well known and semi legendary beast known as the Monster of Glamis. It's said that the creature was supposed to have been the hideously deformed heir to the Bowes-Lyon family and who was, according to popular rumor, born in about 1800, and died as recently as 1921."

Downes digs further into the puzzle:

Legend has it that the monster was supposed to look like an enormous flabby egg, having no neck and only minute arms and legs but possessed incredible strength and had an air of evil about it. Certainly, there is a family secret concerning the monster, which is only told to the male heir of the Bowes-Lyon family when they attain majority. But according to the author Peter Underwood, who has looked into this case, the present Lord Strathmore knows nothing about the monster, presumably because the creature has long been dead, but he always felt that there was a corpse or coffin bricked up behind the walls.

There is another matter worth noting, too, that may be of deep significance and relevance to Bigfoot: According to James Wentworth Day, an author who extensively researched and wrote about the legend, the creature of the castle was "hairy as a doormat."

According to folklore and oral tradition, the existence of the creature was allegedly known to only four men at any given time, namely the Earl of Strathmore, his direct heir, the family's lawyer, and the broker of the estate. At the age of twenty-one each succeeding heir was told the terrible secret and shown the rightful—and horrendously deformed—Earl, and succeeding family lawyers and brokers were also informed of the family's shocking secret. As no countess of Strathmore was ever told the story, however, Lady Strathmore, having indirectly heard of such rumors, quietly

A monster that was said to be "hairy as a doormat" and shaped like an "enormous flabby egg" was said to have once inhabited Glamis Castle in Scotland. It might have actually have been a deformed member of the Bowes-Lyon family that lived there in the nineteenth century.

approached the then broker, Mr. Ralston, who flatly refused to reveal the secret and who would only say by way of a reply: "It is fortunate you do not know the truth for if you did you would never be happy."

Was the strange creature of the castle a terribly deformed soul with some bizarre genetic affliction, a captured wild man or something else? While the jury, inevitably, remains steadfastly out, it's an intriguing reality that in 1912, in his book, *Scottish Ghost Stories*, Elliott O'Donnell published the contents of a letter that he had received from a Mrs. Bond who had spent time at Glamis Castle and who underwent an undeniably weird encounter. In her letter to O'Donnell, rather notably, she described a somewhat supernatural encounter with a beast possessed of distinct ape-like qualities.

Mrs. Bond wrote to O'Donnell the following words:

It is a good many years since I stayed at Glamis. I was, in fact, but little more than a child, and had only just gone through my first season in town. But though young, I was neither nervous nor imaginative; I was inclined to be what is termed stolid, that is to say, extremely matter-of-fact and practical. Indeed, when my friends exclaimed, "You don't mean to say you are going to stay at Glamis! Don't you know it's haunted?" I burst out laughing. "Haunted!" I said, "How ridiculous! There are no such things as ghosts. One might as well believe in fairies."

Of course I did not go to Glamis alone—my mother and sister were with me; but whereas they slept in the more modern part of the castle, I was, at my own request, apportioned a room in the Square Tower. I cannot say that my choice had anything to do with the secret chamber. That, and the alleged mystery, had been dinned into my ears so often that I had grown thoroughly sick of the whole thing. No, I wanted to sleep in the Square Tower for quite a different reason, a reason of my own. I kept an aviary; the tower was old; and I naturally hoped its walls would be covered with ivy and teeming with birds' nests, some of which I might be able to reach—and, I am ashamed to say, plunder—from my window. Alas, for my expectations!

Although the Square Tower was so ancient that in some places it was actually crumbling away—not the sign of a leaf, not the vestige of a bird's nest could I see anywhere; the walls were abominably, brutally bare. However, it was not long before my disappointment gave way to delight; for the air that blew in through the open window was so sweet, so richly scented with heather and honeysuckle, and the view of the broad, sweeping, thickly wooded grounds so indescribably charming, that, despite my inartistic and un-poetical nature, I was entranced—entranced as I had never been before, and never have been since. "Ghosts!" I said to myself. "Ghosts! How absurd! How preposterously absurd! Such an adorable spot as this can only harbor sunshine and flowers."

I well remember, too—for, as I have already said, I was not poetical—how much I enjoyed my first dinner at Glamis. The long journey and keen mountain air had made me hungry, and I thought I had never tasted such delicious food—such ideal salmon (from the Esk) and such heavenly fruit. But I must tell you that, although I ate heartily, as a healthy girl should, by the time I went to bed I had thoroughly digested my meal, and was, in fact, quite ready to partake of a few oatmeal biscuits I found in my dressing-case, and remembered having bought at Perth.

It was about eleven o'clock when my maid left me, and I sat for some minutes wrapped in my dressing gown, before the open window. The night was very still, and, save for an occasional rustle of the wind in the distant tree-tops, the hooting of an owl, the melancholy cry of a peewit and the hoarse barking of a dog, the silence was undisturbed.

The interior of my room was, in nearly every particular, modern. The furniture was not old; there were no grim carvings; no grotesquely-fashioned tapestries on the walls; no dark cupboards; no gloomy corners—all was cozy and cheerful, and when I got into bed no thought of bogle or mystery entered my mind.

In a few minutes I was asleep, and for some time there was nothing but a blank—a blank in which all identity was annihilated. Then suddenly I found myself in an oddly-shaped room with a lofty ceiling, and a window situated at so great a distance from the black oaken floor as to be altogether inaccessible from within. Feeble gleams of phosphorescent light made their way through the narrow panes, and served to render distinct the more prominent objects around; but my eyes struggled in vain to reach the remoter angles of the wall, one of which inspired me with terror such as I had never felt before. The walls were covered with heavy draperies that were sufficient in themselves to preclude the possibility of any save the loudest of sounds penetrating without.

The furniture, if such one could call it, puzzled me. It seemed more fitted for the cell of a prison or lunatic asylum, or even for a kennel, than for an ordinary dwelling-room. I could see no chair, only a coarse deal table, a straw mattress, and a kind of trough. An air of irredeemable gloom and horror hung over and pervaded everything. As I stood there, I felt I was waiting for something—something that was concealed in the corner of the room I dreaded. I tried to reason with myself, to assure myself that there was nothing there that could hurt me, nothing that could even terrify me, but my efforts were in vain— my fears grew.

Had I had some definite knowledge as to the cause of my alarm I should not have suffered so much, but it was my ignorance of what was there, of what I feared, that made my terror so poignant. Each second saw the agony of my suspense increase. I dared not move. I hardly dare breathe, and I dreaded lest the violent pulsation of my heart should attract the attention of the

A monster that was said to be "hairy as a doormat" and shaped like an "enormous flabby egg" was said to have once inhabited Glamis Castle in Scotland. It might have actually have been a deformed member of the Bowes-Lyon family that lived there in the nineteenth century.

Unknown Presence and precipitate its coming out. Yet despite the perturbation of my mind, I caught myself analyzing my feelings. It was not danger I abhorred so much, as its absolute effect—fright. I shuddered at the bare thought of what result the most trivial incident—the creaking of a board, ticking of a beetle, or hooting of an owl—might have on the intolerable agitation of my soul.

In this unnerved and pitiable condition I felt that the period was bound to come, sooner or later, when I should have to abandon life and reason together in the most desperate of struggles with—fear. At length, something moved. An icy chill ran through my frame, and the horror of my anticipations immediately reached its culminating point. The Presence was about to reveal itself. The gentle rubbing of a soft body on the floor, the crack of a bony joint, breathing, another crack, and then—was it my own excited imagination—or the disturbing influence of the atmosphere—or the uncertain twilight of the chamber that produced before me, in the stygian darkness of the recess, the vacillating and indistinct outline of something luminous, and horrid? I would gladly have risked futurity to have looked elsewhere—I could not. My eyes were fixed—I was compelled to gaze steadily in front of me.

Slowly, very slowly, the thing, whatever it was, took shape. Legs—crooked, misshapen, human legs. A body—tawny and hunched. Arms—long and spidery, with crooked, knotted fingers. A head—large and bestial, and covered with a tangled mass of grey hair that hung around its protruding forehead and pointed ears in ghastly mockery of curls. A face—and herein was the realization of all my direst expectations—a face—white and staring, pig-like in formation malevolent in expression; a hellish combination of all things foul and animal, and yet withal not without a touch of pathos.

As I stared at it aghast, it reared itself on its haunches after the manner of an ape, and leered piteously at me. Then, shuffling forward, it rolled over, and lay sprawled out like some ungainly turtle—and wallowed, as for warmth, in the cold grey beams of early dawn. At this juncture the handle of the chamber door turned, someone entered, there was a loud cry—and I awoke—awoke to find the whole tower, walls and rafters, ringing with the most appalling screams I have ever heard—screams of something or of someone—for there was in them a strong element of what was human as well as animal—in the greatest distress.

Wondering what it meant, and more than ever terrified, I sat up in bed and listened—listened whilst a conviction—the result of intuition, suggestion, or what you will, but a conviction all the same—forced me to associate the sounds with the thing in my dream. And I associate them still.

Gnena

See: Senegal's Savage Ape

Government Agents and Bigfoot

In 1954, a very strange and somewhat fragmentary story surfaced from C. S. Lambert, who commented on his apparent knowledge of what was perceived as Bigfoot activity near Vancouver:

> After a series of alarming reports that these giants were prowling around Harrison Mills, 50 miles East of Vancouver, disturbing the residents by their weird wolf-like howls at night, and destroying property, a band of vigilantes was organized to track the marauders down. However, no specimen of the primitive tribe was captured, and many white people became openly skeptical of the existence of the giants.

> According to Allen Roy Evans, in the *Montreal Standard* ("B.C.'s Hairy Giants"), the Indians are now very sensitive to any imputations cast upon their veracity in this matter. During the nineteenth century they were ready to tell enquirers all they knew about the Susquatch [sic] men; but today they have become more reserved, and talk only to Government agents about the matter. They maintain that the "Wild Indians" are divided into two tribes, whose rivalry with each other keeps their number down and so prevents them becoming a serious menace to others.

> Expeditions have been organized to track down the Susquatch [sic] men to their lair in the mountains; but the Indians employed to guide these expeditions invariably desert before they reach the danger zone. However, certain large caves have been discovered, with man-made walls of stone inside them, and specially-shaped stones fitted to their mouths, like doors. The difficulty in the way of penetrating to the heart of the Morris Mountains district is very great. The terrain is cut up by deep gorges and almost impassable ravines; it is easy to get lost, and hard to make substantial progress in any one direction for long.

It's a great pity that Lambert did not expand on certain points contained in his account, such as who, exactly the "government agents" to whom he referred were. Why, exactly, might they have been interested in the Bigfoot phenomenon in the first place? Where, exactly, were these large caves? Can they be found today? The questions and implications surrounding Lambert's communication are many. The answers, however, are not.

Green Man of the Woods

Elizabeth Randall has dug very deeply into the largely (but not exclusively) British phenomenon of what has become known as the Green Man. It is a decidedly wild character linked with places perceived as magical, such as woods, glades, and streams, and whose very image provokes thoughts of ancient, proto-humans roaming the land.

Randall says:

Usually these figures are male, although there are a very few Green Women, together with green cats, green demons, and green lions. The Green Man can appear in different forms, although there are three types that are normally represented. These are the Disgorging Head, which emits foliage from the mouth; the Foliate Head, which is entirely covered in green leaves; [and] the Bloodsucker Head, which has foliage emerging from all the facial outlets.

As for the point of origin for the phenomenon, Randall suggests that the Green Man quite possibly surfaced out of the mythology of fantastic deities and mighty gods in very early times. Perhaps, in the British Isles, she muses, the Green Man arose from the Celtic god of light, Lud (also referred to as Lug or Lyg). On a similar track, in 1942, at West Row, Suffolk, England, a silver salver, which dated from the fourth century, was found and, today, comprises an integral and important part of what has become known as the so-called Mildenhall Treasure. The salver in question, which was uncovered at the site of an old Roman villa and is now on display at the British Museum, contains an intriguing image. It resembles a partly leafy mask thought to represent Neptune—the Roman god of the sea and the water—with the foliage being seaweed. But it is definitely Green Man-like in its appearance.

Randall has far more to say, too, of a nature that provides us with a solid body of data and history on the mysterious figure:

Carved depictions of the Green Man can be found not only in churches but also in secular buildings. Plus, it is a common name for a public house, where it would appear on inn signs that, occasionally, show a full figure instead of simply a head. The motif can be found right across the world and is, more often than not, related to natural vegetative divinities from throughout the ages. It is first and foremost a symbol of rebirth that represents the spring cycle of growth. From Asia to Europe there are representations of the image. From the second century to the modern day the Green Man can be associated with similar beliefs.

A statue honoring the magical Green Man was installed at the Dovecote Lane Recreation Ground in Beeston, England, around 2009.

It may surprise some to learn that while the Green Man—as a specific entity of traditional British folklore, at least—certainly has ancient origins, the usage of those two combined words (*Green* and *Man*, in the particular context they appear in this book to explain the nature of the phenomenon), is most certainly not old in the slightest. Randall demonstrates this clearly:

> The first person to use the term Green Man was Lady Raglan, wife of Major FitzRoy Richard Somerset, 4th Baron Raglan. At one time he was the President of the Folklore Society. And, in 1939 his wife, Lady Raglan, created the phrase Green Man in her one and only article that appeared in the *Folklore* journal. She invented the term to define the leaf-decorated heads seen in English churches, and to this day her theory concerning where they come from is still discussed.

So, yes, the name most certainly is recent. But the motif is far, far less so. Randall shows that, the name issue aside, its origins are just about as long as they are winding and open to question and debate: "On the surface it seems these images are pagan, but they can often be found in ecclesiastical buildings from the eleventh century onwards. Many look either unsettling or mystical, which is sometimes thought to show the vitality of the Green Man in that it was capable of enduring as a character from pre-Christian traditions. This was probably due to the fact that in early Christianity old symbols were often incorporated into the newer religion. And, from around the 14th Century on they were also included simply as decoration in things such as manuscripts, stained glass, and other items.

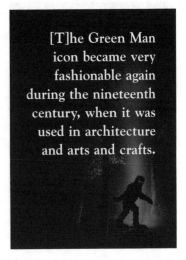

[T]he Green Man icon became very fashionable again during the nineteenth century, when it was used in architecture and arts and crafts.

Randall also notes that in Britain, at least, the Green Man icon became very fashionable again during the nineteenth century, when it was used in architecture and arts and crafts. Moreover, to this day, the image is still used as decoration in many parts of the world by artists using many different types of media, including literature.

There is another aspect to the mystery, too, as Randall also makes clear:

> The expression shown on the faces of many Green Men found in churches seems to suggest some form of torture. It may be that such expressions were to remind people of sin and that their souls would burn in hell if they committed such transgressions. As the image also represents renewal and rebirth, in a church the image might be a sign of resurrection where it appears, especially when found on tombs. It might also be a sign of creation. Or, it may just be a sign of nature and fertility.

Randall also has much to say on the connections between the Green Man and churches: "It is thought that the Celts adorned their victim's head with leaves, which might lead us to speculate that the Green Man has Celtic origins; however the first depictions of Green Men come from Classical Roman times. But, if it is Celtic then, where it is shown next to, or above, doors it might be to protect the building from evil spirits.

> However, the problem remains that in the very early years of the Church, and when it took over in Britain, all pagan images were destroyed and banned. So it's hard to see how the Green Man should then have been

included in church architecture. And yet, there are no accounts from Mediaeval Times that tell us how the image of the Green Man came to be included in churches. Regardless of what the Green Man was intended to represent in church architecture current congregants see him as the archetype of our oneness with the earth. And, for Wiccans and Neo-pagans he portrays an earth-centered idea of male divinity.

She adds:

Today, the symbolism of the Green Man has come to mean the relationship between man and nature. It reveals an essential basic pattern deep in the human mind. It has become an archetype that is common to all and represents a profoundly sympathetic feeling for, and with, nature. This has probably arisen from our current concerns about the ecology, and environment, of Planet Earth.

... sightings have been made of a creature sounding suspiciously like Bigfoot from within what is left of Sherwood Forest....

Researcher Luke Mastin notes that the Green Man phenomenon has been linked to some famous and infamous characters over the years, including a particularly acclaimed one that practically everyone will instantly recognize:

Although best known as the heroic, bow-wielding outlaw of English folklore since the 14th century, along with his green-garbed band of Merry Men and the beautiful and virtuous Maid Marian, Robin Hood (originally a contraction of Robin of the Wood) was also traditionally seen as a protector of the old ways and of the woods and forests.

According to a curious and swirling mix of history and mythology, it transpires that, for a number of years, sightings have been made of a creature sounding suspiciously like Bigfoot from within what is left of Sherwood Forest, a royal forest located in Nottinghamshire known as the home of the famous and heroic Robin of Loxley, far better known as the aforementioned Robin Hood.

Chris Mullins, who has investigated many reports of Bigfoot in Britain, said of the Sherwood Forest controversy: "While having some reservations myself, I believe it's feasible. Wild men could still exist in our time. Notts [Nottinghamshire] and Derbyshire are known for their underground caves and catacombs, explored and unexplored, and the woods could conceal a lot."

Not everyone is quite so open to such possibilities. In 2002, Izi Banton, the manager of the Sherwood Forest Visitor Centre, said of the rumored man-beast: "I think its existence is highly unlikely. We have one eccentric who wanders around wearing part of a tree on his head, so they might have spotted him."

Sherwood Forest, then, may or may not be home to far stranger puzzles than merely the man who supposedly stole from the rich and gave to the poor.

Guije

See: Cuba's Very Own Bigfoot

Hairy Hands on the Highway

Barely one decade into the twentieth century, an old road, situated between a pair of old English villages, became the site of a series of macabre and creepy deaths. The road in question was the B3212, which runs through the villages of Two Bridges and Post Bridge. Both the road and the villages can be found in the English county of Devon, and specifically in Dartmoor, where Sir Arthur Conan Doyle set his classic Sherlock Holmes novel of 1902, *The Hound of the Baskervilles*. This is notable, since Holmes would have been the ideal person to investigate the case—had he not just been a fictional creation, of course.

As for those deaths, they were caused by a large pair of disembodied, apelike hands that materialized inside people's cars—and even on the handlebars of their motorbikes—and forced them off the road, more often than not killing the driver and injuring the passengers. Thus was born the legend of what quickly became known as the "Hairy Hands."

The people of Two Bridges and Post Bridge had been aware of what was afoot since at least 1908, but, being close-knit and deeply afraid of the paranormal strangeness that enveloped mysterious, foggy Dartmoor, they largely chose to remain silent on the unsettling affair. That is, until 1921, when the media caught up with what was afoot.

One morning in June 1921, Dr. E. H. Helby, a medical officer at the nearby Dartmoor Prison, lost his life after crashing his motorcycle on the B3212. At the time, Helby's two young children were with him—travelling in a sidecar. Fortunately, both survived the incident and were later able to report that, only moments before the crash

Sir Arthur Conan Doyle set his classic tale *The Hound of the Baskervilles* in Dartmoor, England, the same place where it is rumored that a pair of disembodied, apelike hands have been murdering people.

occurred, they could see their father struggling with the handlebars and screaming: "Let go! Let go!"

Two months later, on August 26, a captain with the British Army, one who the local newspaper referred to as a "very experienced rider," nearly lost his life on the very same stretch of the B3212. The captain was able to tell both the media and the police his bizarre story:

It was not my fault. Believe it or not, something drove me off the road. A pair of hairy hands closed over mine. I felt them as plainly as ever I felt anything in my life—large, muscular, hairy hands. I fought them for all I was worth, but they were too strong for me. They forced the machine into the turf at the edge of the road, and I knew no more till I came to myself, lying a few feet away on my face on the turf.

Then there was the matter of the hellish happenings of July 1924. On this occasion, the witness was Theo Brown, an acclaimed collector of, and expert on, Devon folklore. Years later, Brown recalled what happened, late one night, on Dartmoor, just a few hundred yards from whereHelby was killed:

I knew there was some power very seriously menacing us near, and I must act very swiftly. As I looked up to the little window at the end of the caravan, I saw something moving, and as I stared, I saw it was the fingers and palm of a very large hand with many hairs on the joints and back of it, clawing up and up to the top of the window, which was a little open. I knew it wished to do harm to my husband sleeping below. I knew that the owner of the hand hated us and wished harm, and I knew it was no ordinary hand, and that no blow or shot would have any power over it.

Almost unconsciously I made the Sign of the Cross and I prayed very much that we might be kept safe. At once the hand slowly sank down out of sight and I knew the danger was gone. I did say a thankful prayer and fell at once into a peaceful sleep. We stayed in that spot for several weeks but I never felt the evil influence again near the caravan. But, I did not feel happy in some places not far off [sic] and would not for anything have walked alone on the moor at night or on the Tor above our caravan.

Then there was the tale told to writer Michael Williams—the author of the book *Supernatural Dartmoor*—by journalist Rufus Endle, who said that while driving near Postbridge on an undetermined date, "a pair of hands gripped the driving wheel and I had to fight for control." Luckily, Endle managed to avoid crashing the vehicle; the hands, meanwhile, mysteriously, and in an instant, vanished into thin air. A very concerned Endle requested that the story specifically not be published until after his death.

Hairy Men of the Old Mines

One of the most thought-provoking theories for Bigfoot's overwhelming elusiveness suggests that the creatures spend a great deal of time living in natural caves and caverns, as well as abandoned old mines. In the early 1900s, a number of stories surfaced in the Oregon press that, upon careful reflection, just might offer support for the intriguing theory that Bigfoot is a creature of the underground. The reports are made all the more significant because they reference in excess of a decade of sightings of a large, hairy creature, all in a specific vicinity where underground digging was known to be widespread.

> The reports are made all the more significant because they reference in excess of a decade of sightings of a large, hairy creature, all in a specific vicinity....

In 1900, a Curry County, Oregon, newspaper reported an amazing story:

The Sixes mining district in Curry County has for the past 30 years glorified in the exclusive possession of a "kangaroo man." Recently while Wm. Page and Johnnie McCulloch, who are mining there, went out hunting McCulloch saw the strange animal-man come down a stream to drink. In calling Page's attention to the strange being it became frightened, and with cat-like agility, which has always been a leading characteristic, with a few bounds was out of sight.

Despite having been given the extremely odd nickname of the "kangaroo man," the newspaper's description of the beast is actually far more Bigfoot-like, as the following extract from the article clearly demonstrates:

The appearance of this animal is almost enough to terrorize the rugged mountainsides themselves. He is described as having the appearance of a man—a very good looking man—is nine feet in height with low forehead, hair hanging down near his eyes, and his body covered with a prolific growth of hair which nature has provided for his protection. Its hands reach almost to the ground and when its tracks were measured its feet were found to be 18 inches in length with five well formed toes. Whether this is a devil, some strange animal or a wild man is what Messrs. Page and McCulloch would like to know.

Four years later, in 1904, the creature—or, at least, another, similar one of its kind—was yet again plaguing the mine-filled area. The press enthusiastically reported on the latest development:

At repeated intervals during the past ten years thrilling stories have come from the rugged Sixes mining district in Coos County, Oregon, near Myrtle Point, regarding a wild man or a queer and terrible monster which walks erect and which has been seen by scores of miners and prospectors.

The appearance again of the "Wild Man" of the Sixes has thrown some of the miners into a state of excitement and fear. A report says the wild man has been seen three times since the 10th of last month.

The first appearance occurred on "Thompson Flat." Wm. Ward and a young man by the name of Burlison were sitting by the fire of their cabin one night when they heard something walking around the cabin which resembled a man walking and when it came to the corner of the cabin it took hold of the corner and gave the building a vigorous shake and kept up a frightful noise all the time—the same that has so many times warned the venturesome miners of the approach of the hairy man and caused them to flee in abject fear.

Mr. Ward walked to the cabin door and could see the monster plainly as it walked away, and took a shot at it with his rifle, but the bullet went wide of its mark. The last appearance of the animal was at the Harrison cabin only a few days ago. Mr. Ward was at the Harrison cabin this time and again figures in the excitement.

About five o'clock in the morning the wild man gave the door of the cabin a vigorous shaking which aroused Ward and one of the Harrison boys who took their guns and started in to do the intruder. Ward fired at the man and he answered by sending a four-pound rock at Ward's head but his aim was a little too high. He then disappeared into the brush.

Many of the miners avow that the "wild man" is a reality. They have seen him and know whereof they speak. They say he is something after the fashion of a gorilla and unlike anything else that has ever been known; and not only that but he can throw rocks with wonderful force and accuracy. He is about seven feet high, has broad hands and feet and his body is covered by a prolific growth of hair. In short, he looks like the very devil.

Maybe, in light of all of the above, our quest to learn the truth of Bigfoot should shift from the woods, the forests, and the mountains to somewhere else entirely: the mysterious, dark underworld beneath our very own feet.

Harry and the Hendersons (1987 movie)

For those who have been lucky (or unlucky) enough to encounter a Bigfoot, the event will likely have been amazing, incredible, nerve-wracking, or downright terrifying. There are very few occasions upon which the witness has claimed the event was amusing or even comical (for one notable exception, see "Mica Mountain Monster"). Indeed, for a funny look at Bigfoot, one largely has to focus on the world of fiction. And, most famously, at *Harry and the Hendersons*.

This 1987 movie, for which Steven Spielberg was executive producer, asks the question: What would you do if Bigfoot moved into your home? Most people would probably flee in terror. Not the Hendersons. They are George (actor John Lithgow), his wife, Nancy (Melinda Dillon), and their two kids, Sarah and Ernie (Margaret Langrick and Joshua Rudoy), who, after a fraught and chaotic start in which they first hit the creature while driving deep in the woods, find themselves forced to take in the giant beast. Cue a great deal of anarchic activity, destroyed furniture, and attempts to try and domesticate Bigfoot. Add to that an old man whose life was changed by Bigfoot, and a near-crazed hunter who wants to bag a Bigfoot for himself—with a fistful of bullets—and you have a movie that is filled with not just laughs, but adventure, intrigue, and even tension.

Evidently, audiences were happy with the non-menacing presentation of Bigfoot: the movie has, so far, grossed in excess of $50 million and prompted the production of a television-based spin-off series of the same name, which aired from 1991 to 1993.

Particularly notable is the matter of "Harry," (as the Henderson family come to name the Bigfoot). He was played by the late Kevin Peter Hall, who was no stranger to portraying huge, forest-dwelling monsters. The 7-foot-2¾-inch-tall Hall was the ideal person to play Harry. He had plenty of practice, too.

The 1987 Steven Spielberg movie *Harry and the Hendersons* portrays Bigfoot as a big, lovable, misunderstood creature

In 1979, Hall took on the role of Katahdin, a monstrous creature of Native American legend, in *Prophecy*. It was a movie based upon a novel of the same name by David Seltzer. In the movie, Katahdin is actually a grossly mutated bear, one that grows to a towering height of around fifteen feet or more, and whose condition is caused by overexposure to mercury in the woods and rivers of Maine. Seeing the giant, hairy creature roaming the woods by night, quickly and easily makes one think of Bigfoot, the very beast that Hall went on to portray eight years later.

In 1987, the same year that Hall played Harry the Sasquatch, he also took on the role of yet another forest-dwelling creature. Whereas Harry was genial and gentle, the character that Hall played against Arnold Schwarzenegger's Dutch, in *Predator*, was very different: it was a lethal, extraterrestrial killing machine that hunted in the rain forests of Central America and wiped out Dutch's handpicked team of mercenaries one by one. Hall played a predator again, in 1990, in *Predator 2*.

Hawaii's Mysterious Menehune

The islands that comprise Hawaii are the reported home of something similar, albeit significantly smaller than Bigfoot. They are the Menehune. Although their average height is said to be barely two to three feet at the maximum, they have physical qualities that suggest they may have a linkage to the human race. Although they are covered in hair and have red-colored faces, their large eyes are reportedly filled with intelligence, and their short noses and pronounced foreheads echo something akin to Cro-Magnon man, rather than a monkey or an ape.

Tales of the Menehune cannot have been influenced by today's fascination for Bigfoot. There is a very good reason for this: reports of the small, hairy residents of Hawaii date back to at least the 1700s. In 1786, for example, a census was held during the reign of King Kaumualii. Of the almost 2,000 people who took part in the census, almost six dozen were said to be of the Menehune tribe! That, alone, suggests they were a form of human, even if clearly not of the *Homo sapiens* variety.

A notable account of a very close encounter with more than twenty Menehune occurred during the latter part of the 1940s, when dozens of school-children—overseen by their superintendent, George London—encountered the chattering group of hairy dwarfs playing on the grounds of an old

This 1946 keepsake bank from Hawaii was fashioned in the form of a Menehune, a kind of small Bigfoot.

church in the Waimea Valley. When they realized they had been seen, the creatures raced for the safety of a tunnel that existed under the old church, suggesting that the Menehune were—and still may very well be—chiefly subterranean in nature.

Hecate Hill (2006 play)

The brainchild of a Dallas, Texas-based author, filmmaker, and artist named Bill Fountain, *Hecate Hill* was a two-act play that did the rounds in Dallas in late 2006. It tells the story of a group of friends who head off for a claustrophobic cabin deep in the backwoods of Atoka County, Oklahoma, where something large, hairy, and violent lurks. Bigfoot is on the loose and he is not a happy soul.

The play begins in a bright and breezy fashion as we get to know the lives and loves of the characters—Skim, Blue, Kylie, Maddie, Liver, and Red Death. But, inevitably, that bright and breezy atmosphere, and the joking around, are soon replaced by something far more frightening. As the gang settles in, fragmentary reports on their radio tell of a giant, hairy creature that has been shot by hunters in Oklahoma, and its body is due to be studied by the world's scientific elite.

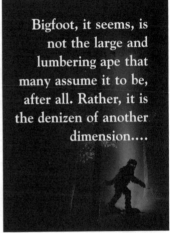

Bigfoot, it seems, is not the large and lumbering ape that many assume it to be, after all. Rather, it is the denizen of another dimension....

As the night progresses, and the group becomes ever more alarmed by the fact that they are out in the woods in an area known for intense man-beast activity, the story develops rapidly: An announcement is made that the president is about to make a speech concerning the historic discovery; CNN will be showing the body of the beast on prime-time television; and Bigfoot, so long the subject of derision and ridicule, is about to be unleashed upon an amazed world.

But then, just before the truth can be revealed, something even stranger happens: All across the world the lights begin to go out. Engines stop running. Frantic voices report that an "electromagnetic pulse"-type weapon is bringing our civilization to a standstill. And, seemingly out of nowhere, strange "shadow-creatures" begin to materialize *en masse* around the planet. Then there is nothing but complete darkness and never-ending radio static. Aside, that is, from the weird, animalistic noise that emanates from the dark woods and reverberates around the cabin.

Bigfoot, it seems, is not the large and lumbering ape that many assume it to be, after all. Rather, it is the denizen of another dimension—a realm that co-exists with ours and where time, as we understand it, is barely a relevant factor. The killing of one of its kind leads the creatures to launch an all-out planetary assault and we, the human race, are soon reduced to—according to the play's publicity blurb —"the bottom of the food-chain."

As the night progresses, and as the menacing growls get ever closer to the cabin, and a thunderous storm of almost apocalyptic levels grows, tensions among certain elements of the group increase until they reach levels of literal terror. But, by now, some of the friends are not so sure that anything untoward has taken place at all—that is, other than an immense and ingenious practical joke perpetrated by the character Blue.

Is the end really nigh for planet earth? Or is this merely Blue's own, unique, and brilliantly executed, homage to Orson Welles's infamous, hysteria-inducing radio production of H. G. Wells's *War of the Worlds*? Indeed, one character proclaims loudly: "This is a really stupid way for the world to end!" And, thus, their—and our—suspicions are reinforced that perhaps all is not quite as it seems. Or is it?

I will not spoil the ending for those who may want to catch *Hecate Hill* for themselves. But it should be noted that this is a story that grips right to the very last scene and remains thought-provoking throughout. Taking nods from Sam Raimi's cult-classic film *The Evil Dead*, and the aforementioned *War of the Worlds*, *Hecate Hill* is an atmospheric production with a writer, cast, and crew who have worked hard to create a story about Bigfoot that does not follow accepted convention and wisdom. And talking of the writer, Bill Fountain elaborated to me in late 2006 on what it was that prompted him to produce, write, and produce *Hecate Hill*:

> All of my life I've been fascinated with the notion of Bigfoot. As a little kid, I remember my great-grandmother in Oklahoma would tell me stories about these giant skunk-apes. She could tell great ghost stories. As a kid, anytime there was a documentary, or pseudo-documentary, on TV I was there. There was always that thing about how something that big couldn't exist. But then another part of me was like: "Please let it be true."

Hibagon

See: Japan's Enigmatic Apes

Hoaxing a Bigfoot Encounter

Quite possibly the strangest of all headlines to ever have graced the pages of a newspaper appeared in England's *Chase Post* on March 23, 2006. It read: "Bigfoot Almost Caused Me to Lose My Baby"! Utterly relishing the opportunity to relate to its readers a tale of proportions that easily surpassed the surreal, the *Post* began as follows:

> Police chiefs have hit out at the dangers posed by the spoof "Bigfoot" craze after a teenager almost lost her baby when a joker clad in a gorilla suit jumped in front of her car. And the concerns have been echoed by a leading councilor and conservationist, who fears the "irresponsible idiots" are causing harm to wildlife as well as people.

No, it was not April Fools' Day, although many might have been forgiven for thinking it was exactly that! As the story went, the controversy kicked off in the heart of the English village of Brocton. It was barely sixty minutes before the witching-hour struck when a nineteen-year-old pregnant girl and her parents were driving through picturesque Brocton, having had a Saturday night out in a restaurant in nearby Milford—a locale whose other brief claim to infamy occurred in September 1990, when Sir Peter Terry, the former governor of Gibraltar, was shot and severely injured at his Milford home by terrorists from the Provisional Irish Republican Army.

When questioned later by police, the girl said:

We noticed a BMW parked in the road. Suddenly it flashed its lights. Just then, out of nowhere, this person dressed in a gorilla suit jumped out in front of our car, flailing their arms like mad. Then they started running at the car like mad. It was terrifying.

She continued:

Looking back it was obviously a fake suit, but late at night, in an isolated area like that, it was a very scary experience. In broad daylight, I suppose it could be quite funny, but this was 11 o'clock at night with no one around. It's very lonely there. If that had been someone with a heart condition, they could've had a heart attack. I screamed so loud. It was a real scare. It left me with fears that the trauma of it could have fatally harmed my baby.

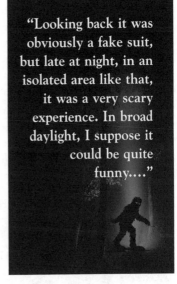

"Looking back it was obviously a fake suit, but late at night, in an isolated area like that, it was a very scary experience. In broad daylight, I suppose it could be quite funny...."

The girl's irate father was up in arms and told the *Chase Post*: "If I'd have caught the idiots, I'd have pasted them."

The local police weren't exactly laughing either. When contacted by the newspaper for comment on the matter, a spokesperson for the Staffordshire Police replied in stern tones:

We take it very seriously because it may result in a Public Order Offence. The person [in the gorilla suit] may very well be in high spirits, but this would be viewed as a criminal offence.

And councilor John Burnett made sure he put in his considerable words, too:

This is the behavior of an irresponsible idiot. At this time of year, there are all manner of ground-nesting birds in that area; the partridge, the pheasant, woodlarks, skylarks—many rare birds whose habitat and nesting could be destroyed by this kind of activity.

Homo floresiensis

In 2004, a remarkable discovery was made in Flores, an island situated east of Komodo, Indonesia, home to the huge, deadly, and fearsome Komodo dragon. It was a discovery of what appeared to be a small human, but which some researchers believed may have been the impetus for the tales of the mysterious ape called Orang-pendek.

In a specially prepared report, crytozoologist Richard Freeman tells the story and reveals the truth of the Orang-pendek angle.

Freeman reveals the remarkable facts:

Some theorize that the Orang-pendek may be a small hominian. As far back as the 1940s William Charles Osman Hill, primatologist, zoologist, and anatomist, postulated that Orang-pendek might have a possible connection to the fossils of *Homo erectus*. Along with the Nittaewo of Sri Lanka, he believed that they might be a dwarf island form of *Homo erectus*. Island dwarfism occurs when a species colonizes an island smaller than the landmass from whence it came. With fewer resources the species' descendants evolve into a smaller species.

The notion of a tiny island hominian was proven in a spectacular manner in 2004. Australian paleontologist Mike Morwood was excavating the Liang Bua cave in the west of Flores when he made a remarkable discovery, an adult skull of a human-like creature, but of tiny proportions. Further excavations uncovered more of the skeleton and a number of other individuals. Most incredibly of all, the remains were not fossilized. Their constitution was likened to wet tissue paper. The bones had to be allowed to dry before they could be excavated. Besides the creatures were tools, weapons, and evidence of fire use.

The creatures were named *Homo floresiensis* and in life would have stood only one meter tall. Despite having a smaller cranial capacity than a chimpanzee, it seems that *Homo floresiensis* was highly intelligent. Not only did it use fire and stone tools, it seems to have hunted pygmy stegodont elephants and giant rodents with which it shared its island home.

A reconstruction by anthropologists of what a *Homo floresiensis* would have looked like about twelve thousand years ago.

Some tried to discredit the find as nothing more than microcephalic examples of modern man. This theory is quite absurd as the skull of *Homo floresiensis* is rounded and not elongated or proportionately tiny in the way microcephalics invariably are. Neither could microcephalics produce the tools that the remains were found alongside. Finally, the idea of a number of microcephalics, a rare condition as it is, all being found in the same cave is patently absurd.

In general, life expectancy for individuals with microcephaly is reduced and the prognosis for normal brain function is poor. The prognosis varies depending on the presence of associated abnormalities.

Recent work seems to suggest that *Homo floresiensis* is even more incredible than we first thought. It now seems that, rather than being a descendent of *Homo erectus* as originally postulated, it was outside of the genus *Homo* and more closely related to the African *Australopithecus*. The last known *Australopithecus*, the *Australopithecus africanus*, died out 1.9 million years ago.

It seems that the Liang Bua population of *Homo floresiensis* was killed during the eruption of a volcano around 12,000 years ago. But anthropologist Gregory Forth and others have suggested that *Homo floresiensis* survived in other parts of Flores until recently and may have been the genesis of the Ebu gogo legends.

Indeed, the Ebu gogo is said to survive in the deep jungles of Flores even today. The legend of the Ebu gogo's destruction by fire may be a distorted retelling of real events. Around 1830 a volcano known as Ebu Lobo erupted, spewing lava for a distance of 4km. The date matches fairly well with the date that the Ebu gogo were supposedly destroyed. Could the localized eruption have killed off a late surviving population of *Homo floresiensis* or have forced them away from the area, leading to the folktale?

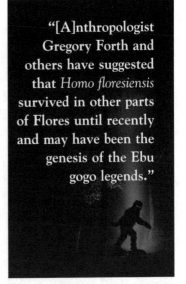

"[A]nthropologist Gregory Forth and others have suggested that *Homo floresiensis* survived in other parts of Flores until recently and may have been the genesis of the Ebu gogo legends."

It seems quite possible that *Homo floresiensis* and the Ebu gogo are one and the same as are the other Flores creatures known under different names. It is also perfectly possible that *Homo floresiensis* is still alive and well on Flores and on other Indonesian islands.

When it was first discovered, many people made the link between *Homo floresiensis* and the Orang-pendek (*see* "Orang-pendek of Sumatra"). Debbie Martyr told me of stories from Sumatra of a race of tiny hairy people. They used tools and fire and lived only in the very deep jungle. But here is the catch, the native people knew them to be totally distinct from the Orang-pendek.

These little people were smaller than Orang-pendek and though hairy, they were much less ape-like. Unlike Orang-pendek they fashioned tools, used fires and lived in small tribes. Orang-pendek has no use of fire. It may use sticks as weapons but—as far as we know—it does not seem to fashion tools. Furthermore, it is solitary.

Homo floresiensis and Orang-pendek do not match up well. The latter is larger, more primitive, and more solidly built. All of the tracks I have seen of the Orang-pendek show an offset big toe, a feature indicative of an ape. All the eyewitness descriptions seem to be recalling an upright ape and not a hominian.

Honey Island Swamp Monster

See: Zoo Escapees

Hoosier Folklore's Baboon-like Beast

In March 1946, *Hoosier Folklore* magazine told its readers of a strange story coming out of southern Illinois:

> Another type of story that is of much more concern to us here in Southern Illinois nowadays is the "strange beast" legend. Every few years some community reports the presence of a mysterious beast over in the local creek bottom.

Although it is difficult to determine just where a story of this sort has its beginning, this one seems to have originated in the Gum Creek bottom near Mt. Vernon. During the summer of 1941, a preacher was hunting squirrels in the woods along the creek when a large animal that looked something like a baboon jumped out of a tree near him.

The preacher struck at the beast with his gun barrel when it walked toward him in an upright position. He finally frightened it away by firing a couple of shots into the air. Later the beast began to alarm rural people by uttering terrorizing screams mostly at night in the wooded bottom lands along the creeks. School children in the rural districts sometimes heard it, too, and hunters saw its tracks.

By early spring of 1942, the animal had local people aroused to a fighting pitch. About that time, a farmer near Bonnie reported that the beast had killed his dog. A call went out for volunteers to join a mass hunt to round up the animal. The beast must have got news of the big hunt, for reports started coming in of its appearance in other creek bottoms, some as much as 40 or 50 miles from the original site.

A man driving near the Big Muddy River, in Jackson County, one night saw the beast bound across the road. Some hunters saw evidence of its presence away over in Okaw. Its rapid changing from place to place must have been aided considerably by its ability to jump, for, by this time, reports had it jumping along at from 20 to 40 feet per leap. It is impossible to say how many hunters and parties of hunters, armed with everything from shotguns to ropes and nets, went out to look for the strange beast in the various creek bottoms where it had been seen, or its tracks had been seen, or its piercing screams had been heard. Those taking nets and ropes were intent on bringing the creature back alive.

Usually this strange beast can't be found, and interest in it dies as mysteriously as it arose in the beginning. About 25 years ago, a "coon hunter" from Hecker one night heard a strange beast screaming up ahead on

> "[A]nthropologist Gregory Forth and others have suggested that *Homo floresiensis* survived in other parts of Flores until recently and may have been the genesis of the Ebu gogo legends."

Prairie du Long Creek. Hunters chased this phantom from time to time all one winter. Their dogs would get the trail, then lose it, and they would hear it screaming down the creek in the opposite direction. It was that kind of creature: you'd hear it up creek, but when you set out in that direction you'd hear it a mile down creek.

Horse Hair Braiding and Bigfoot

Beyond any shadow of a doubt, one of the strangest claims made about Bigfoot is that the creatures have a particular liking for braiding the manes of horses! While it's a scenario that, at first glance, sounds manifestly absurd, the fact is that throughout recorded history there are stories of strange creatures with a fascination for horse-braiding, with Bigfoot and its mysterious ilk leading the pack.

The leading expert in this curious field is Lisa Shiel, author of *Backyard Bigfoot* and *Forbidden Bigfoot*. Shiel, whose books chronicle her very own encounters with Bigfoot, says:

> I first encountered the mane braiding phenomenon while living in Texas. In the beginning, I allowed myself to dismiss them as natural tangles or perhaps the handiwork of the neighbors' children. As time went on, however, I found it more and more difficult to stick to my original hypothesis.

Indeed, in the 2000s, and particularly 2005, Shiel experienced numerous examples of horse-braiding when Bigfoot activity in her vicinity was at its height. Before dismissing this odd aspect of Bigfoot lore out of hand, it's worth noting there is nothing new about the phenomenon. In the 1200s, the Bishop of Paris (William of Auvergne) wrote of a fairy queen whose female underlings would stealthily enter stables in the dead of night, "with wax tapers, the drippings of which appear on the hairs and necks of the horses, whilst their manes are carefully plaited."

Even William Shakespeare got in on the act. In *Romeo and Juliet*, Shakespeare wrote of "elf-locks," which, essentially, were the work of supernatural sprite-like creatures that braided horses.

Ebenezer Cobham Brewer's *Dictionary of Phrase and Fable* talks about the "Hag's knot," which he describes as "Tangles in the manes of horses, etc., supposed to be used by witches for stirrups."

Similarly, author Newbell Nil Puckett said:

When you find your hair plaited into little stirrups in the morning or when it is all tangled up and your face scratched you may be sure that the witches have been bothering you

In a truly bizarre twist concerning Bigfoot, it seems that some of the hairy creatures like to braid the manes of horses!

Is it feasible that these stories of fairies, elves, witches, and other supernatural entities braiding the manes of horses were, in reality, distortions of braiding undertaken by cryptid apes, such as Bigfoot?

at night…. Horses as well as humans are ridden; you can tell when the witches have been bothering them by finding "witches stirrups" (two strands of hair twisted together) in the horses' mane. A person who plaits a horse's mane and leaves it that way is simply inviting the witches to ride, though they will seldom bother the horses except on very dark nights, and even then have a decided preference for dark colored horses. In England and Scotland, such "fairy stirrups" are attributed to the pigsies (piskies) riding the animals.

Is it feasible that these stories of fairies, elves, witches, and other supernatural entities braiding the manes of horses were, in reality, distortions of braiding undertaken by cryptid apes, such as Bigfoot? Certainly, there is no shortage of cases in support of such a scenario.

In 2012, researcher Robert Lindsay wrote: "One of the very strange stories that I leaked a while back was that [Melba] Ketchum, who is in charge of the Bigfoot DNA study, stated that Bigfoots at a site she is leasing in Texas had braided the manes on her horses. This report was met with quite a bit of ridicule at the time, and it was never confirmed by Ketchum to my knowledge (*see* "Ketchum, Dr. Melba").

Via a confidential source, I recently received three photos of what is reportedly one of Melba's horses showing braiding of the horse's mane. There are three photos in total. The person is close to the Ketchum Project and states that the photos are indeed from one of Melba's horses.

And it's not just in the United States that such things are reported. Shiel reported:

In the Americas, folk tales speak of hairy dwarves that live in remote canyons and valleys in the Andes. Locals say these mini-Bigfoot love to ride horses, but their small stature makes it impossible for them to ride on the horses' backs. The creatures braid locks of mane into stirrups so that they may enjoy horseback riding.

Russia has also been the site of such activity. Author George M. Eberhart said:

While he remained hidden in a barn in Kuruko ravine, Kabardin-Balkar Republic, Russia, on August 25, 1991, biologist Gregory Panchenko observed an Almasti enter through a window and plait a horse's mane. The horse did not offer any resistance. After a short time, during which it made high-pitched, twittering sounds, the Almasti departed through an open window above the barn door. Panchenko verified that the horse's mane had new and clumsily plaited braids that were not there the day before.

In Dorset, United Kingdom—the site of many so-called "wild man" reports in centuries long gone—there was a spate of mysterious hair-braiding of horses in 2009. Even the British Police Force found itself plunged into the heart of the mystery. Police constable Tim Poole, one of the officers who investigated the Dorset cases, said:

We have some very good information from a warlock that this is part of a white magic ritual and is to do with knot magick.

It would appear that for people of this belief, knot magick is used when they want to cast a spell. Some of the gods they worship have a strong connection to horses so if they have a particular request, plaiting this knot in a horse's mane lends strength to the request. This warlock said it is a benign activity, albeit maybe a bit distressing for the horse owner.

Howard-Bury, Lt. Col. C. K., Yeti Encounter

Lieutenant Colonel Charles K. Howard-Bury was a man who played a notable role in the subject of cryptid apes. He led the very first Everest Reconnaissance Expedition in 1921. It was while at a height of around 20,000 feet that Howard-Bury came across some unusual footprints in the snow. While he suggested a logical explanation for the prints, his comments make for notable reading. And, there is no doubt that regardless of what the tracks were really made by, the Howard-Bury affair was a defining moment in Yeti history and lore. He said:

This photo was taken in 1921 of the Mount Everest expedition's base camp. In the back row are (left to right) naturalist Dr. Sandy Wollaston, Charles Howard-Bury, geologist Alexander Heron, and mountaineer Harold Raeburn; seated left to right George Mallory, surveyor Edward Wheeler, Guy Bullock, and surveyor Henry Morshead.

> "We were able to pick out tracks of hares and foxes, but one that at first looked like a human foot puzzled us considerably."

On September 22, leaving Raeburn behind, Mallory, Bullock, Morshead, Wheeler, Wallaston and myself started off to Lakhpa La camp. We left the 20,000-foot camp in 22 degrees of frost at four o'clock in the morning, accompanied by twenty-six coolies, who were divided up into four parties, each of which was properly roped. It was a beautiful moonlight night, and the mountains showed up nearly as brightly as in the daytime. We rapidly descended the 200 feet from our terrace to the glacier, when we all "roped up."

The snow on the glacier was in excellent condition, and as it was frozen hard we made good progress. Dawn overtook us on the broad flat part of the glacier, the first of the sun falling on the summit of Mount Everest, which lay straight in front of us, and changing the color of the snow gradually from pink to orange, all the time up sharp and clear in the frosty air.

We mounted gradually past Kartse, the white conical-shaped peak climbed by Mallory and Bullock a month ago from the Kama Valley. We wended our way without much difficulty through the ice-fall of the glacier, below some superbly fluted snow ridges that rose straight above us. Then followed a long and at times a somewhat steep climb over soft powdery snow to the top of the grass.

And then, normality was utterly shattered, when something very strange occurred, as Howard-Bury duly recorded in his diary:

Even at these heights we came across tracks in the snow. We were able to pick out tracks of hares and foxes, but one that at first looked like a human foot puzzled us considerably. Our coolies at once jumped to the conclusion that this must be "The Wild Man of the Snows," to which they gave the name of Metoh-kangmi, the Abominable Snowman who interested the newspaper so much. On my return to civilized countries I read with interest delightful accounts of the ways and customs of this wild man whom we were supposed to have met.

As noted above, Howard-Bury was not personally convinced he had stumbled on real Yeti prints, even though he personally described them as looking like "a human foot." On this issue, he elaborated:

These tracks, which caused so much comment, were probably caused by a large "loping" grey wolf, which in the soft snow formed double tracks rather like those of a barefooted man. Tibet, however, is not the only country where there exists a bogey man. In Tibet he takes the form of a hairy man who lives in the snows, and little Tibetan children who are naughty and disobedient are frightened by the wonderful fairy tales that are told about him. To escape from him they must run down the hill, as then his long hair falls over his eyes and he is unable to see them. Many other such tales have they with which to strike terror into the hearts of bad boys and girls.

Human–Bigfoot Offspring

There are a number of ancient stories and contemporary accounts—from all across the world—of girls and women kidnapped by Bigfoot-type creatures, made pregnant by the hairy monsters, and ultimately giving birth to half-human, half-Bigfoot, freakish things of a nightmarish nature. If there is even a modicum of truth to these tales, then it goes without saying that these unknown animals are clearly of the human family—despite their savage, hairy appearance.

A particularly bizarre story that falls into this category was published in a Chinese newspaper, the *World Journal*, in October 1997. Translated into English, it reads as follows:

> A woman, who works for the Bigfoot Research Center in China, was going through the belongings of her recently deceased father. Her father had been with the Wildlife Research Center in China. Among the belongings she found a video tape taken in 1986.

The story continued that the tape showed something strange and disturbing: an unusual-looking man, who stood about six feet five inches in height, who had a small head, and arms of a noticeably long length. He was also reported to have had a tail-like protuberance from the base of his spine.

According to the account, the man's appearance was not caused by a rare genetic defect, as one might suppose, but something acutely different:

> The mother of the "boy" was still alive when the video was taken. The mother states that she had been kidnapped or abducted by a "wild man" after the death of her husband, and the boy was an offspring of her relationship with the wild man. The woman previously had a son by her husband. The son was an officer in the army, and he persuaded his mother to tell her story to the Wildlife Research people. She told her story under the condition that the research people would not reveal her identity while she was alive because she was ashamed of what had happened.

Truth or tall tale, it's just one of many eerily similar cases that suggest that Bigfoot may be far more human than ape-like.

Hypertrichosis and Hair-covered Man-Things

Today, Jonathan Downes is the director of the Centre for Fortean Zoology, which undertakes worldwide investigations of unknown animals. Back in 1982, however, Downes was a psychiatric nurse at an old and imposing-looking hospital in the English southwest called Starcross Hospital. In the 1800s it had what today would be considered a politically incorrect name—the West Counties Idiot Asylum. While he was employed at the hospital, Downes was given a fascinating story by a senior doctor who was, at that time, fast approaching retirement. It was a story of definitive cryptozoological proportions, one that may have had a bearing on the Bigfoot controversy in the United Kingdom, and which occurred at the height of the Second World War.

I interviewed Downes a number of years ago about this affair and he told me this fascinating saga:

> There had, apparently, been a number of occasions when captured German aircrew and pilots who had been shot down over South Devon or the English Channel were kept, temporarily, in a remote wing of Starcross Hospital—which is roughly ten miles from the city of Exeter—until they could be transferred to the prisoner of war camp high above Starcross on the Haldon Hills.

On one particularly memorable occasion, Downes revealed, a man was seen racing through the woods, and, as a German plane had been shot down that same night, it was a natural assumption that the man was the German pilot, who, presumably, had parachuted out of his plane before it crashed. Back to Downes:

> The old man who told me the story was actually one of the Home Guards [a body created by the British government to help defend the nation if German troops ever managed to invade the British Isles—which they did not]. He told me that one of the party had been a teacher in Germany before the war and could speak the language. He ordered the man to stop, but the fugitive ignored him. The captain was an educated man, and had no intention of using force to capture the fugitive unless it was absolutely necessary. A man with a shotgun—a local farmer, who had lost two of his sons in the desperate weeks leading up to Dunkirk—raised his weapon and fired. The dark figure ahead of them let out a grunt of agony and fell to the ground.

As the unit reached the man, and one illuminated the area with a flashlight, it immediately became clear that the shot, injured man was no Nazi pilot; he was naked and covered in hair. Downes continued:

> Apparently, the doctor told me, the badly injured wild man was taken to Starcross Hospital in the middle of the night, and all efforts were made to make him comfortable. Then, in the early hours of the morning, apparently an unmarked black van arrived, and two men in uniform and another wearing a long white coat, manhandled the mysterious victim onto a stretcher, loaded him into the back of the van, and took him to an unknown destination. My informant never heard anything about the case again. He did hint, however, that the authorities warned everybody involved to say nothing.

Was the hair-covered creature actually a British Bigfoot? Might it have been a definitive wild man? Incredibly, could it have been part of a still-surviving, relic population of primitive humans, such as Neanderthal man, presumed to have become extinct thousands of years earlier? Those questions would likely have been pondered for years had it not been for the fact that Downes cracked the case. He revealed the next part of the story:

> In the early weeks of 1983, I found myself going through the voluminous filing cabinets that held over a century's worth of patient records at Starcross. This was part of my training as a psychiatric nurse. And, although I was supposed to be looking for the distribution of different syndromes of mental and physical handicap from which the patients at Starcross Hospital suffered, much to my surprise I found what I strongly suspected to be the solution to my then forty year old mystery.

Downes discussed the files:

> Several members of the family suffered from … congenital, generalized, hypertrichosis, commonly known as Wolf-Man Syndrome. In extreme cases, this disease not only causes bizarre behavior and radical mood swings, but the body of the victim becomes excessively hairy. Although several people from the family had been diagnosed as suffering from this syndrome, there were no hospital records absolutely proving that they had been resident at a hospital after the First World War [which ended in 1918].

> What I did find out, however, was that the bloodline definitely had not died out. The family was still very important in the Devon area. They were notable benefactors to local charities, and, at one time, at least, members of the family had been on the governing board of Starcross Hospital itself.

Downes concluded:

> I thought it was quite likely that the unruly rabble that had accompanied the Home Guard on that fateful night in 1942 had actually shot a member of the ruling family—in the mistaken belief that he was a German airman. This would explain everything. It would explain why the whole affair had been shrouded in secrecy. In those days, the part of the landowner and the patrician establishment was far greater than it is today.

> There is still a stigma surrounding mental illness, mental handicap, and disability. This poor idiot, covered in hair, was still a member of the fami-

The genetic condition of hypertrichosis has been known for centuries. One famous case was Petrus Gonsalvus (Pedro Gonzales), who was born in the Canary Islands in 1537. Four of his children also inherited "Wolf-Man Syndrome."

ly who, after all, still paid the wages of most of the members of the posse that had hunted him down. Especially at a time when the nation was facing the deadly peril of the Nazi hordes, the powers-that-be would not have wanted the populace at large to be aware that one of their own was an unstable, dangerous, hair-covered lunatic who had escaped from his care and was wandering, naked and belligerent, across the countryside.

A case that could have languished for years in a file titled "British Bigfoot, 1942" ended up being nothing of the sort. It was not a tale of a hair-covered monster, but of a tragic man who found himself a victim of both circumstances and an unfortunate, rare medical condition.

India's Cryptid Apes

The Mande Burung (which translates into English as "Forest Man") is the closest thing that India has to the Abominable Snowman. In fact, given the near proximity between India and Tibet, it's entirely possible that the creatures are actually one and the same, but given different names by their respective people. Most witnesses to the Mande Burung describe a terrifying, intimidating beast of around ten feet tall and with a coat of black hair.

Fortunately, we are not reliant on ancient, impossible-to-investigate reports to make a case for the existence of the Mande Burung. In 2003, for example, what may very well have been a juvenile Mande Burung was encountered in Jammu and Kashmir. One of the witnesses, twenty-year-old Raja Wasim, encountered a black, hair-covered man-thing of about four feet in height on his uncle's farm. It glared at him in decidedly menacing fashion. In Wasim's own words:

> There is no mistake about what I saw. The monster had the face of a man with monkey-like features. It was the Snowman. It pounced on me and I jumped back on the veranda, shouting for help. My uncle and his family rushed to my rescue and the monster lazily walked away. It was hardly frightened by the commotion.

Wasim's uncle, Muhammad Shafi, commented on the fact that the animal did, at one point, exhibit fear, specifically when the family lit fires to keep it at bay. Another of those who encountered the creature was eighty-nine-year-old Rehman Magray. He said: "In our youth there used to be very heavy snowfall. Almost regularly, the Snowman would visit this village and others close to the mountains where heavy snow made feeding difficult for them during harsh winters."

In 2001, the people of East Delhi were plunged into a state of hysteria when a creature that became known as the Monkey-Man became briefly infamous. Late on the night of May 13, a large ape- or monkey-like animal came leaping out of the darkness of the slum-like environment, provoking chaos and terror in the process. Coated in hair and standing four to five feet tall, it mercilessly attacked its victims with sharp claws and even sharper fangs. People—quite literally—stampeded out of the area, fearful of being pounced on and killed.

The police were quickly on the scene, which was very fortunate, since, in the days that followed, the terror grew and the people of Delhi quickly set up vigilante-type groups to try and track down the hostile horror. When a number of normal, everyday citizens were beaten up by near-maniacal crowds—who mistook them for the Monkey-Man—police swiftly sought to squash the anarchy. They succeeded. The Monkey-Man disappeared as quickly as it had first surfaced.

Clearly, much of the Monkey-Man phenomenon was provoked by wild hysteria, inflammatory rumors, and not much else. That's not to say that a legitimate creature of some kind did not provoke the initial reports, but what followed soon afterwards was clearly propelled by fear and groundless tales that spread like wildfire. Such is the effect that cryptid apes can have on the populace.

Indonesia's Mysterious Ape

Situated in southeast Asia and Oceania, Indonesia is made up of thousands of islands. One of those islands is Flores, covering more than 5,000 square miles and which has a population of close to two million. Its wild animal population is notable and includes the deadly Komodo dragon and the huge Flores giant rat. Flores may be home to something far stranger, too.

The Nage people of Flores tell of a somewhat human-like ape called the Ebu gogo. As with so many of the smaller variety of creatures described within the pages of this book, the Ebu gogo was covered in hair, had distinct ape-like qualities, but walked upright, like a human. At barely three feet tall, they were hardly on a par with Bigfoot, but for the Nage people, the creatures generated a great deal of folklore and history.

According to legend, the presence of the animals was first noted when a tribe of people set up a village in an area known as Ua, at some point in the 1700s. All of the Ebu gogo on Flores lived deep inside an extensive network of caves, somewhere in the central part of the island, which extended almost a mile in length. Reportedly, the colony ran to around four dozen creatures. It wasn't long before curiosity got the better of the Ebu gogo and they made regular visits to the village perimeter, watching the people from a safe distance.

Over time, the Ebu gogo gained more confidence and, finally, were invited to partake in a village feast. By all accounts, they ate and drank heartily, hence the name given to them by the villagers, which translates as "ancestor who eats everything."

As a demonstration that the Ebu gogo were something more than mere unknown apes, they loved to dance, had their own fairly complex language, and could even mimic—to an eerie degree—the words of the Nage people, though it's debatable as to how much they understood.

It wasn't long, however, before matters began to deteriorate and tensions grew. Not content with the large banquets that the Nage invited the Ebu gogos to attend, the greedy creatures began raiding the farms of the villagers, grabbing crops and killing animals for food. According to legend, two children

The Nage tribespeople of the remote island of Flores in Indonesia tell of the Ebu gogo, a creature that looks very much like an ape but walks erect.

of the village were seized by the Ebu gogo and taken to the caves, where the ape-men demanded the children show them how to make fire. Fortunately, the terrified children managed to escape, fleeing back to the safety of the village.

For the folk of Ua, enough was enough. They decided that the Ebu gogo had to be exterminated, one way or another. They devised a plan: the village elders invited the creatures to a massive feast, one in which the Ebu gogo were encouraged to drink as much powerful wine as they could. The ever-hungry beasts obliged and were soon stuffed and drunk. At the end of the night, the beasts staggered back to the caves and fell into deep, alcohol-induced sleeps.

Then, when the Ebu gogo were out for the count, the villagers hauled a huge amount of palm fiber to the cave, set it on fire, and asphyxiated the creatures as they slept. Reportedly, however, two of the Ebu gogo—a male and a female—were seen fleeing into the woods, which suggests the that they may not have become extinct, after all.

There is an intriguing footnote to the story of the Ebu gogo of Flores. In 2003, at a cave called Liang Bua, in western Flores, the skeletal remains of a number of creatures dubbed "Hobbit" were found. Examinations of the bones showed they were approximately three-feet-three-inches tall and were humanoid creatures. They were given the official title of *Homo floresiensis*. (see "*Homo floresiensis*") Vindication for the tales of the Nage tribespeople? Possibly, yes.

Infrasound and Bigfoot

There are far more than a few reports on record where witnesses in close proximity to Bigfoot have reported feeling inexplicably terrified, nauseous, confused, disoriented, dizzy, light-headed, and physically unable to move. This may not be due to sheer terror and the pounding flood of massive amounts of adrenalin coursing through the bloodstream. The culprit may be something called infrasound. In simple terms, infrasound is an extremely low frequency sound, one which is significantly lower than 20 Hz, which is the typical extreme of human hearing.

A number of animals use infrasound as a means to communicate with each other. The long list includes giraffes, whales, and elephants. It's a form of communication in the animal kingdom that can be highly effective across large distances, sometimes in excess of one hundred miles. There is another important aspect of infrasound: when it is directed at humans it can provoke a wealth of unsettling physical sensations, as well as hallucinations of both the audio and visual kind. "Mysteriously snuffed out candles, weird sensations, and shivers down the spine may not be due to the presence of ghosts in haunted houses but to very low frequency sound that is inaudible to humans," reported the Associated Press in September 2003, continuing:

> British scientists have shown in a controlled experiment that the extreme bass sound known as infrasound produces a range of bizarre effects in people including anxiety, extreme sorrow and chills—supporting popular suggestions of a link between infrasound and strange sensations.

> Normally you can't hear it," said Richard Lord, an acoustic scientist employed at the National Physical Laboratory in England who worked on the project.

"Some scientists have suggested that this level of sound may be present at some allegedly haunted sites and so cause people to have odd sensations that they attribute to a ghost—our findings support these ideas," added Professor Richard Wiseman, a psychologist working at the University of Hertfordshire in the U.K.

So much for ghosts, but what about Bigfoot?

Melissa Adair, an expert on the hairy thing of the woods, said:

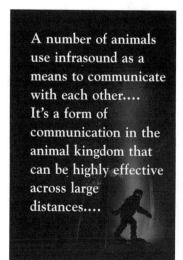

> A number of animals use infrasound as a means to communicate with each other.... It's a form of communication in the animal kingdom that can be highly effective across large distances....

> People who work with elephants have reported, nausea, dizziness, vomiting, disorientation and weakness as a result of being exposed to the infrasound that elephants produce. The known effects of infrasound on humans include feelings of intense fear or awe. Bigfoot researchers have reported similar symptoms that seem to come on suddenly when out in the field. Are we being "zapped"???

> We just might be....

Sasquatch expert Scott Carpenter said of his very own encounter with a Bigfoot:

> I am not an acoustic expert or a scientist. My findings are based on observation and common sense. I think that I was under the influence of infrasound during my encounter with the Bigfoot on April 30th, 2010. The Bigfoot manipulated my perception and sanitized my memory. Even more disturbing was the fact that I did not react to observing the Bigfoot. I had to have initially recognized what it was and where it was hiding. I made

two attempts to zoom in on the Bigfoot and get a close up video. Sometime during this process I was subjected to the influence of infrasound and strongly influenced or "brain washed" into walking off. It is almost like my memory was wiped clean and I was given instructions to leave and I did.

Similarly, "Miss Squatcher" noted the adverse effects of seeking Bigfoot in Elbow Falls, Alberta, Canada, in June 2013. She said:

I felt as if my chest was heavy, my breathing was shallow and I could hardly catch my breath. I stood up from examining the scat and scanned my surroundings, the sensation of my pulse pounding in my head. I saw nothing. I could feel panic setting in. I was on the edge of a full-blown panic attack and had the unrelenting feeling that I needed to leave the area, NOW. My anxiety was increasing and I shared this with the others. They were startled when I took out my compass, oriented myself in the direction we had come and started walking straight through the bush. "I have to leave, I don't feel right."

She added, and not without significance: "Was there a Bigfoot nearby producing infrasonic waves to scare the heck out of us? We will never know for sure. But I can say with certainty that something out there made me feel more fear and panic than I have ever felt before."

It should be noted that not every Bigfoot investigator is convinced that Sasquatch uses infrasound to dissuade people from seeking it and pursuing it. One of those is Lisa Shiel, the author of such books as *Backyard Bigfoot* and *Forbidden Bigfoot*. She observed:

People who report feeling anxious or afraid when near a Bigfoot may simply be anxious and afraid because they are near a Bigfoot. I've seen plenty of strange things in my life, and often I feel anxious when those things happen. It's a natural human response. Must we attribute such responses to a poorly understood type of sound waves?

It's a fair question, one upon which the Bigfoot-seeking community has no solid consensus.

Inter-dimensional Bigfoot

The vast majority of Bigfoot researchers subscribe to the viewpoint that Bigfoot is nothing stranger than a giant ape that science and zoology have yet to conclusively classify. There is, however, a small body of data that suggests Bigfoot is something far stranger than just a regular ape.

Peppered throughout Bigfoot lore and history are stories of the beasts vanishing in flashes of light, fading away into nothingness, and becoming invisible to the human eye. This has given rise to an intriguing theory: that Bigfoot has the ability to traverse multi-dimensions. In other words, while the creatures may be comprised of flesh and

A theory that might be a little out of this world is that Bigfoot comes from another dimenstion, which could explain witness testimony about how the cryptid ape manages to vanish in the wink of an eye.

blood, their overwhelming elusiveness may be due to the fact that they are only temporary visitors to our realm of existence.

A perfect example has been recorded by Jack Lapseritis, author of *The Psychic Sasquatch*. He tells the story of a group of people who had an amazing encounter with a Bigfoot. The story came from a Mrs. Jeffrey, and whose story Lapseritis summarizes as follows:

> After returning from a long hike, the group was stunned when a nine-to-ten foot Sasquatch stepped out in front of them a short distance away. Then, in the twinkling of an eye, the Bigfoot completely disappeared in front of the witnesses! The witnesses insisted that it literally dematerialized! Mrs. Jeffrey reported that she was so awed at what she saw, that when they returned home, she did not leave the house for two weeks. The woman was in such a total state of shock that she did not return to the area for some time.

Ronan Coghlan is the author of a number of acclaimed books, including *A Dictionary of Cryptozoology* and, with coauthor Gary Cunningham, *The Mystery Animals of Ireland*. In a 2012 interview with me, Coghlan provided his views on the nature of Bigfoot and what he believes may be evidence of a link between the phenomenon and that of multi-dimensions. His words are primarily focused on Bigfoot in Britain, but they could quite easily apply to the creatures seen anywhere.

"The idea that there is a viable, reproducing population of apes or humanoids in Britain is totally risible; it just couldn't be. So, alternative explanations for their presence are to be sought," begins Coghlan. "A lot of the British reports seem to be quite authentic. So, there probably are actual beasts or humanoids out there. And the question is: How did they arrive there in the first place?"

Coghlan answers his question with the following words of reply: "It's now becoming acceptable in physics to say there are alternative universes."

He continues on this controversial but thought-provoking path:

The main pioneer of this is Professor Michio Kaku, of the City College of New York. He has suggested that not only are there alternate universes, but when ours is about to go out in a couple of billion years, we might have the science to migrate to a more congenial one that isn't going to go out. I think he expects science to keep improving for countless millennia, which is very optimistic of him, but whatever one thinks about that, the idea of alternative universes is now gaining an acceptance among physicists, and he's the name to cite in this area.

The subject is far from one lacking in mysteries and questions, however, as Coghlan acknowledges:

Now, how do you get into, or out of, alternative universes? Well, the answer is quite simple: You have heard of worm-holes, I'm sure? No one has ever seen a worm-hole, I hasten to add. They are hypothetical, but mainstream physicists say they could be there, and there's one particular type called the Lorentzian Traversable Worm-hole. Physicists admit there is a possibility that this exists, and it would be like a short-cut, from one universe to another. Thus, for example, it's rather like a portal: Something from the other universe would come through it. Or, something from another planet could come through it.

Turning his attentions towards the links between worm-holes and bizarre beasts, Coghlan comments:

If there are any of these worm-holes on Earth, it would be quite easy for anything to come through, and it's quite possible any number of anomalous creatures could find their way through from time to time. You remember John Keel and his window-areas? That would tend to indicate there's a worm-hole in the vicinity; such as Point Pleasant, West Virginia, where the Mothman was seen.

I have the distinct suspicion we are dealing with window-areas that either contact some

Physicists such as Professor Michio Kaku of the City College of New York have suggested that we live in just one of many alternate universes. Could there be a connection between alternate universes and Bigfoot?

other planet, or they contact another universe. My money is on the other universe, rather than the other planet, to be honest with you. Either a short-cut through time, or a short-cut through space, is recognized as possible these days. This is kind of cutting-edge physics, as it were.

Now, the other one isn't cutting-edge physics at all. It's my own little theory. I think, looking at a great many legends, folk-tales, and things of that nature, it is possible to vibrate at different rates. And if you vibrate at a different rate, you are not seen. You are not tangible. And, then, when your vibration changes, you *are* seen, and you *are* tangible; maybe that this has something to do with Bigfoot appearing and disappearing in a strange fashion.

> "... if UFOs travel by worm-holes, and if Bigfoot does the same, that might allow for a connection between the two."

And, finally, on the question of UFOs: Quite a large number of Bigfoot-type creatures have been seen in the vicinity of UFOs. I'm not saying there's necessarily a connection between the two, but they do—quite often—turn up in the same areas. Now, if UFOs travel by worm-holes, and if Bigfoot does the same, that might allow for a connection between the two. They might not be mutually exclusive.

The final word, on Bigfoot's curious ability to disappear before people's eyes, goes to Sharon Eby Comet, who has extensively studied this controversial angle. She says in response to the question of how, exactly, Bigfoot performs its vanishing act:

> Possible answers now include: induced transparency and/or the appearance of such, going through time or locality-exchange portals, H2S "hypnosis" (only possible in some cases), and IR/UV/ELF/VLF (electromagnetic spectrum) camouflage.

> These hypotheses are part of science, not "magic," and perhaps may even explain some of the seemingly paranormal accounts of Bigfoot sightings worldwide ... at least in part. Until a heavy load of field documentation is properly done around the globe, and compared, then all is still speculation. In essence, my own view of paranormal is just "outside of what is expected" so we now *must look in new places for answers to old questions*, because obviously the places we've been looking in up to now have all been—at least partially—wrong, or most Bigfoot researchers would be a lot further along by now!

Invisibility

Most investigators of the Bigfoot and cryptid ape phenomena take the view that the beasts they seek are flesh and blood animals that have been incredibly lucky, in terms of skillfully avoiding us, or getting captured and killed. There is, however, another theory that may explain how and why Bigfoot always eludes us, at least when it comes to securing hard evidence of its existence. It's a theory that posits the creatures have the ability to become invisible—that's to say, they can "cloak" themselves so that we do not see them. It's a theory that the bulk of Bigfoot enthusiasts have absolutely no time for. It is a fact, however, that regardless of what people think of the theory, there is certainly no shortage of reports.

The website *Native Languages* notes:

The Bigfoot figure is common to the folklore of most Northwest Native American tribes. Native American Bigfoot legends usually describe the creatures as around 6–9 feet tall, very strong, hairy, uncivilized, and often foul-smelling, usually living in the woods and often foraging at night.... In some Native stories, Bigfoot may have minor supernatural powers—the ability to turn invisible, for example—but they are always considered physical creatures of the forest, not spirits or ghosts.

Native Americans aren't the only people who hold such beliefs. *Bhutan Canada* says:

In 2001, the Bhutanese Government created the Sakteng Wildlife Sanctuary, a 253 square-mile protected habitat for the Migoi. The sanctuary is also home to pandas, snow leopards, and tigers but the Bhutanese maintain that the refuge was created specifically for the Migoi. Migoi is the Tibetan word for "wild man" or more common to Western culture, the Yeti. The Yeti, often called the Abominable Snowman in the west and referred to as the Migoi by the Bhutanese, is a bipedal ape like creature that is said to inhabit the Himalayan region of Nepal, Tibet, and Bhutan. The Migoi is known for its phenomenal strength and magical powers, such as the ability to become invisible and to walk backwards to fool any trackers.

Davy Russell, who, in 2000, penned an article titled "Invisible Bigfoot", refers to an incident that occurred in North Dakota in 1977 that may be relevant to this particularly charged area of research:

A Bigfoot-type creature was spotted throughout the afternoon and into the evening. Locals, along with the police, staked out the area to search for the mysterious creature. A rancher named Lyle Maxon reported a strange encounter, claiming he was walking in the dark when he plainly heard something nearby breathing heavily, as if from running.

Russell continued that Maxon shone his flashlight in the direction of where the sounds were coming from, but nothing could be seen. Puzzled and disturbed by the encounter, Maxon gave serious thought to the possibility that the beast had the ability to render itself invisible to the human eye.

In April 2012, researcher Mi-Lin said:

This past week, I had several wonderful conversations with a gentleman named Thomas Hughes. Thomas has been communicating with numerous Sasquatch since his first encounter in April 2008. He has a wealth of knowledge about their existence and whereabouts, some of which he shared with me.

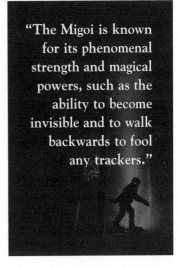

"The Migoi is known for its phenomenal strength and magical powers, such as the ability to become invisible and to walk backwards to fool any trackers."

Sasquatch are gentle and playful giants. They range in height from 6–15 feet and live to an age of approximately 120–140 years. They are natural pranksters and are caretakers of Mother Earth. What I mean by caretakers is that they have adapted themselves to the planet instead of trying to change the environment to suit them....

She added that Hughes told her: "They have the ability to raise their frequency just enough to be able to become invisible to humans. They fear humans—seeing them as their greatest threat. So, most of the time, they go invisible when humans are around to avoid being hunted and killed. Sasquatch are aware they are seen from time to time."

On a similar path, *Soul Guidance* offers that Bigfoot is

... able to shift the frequency of their physical body, by which it phases out of this physical dimension, and thus enters another dimensional world that lies behind this one....

Bigfoot can also shift partially, so they become invisible but are still partially in this physically world. In this partial state, they can follow someone around, invisibly, and their movements can be heard and seen. In this partial state, they can walk through walls; and they can sometimes be seen as being transparent, or just the outline of their body. For example, bushes move aside when they step through. When they appear or disappear, their eyes often turn red, probably a characteristic of the shifting frequencies....

Then there is the matter of Bigfoot invisibility in the world of entertainment. From 2000 to 2002, the Syfy Channel ran a series called *The Invisible Man*. It focused on the exploits and adventures of Darien Fawkes (played by Vincent Ventresca), a thief who is recruited into the top secret world of espionage and assassination. Fawkes is subjected to advanced, fringe surgery, which involves the implantation into his brain of something called the "Quicksilver gland." It's a gland that has the ability to secrete a substance—Quicksilver—that has light-bending abilities when it secretes through the skin, thus creating a form of invisibility.

In series two of *The Invisible Man*, we learn that although the Quicksilver gland was being created and synthesized artificially, its development was prompted by the recovery of a Bigfoot corpse and the deduction that its own Quicksilver gland is what has allowed the creatures to remain almost 100 percent elusive. Fiction paralleling an astonishing truth? It's a question to ponder deeply.

Ireland's Man-Ape

Neil Arnold, a long-time researcher of mysterious creatures, says: "There is nothing like a chilling ghost story," adding that "one of my favorite ghoulish tales comes via Reverend Archdeacon St. John D. Seymour, and concerns a bizarre entity once said to have haunted an Irish castle."

The story, Arnold notes, "is mentioned in *True Ghost Stories* by Marchioness Townshend and Maude Ffoulkes, who comment that 'the truth of this story was vouched for to Mr. Reginald Span by the Vicar of the Anglican Church, Arizona, as it happened to some friends of his when they once rented a picturesque castle in the South of Ireland.'"

And, with that said, read on....

So the very weird saga goes, late one particular night, many years ago, a certain "Mrs. A" was sitting alone in one of the castle's bedrooms, awaiting the return of her husband. Suddenly, there was the distinct and unmistakable sound of one of the doors banging in the corridor outside the room. More disturbingly, footsteps could be heard, too. Someone or *something* was creeping around the old castle. Grabbing a lit candle, Mrs. A carefully and slowly opened the door and, to her eternal horror, saw a darkened, shadowy form heading towards the staircase.

Evidently, the entity realized its presence had been noticed, and it turned to face the by-now fear-stricken Mrs. A. It was at this point that her terror was elevated to stratospheric proportions: The thing was apparitional in nature and possessed the head of a man, but the body of a mighty, hair-covered ape. For a moment or several, it glared malevolently at Mrs. A, before vanishing into nothingness. The story is not over, however.

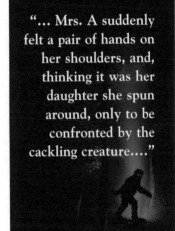

"... Mrs. A suddenly felt a pair of hands on her shoulders, and, thinking it was her daughter she spun around, only to be confronted by the cackling creature...."

Several nights later, the woman's husband also saw the animal-man, after his attention was drawn to the shadows of the landing, from where distinctly unsettling and creepy laughter was emanating. On looking up, Mr. A was confronted by a beast that—just as the man's wife said—had the body of a large and hairy ape and the head of a man—and a most ugly man, too.

Interestingly, Mr. A evidently got a better look at the creature than did Mrs. A, and he could see that the hair of the monster appeared to be of a reddish brown color. In what sounds like some sort of bizarre nightmare, as the man headed up the stairs to confront the man-thing, the terrible laughter got louder and echoed through the old halls of the castle. Not surprisingly, at the last moment the man thought far better of his actions and raced for the safety of the bedroom.

For a few days, things were mercifully quiet. This did not last long, however. While arranging flowers one afternoon in the drawing-room, Mrs. A suddenly felt a pair of hands on her shoulders, and, thinking it was her daughter she spun around, only to be confronted by the cackling creature, looming over her at a height that easily exceeded six feet.

Mrs. A screamed for help, and, as a friend came running, the strange and unearthly entity vanished into absolute nothingness—just as it had before. And, for the family, by now enough was well and truly enough: They packed their bags and returned to the United States.

Perhaps of relevance to this story, noted author and paranormal investigator Ronan Coghlan said: "There is an Irish word, *gruagach*, which can mean a magician, giant or ogre, but that actually means 'the hairy one.' The question must be asked if this contains any sort of reminiscence of hairy man-beasts prowling the Irish countryside."

It may very well, given what Coghlan said next: "A Norse work of the 13th century mentions the capture of a wild man in Ireland with a mane running down its back." The work in question was called *Konungs Skuggsja*, or, alternatively, *Speculum Skuggsjo*, and describes the Irish wild man by the name of the gelt, and his peculiar condition as geltacht."

A careful examination of the old book reveals the following about this Irish entity:

There is also one thing which will seem very wonderful about men who are called gelt. It happens that when two hosts meet and are arrayed in battle-array, and when the battle-cry is raised loudly on both sides, that cowardly men run wild and lose their wits from the dread and fear which seize them. And then they run into a wood away from other men, and live there like wild beasts, and shun the meeting of men like wild beasts.

"And it is said of these men that when they have lived in the woods in that condition for twenty years then feathers grow on their bodies as on birds...."

And it is said of these men that when they have lived in the woods in that condition for twenty years then feathers grow on their bodies as on birds, whereby their bodies are protected against frost and cold, but the feathers are not so large that they may fly like birds. Yet their swiftness is said to be so great that other men cannot approach them, and greyhounds just as little as men. For these people run along the trees almost as swiftly as monkeys or squirrels.

Now, however, when he arrived out of battle, it was seldom that his feet would touch the ground because of the swiftness of his course, and when he did touch it he would not shake the dew from the top of the grass for the lightness and the nimbleness of his step. He halted not from that headlong course until he left neither plain, nor field, nor bare mountains, nor bog, nor thicket, nor marsh, nor hill, nor hollow, nor dense-sheltering wood in Ireland that he did not travel that day, until he reached Ros Bearaigh, in Glenn Earcain, where he went into the yew-tree that was in the glen.

Thereafter, we are told, the gelt lived as a definitive outcast, roaming the land of Ireland in search of three things, and three only: water to drink, water-cress to dine upon, and ivy-bushes on which to sleep.

Isnachi of Peru

A strange denizen of the dark, jungle-saturated mountainous regions of Peru, the Isnachi is a beast that is seemingly wholly monkey-like in nature and appearance. Unlike some of the beasts cited in the pages of this book, it appears to completely lack human-like traits. Very much like a chimpanzee in size, the Isnachi is noted for its large, barrel-like chest and huge, powerful arms. Rather oddly, it has a long pig-like or dog-like snout, giving it somewhat of an orangutan-like appearance, even though it is perceived as a monkey, rather than as an ape.

Little more is known of the Isnachi—chiefly because of the fact that it rarely, if ever, descends below seldom-travelled landscapes of around 1,500 meters—aside from the fact that when it finds itself confronted by people, the creature displays extreme states of aggression.

Ivanov, Ilya, and Ape–Human Hybrids

Quite possibly, the closest real-world equivalent to the fictional Dr. Frankenstein of Mary Shelley's classic novel from 1818, *Frankenstein*, was a Russian scientist who had a disturbing fascination with the idea of hybridizing different kinds of animals. It was a fascination that bordered upon being a dangerous, crazed obsession. The man's name was Ilya Ivanov (1870–1932) , who entered this world in August 1870, in the Russian town of Shchigry. He was not destined to remain in his small-town environment, however. Ivanov obtained his professorship in 1907 and took employment at an animal sanctuary located in the province of Kherson Oblast, Ukraine. It was here that Ivanov's dark and disturbing research began.

Ivanov's initial work was focused on horses. He developed the idea of inter-breeding racehorses, to the point where, eventually, he would end up with what we might call the ultimate "super-horse," one that could outrun, and outperform, just about any other horse on the planet. It was, as one might imagine, a program that did produce fine racehorses, but they were nothing out of the ordinary. Something that was very much out of the ordinary was Ivanov's next target of interest: fusing apes and humans into one.

Just a few years after the "super-horse" saga caught the attention of the Russian government's Academy of Sciences, Ivanov was given a sizable grant by the academy to research the feasibility of creating something akin to an ape-man. It was a monstrous, abhorrent idea—but that didn't stop it from proceeding. Indeed, significant funding was provided to Ivanov, as was a wealth of medical

Russian biologist Ilya Ivanov conducted infamous research in interspecies insemination and hybridization.

equipment and even newly constructed laboratories from where the terrible experiments could take place. The labs were not situated in the heart of the Soviet Union, however. The huge funding allowed for the construction of several facilities in Kindia, French Guiana. And, thanks to the help of the Pasteur Institute, the work began, in early 1926.

Within months, Ivanov was delving into extremely controversial areas, as author Stephanie Pain noted:

> Ivanov passed the summer in Paris, where he spent some of his time at the Pasteur Institute working on ways to capture and subdue chimps, and some with the celebrated surgeon Serge Voronoff, inventor of an increasingly fashionable "rejuvenation therapy." In a now notorious operation, Voronoff grafted slices of ape testes into those of rich and ageing men hoping to regain their former vigor. That summer, he and Ivanov made headlines by transplanting a woman's ovary into a chimp called Nora and then inseminating her with human sperm.

Ivanov's team utilized both chimpanzees and gorillas in their experimentation—all of which was focused upon trying to successfully impregnate ape and chimpanzee females with human male sperm. In one regard it made great sense: chimpanzees, for example, have a DNA sequence that is around 95 percent identical to that of the human race. What seemed promising on paper and in theory, however, proved to be far less promising in reality. That's to say, none of the attempts at impregnation worked. Ivanov was not dissuaded, however. He decided to take a different approach—a very dangerous and even unethical approach.

> If the process of impregnating apes with human sperm wasn't going to work, thought Ivanov, why not impregnate human women with ape sperm? This is precisely what Ivanov did—on local tribeswomen.

If the process of impregnating apes with human sperm wasn't going to work, thought Ivanov, why not impregnate human women with ape sperm? This is precisely what Ivanov did—on local tribeswomen. It seems, from the surviving records, that little, if any, thought was given to (a) the moral aspects of all this (or, to be correct, the profound lack of morals); and (b) the trauma that the women might experience, in the event that they gave birth to freakish, half-human, half-ape abominations. Despite this approach, and regardless of whether or not the animals used were gorillas or chimpanzees, failure was the only outcome.

Ivanov was not still deterred. He returned to his native Soviet Union, secured further funding, and established several other labs. Rather intriguingly, several of the locations of the installations were kept secret—perhaps, to ensure that outraged locals didn't take to storming them, fearful of what was afoot in their towns and cities. Nevertheless, it is a fact that at least one facility was built—underground—in the town of Sukhumi, Georgia. We know this as, just a few years ago, a number of ape skeletons were unearthed there when workmen digging underground stumbled upon one of the nightmarish labs.

It is, perhaps, not a surprise to learn that the experiments undertaken in Sukhumi failed as abysmally as those attempted in French Guiana. The Soviet government was hardly pleased with the outcome and, under the ruthless command of Josef Stalin, its agents arrested Ivanov. It was December 31, 1932, when Ivanov found himself in distinctly hot water. It soon became scalding: he received a five-year term in prison, dying just two years into his sentence, which had been changed to exile, rather than jail, shortly after being sentenced.

Pawel Wargan, who has extensively studied the work of Ivanov, noted:

Interspecific hybridization was seen to hold great potential. Animals that combined the strongest qualities of two species could become popular house pets. The Soviet media was keen to suggest that a new species, uniting human strength with the subservience and agility of an ape, could form a more obedient workforce and a stronger army. The Soviet Union was caught in a genetic manipulation mania, much to the amusement of one novelist—Mikhail Bulgakov wrote of a canine that became a Soviet bureaucrat after being subject to a transplant of human testicles. The buildings on this hill above Sukhumi were to be the Soviet answer to Charles Darwin's insights, where chimeras were born and biology became another tool in the propagandist's arsenal.

The final word goes to Jerry Bergman, Ph.D., who said:

In the end, the research failed and has not been attempted again, at least publicly. Today we know it will not be successful for many reasons, and Professor Ivanov's attempts are, for this reason, a major embarrassment to science. One problem is humans have 46 chromosomes—apes 48—and for this reason the chromosomes will not pair up properly even if a zygote is formed. Another problem is a conservatively estimated *40 million* base pair differences exist between humans and our putative closest evolutionary relatives, the chimps. These experiments are the result of evolutionary thinking and they failed because their basic premise is false.

Jacko

It was a story that surfaced in 1884—a story that, if true, suggested something deeply strange was afoot in Yale, British Columbia. On Independence Day 1884, the *Daily Colonist* newspaper published a story titled: "What is it? A Strange Creature Captured above Yale. A British Columbia Gorilla." Supposedly, the curious creature had been caught on June 30 and held in a nearby jail.

The startling saga began:

In the immediate vicinity of No. 4 tunnel, situated some twenty miles above this village, are bluffs of rock which have hitherto been unsurmountable, but on Monday morning last were successfully scaled by Mr. Onderdonk's employees on the regular train from Lytton. Assisted by Mr. Costerton, the British Columbia Express Company's messenger, and a number of gentlemen from Lytton and points east of that place who, after considerable trouble and perilous climbing, succeeded in capturing a creature which may truly be called half man and half beast.

The story continued:

Ned Austin, the engineer, on coming in sight of the bluff at the eastern end of the No. 4 tunnel saw what he supposed to be a man lying asleep in close proximity to the track, and as quick as thought blew the signal to apply the brakes. The brakes were instantly applied, and in a few seconds the train was brought to a standstill. At this moment the supposed man sprang up, and uttering a sharp quick bark began to climb the steep bluff.

Conductor R. J. Craig and Express Messenger Costerton, followed by the baggage man and brakemen, jumped from the train and knowing they were some twenty minutes ahead of time immediately gave chase. After five minutes of perilous climbing the then supposed demented Indian was corralled on a projecting shelf of rock where he could neither ascend nor descend. The query now was how to capture him alive, which was quickly decided by Mr. Craig, who crawled on his hands and knees until he was about forty feet above the creature. Taking a small piece of loose rock he let it fall and it had the desired effect of rendering poor Jacko incapable of resistance for a time at least.

The beast was quickly named Jacko and a legend was born. The newspaper told its no-doubt amazed readers that Jacko

… has long, black, strong hair and resembles a human being with one exception, his entire body, excepting his hands, (or paws) and feet are covered with glossy hair about an inch long. His fore arm is much longer than a man's fore arm, and he possesses extraordinary strength, as he will take hold of a stick and break it by wrenching or twisting it, which no man living could break in the same way.

> **"… [Jacko is] becoming daily more attached to his keeper, Mr. George Telbury, of this place, who proposes shortly starting for London, England, to exhibit him."**

Since his capture he is very reticent, only occasionally uttering a noise which is half bark and half growl. He is, however, becoming daily more attached to his keeper, Mr. George Telbury, of this place, who proposes shortly starting for London, England, to exhibit him. His favorite food so far is berries, and he drinks fresh milk with evident relish. By advice of Dr. Hannington raw meats have been withheld from Jacko, as the doctor thinks it would have a tendency to make him savage.

The Daily Colonist concluded:

The question naturally arises, how came the creature where it was first seen by Mr. Austin? From bruises about its head and body, and apparent soreness since its capture, it is supposed that Jacko ventured too near the edge of the bluff, slipped, fell and lay where found until the sound of the rushing train aroused him.

Mr. Thos. White and Mr. Gouin, C. E., as well as Mr. Major, who kept a small store about half a mile west of the tunnel during the past two years, have mentioned having seen a curious creature at different points between Camps 13 and 17, but no attention was paid to their remarks as people came to the conclusion that they had either seen a bear or stray Indian dog. Who can unravel the mystery that now surrounds Jacko! Does he belong to a species hitherto unknown in this part of the continent, or is he really what the train men first thought he was, a crazy Indian!

Five days later, the article was denounced by the *British Columbian* newspaper. Its staff was very vocal about how the *Daily Colonist* had fallen for such a tall tale. The *Mainland Guardian* had similar, sharp words for the *Daily Colonist's* story, too:

The "What Is It" is the subject of conversation in town. How the story originated, and by whom, is hard for one to conjecture. Absurdity is written on the face of it. The fact of the matter is, that no such animal was caught, and how the *Colonist* was duped in such a manner, and by such a strange story, is strange.

If the story did have any truth to it, unless the beast was a juvenile Bigfoot, then it was clearly something else entirely. Dr. Grover S. Krantz said of the animal dubbed "Jacko":

It was described as being wild, hair covered, long armed, and very strong. Reportedly it measured 4 feet 7 inches tall and weighed 127 pounds. It was captured on the Canadian Pacific Railroad, near Yale, B.C., while this line was still under construction.... Very little additional information is available on it.... Its fate is unknown, assuming that it ever existed at all.

Today, the case of Jacko is one that is still championed by a handful of Bigfoot researchers and wholly dismissed by many others. Some are situated somewhere between both camps, chiefly as a result of the fact that regardless of whether or not the Jacko story has merit, British Columbia has a long tradition of man-beast encounters of the Bigfoot variety.

The final word goes to Bigfoot authority Loren Coleman:

Unfortunately, a whole new generation of hominologists, Sasquatch searchers, and Bigfoot researchers are growing up thinking that the Jacko story is an ironclad cornerstone of the field, a foundation piece of history proving that Sasquatch are real. But in reality Jacko seems to be a local rumor brought to the level of a news story that eventually evolved into a modern fable.

Japan's Enigmatic Apes

What is particularly intriguing, but also puzzling, about the Hibagon of Japan is that sightings of the roughly five-foot-tall creature did not begin until the dawning of the 1970s. In pretty much every other location on the planet, however, the lore and legends of cryptid apes date back centuries. While there is no solid answer as to why the Hibagon seemingly surfaced out of nowhere, that does not detract from the significance of the encounters. The date was July 20, 1970, and the location was Japan's Mount Hiba, which is situated within the Hiba-Dogo-Taishaku Quasi-National Park.

One of the many witnesses who saw the creature, Yokio Sazawa, said that as he dug for sweet potatoes in Mount Hiba's foothills: "All of a sudden, this thing stood before me. It was about five feet tall with a face like an inverted triangle, covered with bristles. Having a snub nose, and large, deep, glaring eyes."

Another witness was Albert Kubo, who said of the beast he encountered:

Snow monkeys (Japanese macaques) are the only wild primate known to live in Japan, so what, exactly, is the Hibagon?

I was petrified, but the stench was what really got to me. He must have bathed in a septic tank and dried off with cow dung. I nearly passed out. Luckily enough, though, I managed to turn and run before it realized I was there. I ran five miles straight home without ever looking back over my shoulder.

More than a dozen sightings were made in 1970, with even more following in the period 1971–1974. Reports then tailed off but resumed again in the early 1980s, at Mitsugi, where a hair-covered ape of broadly human proportions was encountered. Interestingly, the witness reported the animal apparently brandishing a stone axe-like weapon.

Zoologist Richard Freeman has studied the reports of the Hibagon and said:

What was the Hibagon? The Japanese macaque, or snow monkey, is the only known species of Japanese monkey, and is found throughout the wilder, mountainous areas of Japan. But the macaque is a quadruped and reaches a size less than half that of Hibagon.

"Another idea," Freeman continues, "is that the Hibagon was an escaped pet chimpanzee. Exotic pets are popular in Japan and, strange as it may seem, a number of these savage and dangerous apes are kept. Chimps can walk on their hind legs for a while but they are knuckle walkers by nature. This clashes with the description of Hibagon as a bipedal creature."

Thus, we are left with a definitive mystery regarding the true nature of the Hibagon.

Jigue
See: Cuba's Very Own Bigfoot

Junjudee
See: Australia's Beast-Men

Kalanoro
See: Madagascar's Primitive People

Kangaroo Man
See: Hairy Men of the Old Mines

Kelly–Hopkinsville Gunfight in the Woods

The subject of UFO research is filled with cases that positively reek of high strangeness. And they don't get much stranger than a very weird incident that occurred on the night of August 15, 1955, in the vicinity of Kelly and Hopkinsville, Kentucky. Depending on whose version of events you accept as the truth, either aliens landed or a band of marauding circus monkeys—painted silver, no less—were on the loose!

Kelly was, and still is, a small, rural town about ten miles from Hopkinsville. They are the kinds of places where people keep to themselves, and nothing of a particularly sensational matter ever happens—apart, that is, from the fateful night of August 15, when absolute chaos broke out. It all went down at the farmhouse of the Sutton family, who had visitors in from Pennsylvania: Billy Ray Taylor and his wife. It was roughly 7:00 P.M. when Billy Ray left the farmhouse to fetch water from the well. And what a big mistake that was.

In mere minutes, Billy Ray was back, minus the water. Terrified, Billy Ray told the Suttons and his wife that as he headed towards the well he saw a significantly sized, illuminated, circular-shaped object come to rest in a nearby gully. As the group tried to figure out what on earth (or off it …) was going on, they mused upon the possibilities of shooting stars, meteorites, and good ol' leg-pulling. By all accounts, it was none of those. In just a few minutes, the Suttons' dog began to bark, growl, and snarl in aggressive, uncontrollable fashion—after which it raced for cover underneath the porch. Clearly, something strange was going down. Exactly how strange soon became very apparent.

> Terrified, Billy Ray told the Suttons and his wife that as he headed towards the well he saw a significantly sized, illuminated, circular-shaped object come to rest in a nearby gully.

Intent on making sure they were in control of the situation, Elmer Sutton and Billy Ray Taylor each armed themselves with a shotgun and headed out into the darkness. In no time, they were confronted by something terrifying: a small, silvery, creature—about three feet tall—that was scurrying towards them with its long, ape-like, arms held high in the air. Sutton did what most folk might do when confronted by a strange, dwarfish thing after sunset: he blasted the beast with his shotgun. To the consternation of both men, the gun had no effect, aside from causing the creature to do a quick, impressive backflip, after which it disappeared into the darkness—for a while.

Rather wisely, Elmer and Billy Ray raced for the safety of the farmhouse and locked the doors behind them. In mere moments, the same creature—or, at least, a very similar one—was seen peering through one of the windows. Elmer's son, J.C., took a shot at it. The only damage was to the window. The small beast scurried away at lightning speed. The curiously named Lucky Sutton and Billy Ray took a tentative walk outside to see if they could see the creature—or creatures. That was a very bad move: as they prowled around the property, a clawed hand came down from the roof and seized Billy Ray's hair and head.

Terrified, Billy Ray pulled away, screaming, to see the creature charge across the roof. To their horror, a second creature was staring at them from the branch of a nearby tree. A second shoot-out achieved nothing, aside from the remarkably weird sight of the creatures floating—rather than leaping or falling—to the ground and then racing into the darkness. The tumultuous events continued throughout the night, with guns firing, and the wizened little beasts creating havoc.

Realizing that the situation might very well go on all night, the group decided there was only one option available to them: they had to flee the farmhouse, which they did in two cars, making their speedy way to the sheriff's office in nearby Hopkinsville. The sheer, collective state of fear into which the Suttons and the Taylors had been plunged immediately convinced the sheriff that whatever had happened, it was no drunken prank.

By the time the sheriff and the family arrived back at the farmhouse, the creatures were gone—they did, however, reappear in the early hours, and conveniently after the police had left. In no time at all, the media heard the story, as did the U.S. Air Force—the latter coming up with a very bizarre explanation as its staff sought to lay matters to rest.

Respected UFO researcher Dr. J. Allen Hynek felt that the witness testimony about the creatures in Kentucky made it unlikely they were escaped monkeys from a a circus.

Before we get to the matter of the explanation, it's important to have a full understanding of the physical appearance of the creatures, drawn from the Suttons and Taylors' memories. All of the strange entities were near-identical: long arms, skinny legs, large ears, and yellow eyes. As for their gait, they moved in a strange, pivoting fashion. And they were all silver in color. Cue the Air Force's best estimate of what really happened.

With absolutely nothing solid to back up its claims, the Air Force suggested the culprits were monkeys, painted silver, that had escaped from a traveling circus! As cryptozoologist Ken Gerhard noted, it's "a theory more ridiculous than the notion of invading aliens." Nevertheless, the Air Force stuck to its guns, with Major John E. Albert being the major proponent of the circus escapee/painted monkeys theory.

Ufologists did not just accept this theory without question. One of the most respected of all UFO researchers was Dr. J. Allen Hynek. He said of his investigation of the Air Force's claim:

I did make an attempt to find out whether there had been any traveling circuses in the area from which some monkeys could have escaped. The monkey hypothesis fails, however, if the basic testimony of the witnesses can be accepted. Under a barrage of gunfire from Kentuckians, over a somewhat extended period, it is unthinkable that at least one cadaver would not have been found. Furthermore, monkeys do not float down from trees: they either jump or fall. And, anyway, I was unable to find any trace of a traveling circus!

The 1955 Kelly-Hopkinsville saga remains unresolved to this day. The fact that the incident began with the sighting of what may well have been a UFO has led flying saucer sleuths to conclude a mini-alien invasion briefly broke out in rural Kentucky. On the other hand, is it possible that the Air Force was, at least, partly on the right track? Could the creatures have been monkeys, after all—not from a circus, but of a very strange kind, perhaps of the anomalous variety described elsewhere in this book?

They are questions that we are unlikely to ever have answers for.

Kenya's Collection of Unknown Apes

The Republic of Kenya is found in east Africa and can boast of being home to more than a few kinds of unidentified, and unacknowledged, apes. Mount Kilimanjaro is the dwelling of the dwarfish Wa-mbilikimo (or Mberikimo), a hairy man-beast with a head full of flowing locks. Perhaps related to the Wa-mbilikimo are the Dokos of Lake Turkana, stories of which surfaced in the nineteenth century. That the Dokos reportedly had their own form of religion suggests they were far more evolved than the average ape—or, quite possibly, were an unknown form of human.

The Maus of Kenya's Mau Escarpment, which runs along Kenya's Great Rift Valley, sound like a combination of both the Doko and the Wa-mbiliki-mo. Short and hairy, they seem to possess profoundly human traits, despite their primitive, animal-like appearances. This is made clear by their reported use of rudimentary tools and fire, and their odd obsession with herding cattle.

One of the most significant accounts of the Mau people came from big game hunter Roger Courtney. In his 1940 book *A Greenhorn in Africa,* he related a number of accounts of sightings of, and confrontations with, the Mau—or "Mau Men," as Courtney was told they were also called. Courtney said that one of his interviewees "went on to tell how his own father, who was driving his sheep to pasture on the slopes of Mount Longenot, fell into the hands of these gnomes when he went into a cave, following the trail of blood left by one of his

Mt. Kilimanjaro in the African nation of Tanzania is the home of the dwarfish Wa-mbilikimo.

sheep that had been stolen. He was stunned from behind, and when he came round he found he was surrounded by strange little creatures."

Courtney added that his source related his father's further words as follows:

The Mau men were lower even than those little people of the forests for, though they had no tails that I could see, they were as the monkeys that swing in the forest trees. Their skins were white, with the whiteness of the belly of a lizard, and their faces and bodies were covered with long, black hair.

Ketchum, Dr. Melba

On November 24, 2012, a controversial press release was issued, one that immediately caught the attention of the entire Bigfoot-seeking community. Its title was *"Bigfoot" DNA Sequenced in Upcoming Genetics Study: Five-Year Genome Study at DNA Diagnostics Yields Evidence of Homo sapiens/Unknown Hominin Hybrid Species in North America.*

It read as follows:

A team of scientists can verify that their 5-year long DNA study, currently under peer-review, confirms the existence of a novel hominin hybrid species, commonly called "Bigfoot" or "Sasquatch," living in North America. Researchers' extensive DNA sequencing suggests that the legendary Sasquatch is a human relative that arose approximately 15,000 years ago as a hybrid cross of modern Homo sapiens with an unknown primate species.

The study was conducted by a team of experts in genetics, forensics, imaging and pathology, led by Dr. Melba S. Ketchum of Nacogdoches, TX. In response to recent interest in the study, Dr. Ketchum can confirm that her team has sequenced 3 complete Sasquatch nuclear genomes and determined the species is a human hybrid:

"DNA sequencing suggests that the legendary Sasquatch is a human relative that arose approximately 15,000 years ago as a hybrid cross of modern Homo sapiens with an unknown primate species."

"Our study has sequenced 20 whole mitochondrial genomes and utilized next generation sequencing to obtain 3 whole nuclear genomes from purported Sasquatch samples. The genome sequencing shows that Sasquatch mtDNA is identical to modern Homo sapiens, but Sasquatch nuDNA is a novel, unknown hominin related to Homo sapiens and other primate species. Our data indicate that the North American Sasquatch is a hybrid species, the result of males of an unknown hominin species crossing with female Homo sapiens."

Hominins are members of the taxonomic grouping Hominini, which includes all members of the genus Homo. Genetic testing has already ruled out Homo neanderthalis and the Denisova hominin as contributors to Sasquatch mtDNA or nuDNA. "The male progenitor that contributed the unknown sequence to this hybrid is unique as its DNA is more distantly removed from humans than other recently discovered hominins like the Denisovan individual," explains Ketchum.

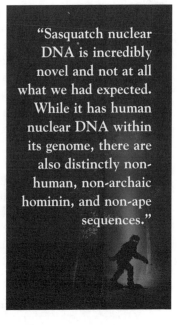

"Sasquatch nuclear DNA is incredibly novel and not at all what we had expected. While it has human nuclear DNA within its genome, there are also distinctly non-human, non-archaic hominin, and non-ape sequences. We describe it as a mosaic of human and novel non-human sequence. Further study is needed and is ongoing to better characterize and understand Sasquatch nuclear DNA."

Ketchum is a veterinarian whose professional experience includes 27 years of research in genetics, including forensics. Early in her career she also practiced veterinary medicine, and she has previously been published as a participant in mapping the equine genome. She began testing the DNA of purported Sasquatch hair samples 5 years ago.

Ketchum calls on public officials and law enforcement to immediately recognize the Sasquatch as an indigenous people:

"Genetically, the Sasquatch are a human hybrid with unambiguously modern human maternal ancestry. Government at all levels must recognize them as an indigenous people and immediately protect their human and Constitutional rights against those who would see in their physical and cultural differences a "license" to hunt, trap, or kill them."

The press release provoked a flood of comments, observations, articles, and blogposts among the Bigfoot-seeking community, with some coming down solidly on Ketchum's side, and others questioning the conclusions reached and the science involved. At the time of writing, the debate shows no signs of going away anytime soon—just like Bigfoot itself.

Khon Paa

In 1835, W. S. W. Ruschenberger penned a book titled *A Voyage Round the World: Including an Embassy to Muscat and Siam*. In the pages of his book, Ruschenberger referenced a curious story from Siam that suggested a strange man-thing was in its midst. He wrote:

Among the strange animals belonging to Siam, there is one described under the name of Khon Paa, which belongs to no known genus of natural history. This animal has been seen by the prince and hundreds of others, yet we must confess, we are inclined to doubt the accuracy of the description.

The Khon Paa resembles a man; it is five feet high, walks erect, has no knee joints, and runs faster than a horse. Should he accidentally fall, he is forced to crawl to a tree or something else, by which he again raises himself on his feet. His skin is transparent as a China horn lantern; his entrails are distinctly seen through it, and his abdomen shines like a looking-glass.

Under the superstitious notion, that the presence of the animal in Bangkok was unlucky, his owners were bambooed, and all their property was confiscated by the king for bringing him there. This treatment caused so much terror, that no one has since ventured to bring a specimen of the beast from his native lurking places.

We should not, perhaps, take literally the claim that the skin of the Khon Paa was transparent and that its entrails could be seen. Almost certainly, this was a folkloric exaggeration. Nevertheless, this does not take away the likelihood that—as Ruschenberger's story makes clear—the creature was all too real, regardless of what it actually was, and perhaps still is.

Kibaan

See: Philippines' Hairy Dwarfs

Kidnapped by Bigfoot

It's one thing to see a Bigfoot. It is, however, quite another thing entirely to claim to have been kidnapped by one and held hostage for several days! That was the controversial claim of Scandinavian Albert Ostman. Although Ostman claimed the traumatic event occurred in 1924, he did not go public with the story until 1957—which is, perhaps, understandable, given its wild nature.

At the time in question, Ostman worked in construction, although his background was as a lumberman. At this time, he decided to try something different, so he did some gold prospecting in the Toba Inlet, situated on the British Columbia coast. It was during the course of the prospecting that Ostman experienced something that made him distinctly troubled and uneasy: someone, or something, had clearly been wandering around his camp while he was on his quest for gold.

Ostman decided he was going to find out the guilty party's identity and, instead of going to sleep, he stayed wide awake in his sleeping bag, with his rifle by his side. Unfortunately, a hard day toiling for gold took its toll and Ostman quickly fell asleep. But not for long: he was jolted from his sleep by the sensation of being scooped up and carried away while still in his sleeping bag. In fact, that's exactly what happened. For roughly three hours or so, Ostman was unceremoniously carried through, up, and down the dark woods by something large and powerful. According to Ostman, he had heard stories of "the mountain Sasquatch giants" from Native

The Toba Inlet in British Columbia is lush and beautiful. Albert Ostman claims he was prospecting for gold in the area in 1924 when he was kidnapped by a Bigfoot.

American sources. Finally, the terror-filled trek came to its end. That much was made clear when the mighty creature relaxed its grip on the sleeping bag and let it drop to the forest floor.

Since the woods were still enveloped by the blackness of night, Ostman could not make out his kidnapper. As dawn broke, that situation radically changed. He found himself confronted by what can only be accurately described as a Bigfoot family: a giant male, a smaller female, and two juveniles, one male and one female. In other words: mom, dad, and the kids. As Ostman looked around, he could see he was deep in the heart of a heavily forested valley that was surrounded by huge mountains. Clearly anticipating the likelihood that Ostman would try and escape, the "Old Man"—as Ostman referred to the huge male—kept careful watch on Ostman, making sure at all times that he didn't try and make a run for it, via the entrance to the valley. That Ostman was held captive for several days ensured he was able to carefully study their habits and appearance. In his own words:

> The young fellow might have been 11–18 years old and about seven feet tall and might weigh about 300 lbs.... He had wide jaws, narrow forehead, that slanted upward ... the old lady could have been anything between 40–70 years old ... she would be about 500–600 pounds. She had very wide hips, and a goose-like walk. She was not built for beauty or speed.

As for the "old man," Ostman stated that he "must have been near eight feet tall. Big barrel chest and big hump on his back—powerful shoulders, his biceps on upper arm were enormous.

Ostman said of their general appearance: "The hair on their heads was about six inches long. The hair on the rest of their body was short and thick in places.... The only place they had no hair was inside their hands and the soles of their feet and upper part of the nose and eyelids.... They were very agile." Ostman was also able to deduce that the creatures were vegetarian.

Although Ostman was kept in the lair of the Bigfoot against his will, he wasn't mistreated. Nevertheless, he had no intention of spending the rest of his life as the equivalent of an animal in the zoo, held captive for someone else's entertainment; in this case, Bigfoot. It transpired that the answer to his freedom came in a decidedly alternative fashion. Every morning, Ostman took a pinch of snuff from his snuff box. He noticed that the "old man" eyed him carefully on each occasion. Finally, when curiosity got the better of him, the immense giant grabbed the box out of Ostman's hands and poured the entire contents into his mouth. In seconds, the beast was doubled up on the floor, rolling in agony, and gulping down water. As the rest of the family raced to help, Ostman saw his chance to make a run for it. He grabbed his gear, fired a shot in the air to scare off the creatures, and raced for freedom. Unsurprisingly, he was not followed, nor did he see the beasts again.

Although the story of Albert Ostman is filled with controversy, it has received support from entire swathes of the Bigfoot research community. British investigators Janet and Colin Bord, said:

> Although Ostman is now dead, John Green, an experienced Bigfoot investigator, knew him for over 12 years and had no reason to consider him a liar. Also, none of those who questioned him, such as a magistrate, zoologist, and primate specialists, could catch him out; and we therefore have no logical option but to assume that his story, fantastic though it may sound, was true.

Similarly, Bigfoot investigator John Napier said of Ostman and his story: "The anatomical peculiarities of the Sasquatch family are expressed in very reasonable terms, and his observations on behavior, if unimaginative, are without obvious inconsistencies."

Ostman was unmoved by the doubters. He had a stock response for anyone who chose to question his account: "I don't care a damn what you think."

King Kong and Beyond

There can be no doubt, whatsoever, that the ultimate giant ape of the fictional variety is King Kong, whose escapades were famously portrayed in the acclaimed, almost legendary, 1933 movie of the same name.

There can be very few people who are unaware of the plotline: a filmmaker named Carl Denham (actor Robert Armstrong) sails to a mysterious island, along with a beautiful blond, Ann Darrow (played by Fay Wray), and various other characters, most of whom end up suffering violent deaths at the hands of the natives, various dinosaurs, and Kong himself. Kong meets his downfall, however, when he is captured, and shipped to New York—where, in a memorable finale, he battles to the death with the U.S. military, atop the Empire State Building, all in the name of his interspecies love for Ann.

King Kong has been remade twice: while the 2005 version—starring Naomi Watts and Jack Black—stays true to the original, the 1976 remake, which starred Jeff Bridges and Jessica Lange, is undeniably awful, and best avoided at all costs. *King Kong* not only provoked a couple of remakes, it also spawned a huge number of movies of the large and anomalous ape variety.

Capitalizing on the success of *King Kong* was *The Son of Kong*, which, like its predecessor, came out in 1933. It was not the huge hit that the studio was anticipating and hoping for. *The Gorilla* (1939), which starred horror maestro Bela Lugosi and dealt with murder, mayhem, and, of course, a wild gorilla, is a forgettable bit of monster mayhem. One year later came *The Ape*, a tale of a man who becomes a gorilla—albeit in a very strange fashion (*see* "The Ape [1940 movie]"). Almost identical to *The Ape*, in terms of its storyline, was *The Ape Man*—which, yet again, starred Lugosi, this time as a scientist who mutated into what can only be described as a definitive half-human, half-ape monstrosity. *Son of Ingagi*, also made in 1940, has at the heart of its action a murderous missing link from Africa. In 1945 no fewer than two movies were released about white-furred gorillas: *White Pongo* and *The White Gorilla* (*see* "White Pongo [1945 movie]"). And the decade was rounded off with *Mighty Joe Young*—a blatant rip-off of *King Kong*, but a movie that, to this day, has a faithful, cult-like following.

Moving onto the 1950s, *Bride of the Gorilla* (1951), which starred Raymond Burr (of *Perry Mason* and *Ironside* fame), told the weird tale of a man transformed into a gorilla via the power of voodoo. In 1952 *Bela Lugosi Meets a Brooklyn Gorilla* is a comedy that fell flat, although it is high on the babe quota.

The 1960s began with *Konga*—a British movie that dealt with a giant gorilla that rampaged around

A poster from the classic 1933 monster movie *King Kong*, starring Fay Wray. A number of remakes and sequels have been made since then because the giant, misunderstood gorilla still holds appeal for many.

London, England—and ended with 1968's *Planet of the Apes*, which brought talking gorillas to the big screen in spectacular style. Two years later, in 1970, *Trog* was released. It is a very bizarre movie that brought together a fierce ape man and legendary actress Joan Crawford, who must have needed the money when she accepted the role, since there seems to be no other earthly reason why she should have taken part in this spectacularly bad piece of cinematic claptrap—which deals with the discovery of the "Trog" of the movie in a cave deep below the English countryside. The 1970s also saw four sequels to the original *Planet of the Apes* movie and two short-lived television series of the same name, one live action and the other cartoon-based.

In the 1980s there was little that was particularly memorable of a cryptid ape nature, aside from the hit movie *Harry and the Hendersons* (1987), a comedy that reaped in almost $50 million at the box office—proof that Bigfoot equals big money (*see* "Harry and the Hendersons [1987 movie]"). The next decade saw the release of *Congo* (1995), a movie version of Michael Crichton's novel of the same name. At the heart of the story is a colony of savage, violent, and previously unknown gray-colored gorillas that jealously guard the lost city of Zinj.

The 2000s didn't just see a huge, mega-bucks version of *King Kong* unleased on the public: the *Planet of the Apes* franchise got a new lease on life, too. In 2001, a highly confusing version of *Planet of the Apes*, with a deeply convoluted plot, surfaced. *Rise of the Planet of the Apes* was next on the list, in 2011, and *Dawn of the Planet of the Apes* was rolled out in July 2014, demonstrating that as far as both the general public and movie moguls are concerned, marauding, fictional apes are as popular today as they were when poor old King Kong, smitten until the very end by Ann Darrow, took his last breath high above New York, way back in 1933.

Kushtaka of Alaska

In 2014, one of the most intriguing Bigfoot-themed books was published—*In Search of the Kushtaka: Alaska's Other Bigfoot*, by Dennis Waller. This is an excellent read for anyone fascinated by cryptozoology in general and Bigfoot in particular. It's also a book that is likely to polarize its readers into two wildly differing camps: (a) those who conclude that the book's alternative take on Bigfoot has merit; and (b) those who have no time for anything beyond the "Bigfoot is just an unknown ape" scenario.

Waller's work is not your average Bigfoot book. And that's not a bad thing at all. As *The Bigfoot Book* demonstrates time and again, the Sasquatch phenomenon is not just strange. Simply put: it's very often downright too strange. We never, ever, find a body. The beast is seemingly impervious to bullets. There are reports of Bigfoot literally vanishing in front of the witness. Bigfoot is seen in the same location and timeframe as other anomalous phenomena. And so on and so on.

In the minds of many, Bigfoot is not just an unknown ape. I don't pretend to have the answers. I do, however, think the body of high-strangeness that surrounds

Bigfoot suggests we need to focus outside of the box when it comes to the matter of what the beast is. Or is not. All of this brings us right back to Waller's book.

What Waller has done is to focus his attentions upon one particularly weird beast possessing far more than a few overtones of the Bigfoot kind. The Kushtaka—or Land-Otter Man—is a creature that plays a major role in the lore, legends, and history of the Tlingit people, Native Americans who had their origins in the rainforests of southeast Alaska. There is, however, something very strange about the Alaskan beast.

It has astounding abilities, including the power to seemingly vanish (and reappear) at will, to shape-shift, to take on the guise of a deceased person, and to engage in telepathic communication. It can also manipulate space and time. Many might be inclined to relegate such tales and claims to the worlds of folklore and myth-making—all without second thought. But not the author.

Waller takes us on a fascinating journey that does not deny the legends and folklore that have become part of the Alaskan Bigfoot puzzle. It is, however, a journey that—to make its point—also

Dennis Waller, author of *In Search of the Kushtaka: Alaska's Other Bigfoot.*

encompasses science. On this latter issue, Waller delves deeply into the domain of String Theory, quantum physics, and multiple-dimensions. In other words, ancient legend may have been borne out of a science that—to a significant degree—still very much eludes us to this day.

It's also a science that spills over into the realms of Shamanic activity, altered states of mind, the afterlife, and creatures that very possibly feast on human life-energy. Add to that the uncanny parallels between the Kushtaka and the "underwater panther" of the northeast Native American people and the "Fox-Snake" of Argentina, the hostility between the beast and dogs, Smithsonian cover-ups, and numerous and baffling disappearances of people across certain parts of Alaska, and what you have is a fascinating study of a vastly under-appreciated mystery.

It's a mystery that demands our attention and which just might shed a great deal of light on the matter of why so many so-called "cryptids" constantly and consistently elude capture or killing on every single occasion.

Regardless of your views on Bigfoot, you should still read *In Search of the Kushtaka*. The fact is that—like it or like it not—too few people in Bigfoot research are willing to tackle the weirder aspects of the mystery. Instead, they prefer to relegate such rogue cases to the domains of mistaken identity, hoaxing, or fantasizing. To his credit, Waller takes a different pathway.

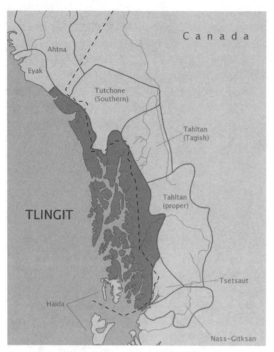

A map showing the area in northwestern Canada (and part of Alaska) where the Tlingit people live. The Tlingits tell of their own version of Bigfoot, called the Kushtaka.

Waller ferrets out fascinating data, provides us with intriguing witness encounters, and offers a body of data that collectively shows we need to broaden our horizons if we are to stand any chance of meaningfully resolving the Bigfoot conundrum. Read Dennis Waller's book. It's a solid, thought-provoking, and mind-bending take on a mystery that is very likely far stranger than any of us currently imagine.

Lake Worth, Texas, Monster

In the very early hours of one particularly fateful morning in the hot and sticky summer of 1969, six petrified residents of the Texan city of Fort Worth raced for the safety of their local police station and related a controversial and amazing story.

John Reichart, his wife, and two other couples were parked at Lake Worth. At the stroke of midnight, a truly vile and monstrous-looking creature came storming out of the thick branches of a large, nearby tree. Reportedly covered in a coat that seemed to be comprised of both scales and fur, it slammed with a crashing bang onto the hood of the Reicharts' car and even tried to grab hold of the not-surprisingly-terrified Mrs. Reichart, before racing off into the pitch-black night and the camouflage of the dense, surrounding trees.

The solitary evidence of its dark and foreboding presence was a deep, foot-and-a-half long scratch along the side of the Reicharts' vehicle. While this specific event rapidly, and unsurprisingly, generated deep media interest, and was actually taken extremely seriously by the Fort Worth police—as prime evidence of this, no fewer than four police cars quickly headed to the scene of the Reicharts' encounter—it was most certainly not the first occasion upon which Fort Worth officialdom had become the recipient of ominous accounts of diabolical beasts roaming around Lake Worth.

Indeed, until the Reicharts' story hit the newspapers, it was a little-known fact that for approximately two months the police had been clandestinely investigating reports of a distinctly weird beast that was said to be spooking the locals on a disturbingly regular basis. While some of the officers concluded that at least some of the sightings might have been the work of local kids running around in ape-costumes, others were not so sure that fakery was a dominating factor and took the Reicharts' story to heart.

For example, Patrolman James S. McGee conceded that the report John Reichart filed with the Fort Worth constabulary was treated very seriously because "those people were really scared."

Hardly surprisingly, the Dallas-Fort Worth media loved the story and did their utmost to promote it. Notably, one particular feature that appeared in the pages of the *Fort Worth Star Telegram* was written by acclaimed author Jim Marrs—very well known today for his books on 9/11, the JFK assassination of November 1963, and countless other conspiracies and cover-ups. The headline that jumped out of the pages of the *Telegram* was a news editor's absolute dream: "Fishy Man-Goat Terrifies Couples Parked at Lake Worth." Beyond any shadow of doubt, this particular story made the Goat Man infamous and feared among the residents of Lake Worth. And it would not be long before the monster's ugly form surfaced once again.

In fact, it was almost twenty-four-hours to the minute: midnight was looming around the corner and the creature was reportedly seen racing across a stretch of road close to the Lake Worth Nature Center. Interestingly, the prime witness, Jack Harris

A photo of Lake Worth in Texas taken by Nick Redfern. Residents were terrorized here in the summer of 1969 by a hulking beast covered by both fur and scales.

of Fort Worth, stated that when he attempted to take a picture of the monster, the flash on his camera failed to work—a phenomenon that is curiously prevalent in mystery animal reports and encounters.

The beast, whatever its ultimate nature and origin, was seen shortly thereafter, charging across the landscape to a nearby bluff, with three dozen hyped-up locals in hot pursuit, and all hysterically baying for the blood of the beast. The Goat Man wasn't about to become the victim of some crazed posse, however. He had an unforeseen ace up his sleeve— towering over the crowd at approximately ten yards, the Goat Man allegedly hurled a huge tire at the group, resulting in the throng wildly scattering in all directions.

One of those present, Jack Harris, said that "everybody jumped back into their cars" and immediately left the area. The Goat Man had won the day. But the story was far from over. Yet more accounts surfaced, with some witnesses stating that the creature had dark fur or hair all over its body, and others maintaining that its coat was overwhelmingly white in color.

Then there were disturbing tales of horrific mutilations of animals in the area: dogs, cats, and more, most of which surfaced amid theories that the Goat Man had made a home—or, more likely, a lair—for himself in a relatively small piece of land called Greer Island, which is connected to the mainland by a small walkway.

The story was on the verge of spinning wildly out of control, when Helmuth Naumer, who was an employee of the Fort Worth Museum of Science and History, offered the theory that the Goat Man was probably nothing stranger than a pet bobcat that someone had clandestinely released into Lake Worth Park, and one that presumably took a great deal of pleasure in jumping onto people's cars at midnight. Precisely how the bobcat was able to change its color from brown to white, or throw a large tire through the air—for what was estimated to be a distance of no less than 500 feet—remained sadly unanswered, however.

It's not impossible that Naumer's theories might indeed have provided answers to the questions that pertained to at least some of the sightings; however, they most assuredly could not explain the truly surreal photo taken by Allen Plaster, who was a local dress-shop owner. Plaster's picture displayed a giant, white-hued beast with a torso that appeared to be constructed out of dozens of cotton balls, atop which sat a truly tiny head. The picture provoked imagery of a Sasquatch-like creature, rather than one of goatish proportions, thus provoking an interesting theory: that the Goat Man of Lake Worth was actually a Bigfoot, possibly migrating through some of the wilder parts of Texas in search of food.

The Legend of Boggy Creek (1972 movie)

Ask the average person to name a Bigfoot movie and, in all likelihood, they will mention *Harry and the Hendersons*. There's little doubt that this 1987 production is the one Bigfoot-based film the general public is most aware of. Ask those within the Bigfoot-seeking community, however, and the response will likely be a very different one. Numerous Sasquatch aficionados have a particular fondness for a 1972 movie titled *The Legend of Boggy Creek*.

What makes the movie stand out from so many others of its type is that *The Legend of Boggy Creek* is based upon real events that occurred in and around the small town of Fouke, Arkansas, in the early 1970s. No one knows more about this than Lyle Blackburn, the author of the book *The Beast of Boggy Creek*.

Blackburn notes that on May 3, 1971, the *Texarkana Gazette* "printed the first in a series of hair-raising reports about a monster that allegedly haunted the woods near Fouke. The monster was said to be a large, hairy ape-like creature that walked upright on two legs. It stood nearly seven feet tall, had glowing red eyes, gave off a rank odor, and occasionally let out a horrifying shriek."

The description of the monster, said Blackburn, "was not unlike that of Sasquatch or Bigfoot, but this creature had a decidedly Southern slant in that it seemed to be leaner, meaner, and hairier. As more reports came in, it was apparent that the *thing*—whatever it was—preferred the proximity of Boggy Creek, a ruddy tributary which snakes up and around Fouke like a long, forked tongue."

It wasn't long before Charles B. Pierce became fascinated by the story of the monster of Boggy Creek, a monster that provoked numerous encounters in the wooded neighborhood in mid-1971 (it should be noted, too, that Blackburn has cataloged reports dating from 1908 to 2010). The story of the making of the movie is almost as fascinating as the story of the creature itself.

Nick Redfern poses with a Bigfoot display in Fouke, Arkansas.

Born in 1938, in Indiana, Pierce moved to Arkansas with his family when he was still a child. Pierce loved movies and television and worked, variously, as an actor, producer, director, and screenwriter. His skills contributed to such well-known television shows as *Remington Steele*, the re-launched, 1980s version of *The Twilight Zone*, and *MacGyver*. It is, however, his 1972 movie, *The Legend of Boggy Creek*, for which Pierce is most remembered.

To say that Pierce was enterprising in his effort to bring his brainchild to fruition is an understatement. Unable to finance the movie himself, he secured six-figure funding from a trucking company. And instead of using a cast filled solely with actors, he elected to use some of the real eyewitnesses to the creature as part of his cast. It was a gamble that could have led to both financial and critical disaster for Pierce. Instead, *The Legend of Boggy Creek*, released on December 6, 1972, achieved cult-like status and reeled in more than $20 million in the process.

Several, best forgotten, sequels followed, none of which achieved the level of the original. Pierce died in 2010. As Lyle Blackburn's work and research demonstrates, however, the beast of Boggy Creek lives on.

Little Red Men of the Delta

I van T. Sanderson was a highly respected monster hunter who became the recipient of numerous stories of unknown humanoids in our midst. One came from a woman who preferred anonymity and who Sanderson only referred to as "Mrs. V. K." Her off-the-record account is, however, in no way tainted by the lack of a name. She wrote to Sanderson in 1959:

> I am a housewife but I majored in biology, attended our state university and have an M.A. in plain zoology. My husband is an experimental chemist and my eldest son is a technician in the Air Force. I come from Mississippi but we have resided here (in Kentucky) for ten years now.
>
> I wonder if you have ever heard of the Little Red Men of the Delta? Nobody thought anything much of them where I was raised except that one had better be careful of shooting one because it might be murder, or so the sheriff might think if anything came off it, but I was surprised to find that the folks hereabout know it too though they took some years to talk about it to me. My husband is a New Englander and these folks don't talk much.
>
> They [the Little Red Men of the Delta] are said to be about the size of a ten year old kid and able to climb like monkeys and to live back from the bayous. They talk a lot but keep out of gunshot range and mostly go into the water. They are people and the muskrat trappers say they often wear scraps of discarded linens, old jeans and such.

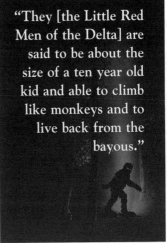

"They [the Little Red Men of the Delta] are said to be about the size of a ten year old kid and able to climb like monkeys and to live back from the bayous."

A reddish creature not unlike that reported to Sanderson by Mrs. V. K. was seen a couple of years later by David Claerr. His encounter, however, occurred in the Detroit, Michigan, suburb of Warren. It was early one summer's morning when Claerr and his brother encountered something monstrous in a "large, uncultivated field covered in thick overgrowth."

Claerr continued that he and his brother heard something smashing its way through the pigweed, while making guttural, muttering sounds. Suddenly, it manifested almost out of nowhere:

> The bizarre creature that suddenly appeared before us had thrust his large head forward on his thickset, furry body, and we could clearly see the surprise and amazement on his face. He looked like a cross between a baboon and a gorilla, with grayish black skin on his face and reddish-tan fur on his

whole body. He gazed at us incredulously with his huge, reddish-amber eyes. He seemed to be about four and a half to five feet tall and stood on two legs. He had long, burly arms, and the skin on his palms was the same grayish-black.

Claerr added:

After about fifteen to twenty seconds of staring at us, the creature quickly turned around and bolted back into thicket. It scrambled away very quickly. This was the type of situation that was difficult to make any sense of. The emotional shock left me feeling numb, and I found myself wanting to just put the whole episode out of my mind. I suspect that my brother felt the same way, because neither of us mentioned it again for quite some time.

Lizard Man on the Loose

In the summer of 1988, a terrifying creature began haunting the woods and little towns of Lee County, South Carolina—and specifically the Scape Ore Swamp area. It quickly became known as Lizard Man, as a result of its alleged green and scaly body.

Bigfoot investigator Lyle Blackburn investigated the Lizard Man stories in South Carolina, publishing a book on the subject in 2013.

For all intents and purposes, it was a case of *The Creature from the Black Lagoon* come to life. A bipedal lizard roaming the neighborhood? Maybe, yes. On the other hand, research undertaken years later suggested that the Lizard Man was something far more akin to Bigfoot. Here is some background on the creature.

It all began—publicly, if not chronologically—when on July 14, 1988, the Waye family phoned the Lee County sheriff's office and made a very strange and disturbing claim. Something wild and animalistic had attacked their 1985 Ford. It looked as if something large, powerful, and deeply savage had viciously clawed, and maybe even bitten into, the body of the vehicle—and particularly so the hood. Somewhat baffled, the deputies responded to the call, nevertheless. Sure enough, the Wayes were right on target: their vehicle was battered and bruised in the extreme. In addition, there were footprints across the muddy area. It was clearly time to bring in Sheriff Liston Truesdale. There was a strong probability that the prints were those of a fox. Larger prints, also found, were suspected of being those of a bear—although some observers suggested they had human qualities.

In such a close-knit neighborhood, it didn't take long before news got around and numerous locals turned up to see what all the fuss was about. It's notable that Sheriff Truesdale told Bigfoot investigator Lyle Blackburn, who wrote the definitive book on the affair—titled, of course, *Lizard Man: The True Story of the Bishopville Monster* (2013)—the following: "While we were there looking over this situation, we learned that people in the Browntown community had been seeing a strange creature about seven feet tall with red eyes. Some of them described it as green, but some of them as brown. They thought it might be responsible for what happened."

A mystery—and a monster—was unleashed.

The publicity afforded the Waye incident prompted someone who ultimately became the key player in the matter to come forward. His name was Chris Davis, age seventeen. Chris's father, Tommy, had seen the sensationalized coverage given by the media to the attack on the Waye's vehicle and contacted Sheriff Truesdale. Specifically, Tommy took his son to tell the police what he had told him. It was quite a story.

> ... Chris saw something looming out of the trees. Large, humanlike in shape, and possessing two glowing, red eyes and three fingers on each hand, it was something horrific.

Back in 1988, Chris was working at a local McDonald's. On the night of June 29—roughly two weeks before the Waye affair exploded—Chris was on the late-shift, which meant he didn't finish work until after 2:00 A.M. His journey home ensured that he had to take a road across a heavily forested part of Scape Ore Swamp. It was just minutes later that he had a blowout. Chris pulled up at a crossroads and, via the bright moonlight, changed the tire. As he finished the job and put the tools back into the trunk, Chris saw something looming out of the trees. Large, humanlike in shape, and possessing two glowing, red eyes and three fingers on each hand, it was something horrific. Chris panicked and jumped in his vehicle and sped off. Based on what Chris had to say next, that was a very wise move:

> I looked back and saw something running across the field towards me. It was about 25 yards away and I saw red eyes glowing. I ran into the car and as I locked it, the thing grabbed the door handle. I could see him from the neck down—the three big fingers, long black nails and green rough skin. It was strong and angry. I looked in my mirror and saw a blur of green running. I could see his toes and then he jumped on the roof of my car. I thought I heard a grunt and then I could see his fingers through the front windshield, where they curled around on the roof. I sped up and swerved to shake the creature off.

The reports didn't end there: Sheriff Truesdale received more reports, to the extent that a near-*X-Files*-style dossier was compiled. It was an official police dossier that contained the fascinating account of Johnny Blythers, who, on July 31, 1990, described for the sheriff's department the events of the previous night:

> Last night about 10:30 P.M., we were coming home from the Browntown section of Lee County. It was me, my mother (Bertha Mae Blyther), [and] two sisters.... I started talking about the time we passed the flowing well

in Scape Ore Swamp. I said "they ain't [sic] no such thing as a Lizzard [sic] Man. If there was, somebody would be seeing it or caught it."

We got up about a mile or mile and one half passed [sic] the butter bean shed, about 50 feet from the dirt road by those two signs, my mother was driving the car.

It was on the right side, it came out of the bushes. It jumped out in the road. My mother swerved to miss it, and mashed the brakes and sped up. It jumped out of the bushes like he was going to jump on the car. When my mother mashed the brakes, it looked like it wanted to get in the car.

Johnny's mother, Bertha Mae, gave her own statement on that terrifying drive through the spooky swamp:

This past Monday night I went to my mother's house in Browntown to pick up my son. We went to McDonald's on Highway 15 near Bishopville to get something to eat. We left there about 20 minutes after 10:00 P.M., was headed home and came through Browntown and Scape Ore Swamp….

We passed the bridge and was down the road near a mile. I was looking straight ahead going about 25 m.p.h., and I saw this big brown thing, it jumped up at the window. I quickly sped up and went on the other side of the road to keep him from dragging my 11 year old girl out of the car. I didn't see with my lights directly on it. It nearly scared me to death.

Then there was the statement of Tamacia Blyther, Bertha's daughter:

> Blackburn suggests that if a Bigfoot dwelled in watery bottomlands, where it might become "covered in algae-rich mud or moss, this could explain its green, wet-like appearance."

Tall—Taller than the car, brown looking, a big chest had big eyes, had two arms. Don't know how his face looked, first seen his eyes. Never seen nothing like it before. I didn't see a tail. Mother says if she hadn't whiped [sic] over he would have hit her car or jumped on it. Mother said she was so scared her body light and she held her heart all the way home.

In addition, Lyle Blackburn has uncovered other reports of the beast—dating from 1986 to well into the 2000s. Two of the key players in this saga are now dead: Johnny Blyther and Chris Davis—the former in a car accident, in 1999, and the latter from a shotgun blast, the result of a drug deal gone bad, almost a decade to the day after Blyther's death.

As for the legendary Lizard Man, what, exactly, was it? Certainly the name provoked imagery of a malevolent scaly, green monster. On the other hand, there were references to the beast having a brown color. All of which leads to Blackburn's conclusions. To his credit, Blackburn undertook a personal, on-site investigation with his colleague, Cindy Lee, and studied all of the evidence in unbiased fashion. Blackburn noted that, despite the undeniably memorable name, the various descriptions of the beast as being brown in color simply did not accord with anything of a reptilian nature.

Blackburn suggests that if a Bigfoot dwelled in watery bottomlands, where it might become "covered in algae-rich mud or moss, this could explain its green, wet-like appearance. It doesn't explain the three fingers, but greenish mud which has dried and cracked could certainly give a scaly appearance."

Certainly, it's a good theory, and far more likely than a huge, bipedal lizard roaming around the swamps of South Carolina.

London Underground Yetis

Britain's famous London Underground serves commuters travelling throughout Greater London, as well as select parts of Buckinghamshire, Hertfordshire, and Essex. It can also claim the title of the world's oldest underground system of its type, given that it opened up for business on January 10, 1863. Today, nearly 250 years after its initial construction, the London Underground has 268 stations and approximately 250 miles of track, making it also the longest sub-surface railway system on the planet. Moreover, in 2007, one million people were recorded as having used the Underground since 1863.

There is something else that is notable—and, in terms of this book, relevant—to the history of the London Underground: in fictional settings it appears in a number of television shows and movies featuring a cryptid ape or wild man.

In 1967 Britain's Hammer Film Productions released the movie *Quatermass and the Pit*. In the United States, it was retitled *Five Million Years to Earth*. Based on a 1950s BBC serial also called *Quatermass and the Pit*, the movie tells the story of a Martian spacecraft that crashed to earth millions of years earlier, and which is only found because its final resting place is deep below what is now London. It's when new digging begins on the London Underground that the unearthly vehicle is found. The British military initially believed it to have been some kind of advanced Nazi craft, left over from World War II. It soon becomes apparent it's nothing of the sort.

Professor Bernard Quatermass (played by Andrew Keir) and paleontologist Barbara Judd (Barbara Shelley) learn that for centuries a particular area of London has been plagued by sightings of strange, ape-like creatures and hideous dwarfs. To their horror, Quartermass, Judd, and her boss, Dr. Mathew Roney (James Donald) deduce that millions of years ago, the visiting Martians—who, we learn, resemble giant-sized grasshoppers—genetical-

The tunnels of the London Underground are home to mysterious creatures and monsters in a number of television shows and science fiction movies.

ly manipulated early primates into something more superior, something that ultimately became us, the human race.

But there's more: a residual Martian energy remains in the old tunnels of the Underground, one that is filled with the memories of the long dead Martians. They are memories that worm their way into the minds of those who stray too close to the alien spacecraft and provoke hallucinations of the creepy, diminutive ape-men. As more people become infected by the ancient memories and become more savage themselves, London begins to descend into overwhelming anarchy. It's up to Quatermass, Judd, and Roney to try and save the day. They do. Only one year later, however, London is again overrun by ape-men—in a totally different piece of on-screen entertainment.

Dr. Who is the world's longest running science fiction series: the BBC began broadcasting it in 1963. In 1968, when the doctor was in his second incarnation—played by actor Patrick Troughton—a still much loved adventure was broadcast: *The Web of Fear*, a six-part story that ran from February 3 to March 9, 1968. It followed on from a previous adventure: *The Abominable Snowman*, which was aired in late 1967. In the first story, the doctor and his comrades, Jamie and Victoria, materialize in the doctor's TARDIS time machine in Tibet—and right in the heart of Abominable Snowman territory.

Unfortunately for the doctor, he becomes the prime suspect in the death of a man who was actually killed by a huge, hairy Yeti. While the doctor is imprisoned, Victoria and Jamie discover huge footprints around the TARDIS and go on a quest to locate the legendary beasts. What follows is a strange story of real flesh and blood Yetis and robot versions that are under the control of the evil Padmasambhava, who has tapped into what is termed the Great Intelligence, a formless, non-physical alien entity that is intent on dominating the Earth. No one will be surprised to learn that the doctor and his friends save the day, and the real Yetis, from the wrath of the Great Intelligence and its robotic snowmen. The success of *The Abominable Snowman* prompted the BBC to deliver a sequel, the aforementioned *The Web of Fear*.

In the new story, the Himalayas have been replaced by London, where the Great Intelligence is hard at work to—yet again—try and make the Earth its own. It's clear from the outset that something menacing is afoot: the city is shrouded in a strange, ominous fog and the London Underground has become infested by a strange fungus that spreads rapidly along the old tunnels. There's something else in the shadowy, coiling tunnels too: an army of robotic Yetis, once again doing the bidding of their ethereal master, the Great Intelligence. Cue a battle between, on one side, the doctor and the military, and on the other, the alien invader and his mechanical man-monsters. No prizes for guessing who wins the day.

Then there is *Death Line* (*Raw Meat* in the States), a 1972 movie that starred horror-film regulars Christopher Lee and Donald Pleasence. In the latter part of the nineteenth century, there is a disastrous collapse while work is taking place to build a new station on the London Underground, specifically at Russell Square, which happens to be a real station. Dozens of workers are assumed to be dead. The company that was hired to do the work goes bankrupt. And, as a result, there is no one around who can dig out the bodies of the dead. It turns out, however, that the victims are not dead, after all. They are trapped, unable to get out.

You can probably see where this is all going: The survivors remain underground, devolving dramatically over the course of several generations—and to the point where, in the early 1970s, when the movie is set, they have become full-blown cannibals, filthy, and dressed in rags. They know their way around the Underground very well, surfacing late at night, when the tunnels are at their absolute quietest, and plucking unfortunate travelers and workers who have the misfortune to cross their paths.

The story of a secret underworld, wild men and women almost of the kind described in many nineteenth-century newspaper reports cited in the pages of this book, police and government cover-ups, and a largely unaware general public, *Death Line* is an oddly unsettling, and often overlooked, saga of how quickly man can become beast, and in just about the worst way possible.

> A story of a secret underworld, wild men and women almost of the kind described in many of the nineteenth-century newspaper reports....

While other productions have focused on the presence of terrible monsters on the London Underground, such as 1981's self-explanatory *An American Werewolf in London* and 2002's *Reign of Fire* (a movie in which fire-breathing dragons decimate the human race), it was from 1967 to 1972 that anomalous apes and savage, devolved humans in the tunnels of old London really caught the public's imagination and attention.

The Long Walk (1956 book)

The Long Walk is a book that was penned in 1956 by Slavomir Rawicz. The highly readable story is told in adventurous, captivating style, and tells of the dicey and daring escape of Rawicz and comrades from a brutal Siberian prisoner of war camp during World War II in 1942. In the book, Rawicz claims that he and his fellow escapees encountered two Abominable Snowmen in the harsh snow, as they hit the road to freedom.

Researchers, however, have questioned the truthfulness of Rawicz's account. It's fascinating, it's eye-opening, and it's almost jaw-dropping. But, is it real? That's the big question. There's no doubt that there are a few significant holes in the story, specifically related to the months-long journey allegedly made from the POW camp to the Himalayas. As far as the Yeti encounter is concerned, we are, unfortunately, only able to take Rawicz at his word—or not, as the case may be.

Rawicz said of the encounter with the pair of extraordinary creatures:

> The contours of the mountain temporarily hid them from view as we approached nearer, but when we halted on the edge of a bluff we found they were still there, twelve feet or so below us and about 100 yards away. Two points struck me immediately. They were enormous and they walked on their hind legs. The picture is clear in my mind, fixed there indelibly by a solid two hours of observation. We just could not believe what we saw at first, so we stayed to watch.

According to Rawicz, the beasts were around eight feet in height, one slightly taller than the other, something that suggested to Rawicz that, possibly, one was male and the other female—although there is no indication he was otherwise able to determine their sex from their physical appearances. Rawicz said that one of the reasons they stopped and watched the massive beasts was because they were on the same "flattish shelf" that he and his fellow prisoners needed to pass along. Rawicz was worried about getting too close to them, preferring instead to watch them for a while, hoping they would finally shamble off and out of sight.

While Rawicz and the rest of the group watched the creatures, they were watching him and his friends as well. Rawicz said, "It was obvious they had seen us, and it was equally apparent they had no fear of us."

> ... Rawicz said the creatures never did drop onto four-limbs; they remained upright and moved around on their legs at all times.

Rawicz said that one of the prisoners, an American, commented that the animals had to be some kind of bear, and was certain that they would soon drop down to all-fours. Certainly, bears will stand on their hind limbs, and they will walk on them, too. That fashion of movement is definitely not their preferred one, however. But Rawicz said the creatures never did drop onto four-limbs; they remained upright and moved around on their legs at all times. He then described the physical appearance of the animals:

Their faces I could not see in detail, but the heads were squarish and the ears must lie close to the skull because there was no projection from the silhouette against the snow. The shoulders sloped sharply down to a powerful chest. The arms were long and the wrists reached the level of the knees. Seen in profile, the back of the head was a straight line from the crown into the shoulders.

Whatever the creatures were, Rawicz was sure of one thing: "We decided unanimously that we were examining a type of creature of which we had no previous experience in the wild, in zoos or in literature."

Rawicz considered the possibility of mistaken identity but dismissed this, although he did note the bear-like qualities of the animals: "It would have been easy to have seen them waddle off at a distance and dismissed them as either bear or big ape of the Orangutan species. At close range they defied facile description. There was something both of the bear and the ape about their general shape, but they could not be mistaken for either."

Rawicz said that the hair color was a combination of brownish-red, grey, and rust. He explained: "They appeared to be covered by two distinct kinds of hair—the reddish hair which gave them the characteristic color forming a tight, close fur against the body, mingling with which were slight greyish tinge as the light caught them."

The story then took on somewhat amusing tones, when Rawicz remarked on what the creatures were doing—which sounded like a loving couple out for a Sunday afternoon stroll in the hills. Maybe that's exactly what it was! Rawicz said:

They were doing nothing but moving around slowly together, occasionally stopping to look around them like people admiring a view. Their heads turned towards us now and again, but their interest in us seemed to be of the slightest.

In conclusion, Rawicz began with a question and duly answered it: "What were they? For years they remained a mystery to me, but since recently I have read of scientific expeditions to discover the Abominable Snowman of the Himalayas and studied descriptions of the creature by native hillmen, I believe that on that day we may have encountered two of the animals. I do insist, however, that recent estimates of their height as about 5 feet must be wrong. The minimum height of a well-grown specimen must be around seven feet.

Today, Slavomir Rawicz's *The Long Walk* remains as controversial as it was decades ago.

Loping Ape-Man of Tengboche Monastery, Nepal

Brigadier General Henry Cecil John Hunt was a highly regarded mountain climber, a noted figure in the British military, and the author of the 1953 book *The Ascent of Everest*. The book told of his 1953 expedition to the mountain. Hunt related a fascinating story of the Yeti that, during his mission to scale Everest, was given to him by the Abbot of the Thyangboche Monastery. Also referred to as the Tengboche Monastery, it stands at a height of almost 14,000 feet in the mountains of Nepal and is dominated by the massive Himalayas—the abode of the Yeti, or Abominable Snowman. Hunt, who, at the time of the expedition worked for Supreme Headquarters Allied Expeditionary Force, said of his visit to the monastery:

> Seated with Charles Wylie and Tensing [Norgay] beside our host, a rotund figure in faded red, I questioned him about the Yeti—better known to us as the Abominable Snowman. The old dignitary at once warmed to this subject. Peering out of the window on to the meadow where our tents were pitched, he gave a most graphic description of how a Yeti had appeared from the surrounding thickets, a few years back in the winter when the snow lay on the ground.

According to the abbot, the creature was grey-haired, about five feet in height, and walked on both two legs and four, in what was described as a "loping" fashion. Evidently, the animal was not hunting for food but happily contented itself by playing in the snow. Despite the apparent non-hostile nature of the good-natured, playful beast, "instructions were given to drive off the unwelcome visitor."

In Hunt's own words: "Conch shells were blown and the long traditional horns sounded. The Yeti had ambled away into the bush."

Henry Cecil John Hunt (seen here, center, in the Caucuses in 1958) learned a fascinating story of the Yeti while on a mission to scale Everest.

Lustleigh Cleave Cave Men

Of relevance to the matter of primitive hominids in the U.K. is the story of a noted Devon folklorist and acclaimed writer, Theo Brown. The author of such titles as *Devon Ghosts* and *Family Holidays Around Dartmoor*, and someone who experienced Devon's notorious Hairy Hands (*see* "Hairy Hands on the Highway"), Brown collected a number of potentially related stories, including one chilling recollection by a friend of hers who had been walking alone at dusk near the Neolithic earthworks at the top of Lustleigh Cleave, which sits on the extreme east side of Dartmoor, England, in the Wrey Valley.

The lush area of Lustleigh Cleave in southwest England has its share of unexplained incidents, including sightings of what appeared to be "cave men."

Lustleigh Cleave is an extraordinarily strange place at the best of times, one where an inordinate number of unexplained incidents and anomalous phenomena seem to take place on an amazingly regular basis. Moreover, the remains of prehistoric stone huts can be seen in the direct vicinity, and an ancient burial monument, Datuidoc's Stone—which is estimated to have originated at some point around 550 to 600 C.E.—still stands today, pretty much as it did all those thousands of years ago.

Jon Downes says of the weirdness that dominates Lustleigh Cleave: "I have got reports of sightings of a ghostly Tudor hunting party, of mysterious lights in the sky, and even the apparitions of a pair of Roman Centurions at Lustleigh Cleave.

But, adds Downes, getting to the most important aspect of the story, "Theo Brown's friend saw, clearly, a family of 'cave men,' either naked and covered in hair or wrapped in the shaggy pelts of some wild animal, shambling around the stone circle at the top of the cleave."

Madagascar's Primitive People

Although there are vague stories suggesting that Madagascar is the domain of several, distinct kinds of anomalous apes, certainly the most talked about is the Kalanoro. Like so many other such creatures in Africa, they are fairly small, falling into the Littlefoot category. These three-toed things reportedly have their own, fairly complex, language and speak in a soft voice that sounds eerily like a woman's. Caves are their chief abodes—that is, when they are not raiding villages for food. A fascinating report of the Kalanoro surfaced in 1886 from G. Herbert Smith:

> We next come to the forest, and from there we get endless stories of the Kalanoro, a sort of wild man of the woods, represented as very short of stature, covered with hair, with flowing beard, in the case of the male, and with an amiable weakness for the warmth of a fire.

> An eye-witness related that once, when spending a night in the heart of the forest, he lay awake watching the fire, which had died down to red embers, when he suddenly became aware of a figure answering to the above description warming himself at the fire, and apparently enjoying it immensely. According to the story, he put a summary end to the gentleman's enjoyment by stealing down his hand, grasping a stick, and sending a shower of red-hot embers on to his unclothed visitor, who, immediately, and most naturally, fled with a shriek.

> Another tells how, on a similar occasion, the male appeared first, and after inspecting the premises and finding, as well as a fire, some rice left in the

pot, summoned his better half; the pair squatted in front of the fire and—touching picture of conjugal affection—proceeded to feed one another!

Malaspina Glacier, Alaska, Monster

In a 1908 edition of the *Alaska-Yukon Magazine*, there appeared a fascinating story from Frank E. Howard. The article told of an incident that occurred during the summer months, just a few years previously. The location was a mountainous region on Alaska's Malaspina Glacier, where Howard was prospecting. As he negotiated the perilous glacier, Howard fell into a deep crevasse. Fortunately, Howard was not injured, but there was a big problem: there was simply no way for him to climb out the same way he had fallen in. So, there was just one option: he had to follow the crevasse, hoping that it would lead downhill and allow him to leave by making his way down the glacier. Thankfully, it did exactly that.

Howard told the magazine:

I arose and started down the slope with the idea of reaching the water and following along its margin while the tide was low, in search of some crevasse leading out into the open bay. I was sure the great cavern was crevassed to the surface at some point beyond.

As I kept going ahead I noticed a gradual increase of light, and in a few more steps, I stood in a broad wall of blue light that came down from above and, looking up, I saw there was no clear opening to the surface. But objects were now revealed some distance around.

At Malaspina Glacier in southern Alaska, Frank E. Howard fell into a crevasse. He managed to find his way out only to encounter a Bigfoot in his path.

Then an object rose slowly out of the glimmer and took form—a spectral thing, with giant form, and lifelike movement. The object rose erect, a goliath in the shape of a man. Then, watching me with a slantwise glance, it walked obliquely from me, until its form faded in the gloom of the cavern.

It's Howard's final words that suggest strongly that the mighty creature was a Bigfoot:

With its shaggy light-colored fur and huge size, the creature in some ways resembled a bear with bluish gray fur, but that it had a roughly human form, and at all times walked erect.

Ed Ferrell, author of the book *Strange Stories of Alaska and the Yukon*, said, "There is no further record of Frank Howard. Yet his account is consistent with other reports of Bigfoot or Sasquatch."

Raincoast Sasquatch author J. Robert Alley commented: "It seems plausible that this event may have happened in some form or another, as described.... At any rate it is an intriguing tale, if not simply a good yarn, and Ferrell's summation, of the creature described as 'consistent with Sasquatch,' seems quite appropriate.

Mande Burung

See: India's Cryptid Apes

Man-Eaters

In 1965, journalist George Draper of the *San Francisco Chronicle* interviewed O. R. Edwards about a startling and highly disturbing Bigfoot sighting that Edwards had back in 1942. According to Edwards, he was hunting with a colleague, Bill Cole, when they encountered what can only have been a Sasquatch, on Oregon's Mount Ashland. Edwards told Draper:

We were both moving slowly and quietly round this patch of brush. Bill went round to the left side. I was on the right. I was sweeping the area ahead with my eyes. On one sweep I caught a glimpse of what seemed like an ape-like head sticking out of the bush. By the time I had brought my head back to focus on the spot, it was gone.

That was nothing compared to what happened next, however:

Then I heard the "pad-pad-pad" of running feet and the "whump" and grunt as two bodies came together. Dashing back to the end of the brush, I saw a large man-like creature covered with brown hair. It was about seven feet tall and it was carrying in its arms what seemed like a man. I could only see legs and shoes. It was heading straight downhill on the run.

> When Edwards realized that Cole was nowhere in sight, he suddenly knew who the man the Bigfoot had abducted was: his very own hunting partner!

I was about thirty feet away and the opening in the brush was only ten to fifteen feet wide. At the speed he was going, it did not leave me much time to make observations. I, of course, did not believe what I had just seen. So I closed my eyes and shook my head to sort of clear things up. I looked down the hill again in time to see the back and shoulders and head of a man-like thing covered with brown hair. It was disappearing into the brush some seventy to eighty yards below.

When Edwards realized that Cole was nowhere in sight, he suddenly knew who the Bigfoot had abducted: his very own hunting partner! Edwards fled the area. As he did so, and to his dismay, he saw two more Bigfoot in a ravine. He raced for his car and didn't look back. Fortunately, Cole managed to escape when the beast dropped him during the course of its fast and furious run, which allowed Cole to charge up the hill and in the direction of his rifle. As it turned out, the gun was not needed: the Bigfoot, and its two comrades, quickly vanished. Rather oddly, neither man talked to each other about what had happened until 1962. Perhaps the silence was due to two things: Edwards was embarrassed and ashamed about having deserted Cole; and, perhaps, in turn, Cole felt no one would believe such an outlandish account if word got out.

There is a far more important issue that needs to be focused upon: namely, the matter of why Cole was abducted in the first place. That the beast was not alone, but was accompanied by two more of its kind, raises the disconcerting possibility that the creatures were hunting for food in the woods, and Cole became their prey—at least, until he was lucky enough to escape from the hairy clutches of the monster and flee for the safety of civilization.

Man-Monkey of the Shropshire Union Canal

Within the worlds of folklore and legend, encounters with magical and monstrous beasts abound at certain, specific locations. They include crossroads, cemeteries, and sites of archaeological significance. Such encounters are also highly prevalent in the vicinity of old bridges. There is, perhaps, no greater example of this latter point than the saga of an infernal, glowing-eyed beast known as the Man-Monkey. It's a creature that lurks in and around the dense, wooded areas of England's Shropshire Union Canal, which was built in the early 1800s.

So far as can be determined, sightings of the man-thing date back to January 1879. It was late on the night of January 21 that a terrible, semi-spectral, ape-like thing burst into view at the large Bridge 39, which spans the Shropshire Union Canal in the vicinity of the picturesque and tranquil village of Ranton, Staffordshire, the origins of which date back to at least the eleventh century.

The story came from a man crossing the bridge with his horse and cart on a cold, windy, moonlit eve—without doubt, the perfect setting for a late-night encounter with something terrible and infernal. As the man reached roughly the halfway point of the large, stone bridge, a hairy, humanoid entity charged out of the trees, in his very direction. Unlike the Bigfoot of the United States, the creature of Bridge 39 was far more like a chimpanzee, in terms of size, stature, and speed. The problem, of course, is that there are no wild chimpanzees in England; or, at least, there shouldn't be. There was another issue, too—a very weird one.

As it charged—and while displaying a pair of large, ominous, staring eyes that glowed silver—the man had the good sense to grab his horsewhip and strike out at the snarling, hairy animal. It did absolutely no good at all. As the man hit the hair-covered

In 1879 a semi-spectral, ape-like creature was seen at Bridge 39 on the Shropshire Union Canal. Other reports of a "Man-Monkey" were also made, and the creature has become the object of much speculation since then.

thing, he was terrified to see his whip pass right through its body, something that suggested it was an entity of spectral, rather than physical, flesh-and-blood proportions.

The man's horse reacted in understandable fashion: it first rose up onto its hind legs, and, then, filled with fear, it broke free of its cart and galloped across the bridge and vanished into the darkness. The man set off in hot pursuit, while the Man-Monkey raced at high speed towards a dirt pathway that led down to the cold waters of the old canal. Thankfully, the man was able to catch up with the horse—which had made its way to the outside of a local inn, one that the man frequented every Friday night. He quickly tied the horse to a post and flung open the door of the pub. In an instant, everyone in the room was silenced. The man, half-crazed by fear, told the crowd what he had seen, something that plunged one and all into states of fear and anxiety.

> Dr. David Clarke noted that the story of the Man-Monkey identifies it "as a human revenant who returns to haunt a bridge in animal form."

For weeks afterwards, the people of Ranton—and other nearby hamlets—had jangled nerves and sleepless nights. The presence of the Man-Monkey caused such a sensation that the local police opened a file on the monster-themed affair. Interestingly, the police heard rumors of earlier encounters with the bridge beast that same month; they were rumors that suggested sightings of the Man-Monkey began just days after a local man drowned after falling into the canal. This provoked an intriguing and unsettling theory.

In his 1912 book *Werewolves*, prestigious author Elliott O'Donnell said:

It is an old belief that the souls of cataleptic and epileptic people, during the body's unconsciousness, adjourned temporarily to animals, and it is therefore only in keeping with such a view to suggest that on the deaths of such people their spirits take permanently the form of animals.

This, O'Donnell said, accounted for the fact that the places where such people died "are often haunted by semi and wholly animal types of phantasm."

Dr. David Clarke noted that the story of the Man-Monkey identifies it "as a human revenant who returns to haunt a bridge in animal form. The manner of its appearance, in the form of 'a strange black creature with great white eyes' and the fear it created by its actions leaping on the back of the horse, resonates with contemporary accounts of ghostly activity elsewhere."

That the human-dead returned in animal form was not the only theory suggested to explain the presence of the Man-Monkey, however. A rumor quickly circulated in the area where a gorilla had escaped from a traveling menagerie that had recently visited the nearby town of Newport. While it's not entirely impossible that just such a creature could have briefly survived in the cold wilds of Staffordshire, it should be noted that the "circus escapee" theory is one that had been trotted out on numerous occasions—and all across the world—to try and rationalize reports similar to that of the Man-Monkey. In nearly all cases, no evidence of any such escapee is found.

There is, however, clearly something supernatural about the Man-Monkey, since sightings of the always solitary beast have continued to be reported into the twenty-first century. And they are almost identical in nature: the location is usually Bridge 39, the monster leaps out of the trees and terrifies the unwary, and it displays qualities and characteristics that are part-flesh and blood and part-spectral. Whatever the true nature of Ranton's resident hairy monster-man, it shows no signs of leaving its tree-covered haunt anytime soon. Should you, one day, find yourself in the vicinity of Ranton, take great care and heed if you are forced to cross Bridge 39—the Man-Monkey may be waiting in the wooded wings, ready to strike at a moment's notice.

Mapinguari of Mato Grosso

The Mapinguari, a terrifying man-beast that has a particular penchant for ripping out the tongues of cattle, is a violent creature that haunts the Mato Grosso, a huge Brazilian state, the name of which translates into English as "thick bushes," and which is dominated by plains, plateaus, and rainforest—ideal locations in which hairy man-beasts can hide and thrive.

Randy Merrill, who has studied the history of the Mapinguari, said that, according to local native legends, the Mapinguari is

a prehistoric cryptid that reportedly lived (and is still reported to live) in the Amazon rain forests of South America, particularly in Brazil and Patagonia. It was consistently described as ... having red hair, long arms, powerful claws that could tear apart palm trees ... a sloping back, a crocodile-like hide that arrows and bullets could not penetrate, a second mouth on its belly and backwards feet (said to make a bottle-shaped footprint).

Readers will, yet again, note the odd reference to the creatures having feet facing backwards. Merrill continued:

It was said to stand up to 6 feet tall when it assumed a bear-like stance on its hind legs, which it did when it smelled a nearby human. It also gave off a putrid, disorienting stench, emitted a frightening shriek, and could move slowly and stealthily through the forest, often surprising unsuspecting locals. Although it was believed to be carnivorous, by all accounts it did not eat humans. Finally, it was said to sometimes speak and to enjoy punishing hunters who violated religious holidays. Certain lore even seemed to link it with the South American werewolf. The more werewolf-like version of the creature is called the "wolf's cape" and is thought to have originally been human.

The late and renowned Dr. Bernard Heuvelmans brought much of the story of the Mapinguari to the attention of the media, the public, and the Bigfoot-hunting community. One story that really stood out occurred decades ago and involved a man identified as Inocencio, an explorer taking part in an expedition on the Urubu River.

Reportedly, Inocencio and his team were in hot pursuit of what were described as a group of mysterious "black monkeys" that they intended to bag and take back to

The late Belgian-French scientist Dr. Bernard Heuvelmans (1916–2012), who was regarded as the father of cryptozoology, brought Mapinguari to the attention of the media.

civilization. Unfortunately for Inocencio, it didn't quite work out as planned. One night, after sunset, something vile and marauding appeared. The hair-raising panic-filled cries of a man echoed through the dense jungle.

Then something worse happened: Inocencio's ears were filled with the sound of heavy feet, resonating loudly on the forest floor. There was no doubt in Inocencio's mind what was going on: a, huge, lumbering, bipedal creature was racing towards him. This was not good news. Suddenly, the loud footsteps were replaced by an ear-splitting silence. To Inocencio's horror, he could see something large, dark, and manlike lurking in the shadows—possibly waiting for the right time to launch an all-out attack. Inocencio was frozen to the spot, fearful of what might happen next. What did happen is that the beast let loose with an almighty, ear-splitting roar.

Acting on instinct, more than anything else, Inocencio fired his rifle in the direction of the creature, which enraged the crazed monster even more, as it hurtled towards him. Fortunately, another bullet deterred the Mapinguari from coming any closer and it vanished into the undergrowth. Showing a high degree of common sense, Inocencio spent the night perched in a high tree, kept awake by the hideous, malevolent roaring of the unknown animal.

When morning finally came, and Inocencio finally plucked up the courage to climb down the tree, the only calling cards of the night's turmoil were splashes of blood on the ground and a strong, sour odor that filled the air. The violent visitor was never identified.

Interestingly, local folklore suggests that the Mapinguari has the ability to make a person disoriented, to induce a nauseous sense of vertigo, and even to instill unconsciousness. This may not be mere myth and legend: it's entirely possible that like its American cousin, Bigfoot, the Mapinguari may have the ability to disable people via the manipulation of infrasound (*see* "Infrasound and Bigfoot").

Although many researchers of the worldwide man-beast mystery believe the Mapinguari may be some form of unknown ape, or even an ape-man, there is another popular theory to explain the existence of the creature in the Mato Grosso.

Ornithologist David Oren, who has extensively traveled the Amazon, believes that the Mapinguari may not be unknown man-beasts, after all, but surviving pockets of massive creatures that are supposed to have become extinct thousands of years ago: giant sloths, possibly Mylodons, that could reach heights of around nine feet and that weighed a hefty 500 pounds.

Cryptid Chronicles notes:

The first rumors that a giant ground sloth species may still exist reached Europe in the sixteenth century. Sailors brought home stories of "water tigers" backed up by fossil bones. In 1789, Dr. Bartolomé de Muñoz found Megatherium bones near what is now Buenos Aires. He gave them to the King of Spain, prompting the King to order a complete specimen of the animal alive or dead. The rumors gained more credence in the late 19th century. The future governor of Santa Cruz province in southern Patagonia, Ramón Lista, was riding in Santa Cruz in the late 1880s when a shaggy red-haired beast resembling what he called a "giant pangolin" trotted across his path.

Craig Woolheater runs the popular website *Cryptomundo*, which is dedicated to the world of unknown animals. In October 2005, Woolheater said:

Ornithologist David Oren theorized that the Mapinguari might be Mylodons, a giant sloth that lived in Patagonia but was thought to be extinct.

Several years back, actually in August of 1999 or so, I ran across a very interesting article in *Discover* magazine. It chronicled an ornithologist named David Oren's treks into the Amazon in search of the Mapinguari, what is thought to be the still living giant ground sloth. The article detailed the derision that Oren suffered from his fellow scientists.

In his article, Woolheater quoted the following from the *Discover* feature:

Oren has gathered a certain amount of derision in the scientific community over the last few years because of his determination to keep tramping through the jungle in search of the giant ground sloth. His detractors suspect he's as likely to find the beast as other adventurers are to find Bigfoot, the mythical creature said to be roaming the wilderness of the Pacific Northwest.

Having read this, Woolheater said:

I felt that this article had many parallels to Bigfoot research. The Mapinguari was known to the locals, much as the anecdotal evidence we are collecting regarding sightings of Bigfoot here in our country.

Woolheater cited another section of the article as being of particular note:

One might argue how much faith Oren should put in anecdotal evidence provided to him by 50 or so people who say they've had encounters with the sloth. Still, it seems odd that scientists, of all people, would question the search for anything thought to be elusive or even impossible to find.

Think of the naysayers who used to scoff every time Carl Sagan said there had to be other planets orbiting other suns in other solar systems; now other planets are discovered so often it's hard to keep track of how many there are.

As Woolheater rightly noted: "People think that every inch of the earth has been explored. Quite the contrary...."

Mawas
See: Mysterious Jungle Races of Sumatra

The Media

On January 3, 1959, an article was written by Betty Allen of the *Humboldt Times* newspaper, titled "Story of Century Old Big Foot in Idaho Adds Color to Legend." The article is important for two reasons: (a) it demonstrates that the Bigfoot mystery is very old; and (b) it is one of the earliest examples of the media using the term "Bigfoot" or "Big Foot." The article states:

> Mrs. Alvin Bortles, Boise, Idaho, discussed an account of a "Big Foot" who lived prior to 1868 in the wilderness of Idaho. The mother of Kenneth Bortles, vice principal of the Hoopa valley high school, Mrs. Bortles said that mysterious tracks of a tremendous size and human shape stirred the residents of Idaho in the early days. Just as with the Big Foot tracks of Northern California's Bluff Creek area, some believed they were genuine, others saw in them a clever hoax.

"The sometimes wanton killings that were the work of almost superhuman strength both with stock and humans, brought about his downfall."

> The "Big Foot" lived in the remote wilderness of Reynold's Canyon now known as Reynold's Creek. A thousand dollars was offered for him, dead or alive. Here the likeness to the local "Big Foot" ended for the "Gigantic Monster," as he was called in Idaho, was a killer. The full extent of the depredations of this Big Foot were never known, for many robberies and murders were attributed to him which he probably did not commit. The sometimes wanton killings that were the work of almost superhuman strength both with stock and humans, brought about his downfall. A thousand dollars was offered for Big Foot dead or alive.

> John Wheeler, a former army man, set out to collect the reward. In the year 1868, he came upon Big Foot and shot him 16 times. Both legs and one arm were broken before he fell to the ground. As he lay there he asked for a drink of water and, because of his great fear, Wheeler shot him, breaking his other arm before giving the water to the creature.

Before he died, he told Wheeler that his real name was Starr Wilkerson and he had been born in the Cherokee nation of a white father. His mother was part Cherokee and part Negro. Even as a very small boy everyone had called him "Big Foot" and made fun of him. At the age of 19 the white girl he loved jilted him for another. Gathering a small band of men about him he killed then, for the sheer love of killing. Later he killed the girl that he had loved.

The foot length of this great giant of a man was 17½ inches and 18 inches around the ball of the foot. His height was 6 feet, 8 inches, with a chest measurement of 59 inches, and his weight was estimated at 300 pounds. He was all bone and sinew, no surplus flesh. He was known to have traveled as far as 60 or 75 miles in a 24-hour period.

Adelaide Hawes gives an account of Starr Wilkerson or "Big Foot" in her book *The Valley of the Tall Grass*, written in 1950.

Although this report suggested that the case may have had a logical explanation, it should be noted that the reference to "mysterious tracks of a tremendous size and human shape" may mean that a genuine Bigfoot was the cause of all the commotion, while the story of the giant Native American was inserted as a means to come up with a rational explanation for what was afoot all those years ago.

Memegwesi

See: Canada's Cryptid Ape-Men

Menehune

See: Hawaii's Mysterious Menehune

Men in Black

Any mention of the legendary and macabre Men in Black (MIB) inevitably evokes imagery of an *X-Files*-type nature—imagery filled with tales of conspiracy and cover-up. It is a fact, however—and a decidedly strange fact, too—that the MIB don't just turn up in UFO-related events. They seem to have a deep fascination for strange creatures, too. In 1967, MIB appeared in Point Pleasant, West Virginia, when sightings of the famous, red-eyed, winged Mothman were at their height. Then, in the early 1970s, a lake-monster researcher named Ted Holiday had an MIB encounter on the shores of Loch Ness. All of which brings us to the MIB-Bigfoot connection.

A particularly strange story that falls perfectly into this category reached my attention in mid-March 2007 and occurred only a week or so earlier. It came from a married couple, Donnie and Lynne, who lived on the outskirts of Oklahoma City. It all began, I was told, in the heart of the Ouachita National Forest in Oklahoma. Certainly, it's a forest that could easily hide many Bigfoot.

The Forest Service says:

The Ouachita National Forest covers 1.8 million acres in central Arkansas and southeastern Oklahoma. Headquartered in Hot Springs, Arkansas, the forest is managed for multiple uses, including timber and wood production, watershed protection and improvement, habitat for wildlife and fish species (including threatened and endangered ones), wilderness area management, minerals leasing, and outdoor recreation. Enjoy camping, hiking, biking, scenic driving, trail riding, water recreation, fishing, hunting, and more!

Donnie and Lynne intended on doing at least several of those things. Instead, however, they encountered the United States' most famous monster. It was around dusk and husband and wife were strolling along the winding paths of the tree-shrouded Ouachita National Recreation Trail when Donnie was suddenly gripped by an overwhelming sense that they were not alone, that their every move was being watched and scrutinized by animalistic eyes. Donnie's sixth-sense was right on target.

In seconds, a hair-covered figure, standing between eight-and-a-half and nine feet tall, emerged from the trees, at a distance of about twenty feet. Neither Donnie nor Lynne had any prior interest in the Bigfoot mystery, but they instantly knew what they were looking at: the legendary Sasquatch. They told me the creature was male: its anatomy made that much clear. Somewhat embarrassed, Lynne said that its "manhood" was visible but tiny. They did not know it, but gorillas, for example, are noted for being far less than well endowed. In that sense, their words on this aspect of the

The Ouachita Mountains are a prime area in western Arkansas for Bigfoot habitat, something that Donnie and Lynne discovered while traveling the recreational trails there.

Bigfoot's appearance actually helped bolster their story. In addition, the creature had a conical head, a huge chest, and thick legs.

Perhaps not surprisingly, seeing the thing at close quarters caused Lynne to fall to the ground, her legs giving way beneath her. Donnie could only stare, with a mixture of awe, fear, and dread. For a moment the Bigfoot merely stared at them, and then something totally unforeseen occurred: Bigfoot spoke to the shocked couple. Not literally, but in a fashion that they could only describe as telepathy.

Both Donnie and Lynne heard the following words fill their heads, but in a soothing, soft, female voice: "Do not be afraid. You will not be harmed. Do not come close." Hardly surprisingly, the pair did exactly what they were told to do. After about twenty seconds, Donnie decided that this was a once-in-a-lifetime chance to capture evidence of the creatures that science and zoology tell us do not exist. He slowly reached into his backpack and pulled out his digital camera.

In a second, the voice filled his head again, although not that of Lynne, interestingly: "Do not." It was as if, Donnie suggested to me, the creature understood perfectly what a camera was and what it could do, and, therefore, instantly took steps to prevent the pair from securing evidence of the beast's existence. The creature then strode towards them, as Donnie also dropped to his knees and the couple clung to each other tightly.

Fortunately, there was no violent attack on them. Instead the Bigfoot leaned in close and, yet again, the couple heard a female voice say: "You will not be hurt and you need not fear. Go. One more time I will see you." They didn't need to be told again and managed to scramble to their shaking legs and backed away, finally breaking into a hysterical run, looking back until the creature could no longer be seen. The weirdness, however, was far from over.

[T]he Bigfoot leaned in close and, yet again, the couple heard a female voice say: "You will not be hurt and you need not fear. Go. One more time I will see you."

Over the course of the next few nights, both Donnie and Lynne had vivid, traumatic dreams of several silver-eyed Bigfoot looming over their bed, warning them never to talk of what they had encountered in the Ouachita National Forest. Notably, on the final night of the nightmarish dreams, Donnie woke up with a sudden jolt as the dream reached its peak and actually saw the creatures in the bedroom—which suddenly dematerialized before his eyes. This led the couple to think that the dreams were not normal dreams based around a recent, traumatic event. They came to believe that Bigfoot can materialize, dematerialize, and even penetrate our dream states.

The pair did not see the creatures again—either physically or in dreams—but there was still more to come. On the next night, both were woken from their slumber in the early hours by a thin beam of light that arced across the darkened bedroom. It was coming through the gap in the curtains of the open window. Donnie raced to the window and caught sight of two things: a number of strange, small balls of light that flitted around the woods surrounding their home; and—illuminated by a bright moon and motion detector lights—a man dressed in a dark suit and trench coat and wearing an old, 1950s-style fedora hat, which is the typical costume of the MIB. Realizing that he had been seen, the MIB retreated into the woods, in the same direction as the eerie globes of light.

A couple more weird things occurred, including several days of static on the couple's landline—another classic aspect of MIB encounters—and strange howling coming from the woods. And then, nothing. Despite having told me of the events—when the creatures had firmly told them never to speak of it—no harm came to Donnie and Lynne. Unfortunately, there were no solid answers for them either.

Metoh-kangmi

See: Howard-Bury, Lt. Col. C. K., Yeti Encounter

Mica Mountain Monster

August 26, 1957, marked the date upon which one of the strangest and most controversial affidavits of all time was prepared and signed. The man who made the sworn statement was William Roe, of Edmonton, Alberta, Canada. The affidavit contained Roe's description of an extremely close encounter with a large, female Bigfoot.

Roe began:

Ever since I was a small boy back in the forests of Michigan, I have studied the lives and habits of wild animals. Later when I supported my family in northern Alberta by hunting and trapping, I spent many hours just observing the wild things. They fascinated me. The most incredible experience I ever had with a wild creature occurred near a little place called Tête Jaune Cache, B.C.E., about 80 miles west of Jasper, Alberta. I had been working on the highway near this place, Tête Jaune Cache, for about 2 years.

In October 1955, said Roe, he

… decided to climb five miles up Mica Mountain to an old deserted mine, just for something to do. I came in sight of the mine about 3 o'clock in the afternoon after an easy climb. I had just come out of a patch of low brush into a clearing, when I saw what I thought was a grizzly bear in the brush on the other side. I had shot a grizzly near that spot the year before.

It soon became apparent that the creature in his midst was no bear:

Roe saw a head and shoulder appear over a rise and could tell that this was no bear.

This one was only about 75 yards away, but I didn't want to shoot it, for I had no way of getting it out. So I sat down on a small rock and watched, with my rifle in my hand. I could just see part of the animal's head and the top of one shoulder. A moment later it raised up and stepped out into the opening. Then I saw it wasn't a bear.

Indeed, that much is clearly evident from the detailed description that Roe provided:

This to the best of my recollection is what the creature looked like and how it acted as it came across the clearing directly towards me. My first impression was of a huge man about 6 feet tall, almost 3 feet wide, and probably weighing near 300 pounds. It was covered from head to foot with dark brown, silver-tipped hair.

Not only was the creature not a bear, it wasn't male, either, as Roe quickly realized:

As it came closer I saw by its breasts that it was female. And yet, its torso was not curved like a female's. Its broad frame was straight from shoulder to hip. Its arms were much thicker than a man's arms and longer, reaching almost to its knees. Its feet were broader proportionately than a man's, about 5 inches wide in the front and tapering to much thinner heels. When it walked it placed the heel of its foot down first, and I could see the grey-brown skin or hide on the soles of its feet.

As Roe revealed next, he had the opportunity to view the animal at almost perilously close quarters:

It came to the edge of the bush I was hiding in, within 20 feet of me, and squatted down on its haunches. Reaching out its hands it pulled the branches of bushes towards it and stripped the leaves with its teeth. Its lips curled flexibly around the leaves as it ate. I was close enough to see that its teeth were white and even. The head was higher at the back than at the front. The nose was broad and flat. The lips and chin protruded farther than its nose. But the hair that covered it, leaving bare only the parts of its face around the mouth, nose and ears, made it resemble an animal as much as a human. None of this hair, even on the back of its head, was longer than an inch, and that on its face much shorter. Its ears were shaped like a human's ears. But its eyes were small and black like a bear's. And its neck also was unhuman, thicker and shorter than any man's I have ever seen.

It's hardly surprising that, as he watched the creature, Roe tried—in vain, it transpires—to rationalize the encounter in rational fashion:

As I watched this creature I wondered if some movie company was making a film in this place and that what I saw was an actor made up to look partly human, partly animal. But as I observed it more I decided it would be impossible to fake such a specimen. Anyway, I learned later there was no such company near that area. Nor, in fact, did anyone live up Mica Mountain, according to the people who lived in Tête Jaune Cache.

Then came the moment that, very possibly, Roe was hoping would not come to pass. The creature suddenly realized it was being watched:

Finally, the wild thing must have got my scent, for it looked directly at me through an opening in the brush. A look of amazement crossed its face. It looked so comical at that moment I had to grin. Still in a crouched position, it backed up three or four short steps, then straightened up to its full height and

Roe wondered if, perhaps, a movie company was making a film featuring a man in a costume, such as this one in Hollywood, but he had to conclude that, no, it was real.

"Although I have called the creature 'it,' I felt now that it was a human being, and I knew I would never forgive myself if I killed it."

started to walk rapidly back the way it had come. For a moment it watched me over its shoulder as it went, not exactly afraid, but as though it wanted no contact with anything strange.

Although the idea of shooting and killing the creature crossed Roe's mind, he quickly backed off from doing so, and explained why:

The thought came to me that if I shot it I would possibly have a specimen of great interest to scientists the world over. I had heard stories about the Sasquatch, the giant hairy "Indians" that live in the legend of the Indians of British Columbia and also, many claim are still, in fact, alive today. Maybe this was a Sasquatch, I told myself. I levelled my rifle.

The creature was still walking rapidly away, again turning its head to look in my direction. I lowered the rifle. Although I have called the creature "it," I felt now that it was a human being, and I knew I would never forgive myself if I killed it.

In mere moments, the encounter would be over. Roe outlined those final seconds:

Just as it came to the other patch of brush it threw its head back and made a peculiar noise that seemed to be half laugh and half language, and which I could only describe as a kind of a whinny. Then it walked from the small brush into a stand of lodge-pole pines. I stepped out into the opening and looked across a small ridge just beyond the pine to see if I could see it again.

It came out on the ridge a couple of hundred yards away from me, tipped its head back again, and again emitted the only sound I had heard it make, but what this half laugh, half language was meant to convey I do not know. It disappeared then, and I never saw it again.

The animal was gone, but Roe was certainly far from finished with it, as he explained in his affidavit:

I wanted to find out if it lived on vegetation entirely or ate meat as well, so I went down and looked for signs. I found it in five different places, and although I examined it thoroughly, could find no hair or shells or bugs or insects. So I believe it was strictly a vegetarian. I found one place where it had slept for a couple of nights under a tree. Now, the nights were cool up the mountain, at this time of year especially, and yet it had not used a fire. I found no signs that it possessed even the simplest of tools. Nor did I find any signs that it had a single companion while in this place.

Roe concluded: "Whether this creature was a Sasquatch I do not know. It will always remain a mystery to me unless another one is found. I hereby declare the above statement to be in every part true, to the best of my powers of observation and recollection."

Migoi

See: Invisibility

Mini-foot of the Woods

In November 2008, an extremely strange story surfaced from Wanstead—a suburban area of London, England. According to witness testimony, a small Bigfoot-type creature was supposedly seen wandering in Epping Forest, a 2,476-hectare area of forestland that, by name at least, was first referenced in the seventeenth century, has existed since Neolithic times, and in the twelfth century, was designated as a Royal Forest by King Henry III.

Author Neil Arnold described how the distinctly odd story began:

The animal was first sighted during early November by eighteen-year-old angler Michael Kent who was fishing with his brother and father in the Hollow Ponds area of Epping Forest, on the border of Wanstead and Leytonstone. The teenager claimed that whilst walking towards his brothers, he heard a rustling in the bushes and saw the back of a dark, hairy animal around four feet in height, that scampered off into the woods.

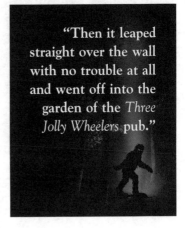

"Then it leaped straight over the wall with no trouble at all and went off into the garden of the *Three Jolly Wheelers* pub."

Another of those that caught sight of the diminutive beast was Irene Dainty, who claimed a face-to-face encounter with the thing on Love Lane, Woodford Bridge. She told the press:

I had just come out of my flat and just as I had turned the corner I saw this hairy thing come out of nowhere. I really don't want to see it again. It was about four feet tall and with really big feet and looked straight at me with animal eyes. Then it leaped straight over the wall with no trouble at all and went off into the garden of the *Three Jolly Wheelers* pub. I was so terrified that I went to my neighbor's house and told her what had happened. She couldn't believe it and asked me if I had been drinking, but I said of course I hadn't—it was only about 3:00 P.M.

Further reports subsequently surfaced, some of which were far more of a four-legged variety, maybe even bear-like, rather than actually being suggestive of Bigfoot. But it was this issue of the "really big feet" that kept the media-driven controversy focused on a mini-Sasquatch. Ultimately, as with so many other similar affairs, sightings of the beast came to an abrupt end and the matter of the Epping Forest monster was never satisfactorily resolved.

Minnesota Iceman

Over the years, various people within the field of cryptozoology have made controversial claims that they have had in their possession the remains of a dead Big-

The Iceman, some speculate, might have been a frozen Neanderthal similar to the ones shown here in a statue display at the Krapina Neanderthal Museum in Croatia.

foot. Thus far, no such claims have been genuine. There is, however, one case that many Bigfoot researchers suspect may be genuine. It's the strange saga of the Minnesota Iceman.

Frank Hansen gained notoriety in the mid-1960s when he maintained that he had acquired the deceased remains of an unusual part-human, part-ape creature. There were problems from the start. Not the least of which was from whom, precisely, Hansen had acquired the body of the beast. The initial story was that the well-preserved corpse was found floating on a block of ice in the ocean waters off of Siberia. Reportedly, it was seen bobbing up and down in the freezing water by the crew of a boat in the area, who wasted no time hauling it aboard.

A second story links the body of the Iceman to Hong Kong, rather than the waters of Siberia. This story maintains that the corpse was found in a Hong Kong deep-freeze and secretly dispatched to the United States. A further theory, that the creature was shot by U.S. troops at the height of the Vietnam War, continues to circulate. Suspicions that the beast was actually slain in Bemidji, Minnesota, by hunter Helen Westring, or was the work of Disney special effects man Howard Ball, also did the rounds for a while. Even the FBI sought to determine if the body was actually human—*Homo sapiens* or something else entirely, maybe even a relic Neanderthal.

Regardless of the origin of the Minnesota Iceman, the word was that the body finally made its way to a still-unknown figure in California, one with a sizeable enough amount of money to allow for the purchase of the potentially priceless remains.

Rumors suggested that the anonymous buyer was actor James Stewart, who was deeply fascinated by the controversy of the Yeti. True or not, the unknown individual made a deal with Hansen to have the latter exhibit the body at a number of state fairs in the United States and Canada. When Hansen received the body, however, he realized this was no monster. Although covered in hair and savage-looking, it had distinct human qualities, too.

Not surprisingly, the cryptozoological community eventually heard of the story and wasted no time in trying to figure out what was going on—and what, exactly, Hansen was displaying for his amazed audiences. Among those who had the opportunity to check out the Minnesota Iceman were two highly regarded cryptozoolgists, Bernard Heuvelmans and Ivan T. Sanderson. They viewed the corpse at Hansen's residence. Both men were sure that what they were looking at had once lived. Even through the ice, the smell of stomach-churning, rotting meat permeated. The body did not appear to be a dummy or special-effects creation. Heuvelmans and Sanderson were excited.

Excitement changed to puzzlement and frustration when the body soon disappeared—back to the unidentified individual who had first placed it in the hands of Hansen. That wasn't the end of the story, however. According to Hansen, after the body was returned to its owner, he received a life-like mannequin of the real Iceman. Hansen happily toured with the mannequin for decades. Today, the fake is on public display at the Museum of the Weird in Austin, Texas. As for the real Minnesota Iceman—presuming it wasn't all just a big con on the part of Hansen—its current resting place remains tantalizingly unknown.

Mississippi's Tusked Ape

It was in 1868 that Franklin County, Mississippi, received a most unwelcome visit from something ape-like and terrifying. It all began when a group of hunters with a pack of dogs in the vicinity of Meadville came across a number of large, human-like tracks, several of which seemed to suggest the feet of the creature faced backwards. As odd as it may sound, tales of backwards-facing feet abound in cryptid ape lore and can be found all around the world.

It was obvious that tracks weren't the only things in evidence: the wild behavior of the dogs made that very clear. Their loud barking suggested that whatever had left the footprints was still around. It was: what was described as a "frightful looking creature," roughly as tall as a grown man, "but with far greater muscular development," appeared out of the trees and stood its ground, staring menacingly at the dogs. Reportedly, the animal had long, coarse hair that flowed from its head to its knees, all of which was a uniform dark brown color. Rather notably, what were described as "two very large tusks" projected from the upper jaw of the animal.

In no time at all, the controversial turned violent and deadly. The beast raced out of the area, towards the Mississippi River, with the hunters and hounds in hot pursuit. Perhaps realizing that it was going to have to make a stand, as the men charged wildly through the woods they suddenly came upon the beast, as if it was seemingly waiting for them. The dogs were let loose, which proved not to be a good thing: the mighty animal grabbed one of the dogs, crushing the poor animal to death in an instant (see "Dogs and Bigfoot"). The men opened

Some species of monkeys and apes have very pronounced fangs, which could be mistaken for tusks.

fire, but the creature skillfully evaded all attempts to kill it, and it was last seen taking an almighty leap into the river, eventually vanishing from sight.

Momo

*See: **Dogs and Bigfoot***

Mono Grande of South America

From various parts of South America, including Colombia, Ecuador, and Venezuela, come stories of a massive, mighty, and extremely violent Bigfoot known as Mono Grande (Big Monkey). One of the most fascinating—but also disturbing and tragic—stories came from Count Pino Turolla, a noted archaeologist who traveled the world, Indiana Jones-style, in pursuit of all things mysterious and fabulous. Turolla (who died in 1984 at the early age of sixty-two) was born in Yugoslavia and later immigrated to Canada. Of note, he developed what became known as the Turolla Control-Descent Parachute used by the U.S. military.

It was while traveling across South America in the 1960s that Turolla first heard of the marauding monster. The information came from Turolla's personal guide, Antonio, who told a shocking story. Some years earlier, Antonio and his two sons traveled to a particular range in Venezuela where they were confronted on the sprawling savannah by a trio of enormous, gorilla-like animals that were around eight feet in height, had long and hanging arms, and tiny heads. They were also armed with large and crudely fashioned wooden clubs. A violent altercation occurred, resulting in one of Antonio's sons being bludgeoned to death by the merciless monsters.

Turolla didn't have time to investigate the matter of the Mono Grande at the time, but half a year later he was back. And this time, it wasn't ancient, historical artifacts that he was looking for: it was for the South American Bigfoot itself. Turolla, Antonio, and three other native men headed off to where Antonio's son lost his life in bloody fashion. The story told by Turolla was terrifying:

> When we set out from the camp, we began hiking southeast across the savanna and after a few hours entered the forest, where we followed a narrow track through undergrowth so thick that it reduced our vision to only a few feet on either side. Only now and then did a small clearing enable us to have a field of view of 6 to 10 meters ahead.

> When we entered the canyon where Antonio had seen the big mono, the Indians became very alert and apprehensive, stepping carefully, and sensing every sound and movement in the brush around them. I was carrying a 3.5 Winchester automatic and kept it at the ready. Tension was mounting as we slowly made our way along the trail. The subdued light created lurking shadows and a mood of mystery.

It was getting toward late afternoon when suddenly we heard a howl, very loud, coming from somewhere in the thick vegetation. The Indians froze. The howl was as loud as the roar of a jaguar, but it was higher and shriller in pitch. It reverberated through the forest, encircling us as if it came from all directions. Something was moving, crashing powerfully through the underbrush.

The Indians turned abruptly and raced back along the trail, yelling at me to follow. But I was frozen in my tracks; my heart beating so hard that I could hear it. Then, suddenly, the howling stopped. I waited, and when I had regained control of my movements, I advanced slowly along the trail, my finger on the trigger of the gun. Then, as I reached a small clearing, the howling started again, in one crescendo after another. But again, as suddenly as it had started, it stopped.

It was then that I saw two furry patches running away from me with a leaping sort of step through the foliage that bordered the clearing. As they bounded across the surface of a group of boulders at the far end of the clearing, I was able to catch a fleeting glimpse of them. They clearly were erect, hairy, apelike creatures, and appeared to be over 5 feet tall. Then they disappeared around the rocks into the jungle, and I heard the cracking sounds of dry twigs and branches as they hastily forged their way through the thick underbrush.

The Mono Grande that Count Pino Turolla encountered in Venezuela were gorilla-like monsters about eight feet in height.

I waited for what seemed an eternity for something else to happen, trying to impress on my mind what I had just glimpsed. I opened my mouth to yell to my companions, but no sound came out. Finally I turned and retraced my steps, and encountered them advancing cautiously back up the trail. "They're gone," I said. No one uttered a word. We continued up the trail. We did not see or hear the creatures again.

Mount St. Helens Eruption and Bigfoot

On May 18, 1980, a devastating natural disaster created an entirely new landscape across a portion of Washington State. Mount St. Helens erupted, killing more

After the catastrophic eruption of Mount St. Helens in Washington State, the federal government launched an operation to look for the remains of Bigfoot that may have been killed. Bigfoot researchers have reportedly been told that the military *did* find several bodies.

than four dozen people, as well as thousands of wild animals. Within the domain of cryptid ape investigations, there are longstanding rumors that the calamitous event also took the lives of more than a few Bigfoot, something that, allegedly, elements of the U.S. government and military sought to keep under wraps. The U.S. Geological Survey (USGS) said of the Mount St. Helens disaster:

> With no immediate precursors, a magnitude 5.1 earthquake occurred at 8:32 A.M. on May 18, 1980 and was accompanied by a rapid series of events. At the same time as the earthquake, the volcano's northern bulge and summit slid away as a huge landslide—the largest debris avalanche on Earth in recorded history. A small, dark, ash-rich eruption plume rose directly from the base of the debris avalanche scarp, and another from the summit crater rose to about 200 m (650 ft) high. The debris avalanche swept around and up ridges to the north, but most of it turned westward as far as 23 km (14 mi) down the valley of the North Fork Toutle River and formed a hummocky deposit. The total avalanche volume is about 2.5 km^3 (3.3 billion cubic yards), equivalent to 1 million Olympic swimming pools.

The landslide removed Mount St. Helens's northern flank, including part of the cryptodome that had grown inside the volcano, noted the USGS, adding that: "The cryptodome was a very hot and highly pressurized body of magma. Its removal result-ed in immediate depressurization of the volcano's magmatic system and triggered pow-erful eruptions that blasted laterally through the sliding debris and removed the upper 300 m (nearly 1,000 ft) of the cone. As this lateral blast of hot material overtook the debris avalanche, it accelerated to at least 480 km per hr (300 mi per hr). Within a few minutes after onset, an eruption cloud of blast tephra began to rise from the for-mer summit crater. Within less than 15 minutes it had reached a height of more than 24 km (15 mi or 80,000 ft).

The lateral blast devastated an area nearly 30 km (19 mi) from west to east and more than 20 km (12.5 mi) northward from the former summit," the USGS noted. "In an inner zone extending nearly 10 km (6 mi) from the summit, virtually no trees remained of what was once dense forest.

And, demonstrating the incredible and deadly power unleashed that day, the USGS said: "Over the course of the day, prevailing winds blew 520 million tons of ash eastward across the United States and caused complete darkness in Spokane, Washing-ton, 400 km (250 mi) from the volcano. Major ash falls occurred as far away as central Montana, and ash fell visibly as far eastward as the Great Plains of the Central United States, more than 1,500 km (930 mi) away. The ash cloud spread across the U.S. in three days and circled the Earth in 15 days.

So much for the official story; now, it's time to take a look at the unofficial one. In many respects, it parallels the claims of U.S. military retrievals of extraterrestrial bodies in the deserts near Roswell, New Mexico, in the summer of 1947. There are stories that the entire oper-ation to recover possibly five or six Bigfoot from the pulverized remains of Mount St. Helens was coordinated by the U.S. Army Corps of Engi-neers (USACE). The USACE notes that its role is to: "Deliver vital public and military engineering services; partnering in peace and war to strengthen our Nation's security, energize the economy and reduce risks from disasters." In other words, the USACE would, indeed, have been the ideal body to have played a central role in the recoveries.

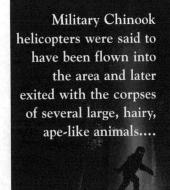

Military Chinook helicopters were said to have been flown into the area and later exited with the corpses of several large, hairy, ape-like animals....

Several of the bodies, Bigfoot researchers have been told, were reportedly found on the 105-mile-long Cowlitz River, in the Cascade Mountains. Military Chinook helicopters were said to have been flown into the area and later exited with the corpses of several large, hairy, ape-like animals hanging from powerful nets strung beneath the helicopters. Their destination remains tantalizingly, and frustratingly, unknown.

In 2012, a story surfaced from a former National Guardsman who maintained that he was actually onsite when at least some of the Bigfoot recoveries occurred—under cover of extensive secrecy. Incredibly, he claimed that not all of the retrieved Bigfoot were dead—some were burned and injured, and a few critically so. Particularly outrageous is the claim that the military had assistance from one or two unharmed Big-foot that helped guide military personnel to the site where the injured, hairy giants lay!

There is absolutely no doubt that the stories of the dead and injured Bigfoot of the Mount St. Helens disaster of May 1980 are fascinating. Admittedly very problematic, however, is the glaring fact that none of the alleged military personnel who divulged such fantastic stories have been willing to reveal their name or proof of employment at a military or government level. Until such identification occurs, the story will likely remain as hazy and controversial as it is sensational and potentially groundbreaking.

Mountain Devils of Mount St. Helens

See: Ape Canyon

Mountain People of Hatzic Lake, British Columbia

Although the exact date is unclear, the following account was prepared in the 1950s by Charley Victor of Chilliwack, British Columbia, Canada:

> I was hunting in the mountains near Hatzic. I had my dog with me. I came out on a plateau where there were several big cedar trees. The dog stood

Charley Victor was hunting near Hatzic Lake in British Columbia when he shot what he believed to be a bear. Wounded, the creature let out a cry and a female "wild person" appeared.

before one of the trees and began to growl and bark at it. On looking up to see what excited him, I noticed a large hole in the tree 7 feet from the ground. The dog pawed and leaped upon the trunk, and looked at me to raise him up, which I did, and he went into the hole.

The next moment a muffled cry came from the hole. I said to myself: "The dog is tearing into a bear," and with my rifle ready I urged the dog to drive him out, and out came something I took for a bear. I shot and it fell with a thud to the ground.

"Murder! Oh my!" I spoke to myself in surprise and alarm, for the thing I had shot looked to me like a white boy. He was nude. He was about 12 or 14 years of age. Wounded and bleeding, the poor fellow sprawled upon the ground, but when I drew close to examine the extent of his injury, he let out a wild yell, or, rather a call as if he were appealing for help. From across the mountain a long way off rolled a booming voice.

Less than half an hour, out from the depths of the forest came the strangest and wildest creature one could possibly see. I raised my rifle, but not to shoot, but in case I would have to defend myself. The strange creature walked toward me without the slightest fear. The wild person was a woman. Her face was almost Negro black and her long straight hair fell to her waist. In height she would be about 6 foot but her chest and shoulders were well above the average breadth.

Regular people descended into states of definitive wildness, or something far stranger? We'll probably never know.

Mowglis

Whether a person believes in Bigfoot, is highly skeptical, or has an open and undecided mind, the fact is that just about everyone is familiar with the word *Bigfoot* itself. But had circumstances not dictated otherwise, the legendary hairy giants of the woods just might have become known by a very different name: Mowglis. The term was briefly used in the early twentieth century—before it was eclipsed by, first, Sasquatch, and then, from 1958 onwards, Bigfoot.

Almost certainly, the name was lifted from Rudyard Kipling's 1894 collection of stories, *The Jungle Book*, which told of the adventures of a young, feral boy named Mowgli, who lives in the wooded wilds of central India.

We see evidence of the word *Mowgli* in a number of newspaper accounts that surfaced in the first decade of the twentieth century. The Ohio-based *Van Wert Daily Bulletin* ran an article on October 28, 1905, with the headline "British Columbia Mowglis: Tribe of Wild Men Roaming Woods and Frightening People."

The article stated:

In the novel *The Jungle Book* by Rudyard Kipling, Mowgli is a wild Indian boy who adapts to living among wolves and monkeys. The name was adopted to describe a strange wild creature found in British Columbia.

James Johnson, a rancher living near Cornox, seven miles from Cumberland, B.C., reports several Mowglis, or wild men, who have been seen in that neighborhood by ranchers, says a Nanaimo (B.C.) correspondent of the *San Francisco Call*. Johnson asserts that they were performing what seemed to be a sort of "sun dance" on the sand. One of them caught a glimpse of Johnson, who was viewing the proceedings from behind a big log. The Mowglis disappeared as if by magic into a big cave.

Thomas Kincaid, a rancher living near French creek, while bicycling from Cumberland, also reports seeing a Mowgli, whom he describes as a powerfully built man, more than six feet in height and covered with long black hair. The wild man upon seeing Kincaid uttered a shriek and disappeared into the woods.

Upon arriving home Kincaid wrote Government Agent Bray of Nanaimo, inquiring if it would be lawful to shoot the Mowgli, as he was terrorizing that vicinity. The government agent replied that there was no law permitting such an act.

It is reported that on a recent hunting expedition up the Quailicum river an Indian saw a Mowgli and, mistaking him for a bear, shot at and wounded him. During the past month no less than eleven persons coming to Nanaimo from Cumberland have seen the wild men. Parties have been organized and every effort is being made to capture the Mowglis.

It's intriguing to note that, as was the case in more than a few early reports of unknown apes in the United States, the Mowglis were tied to the presence in the area of a "big cave." Further proof, perhaps, of their predilection for a life spent largely under the surface of the planet.

Less than one year later, the *Yukon World* published a story of the Mowglis in August 1906. The headline was "Alberni Has a Wild Man Vancouver Island Mowgli Said to Be No Myth—Seen by a Prospector Recently."

The newspaper recorded:

The famous Vancouver island mowgli is no myth. A prospector is now in Vancouver who says he saw the wild man at Alberni a few days ago. He will not allow his name to be used, asserting that he [was] "not looking for notoriety." He says: "A few days ago myself and another prospector dropped right onto the wild man on the shores of Horn lake, Alberni. The mowgli was clothed in sunshine and a smile except that his body was covered with a growth of hair much like the salmon berry-eating bears that infest the region. The wild man ran with astonishing agility as soon as he saw us. We found the wickieup in which he had been sheltering and also many traces of where he had been gathering roots along the lake bank for sustenance. That wild man is no figment of the imagination. You can take my word for that."

As fascinating as both newspaper accounts were, the word "Mowgli" was never embraced in the style, and certainly not to the scale, that Bigfoot was, decades later.

Mozambique Mysterious Animal

In 1938, a startling letter was published in the pages of *Discovery* magazine. It was written by British Army officer Cuthbert Burgoyne. According to Burgoyne, in 1927 he had a close encounter with a pair of unknown apes or monkeys while aboard a Japanese cargo boat that was heading for Portuguese East Africa. They were, apparently, known locally as Agogwes.

In Burgoyne's own words:

We were sufficiently near to land to see objects clearly with a glass of 12 magnifications. There was a sloping beach with light brush above, upon which several dozen baboons were hunting for and picking up shellfish or crabs, to judge by their movements. Two pure white baboons were amongst them. These are very rare but I had heard of them previously.

Then, as Burgoyne noted, something amazing happened:

As we watched, two little brown men walked together out of the bush and down among the baboons. They were certainly not any known monkey and they must have been akin or they would have disturbed the baboons. They were too far away to see in detail, but these small human like animals were probably between 4 and 5 feet tall, quite upright and graceful in nature.

At the time I was thrilled as they quite evidently were no beast of which I had heard or read. Later a friend and big game hunter told me he was in Portuguese East Africa with his wife and three other hunters, and saw mother, father and child, of apparently similar animal species, walk across the further side of a bush clearing. The natives loudly forbade him to shoot.

Myakka Skunk Ape Photographs

Of the many and varied photographs that purport to show real, unknown apes, two of the most talked about, dissected, and studied are those that have become

This is one of the photos provided, anonymously, to the Sarasota County, Florida, police in 2000, along with a letter describing the encounter. The ape-like creature looks like an orangutan, but the police never followed up to learn for certain.

known as the Myakka Skunk Ape photographs. Myakka is a reference to the Myakka River and Myakka State Park that, geographically speaking, dominate the area where the creature was seen. The controversy began on December 22, 2000, when an anonymous letter, and a pair of undeniably sensational photographs, were mailed to the Sarasota County, Florida, police department, which, it's believed, is the same county in which the source of the photos lived. The woman with the potentially priceless photos and tale to tell, said to the police:

Dear Sir or Madam

Enclosed please find some pictures I took in late September or early Oct 2000. My husband says he think[s] it is an orangutan. Is someone missing an Orangutan? It is hard to judge from the photos how big this orangutan really is. It is in a crouching position in the middle of standing up from where it was sitting. It froze as soon as the flash went off. I didn't even see it as I took the first picture because it was so dark. As soon as the flash went off for the second time it stood up and started to move. I then heard the orangutan walk off into the bushes.

From where I was standing, I judge it as being about six and a half to seven feet tall in a kneeling position. As soon as I realized how close it was I got back to the house. It had an awful smell that lasted well after it had left my yard. The orangutan was making deep "woomp" noises. It sounded much farther away then [sic] it turned out to be.

The woman then expressed her concerns about the presence of the beast:

If I had known it was as close to the hedge roll as it was I wouldn't have walked up as close as I did. I'm a senior citizen and if this animal had come out of the hedge roll after me there wasn't a thing I could have done about it. I was about ten foot away from it when it stood up. I'm concerned because my grandchildren like to come down and explore in my back yard. An animal this big could hurt someone seriously.

From the woman's next words, it appears pretty clear that the reason why she had been targeted by the visitations was for food. She explained to the police:

For two nights prior, it had been taking apples that my daughter brought down from up north, off our back porch. These pictures were taken on the third night it had raided my apples. It only came back one more night after that and took some apples that my husband had left out in order to get a better look at it. We left out four apples. I cut two of them in half. The orangutan only took the whole apples. We didn't see it take them. We waited up but eventually had to go to bed. We got a dog back there now and as far as we can tell the orangutan hasn't been back.

Please find out where this animal came from and who it belongs to. It shouldn't be loose like this, someone will get hurt. I called a friend that used to work with animal control back up north and he told us to call the police. I don't want any fuss or people with guns traipsing around behind our house. We live near I75 and I'm afraid this orangutan could cause a serious accident if someone hit it. I once hit a deer that wasn't even a quarter of this size of this animal and totaled my car.

She concluded: "At the very least this animal belongs in a place like Bush [sic] Gardens where it can be looked after properly. Why haven't people been told that an animal this size is loose? How are people to know how dangerous this could be? If I had known an animal like this was loose I wouldn't have aprotched [sic] it. I saw on the news that monkeys that get loose can carry Hepatitis and are very dangerous. Please look after this situation. I don't want my backyard to turn into someone else's circus.

God Bless.

I prefer to remain anonymous.

It appears that the police did very little beyond finding the pictures interesting and humorous. No doubt, the pictures were a welcome break from the world of crime-fighting! It was not until early January 2001 that matters were taken to another level. That's when David Barkasy, who ran the Silver City Serpenarium in Saratosa, was informed by the police of the anonymous letter and the accompanying photos. Barkasy quickly contacted Bigfoot authority Loren Coleman, who revealed the astonishing saga to the public.

> If not an orangutan per se, the creature may, as Coleman noted, fall into the category of "unknown orangutan relatives."

Of course, the big question is: what do the photos show? Certainly, the creature looks very much like an orangutan, but is that really what it was? The anonymous woman's words—"I judge it as being about six and a half to seven feet tall"—would definitely rule out an orangutan as being the culprit, providing her judgment of the size of the animal was accurate. From a distance of around only ten feet, it's a fairly safe guess that the woman was not in error. If not an orangutan per se, the creature may, as Coleman noted, fall into the category of "unknown orangutan relatives."

Then there is the matter of the woman herself. Although, to this day, she remains unidentified, there is one important thing—beyond the photos, naturally—that suggests she was speaking the truth. Recall that she told the police "we live near I75." It turns out that Barkasy was able to determine—as a result of studying the processing number on the images—that the development of the pictures was undertaken, in December 2000, at an Eckerd photo laboratory near an exit off I-75, specifically at the intersection of Fruitville and Tuttle roads.

While there remains no hard and fast consensus on what the creature was, the photos continue to impress Bigfoot seekers, years after they were taken.

Mysterious Jungle Races of Sumatra

The Orang-pendek is, certainly, the most well-known mystery ape said to dwell deep in the dense forests of Sumatra. It's far from being alone, however. In July 1932, the *Singapore Free Press and Mercantile Advertiser* newspaper ran an article titled "Mysterious Jungle Races of Sumatra: Giants and Pigmies, Guard Swine and Have Their Heels in Front." One of the creatures to which the article referred was Orang-lecho, which, according to the newspaper, dwelled in the western parts of Sumatra, and specifically in Gunong Gedang Bondjol and Lubok Sepaking.

Reportedly, the Orang-lecho lived in fear of humans, were short in stature, ate fruit and fish, and possessed a complex language, which they spoke at "a terrible speed." The writer of the article said: "Whenever they see a human being they will shout out 'Derangka! Derangka! Derangka!' which probably means a human being. When they hear this warning note from their friends they immediately fly into forests, and are never found."

Then there was the Si Bigau, which, rather intriguingly, the newspaper described as "one of the species of Orang-pendek," which suggests a knowledge of more than one kind of the creature. Reportedly, the Si Bigau were quiet, retiring animals—"about the height of a child of three or four years of age"—that preferred their own company. Rather curiously, they spent much of their time herding wild pigs—something with which, by all accounts, they had an obsession.

The *Singapore Free Press* continued: "According to old hunters, any swine that is under guardianship of the Si Bigau will never be caught, no matter how good are the hounds, for the swine will follow the swift flight of Si Bigau into the thickest part of the forest.

Much larger than the Si Bigau and the Orang-lecho was the Mawas, said to be "the same height as that of a human being." Not only that, the Mawas physically resembled the human race to an uncanny degree, except for the fact that they were covered in hair. They shunned clothing and reportedly had feet that faced backwards.

Even bigger than the Mawas were the Raksaska, described by the newspaper as being "very tall" and "meters high." Interestingly, they were said to live in primitive, house-like structures deep within the "big virgin jungles."

Native Americans, Bigfoot, and Aliens

Although the term *Bigfoot* was not coined until the late 1950s, it is a fact that reports of giant, hairy, humanoid creatures inhabiting the wilder, mountainous, and forested areas of the United States date back to the earliest years of Native American culture. Loren Coleman, one of the world's leading authorities on Bigfoot, says:

> When Europeans colonized from the East to the West, their initial encounters were with the rare, eastern Bigfoot, which the natives they met spoke about. The first Americans acknowledged these hairy races, and their tales come down to us in the records that ethnographers, folklorists, and anthropologists have preserved in overlooked essays on hairy-giant legends and myths.

There is, however, something very intriguing about the Native American beliefs in Bigfoot. They suggest the creatures are far more than they appear to be. That's to say, they do not just represent an undiscovered kind of North American ape, but rather something directly linked to the UFO phenomenon. Given the fact that reports exist of Bigfoot from centuries ago, as astonishing as it may sound, Bigfoot, according to some eyewitnesses and investigators, may be an ancient alien.

The *Native Languages* website states:

> The Bigfoot figure is common to the folklore of most Northwest Native American tribes. Native American Bigfoot legends usually describe the creatures as around 6–9 feet tall, very strong, hairy, uncivilized, and often foul-smelling, usually living in the woods and often foraging at night…. In

some Native stories, Bigfoot may have minor supernatural powers—the ability to turn invisible, for example—but they are always considered physical creatures of the forest, not spirits or ghosts.

That is where the intertribal Bigfoot similarities end, however. In the Bigfoot myths of some tribes, Sasquatch and his relatives are generally shy and benign figures—they may take things that do not belong to them or even kidnap a human wife, but do not harm people and may even come to their aid. Sometimes Bigfoot is considered a guardian of nature in these tribes. These more benevolent Bigfeet usually appear alone or in a small family unit, and may exchange gifts or use sign language to communicate with Native American communities. But Bigfoot legends from other tribes describe them as malevolent creatures who attack humans, play dangerous tricks on them, or steal children; they may even eat people. These more dangerous Bigfoot monsters, known as Stick Indians or Bush Indians, are sometimes found in large groups or even villages, which engage in warfare with neighboring Indian tribes.

One of the most fascinating cases of relevancy came from James C. Wyatt, of Memphis, Tennessee, who shared with paranormal expert Brad Steiger a copy of Wyatt's grandfather's journal from 1888. It described the old man's exposure to the Bigfoot phenomenon, way back in the nineteenth century. The location was the Humboldt Meridian, in northwestern California. It was while in the area, on one par-

Paranormal researcher and author Brad Steiger recorded a tale from James C. Wyatt about how Wyatt's grandfather encountered a Bigfoot in the 1880s.

ticular day, that Wyatt's grandfather encountered a tribesman carrying a plate of raw meat. Puzzled, he asked what it was for. After pondering for a while, the man motioned Wyatt Sr. to follow him. On arriving at a cave built into a cliff face, he was shocked to see a huge, hair-covered, man-like beast. It was, however, quite docile and enthusiastically ate the meat provided for him.

It was then that Wyatt's grandfather got the full story. The beast—nicknamed "Crazy Bear"—had supposedly been brought to the forests "from the stars." A "small moon" had descended, ejecting both the creature and several others of its kind. The "moon" was reportedly piloted by very human-looking entities that always waved at the Indians as they dumped the hairy beasts on their land.

Wyatt asked Steiger: "Who is to say the Crazy Bears weren't exiled to our planet for some crime or other infraction of the laws of another planet?"

On a very similar path, respected investigator Lon Strickler said:

Researcher and author Kewaunee Lapseritis maintains that the Bigfoot race was brought to Earth by the "Star People," long before human civilization even existed. His evidence is the creature's use of telepathic communications, alleged hundreds of joint Bigfoot-UFO sightings going back over a hundred years, and theoretical physics.

He also stated that conventional Bigfoot investigators have not found the creature because they are limited in their belief that Bigfoot is "simply a relic hominid that never became extinct."

"That really may be true," Lapseritis said in an interview. "But in addition to that, (Bigfoot) may literally be, as I've discovered, a paraphysical, interdimensional native people that have told me and other people telepathically that they were brought here millions of years ago by their friends, the Star People."

Strickler adds:

I recently received a telephone call from a woman in British Columbia who said she was the daughter of a Kootenai shaman. She stated that most Native tribes seem to believe Sasquatch is a non-physical creature. Some tribal elders mention that they have seen the creature shapeshift into a wolf. She said her father thought that the creatures lived in another dimension from our physical plane, but can come here as it wishes.

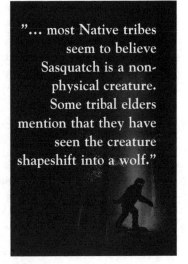

"… most Native tribes seem to believe Sasquatch is a non-physical creature. Some tribal elders mention that they have seen the creature shapeshift into a wolf."

Going back to the aforementioned Lapseritis, it's worth expanding on his views on the Bigfoot phenomenon. When the creatures were brought to our world by visiting extraterrestrials in times long past, says Lapseritis....

… some were genetically "modified" and released. Zecharia Sitchin practiced real science by correctly interpreting the Sumerian cuneiforms, which others in mainstream science could not understand. Sitchin opened the doors to reality for a lot of people. According to his work, all of us were genetically engineered. Some humans have the soul of an ET or Sasquatch/Ancient One. Contact with the right people is important to the Sasquatch. Some humans ("hairless ones") have the skills needed to put out the truth. The Sasquatch say we are living a lie, in an illusion created by our so-called "modern" society. Our government and our religions are the true illusionists, perpetrating a diversion away from who we really are, in order to control the masses. More and more people are being contacted. We have all come here to learn critical lessons. I have come to understand, and to piece together all that they have told me and the other contactees.

The New Daughter (2009 movie)

The *New Daughter* is a 2009 movie that did not catch the attention of the cinema-going general public upon its release, which is unfortunate, since it is a skillfully made movie, one that is high on tension and atmosphere and that has a notable cast. It's also a movie that should be watched—and appreciated—by those fascinated by the Bigfoot mystery, since it deals with the matter of primitive humans living alongside us in the woods. The movie stars Kevin Costner, Samantha Mathis (of *American Psycho*), and Ivana Baquero, who played the lead role in Guillermo del Toro's acclaimed fantasy-themed movie of 2006, *Pan's Labyrinth*.

Costner's character, John James, has recently split up with his wife and moves with his children, Louisa (Baquero) and Sam (Gattlin Griffith), to a small, isolated town surrounded by dense woodland. This sets the scene for the menace that soon follows.

It's clear from the beginning that the relationship between John and his children is strained: Louisa resents being taken out of her old school and losing all her old friends. Sam is the quieter one of the two, but is traumatized by his parents' divorce and clings to his father for support. Almost immediately, we come to realize that there is something very strange about the house into which the James family has moved.

On the very first night, we catch a shadowy glimpse of a strange, humanoid creature clambering across the roof of the huge house, the sounds of which catch Louisa's attention. On top of that, John learns—to his anger, since his realtor made no mention of it—that the previous owner disappeared under mysterious circumstances. The unsettling atmosphere only increases when Louisa's pet cat is found dead by John, torn to pieces, as if by a wild animal. He chooses to bury the body without telling his children.

With no friends in the area, Louisa and Sam decide to explore the woods that surround their home. On doing so, they stumble upon a strange, grassy mound, about fifteen feet high, one that clearly looks to have been constructed, rather than being a natural formation. They quickly call their father to the scene. Sam immediately feels disturbed by the mound and refuses to go near it, whereas Louisa is oddly drawn to it. And that's when the trouble starts.

Tensions grow higher when the children start at their new school. Neither Sam nor Louisa are looking forward to it, especially Louisa, who notes the instant attraction between her father and Sam's teacher, Cassandra Parker. When the school day is finally over, Louisa visits the mound, and lays down on top of it. Suddenly, hostile, animalistic sounds fill the air. Only later do we find out why.

Later that evening, John is puzzled by the sight of a trail of muddy footprints that extend from the front door to Louisa's room. Unbeknownst to John, his daughter is in the shower, washing off her mud-covered body. Hours later, John finds Louisa sleepwalking, which deeply worries him. He's also concerned by the discovery, in Louisa's room, of a crudely fashioned doll, made from straw. John helps his daughter return to her bed and she quickly resumes her regular sleep. The following morning, Louisa is normal, and, when pressed by John, she does not recall sleepwalking.

Louisa begins to have trouble at school, and particularly so with one of the girls in her class. Her eating habits change, to the extent that she begins to eat her food solely with her fingers, savagely biting at, and chewing on, her dinner like a wild animal. John looks on, exasperated and angry, but he puts it all down to teenage rebellion and the stress caused by the divorce. He soon finds out how very wrong he is.

John and Cassandra meet for dinner, during which the matter of Louisa's odd behavior comes up. Cassandra, too, believes that everything is down to hormones and John's recent split from his wife. John's perspective changes drastically, when, as he drives home and passes through the woods that surround the property, a strange, darkened form races across the road. John screeches to a halt and gets out of the car. He cautiously peers into the dense forest, only to find himself seemingly stalked by something savage and animalistic. As he jumps back into his vehicle, the driver's side window is smashed by a rock thrown from the darkness. Racing into the house and locking the door, John warns Louisa to keep away from the woods and the mound. By now, however, her curious behavior is becoming more and more unsettling, as she descends into a state of near-savagery.

As John decides to dig further into the history of the house, he learns that not only did the previous owner, Sarah Wayne, vanish, she also locked her daughter in her bedroom before she fled the property. Even more disturbing, the daughter subse-

Actor Kevin Costner starred in the 2009 film *The New Daughter.*

quently went to live with her grandfather, Roger Wayne. When John visits him, Wayne tells him that he killed his own granddaughter in a fire. The reason for Wayne's crazed action: she was changing into … something else. John flees from the deranged Roger Wayne and races for home, where Louisa and Sam have been left with an elderly babysitter—who is savagely attacked and killed by an unseen predator as she smokes on the porch late at night.

With the disappearance of the sitter—something that brings the local police into the story—John begins to dig further into the matter of the curious mound, to which Louisa is so oddly, and unsettlingly, attached. During the course of his research into the mound, John speaks with Professor Evan White, who reveals the folklore and mythology behind the many similar mounds that extend across the United States. They are said to be the work of an ancient race of semi-human, primitive beings that live in forested areas and dwell in underground tunnels and hollows, access to which is made via the above-ground mounds.

More disturbing, the mound-dwellers—all of whom are male—require a female mate to ensure that a new, healthy lineage comes into being. Although John cannot find himself fully able to believe that Louisa has been chosen for such a task, any more than he can accept the existence of the primal monsters said to lurk below, he asks a friend to tear down the mound—but not before Professor White arrives and begs him to reconsider. John does not: as his workman proceeds to tear down the mound with his bulldozer, White's assistant lets out an ear-splitting scream; the mutilated body of the babysitter is seen, semi-buried, in the dirt and grime.

Police officer Ed Lowry (actor Erik Palladino) gets involved, only to lose his life to one of the creatures in the woods, as he and John are driving to the family home. As John bursts through the front door, he is confronted by a scene of carnage: Cassandra is lying on the kitchen floor, dying from a gaping wound to her neck. Sam is in a state of shock and fear. Louisa, meanwhile, is no longer recognizable as John's daughter: her mind has been transformed into something else.

A fierce battle for survival begins as three of the mound-monsters invade the home, and John finally realizes that the proto-humans are not the stuff of folklore and mythology, but of deadly reality. He blasts them with his shotgun, telling Sam to stay where he is, while he, John, goes off in pursuit of Louisa. He knows exactly where he will find her: the mound.

John finds a way into the mound and is plunged into a nightmarish, underground realm filled with muddy, dirty tunnels, a maze-like construction that extends dozens of feet underground and in which live the mound-dwellers. He finds Louisa and drags her to the surface, fighting off the crazed creatures as he does so. The fight for survival is not over, however. As John stares at Louisa, he sees she is beginning to physically change—into a female equivalent of the primitive people he knows he must destroy. A look of utter despair comes over John's face as blows up the mound with a large canister of diesel—killing not just the creatures, but himself and Louisa, too.

The final scene of the movie is that of Sam, exiting the house and searching for his dad and sister, only to be surrounded by several mound-dwellers that surface out of the woods.

For Bigfoot enthusiasts, *The New Daughter* is a movie to which they should be able to relate. The movie's theme—of an unknown, and unclassified, humanoid inhabiting the woods and forests of the United States—has deep parallels with the Sasquatch conundrum, as does the way in which the creatures are shown to be not folkloric, but all too terrifyingly real.

Njmbin

See: Australia's Beast-Men

Nyalmo

Bernard Heuvelmans, one of the most important figures in the field of cryptozoology, said that during the course of his research into the Yeti of the Himalayas, he had learned of three kinds of creature that roamed the vast mountains.

"This opinion," said Heuvelmans, "was confirmed in 1957 by a Tibetan lama called Punyabayra, high priest of the monastery at Budnath, who spent four months in the high mountains and brought back the surprising but valuable information that the Tibetan mountain people knew three kinds of snowmen."

There was the *rimi*, a man-beast of close to three meters in height that dwelled in the Barun Khola valley, in eastern Nepal, and which was specifically omnivorous. Then there was the rackshi bompo, a beast of roughly human proportions, and which Heuvelmans said "must be the Sherpas' reddish *yeh-teh* or *mi-the*, which leaves the footprints 20 to 23 cm long that the *Daily Mail* expedition … found in such quantity." Finally, there was the imposing and terrifying Nyalmo.

Heuvelmans came straight to the point: "The *nyalmo* are real giants, between 4 and 5 m high, with enormous conical heads." He continued: "They wander in parties among the eternal snows above 4000m. In such empty country it is hardly surprising that they should be carnivorous and even man-eating."

Heuvelmans asked of the Nyalmo: "Do they really exist, or are they just a myth?" He admitted to having heard of accounts of Yetis with feet around 45 to 60 cm in length, but he was careful to qualify this by stating that "the evidence is far too slender for us to draw any satisfactory conclusions. Possibly the *nyalmo* are an invented addition based on the belief that *Yetis* increase in size the higher you go.

This May 1960 issue of *Radar* magazine shows a Yeti attacking Tibetan refugees. Note the distinctively conical shape of the Yeti's head.

Loren Coleman said: "When [Sir Edmund] Hillary went to the Himalayas to look for the Yeti, he and his collaborator, journalist Desmond Doig, noted that there were several unknown primates said to be there still undiscovered in any formal way. Among the varieties was one called the 'Nyalmo.' Hillary and Doig learned of the Nyalmo in north-central Nepal. It was said to be 'giant-sized (up to twenty feet tall), manlike, hairy, and given to shaking giant pine trees in trials of strength while other Nyalmos sit around and clap their hands.'"

The matter of the curious behavior of the Nyalmos—to which Coleman refers—was most graphically told by Jean Marquès-Rivière. It was in 1937 that the details of Marquès-Rivière's account first surfaced, one that was eagerly picked up on by Bernard Heuvelmans. According to Marquès-Rivière, he had occasion to speak with an Indian pilgrim who personally encountered a group of Nyalmo in the wilds of Nepal. *Crypto Journal* describes the extraordinary encounter in a fashion that suggests the beasts have a high degree of intelligence and may even have some form of spiritual belief-system:

> The creatures were standing as they formed a circle and were chanting, as if they were doing a religious ritual or something of that sort. One of the Yeti-like creatures was enthusiastically beating a hollow trunk of a tree, like a man hitting his drums to create some music. The others continued their "chants," but their faces seemed to be filled with a sad expression.

A 1979 drawing by Edwin Duesiester based on descriptions provided by Sir Edmund Hillary and Desmond Doig of the Yeti they saw.

With this sight, the adventurers thought that the creatures acted like typical persons and that they should not be feared. But eventually, fears set in due to the creatures' massive build, they decided to walk away stealthily to avoid conflict.

What may very well have been a description of the huge, and reportedly extremely dangerous and violent, Nyalmo came from Charles Stonor, a former assistant curator of the London Zoo in England, who embarked on a quest for the truth of the Yeti in December 1953, an expedition that was organized and funded by the British *Daily Mail* newspaper. While in Darjeeling, Stonor was told of a creature known as the Thloh-Mung that, with hindsight, may very well have been the Nyalmo.

The story told to Stonor went like this:

Long ago there was a beast in our mountains, known to our forefathers as the Thloh-Mung, meaning in our language Mountain Savage. Its cunning and ferocity were so great as to be a match for anyone who encountered it. It could always outwit our Lepcha hunters, with their bows and arrows. The Thloh-Mung was said to live alone, or with a very few of its kind; and it went sometimes on the ground, and sometimes in the trees.

The account continued: "It was found only in the higher mountains of our country. Although it was made very like a man, it was covered with long, dark hair, and was more intelligent than a monkey, as well as being larger.

It seems that, to a significant degree, the beasts were fighting for their very survival: "The people became more in number, the forest and wild country less; and the Thloh-Mung disappeared. But many people say they are still to be found in the mountains of Nepal, away to the west, where the Sherpa people call them the Yeti."

Ohio Sasquatch

"**B**igfoot Sightings Scare Socks Off Pair" was the eye-catching headline that leapt out of the pages of the June 24, 1980, edition of the *Ohio Daily News* that was published out of Dayton. It so happens that Ohio has a long history of reports of hairy man-beasts, some of which date back to the nineteenth century. The article began: "Does Logan County have a 'Big Foot' [sic] stalking its wooded hills between West Mansfield and the Union County Line?"

It was a question prompted by something intriguing that occurred only days earlier. An off-duty police officer, Ray Quay, who worked out of Russell Point, ran into a huge, seven-foot-tall Sasquatch in his barn late at night—(the man's barn, not Bigfoot's). The officer was so certain about what he had seen that he was willing to speak on the record, rather than under a cloak of anyonymity. Quay's encounter was quickly the subject of an investigation by sheriff's deputies. The exact location of Quay's encounter was adjacent to a stretch of road near West Mansfield. Not surprisingly, Quay told the press he was "dumbfounded" by what he had seen.

> A number of clawed, four-toed prints were found in the direct area, measuring sixteen inches in length and four inches in width.

He also informed the media:

I was unloading eight pigs I had bought about 11 P.M. I shut off the light in the barn and went around the corner to see what my two dogs were raising Cain about. They never bark when I'm around. I stepped around the corner of the barn and saw this hairy animal. I thought it was a man so I hollered at him. It took off and I've got some weeds out back I haven't mowed and they are waist high or higher and the creature went through them with no problem.

Four deputies responded and scoured the area. Although the beast was not found, another witness was: Patrick Poling, who lived east of West Mansfield. Two nights later, he, too, saw a massive, hairy ape-like creature that resembled the description provided by Officer Quay. The monster may have remained elusive, but its tracks certainly weren't. A number of clawed, four-toed prints were found in the direct area, measuring sixteen inches in length and four inches in width. Whatever the beast was, it came and went in rapid fashion, leaving nothing but a stunned and frightened neighborhood in its wake.

Ohio's "Gorilla"

The following account, which appeared in the pages of the January 23, 1869, edition of the *Minnesota Weekly Record*, sounds as bizarre as it does unlikely. That doesn't mean it's not true, however. Under the eye-catching headline of "A Gorilla in Ohio", it reads thus:

> Gallipolis [Ohio] is excited over a wild man, who is reported to haunt the woods near that city. He goes naked, is covered with hair, is gigantic in height, and "his eyes start from their sockets." A carriage, containing a man and daughter, was attacked by him a few days ago. He is said to have bounded at the father, catching him in a grip like that of a vice, hurling him to the earth, falling on him and endeavoring to bite and scratch like a wild animal.

The story continues:

> The struggle was long and fearful, rolling and wallowing in the deep mud, suffocated, sometimes beneath his adversary, whose burning and maniac eyes glared into his own with murderous and savage intensity. Just as he was about to become exhausted from his exertions, his daughter, taking courage at the imminent danger of her parent, snatched up a rock and hurling it at the head of her father's would be murderer, was fortunate enough to put an end to the struggle by striking him somewhere about the ear.

Evidently that worked, and the terrifying incident came to a sudden halt in decidedly docile fashion: "The creature was not stunned, but feeling unequal to further exertion, slowly got up and retired into the neighboring copse that skirted the road."

Old Ned's Devil

In a somewhat strange and roundabout way, the following story has a connection to both me and to the Man-Monkey of England's Shropshire Union Canal (*see* "Man-Monkey of the Shropshire Union Canal"). It was a story that came to me via my father, Frank Redfern, who got it from a close friend of his named Eddie. The two of them, to this very day, work together on weekends as volunteer guides at a military aerospace museum at Royal Air Force Cosford, in Shropshire, England. Eddie knows that I have a somewhat unusual job and passion, and a few years ago he shared with my father a story, the origins of which date back to the nineteenth century and to Eddie's great-uncle.

That the story related to an incident involving something that was rumored to be an out-of-place monkey roaming around just outside the English city of Birmingham certainly made me take notice, since I grew up less than ten miles from Birmingham. Here is the story, in the words of legendary cryptozoologist and friend Dr. Karl Shuker—the author of *Karl Shuker's Alien Zoo* and many more titles—with whom I shared the known details in 2007:

> Around the end of the nineteenth century, Eddie's great-uncle Ned was driving a pony and trap on Rolfe Street, Smethwick, late one night when he heard some strange noises behind him. Suddenly, a weird-looking animal leapt out at him, but he supposedly fought it off with his horse-whip. The creature was killed, placed in a glass case, and displayed in the Blue Gate pub on Rolfe Street for some time, where the locals dubbed it "Old Ned's Devil." Sadly, however, this mystifying specimen, for which no morphological description exists, apparently vanished years ago, and nothing more is known of it.

Professor Carl Chinn, a writer, educator, columnist, historian, and radio presenter, is an expert on the history of Black Country. Karl Shuker consulted Chinn about Ned's Devil.

The story, of course, with its attendant tale of the man sat atop a trap and striking the beast with his whip, is incredibly reminiscent of the January 1879 saga of the Man-Monkey at Bridge 39 on the Shropshire Union Canal, which means we cannot rule out the possibility that, in some poorly understood fashion, the tale of old Ned's Devil might be a distorted story of the beast of the Shropshire Union Canal. But, for now anyway, let's give it some degree of benefit of the doubt.

Recognizing the potential significance of the affair, Karl Shuker began to make inquiries of his own. He wrote about it on his blog, in the hope it might bring forth additional data (it did not), and he also emailed the scant details to Professor Carl Chinn, the leading historian of the Black Country, which encompasses such locales as Sandwell, Dudley, Wolverhampton, Walsall, and the outskirts of Birmingham. Unfortunately, even the attempts of Professor Chinn failed to open any more doors, and, today, the story remains very much in stalemate mode, just as it was when Eddie told my father in 2006.

Orang-Cooboo and Orang-Googoo

Long before the Orang-pendek (*see* "Orang-pendek of Sumatra") was on anyone's radar, there was talk of other entities inhabiting the jungles of Sumatra. In his 1784 book, *The History of Sumatra*, William Marsden told a fascinating story. Marsden—who worked for the East India Company—said:

In the course of my inquiries among the natives, concerning the aborigines of the island, I have been informed of two different species of people dispersed in the woods, and avoiding all communication with the other inhabitants. They are called the Orang Cooboo and the Orang Googoo.

Marsden said that both species existed in significant numbers, particularly so in the regions between Palembang and Jambie. He also commented on stories he had heard, specifically concerning how some of the creatures had been captured and used as slaves, and how a man at Laboon had wed a "tolerably handsome Cooboo girl."

According to Marsden, both the Cooboo and the Googoo possessed a language and fed "promiscuously" on just about anything and everything they could get their hands on, including deer, snakes, and wild hogs. As for their appearance, Marsden described the Googoo as being far fiercer in nature than the Cooboo and added that their bodies were covered in long hair. More controversially, Marsden added that:

There have not been above two or three instances of their being met with by the people of Laboon and one of these was entrapped many years ago.... He had children by a Laboon woman, who were also more hairy than the common race.

Marsden concluded:

The reader will bestow what measure of faith he thinks due, on this relation, the veracity of which I do not pretend to vouch for. It probably has some foundation in truth but is exaggerated in the circumstances.

My good friend and former zookeeper Richard Freeman says of this saga:

The Orang Cooboo of which Marsden speaks are, in fact, the Kubu people, the aboriginal inhabitants of Sumatra. The idea of an Orang-pendek—if indeed it is an anthropoid ape—mating with a human woman and her bearing its children is absurd, but it is a folkloric motif found wherever hairy, man-like creatures are reported. The story has analogues in stories of the Yeti, Sasquatch, the almasty of central Asia, the di-di of South America, and many others.

Astonishingly, Sumatra appears to be filled to the brim with mysterious, hairy hominids, many clearly displaying notable differences in their appearances. It is, of course, possible that all of the reports can be attributed to the Orang-pendek and nothing else. On the other hand, however, some cases do appear to imply the presence of at least several kinds of unknown ape on Sumatra. Two classic examples come from a highly credible source, L. C. Westenenk, who served as the governor of Sumatra in the early twentieth century. Of the first case, which occurred in 1910, Westenenk said:

A boy from Padang employed as an overseer by Mr. van H ... had to stake the boundaries

William Marsden (1754–1836) was an English orientalist and linguist who was one of the first Westerners to make a serious study of Indonesia.

of a piece of land for which a long lease had been applied. One day he took several coolies into the virgin forest on the Barissan Mountains near Loeboek Salasik. Suddenly he saw, some 15m away, a large creature, low on its feet, which ran like a man. It was very hairy and was not an Orang-utan; but its face was not like an ordinary man's.

Clearly, the reference to a "large creature" does not fit the description of Orang-pendek, which is of distinctly small stature. The next case that Westenenk heard of took place seven years later, in 1917. The witness was one Mr. Oostingh, a coffee-plantation owner based in Dataran. The location was the forest of Boekit Kaba, where Oostingh encountered something remarkable. Westenenk made careful note of Oostingh's exact words:

Oostingh compared the creature he saw to perhaps being like a large siamang because the beast had very long arms.

[The creature's] body was as large as a medium-sized native's and he had thick square shoulders, not sloping at all. The color was not brown, but looked like black earth, a sort of duty black, more grey than black. He clearly noticed my presence. He did not so much as turn his head, but stood up on his feet: he seemed quite as tall as I, about 1.75m.

Oostingh then suddenly became deeply concerned by the strange beast in his midst:

Then I saw that it was not a man, and I started back, for I was not armed. The creature took several paces, without the least haste, and then, with his ludicrously long arm, grasped a sapling, which threatened to break under his weight, and quietly sprang into a tree, swinging in great leaps alternately to right and to left.

For those who might be inclined to think that Oostingh encountered nothing stranger than an orangutan, it's important to note what he had to say next:

My chief impression was and still is "What an enormously large beast!" It was not an Orangutan; I had seen one of these large apes before at the *Artis*, the Amsterdam Zoo. It was more like a monstrously large siamang, but a siamang has long hair, and there was no doubt it had short hair. I did not see the face, for, indeed, it never once looked at me.

Orange-Red-Colored Sasquatch

"**D**ear Sir, My name is James Meacham, I read the article that you wrote for *True Magazine*," began Meacham in a 1960 letter to Bigfoot investigator Ivan T. Sanderson. The letter continued:

I have been planning on going to California in the same area that your article was about. I was a little surprised to read about such a creature as an Abominable Snowman living so close to where I intended to visit. I have always liked to explore places that other people care little about.

I would like to know all you can tell me about this creature if you can tell anything more than you did in the article. I am sure a man of your standing must have more information about this subject than was in those few pages. I will gladly pay the postage on the information you can send. I cannot offer more because I am not working at the present.

I have met a few strange things in my life; as I am still young, there are many more I will probably see. I would like to know if you can tell me anything about a creature that looks like a small ape or a large monkey that has hair the color of fur a reddish orange color. I saw such a creature when I was 15. A friend was with me but did not see it. Whatever it was did not have a tail like a monkey but it did swing like one by its arms.

This may sound like something that I thought I saw but really didn't which I would believe except for a few details. I had a .22 caliber semi-automatic with me. I watched this thing for about 5 minutes so I have to believe it. I put fourteen .22 long-rifle shells into whatever it was. From where I was standing I couldn't have missed. We found 1 bullet in the tree trunk so 13 of them hit it. The part that sounds more impossible is that whatever it was, did not even move while 13 bullets went into it. If I had missed all 14 bullets would have gone into the tree trunk. I have told many people about this but nobody believes it. We found a few hairs where I had shot, but nothing else except the bullet. There was not a trace of blood.

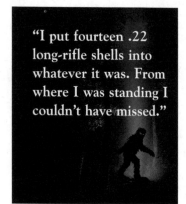

"I put fourteen .22 long-rifle shells into whatever it was. From where I was standing I couldn't have missed."

My partner thinks it was a squirrel but no squirrel grows that big. If it had been one, 2 of those bullets would have stopped it dead. Whatever it was did not even move till I headed for the tree. It traveled through those trees like an express train. I could hear the leaves rattle but could not see it. I searched for it for a long time after that but never saw it again. No one in that area knows anything about it or has ever seen it.

It had a cry that was enough to drive a person crazy. That was almost 3 years ago and I still wake up in my sleep sometimes when that sound comes back to me. If you can give me any advice as to what it could have been I will greatly appreciate it. If I had not shot it myself I would not believe it, not being able to find any blood.

I know you must receive a lot of letters about this sort of thing, but all I want to know is what animal in a marsh near Jackson, Tenn. could hold 13 long-rifle shells without even moving till you start to come after it? That is what started me looking for things most people think cannot possibly exist. Yours truly, James M. Meacham.

Orang-lecho

*See: **Mysterious Jungle Races of Sumatra***

Orang-pendek of Sumatra

Next to Bigfoot and the Abominable Snowman, probably the most talked about cryptid ape is the Orang-pendek, a small, bipedal creature that dwells in the thick forests of Sumatra. Although expeditions to find the creature have come to the fore in the last couple of decades, the people of Sumatra have a history and lore of the animal that date back to the beginnings of recorded history on the island.

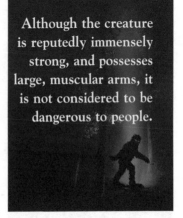

Although the creature is reputedly immensely strong, and possesses large, muscular arms, it is not considered to be dangerous to people.

Given that the Orang-pendek walks upright, just as we do, and stands at a height of four and a half to five feet, its name is highly appropriate. In English, it translates to "short man." Most witnesses to the creature describe it as having black or brown hair, but a minority of cases have also reported a somewhat reddish colored hair as well. Also echoing the idea of the Orang-pendek having somewhat human qualities, it is sometimes said to have a head of long, flowing hair extending to the shoulders—but which may actually be something more akin to a mane.

Not only do the Orang-pendek do an excellent job of avoiding people, while living, hunting, and feeding in the thick, mysterious forests, by all accounts they do a good job of avoiding each other, too. Indeed, most reports describe a creature that seems to be overwhelmingly solitary—aside, of course, from when it's mating. This differs from many apes, which are highly social animals that live in groups. Interestingly, however, the image of Orang-pendek being a loner very closely mirrors the life of Bigfoot, another anomalous ape seen more often than not on its own.

Although the creature is reputedly immensely strong, and possesses large, muscular arms, it is not considered to be dangerous to people. Certainly most witnesses who have encountered the beast at close quarters have said that when it is seen it tries to escape, rather than going on the attack. That said, there are a few reports of Orang-pendek hurling stones and rocks at people, but such reports are definitely in the minority. The Orang-pendek's diet is said to consist of vegetables and fruit, followed by tubers and fish.

A study of the history of the people of Sumatra demonstrates that the existence of small, hairy, human-like animals on the island has been accepted for centuries. That different regions have different names for the creatures has led to an interesting concept: that there might be more than one kind of cryptid ape on Sumatra. Of course, the likelihood is that despite the differences in name, the animals are one and the same. That is far from certain, however, chiefly because some of the reports from Sumatra describe animals as ape-like, whereas others resemble humans, both physically and in terms of their actions.

The long list of witnesses to the Orang-pendek is filled with highly credible individuals. In the summer of 1927, the Orang-pendek was encountered by A. H. W. Cramer, who was employed by a plantation company and who got within thirty feet of the creature, near Kerinci. The animal was short and was noted for its long hair and its eerily human-like footprints.

Not long afterwards, Sergeant-Major Van Esch of the Topographical Service had his own sighting, near a large, jungle-surrounded cliff in Surulangun. As the creature—seemingly oblivious to the presence of Van Esch—sauntered along, the Sergeant-Major could see its huge, muscular chest, wide head, dark skin, and large fangs.

> "From further examination the print did not match any known primate species and I can conclude that this points towards there being a large unknown primate in the forests of Sumatra."

A respected explorer named Benedict Allen heard numerous stories of sightings of the Orang-pendek during the Second World War. One of them concerned the rare sight of an entire group of Orang-pendek violently hurling sticks at workmen on the Trans-Sumatran Highway.

There is no doubt, however, that the most important figure in the controversial saga of the Orang-pendek is Debbie Martyr. Her quest to uncover the truth of the Orang-pendek began in the latter part of the 1980s. In July 1989, Martyr visited Sumatra as a travel writer. While Martyr was camped on the slopes of Mount Kerinci, her guide told her of the Orang-pendek—and that he had even seen the creature on a couple of occasions.

It was, for Martyr, the beginning of an extensive study for the truth of the Orang-pendek, a study that has resulted in the collection of notable evidence and even a firsthand encounter. Among the evidence was the cast of what was believed to be the print of an Orang-pendek. It was shared with Dr. David Chivers, of the University of Cambridge, England, who commented that:

> ... the cast of the footprint taken was definitely an ape with a unique blend of features from gibbon, orang-utan, chimpanzee, and human. From further examination the print did not match any known primate species and I can conclude that this points towards there being a large unknown primate in the forests of Sumatra.

Most significant of all was Martyr's own sighting of such an animal, which she describes as follows:

> I saw it in the middle of September, I had been out here [on Sumatra] for four months.... When I saw it, I saw an animal that didn't look like anything in any of the books I had read, films I had seen, or zoos I had seen. It did indeed walk rather like a person and that was a shock.

She added that, in terms of appearance, the Orang-pendek was a "relatively small, immensely strong, non-human primate.... It is built like a boxer, with immense upper body strength…. It was a gorgeous color, moving bipedally and trying to avoid being seen."

Richard Freeman, the zoological director of the Centre for Fortean Zoology, believes that it is only a matter of time before the existence of Orang-pendek is proved, once and for all, and conclusively.

Orang-pendek, the Centre for Fortean Zoology Expedition, 2009

On September 3, 2009, Richard Freeman, the zoological director of the Centre for Fortean Zoology, emailed me the following information:

> After two previous expeditions to the Indonesian island of Sumatra on the track of the upright walking ape know as orang-pendek (short man) the CFZ will be returning for a third expedition beginning on September the 13th.

> Adam Davis, Dr. Chris Clark, Dave Archer and myself will be spending two weeks in the jungle in search of the orang-pendek. Past expeditions have concentrated on Gunung Tuju (the lake of seven peaks) in Kerinchi National Park. This time the better part of the expedition will be spent with the Kubu people in the lowland jungles. Back in 2004 Chris and I spent a day with these people and Nylam their chief.

> The Kubu are the original inhabitants of Sumatra. The modern Indonesians arrived relatively recently from Malaya. They are far taller and more slender than the average Sumatran. They have oriental features but the men have curly hair almost like Africans. Until recently the Kubu live totally wild in the jungle. Now they have houses but still spend months on end in the deep rain forest.

> Nylam told us of his own encounter with an orang-pendek a few years back. He and his warriors had also seen ten meter long serpents that they described as having horns like an ox! We will be working with the Kubu to search for orang-pendek and the horned serpents (the Kubu call them Nagas).

> Apparently there have been a number of sightings of the short man in the area recently. We intend to make our HQ in the "garden," a semi cultivated area that abuts the true jungle. We hope to record some of their culture and folklore as next to nothing has been written on Kubu beliefs. Towards the end of the trip we will return to Gunung Tuju where the creature has also been seen recently.

> They say three's the charm and third time lucky so keep your fingers crossed!

Richard Freeman is the director of the Centre for Fortean Zoology in England.

On September 29, there was a significant breakthrough in the CFZ's hunt for the Orang-pendek, as Freeman revealed:

We are just back from the jungle and have amazing news but don't release it till tomorrow when we will be out of Indonesia. Dave Archer and Sahar the guide saw orang-pendek! It was squatting in a tree around 100 feet from them. It was the size of an adult chimp and dark brown in color. They could not see the face, hands or feet. Its head was shaped more like a gorilla's than a chimp's and it lacked the long mane of hair some witnesses describe. A darker strip was visible on the back. It had broad shoulders and the upper half of the body, including the head, was 40 inches (we measured afterwards). The coat was thick, like a mountain gorilla's.

We have hair samples and rattan that the orang-pendek was chewing on. Sahar saw it jump down and walk away on two legs. Dave missed a photo opportunity when he tried to get a better vantage point. We found and photographed very clear footprints in a different area but could not cast them as we couldn't get hold of any plaster of Paris. We collected many hairs from this area.

Dampness screwed the moving camera's battery. It was virtually dead within 48 hours of us reaching Gunung Tuju. We took lots of photos. Dave's moving camera was drained by humidity too. We have some film but not a vast amount. We filmed a big cat sequence.

Loads of adventures happened including almost sinking in flooded canoes, thinking we had OP cornered up a tree and clothes being soaked in raw sewage! The rattan will probably have OP DNA on it like a mouth swab. These are the best results from any expedition ever.

Freeman's news was hastily followed by a press release from the CFZ's director, Jonathan Downes:

The Centre for Fortean Zoology (CFZ) is the world's largest mystery animal research group. A group of four British explorers and scientists from the CFZ have just returned from the jungles of Sumatra having spent two weeks in the rain-forest on the track of the orang-pendek, an unknown species of upright walking ape.

They have brought back some incredible news.

CFZ member Dave Archer and local guide Sahar saw the creature at a distance of around 100 feet as it squatted in a tree. Dave describes it as broad shouldered, with a large head, black skin and dark brown hair. A line of darker fur was visible on the spine. He likened the coat of the creature to that of a mountain gorilla. Sahar saw the creature jump down from the tree and walk away on its hind legs. It was the size of an adult male chimpanzee.

Next to the tree was some rattan vine that the animal was apparently chewing. Expedition leader Adam Davis has preserved part of the plant in ethanol in the hope that it contains cells from the animal's mouth.

The team also found and photographed several sets of tracks made by creatures. Expedition zoologist Richard Freeman confirmed that they matched no known creature in the area. The prints were six to seven inches long with a narrow heel and wider front. The big toe is well separated.

> **"The prints were six to seven inches long with a narrow heel and wider front. The big toe is well separated."**

Hair samples were taken from a tree close to the tracks. A number of the hairs contain medullas that the team hopes will contain orang-pendek DNA. The samples will shortly be sent off to experts around the world for analysis.

If the samples turn out to be from a new species Freeman suggests the scientific name of *Pongo martyri* in honor of the English researcher Debbie Martyr who has done more than anyone else to look into this zoological mystery.

The CFZ has plans for further expeditions, which they hope will vindicate their quest to unravel the mystery of the Orang-pendek.

Orestimba Creek Monster

In 1870, a California-based newspaper, the *Antioch Ledger*, published the fascinating account of a man named de Groot, a hunter who may very well have had a close encounter of the large and hairy kind. The incident reportedly occurred in the previous year at Orestimba Creek, Stanislaus County, California. As with many of the accounts cited in this book, it clearly demonstrates that sightings of anomalous, large apes in the United States are nothing new.

De Groot said:

Last fall I was hunting in the mountains about 20 miles south of here, and camped five or six days in one place, as I have done every season for the past 15 years. Several times I returned to camp, after a hunt, and saw that the ashes and charred sticks from the fireplace had been scattered about. An old hunter notices such things, and very soon gets curious to know the cause. Although my bedding and traps and little stores were not disturbed, as I could see, I was anxious to learn who or what it was that so regularly visited my camp, for clearly the half burnt sticks and cinders could not scatter themselves about.

I saw no tracks near the camp, as the hard ground covered with leaves would show none. So I started in the circle around the place, and 300 yards off, in damp sand, I struck the tracks of a man's feet, as I supposed, bare and of immense size. Now I was curious, sure, and I resolved to lay for the barefooted visitor. I accordingly took a position on the hillside, about 60 or 70 feet from the fire, and, securely hid in the brush, I waited and watched. Two hours and more I sat there and wondered if the owner of the feet would come again, and whether he imagined what an interest he had created in my inquiring mind, and finally what possessed him to be prowling about there with no shoes on.

"... I saw the object of my solicitude standing beside the fire and looking suspiciously around. It was the image of a man, but could not have been human."

The fireplace was on my right, and the spot where I saw the track was on my left, hid by the bushes. It was in this direction that my attention was mostly directed, thinking the visitor would appear there, besides, it was easier to sit and face that way. Suddenly I was surprised by a shrill whistle, such as boys produced with two fingers under their tongues, and turning quickly, I [exclaimed]: "Good God!" as I saw the object of my solicitude standing beside the fire and looking suspiciously around. It was the image of a man, but could not have been human.

I was never so benumbed with astonishment before. The creature, whatever it was, stood fully 5 feet high, and disproportionately broad and square at the fore shoulders, with arms of great length. The legs were very short and the body long. The head was small compared with the rest of the creature, and appeared to be set upon the shoulders without a neck. The whole was covered with dark brown and cinnamon colored hair, quite long on some parts, that on the head standing in a shock and growing close down to the eyes, like a Digger Indian's.

As I looked he threw his head back and whistled again, and then stopped and grabbed a stick from the fire. This he swung round, until the fire at the end had gone out, when he repeated the maneuver. I was dumb, almost, and could only look. Fifteen minutes I sat and watched him as he whistled and scattered my fire about. I could easily have put a bullet through his head, but why should I kill him? Having amused himself, apparently, as he desired, with my fire, he started to go, and, having gone a short distance returned, and was joined by another—a female, unmistakably when both turned and walked past me within 20 yards of where I sat, and disappeared in the brush.

I could not have had a better opportunity for observing them, as they were unconscious of my presence. Their only object in visiting my camp seemed to be to amuse themselves with swinging lighted sticks around. I have told this story many times since then, and it has often raised an incredulous smile; but I have met one person who has seen the mysterious creatures, and a dozen of whom have come across their tracks at various places between here and Pacheco Pass.

Of particular interest in this case is the height of the Bigfoot. Or, rather, its profound lack of height. At just around five feet tall, it hardly resembled the classic seven-to-eight-feet-tall Bigfoot of the Pacific Northwest. Unless, of course, what de Groot encountered was a juvenile Bigfoot. That the creature seemed to enjoy playing with the fire, and whistling at the same time, is, perhaps, an indication it was, indeed, a youngster, roaming around and having a bit of fun.

Ouija Boards, Séances, and Sasquatch

The late Stan Gooch, the author of a number of books, including *Creatures from Inner Space* and *The Paranormal*, told of his encounter with what seemed to be a Neanderthal man at a séance held at a house in the English city of Coventry in the 1950s. In Gooch's very own words, during the course of the séance, something both primitive and primeval materialised before the shocked attendees:

> This was a crouching ape-like shape, which became clearer as the moments passed. I guess it approximated to most people's idea of what an ancient cave man would look like. Yet one could not make out too much detail—the eyes were hidden, for example. It stood in half shadow, watching us, breathing heavily as if nervous. I must say, though, that I sensed rather than heard the breathing. I could not decide whether our visitor was wearing the skin of some animal, or whether it had a rough coat of hair of its own.

All attempts to question the man-beast, and have it join the circle, were utterly fruitless, and, eventually, it melted away into nothingness. Nevertheless, Gooch never forgot the experience and later mused upon the notion that what he had seen on that fateful evening was a "classic Neanderthal."

Rather interestingly, Gooch, in his later years, penned a number of books, including *The Neanderthal Question* and *The Neanderthal Legacy*, which theorized that *Homo sapiens* are the result of a hybrid mix of Cro-Magnon man and Neanderthal man.

A somewhat similar event occurred in 1985, in Rochester, New York. The story comes from a woman named Laura who, at the time, was in her mid-teens. On one particular Friday night, when her parents were out for the evening and weren't due back until well after midnight, Laura arranged for several of her friends to come over for a slumber party. Laura wasn't aware until her friends arrived that her friend Brooke brought a Ouija board for additional entertainment.

For the four girls—Laura, Alison, Brooke, and Beth—it was the perfect way to have a diversion from school, homework, and boyfriend dramas. By Laura's own admission, none of the girls had any clue about how to use a Ouija board in the slightest. In fact, Brooke aside, not a single one of them had even seen such a board in person

Could using a Ouija board have somehow summoned a Bigfoot to come to a home in Rochester, New York?

before. Great fun resulted from asking the board about sex, boys, and their future escapades. Things got a bit more serious when each one attempted to contact a dead relative: somewhat of a dark and unsettling atmosphere briefly enveloped the four friends, causing them to suspect they had opened a paranormal portal to something malevolent. Quite possibly, that is exactly what happened.

Although nothing else strange occurred that night, by the next day Laura was unable to shake off the odd sensation that had the girls briefly concerned the night before. The next night, something terrifying occurred, which, in hindsight, Laura was convinced resulted from using the Ouija board.

Just after going to bed, Laura heard from outside the window the shrill, banshee-like wail of a creature she had never heard before. Since the house backed onto woodlands, she was used to seeing wildlife, but this was clearly something different. She peered out of her bedroom window, into the heart of the darkness and the old oaks, but could see nothing.

It was in the early hours of the morning that something terrifying occurred: an abomination was about to put in an appearance. Laura was woken from her sleep by a noxious, sickly smell that filled her bedroom. She was about to turn on the light when, thanks to light given off by the moon's illumination, she saw something standing in the corner of the room.

Laura, hardly surprisingly, tried to scream but nothing came out. It was, she said, as if something was preventing her from making any noise; it was as if her mind and body were under the control of the awful, shadowy thing that glared at her from the darkness. To Laura's even greater terror, the beast began to move towards the bed, slowly and silently. She could then, finally, see what it was that had invaded her bedroom: it was a large, black-haired beast that looked like a cross between a man and a huge ape. Its thick, long arms hung by its side, and its silvery eyes stared at her, showing no sign of emotion whatsoever.

The creature then moved closer still, around to the side of the bed and bending forward. Its face was barely six inches from Laura's, at which point she could see that the thing before her was a form of primitive human, or a classic ape-man. For a few moments—but which, to Laura, seemed like minutes—the creature continued to stare, not making any sounds or movements at all. Then, it retreated into the shadows of the corner of the room, not once taking its eyes off Laura. Finally, the ape-man melted into the shadows and was gone. Oddly, the sickening smell, despite having dominated the room throughout the encounter, also vanished in moments.

To this day, Laura believes that the manifestation of the spectral, Bigfoot-like thing was directly linked to the previous night's events when the girls chose—probably most unwisely—to open a door to what might be termed "the other side." Laura's theory is that the creature had no intention of hurting her, but appeared as a warning not to get involved in things one has no control over—in this case, dabbling recklessly with a Ouija board. You may not be surprised to learn that Laura's 1985 experience with the board was both her first and last time.

Pamir Mountain Monster

A massive range that covers parts of China, Pakistan, Kyrgyzstan, Afghanistan, and Tajikistan, the Pamir Mountains are home to a number of accounts of Bigfoot-like animals of both a short and large stature. A particularly credible case that falls into the former category occurred in the latter part of 1925. General Mikhail Stepanovich Topilski was leading a unit in search of a pocket of anti-Soviet guerrillas who were hiding out in the western segment of the Pamir range.

While hunting down the guerrillas, Topilski and his party heard a number of stories from local villagers of creatures that dwelled in the more isolated regions of the mountains and which displayed both human- and ape-like qualities. They were somewhat doubtful of the tales—at least, until they came across human-like footprints negotiating decidedly treacherous snow-covered cliffs and slopes.

Things really came to a head when Topilski and his men finally caught up with the guerrillas, who were hiding out in a large cave. A firefight began, resulting in multiple deaths among the guerrillas, some by bullets and others by falling ice provoked by the firing. Among the survivors, however, was a man who told a strange tale to Topilski and his team. He described weird, ape-man-like creatures that had attacked the guerrillas with clubs, one of which, the man said, was killed in the ice fall.

Topilski wasted no time in ordering his men to dig deep and find the corpse. They did. Topilski described the shocking discovery of the creature as follows:

The body belonged to a male creature 165–175cm tall, elderly or even old, judging by the greyish color of the hair in several places. The chest was

In 1925 a unit of Soviet soldiers led by General Mikhail Stepanovich Topilski were looking for guerillas in the Pamir Mountains in Central Asia, where they found a dead ape-man creature.

covered with brownish hair and the belly with greyish hair. The color of the face was dark and the creature had neither beard nor moustache. The dead creature lay with its eyes open and its teeth bared. The prominent cheekbones made the face resemble the Mongol type of face. The creature had a very powerful broad chest and well developed muscles. We didn't find any anatomical differences between it and a man.

Topilski was all set to skin the animal and bring its hide back to civilization. He chose not to, however, as a result of the eerie, human-like qualities that the creature possessed. As a result, Topilski ordered his men to bury the corpse. Interestingly, when, shortly afterwards, Topilski's team met with the Baluchi people of the area, the latter expressed amazement that the group had not all fallen victim to the marauding and ferocious man-beasts.

Another account, from geologist B. M. Zdorik, focused on a creature of the Pamir Mountains known as the Dev. In the fall of 1929, Zdorik learned of the Dev: "a thickset man" that lived in the mountains, that walked in bipedal fashion, but that was "covered with brown or black hair." Reportedly, an adult Dev was captured on the slopes near Tutkaul in 1928. For around two months the animal-man was kept prisoner and fed on raw meat and barley cakes. One day it escaped and fled back to its home, high in the wild mountains, never to be seen again.

Given that the Pamir Mountains cover parts of Pakistan, it is likely that what has been seen in the mountains is the same creature, known as the Bar-manu, reported in other parts of Pakistan. As recently as 1987, reports of encounters with this particularly violent monster have surfaced, specifically from around northern Kashmir.

Pantyffynon Man of the Woods

On April 29, 2009, the United Kingdom's *Daily Mail* newspaper published an article with the eye-catching and lengthy headline "Police Launch Hunt for 'Wolfman' behind Mini Crimewave Who Lives on Rabbits and Berries in Woods." The *Mail's* article began in intriguing, scene-setting style: "The one man mini-crime wave is also suspected of a string of thefts of shopping from parked cars and clothes from washing lines during his furtive forays into the civilized world over the last two years."

Police have tried to catch him during searches on foot and have even sent up a helicopter with heat-seeking equipment to track him down, but he has so far always managed to avoid capture. He knows the miles of paths through the dense woodland near Ammanford, South Wales, where he lurks, so well that even when officers are on his trail, he manages to give them the slip. Abandoned hideouts made from board with plastic roofs have been found, suggesting he moves around to avoid arrest.

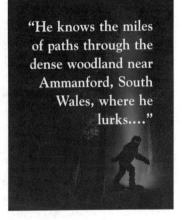

"He knows the miles of paths through the dense woodland near Ammanford, South Wales, where he lurks...."

In the tiny hamlet of Pantyffynon, which was one of the mystery-man's favorite hunting grounds, outraged and worried locals planned on taking action of their very own to seek out the strange and elusive man of the woods. Planning a course of attack combined the proactive approach taken by "V" in the *V for Vendetta* film and the breathless antics of torch-wielding eastern Europeans in old 1930s and 1940s black-and-white monster movies; the people of Pantyffynon were almost baying for the wild man's blood. One villager said, ominously: "We want him caught before something serious happens."

For their part, the local police vaguely vowed to apprehend the man "sooner or later" and loudly appealed to locals not to scour the woods themselves. As evidence of this, Sergeant Charles Gabe sternly warned any would-be heroes "not to take the law into their own hands or approach this man."

Sergeant Gabe added:

We've found one or two hides where we believe he has been sleeping. We think he catches rabbits and eats berries or whatever else he can get his hands on. But although we've had the police helicopter overhead using heat-seeking equipment we've still been unable to locate him. This is a massive thickly-wooded area—and one he obviously knows well. On one occasion a couple of our guys came close to nabbing him but he scarpered back into the woods. But we are sure he will be caught sooner or later.

When questioned for comment, local councilor Hugh Evans said:

It's a very strange case and no one seems to know who he is. But he must be a bit of a *Rambo* type and pretty tough to have survived the bitterly cold winter living out in the open. The area where he is living is thickly-wooded and forested—the sort of area where it is easy to disappear.

Evoking surreal imagery of some Stone Age-type character, the *Daily Mail* added: "'The Wolfman' lives in the woodland on an area of reclaimed coal slagheaps known locally as 'The Tips.'"

Meanwhile, a Dyfed-Powys police spokesman tactfully said, in typically bureaucratic terminology that was suggestive of far more than they were willing to impart at the time: "We want to question him over several alleged incidents."

For a while the wild man and his equally wild antics vanished—perhaps into the underground lair that many believed had become his home. He wasn't destined to stay buried for too long, however. In the latter part of 2010, the mystery man resurfaced from the heart of those dark woods.

"The hunt for a West Wales 'wolfman' is back on—after walkers stumbled across what is thought to be his lair," noted *Wales Online* on October 10, 2010. The "unknown vagrant," it was reported, was up to his old tricks, which led to the revelation that "officers from the Dyfed-Powys force this week confirmed they are looking into possible fresh sightings after walkers reported stumbling across a woodland shack stuffed with food, clothes and electrical equipment."

One of those who spoke publicly on the return of the wild man was John Jones, a builder from Pantyffynon, who told *Wales Online*:

> We've been told that some walkers found a tin shed full of food and clothes, so we assume that is one of his hideouts. Lots of people have been looking for where he is, but the woodland is so dense it's not an easy place to search. There have been one or two sightings of this longhaired, bearded person who is so scruffy and unkempt; he's like a wild man.

There was also talk of milk being stolen, of food taken from freezers in outside storage areas in the dead of night, and of what were intriguingly, but briefly, described as "odd sightings." But was the wild man simply some eccentric, solitary soul who had decided to leave the restrictive boundaries and conventions of society far behind him? Not everyone was quite so sure that's all he was.

Gwilym Games, a regional representative in Wales for Jonathan Downes's Centre for Fortean Zoology, noted, "There is a long history of werewolves in Wales and even an earlier mention in the Amman valley." Despite this undeniably intriguing aside, nothing else surfaced on this aspect of the mysterious matter, and once again the wild man vanished into obscurity, or, far more likely, into the heart of the thick woods that dominate the area.

The police continued on their plodding path of "making enquiries." They proved to be utterly fruitless. But there was one further development in the story. One week after the *Wales Online* article surfaced, Pantyffynon attorney Peter Rhys Jones said that the wild man was harmless, and was simply an ex-serviceman who Jones had once represented. Once again, things then went quiet for a while. But in 2012, there was a dramatic development in the story that confirmed what Rhys Jones had to say about the man's military background.

In February of that year, it was revealed that the man living wild was Wayne John Morgan, aged thirty-seven, formerly of the British Army and someone well-trained to survive in the harsh and unforgiving wilds of the Welsh outdoors. A police spokeswoman said, "He has not been seen by his family for four years, but now concerns have been raised about his welfare." He added that "as he is living rough, he may be hungry and on the look-out for food. If you are suspicious that any food items are missing from your stores, or whether any outbuildings such as garden sheds and garages have been disturbed, then please contact us."

Mike Lewis, editor of the *South Wales Guardian*, reacted to that news:

Some speculators thought that the Pantyffynon wild man might have been a werewolf of some kind.

> One magazine specializing in the paranormal even sent a reporter to assess whether this was a real-life werewolf.... But strip away the legend and what's left? A missing man, a police appeal and a worried family anxious for news. The *Guardian* has covered some strange stories during my five years at the helm, but the one about "The Wolfman" of Pantyffynnon tips must rank among the strangest.

By May, with still no news—despite fairly widespread, renewed media publicity—things were looking bleak. The local press highlighted the opinion of people in the area that there was "no chance" Morgan was still hiding in the woods—citing the then recent, bitterly cold weather as one reason—while his obviously very anxious family prayed and hoped for good news. At the time of writing, unfortunately, that is where matters still stand in this tragic and sad affair.

Pastrana, Julia

Julia Pastrana (1834–1860), a Spanish dancer, was a remarkably fine woman, but she had a thick masculine beard and a hairy forehead; she was photographed, and her stuffed skin was exhibited as a show; but what concerns us is that she had in both the upper and lower jaw an irregular double set of teeth, one row being placed within the other, of which Dr. Purland took a cast. As a result of her redundant teeth, her mouth projected and her face had a gorilla-like appearance.

Nineteenth century Spanish dancer Julia Pastrana likely suffered from the genetic conditions of gingival hyperplasia and hypertrichosis, which gave her an apelike appearance.

Those are the words of Charles Darwin, who formulated the theory of evolution. They were written in Darwin's 1868 book, *The Variation of Animals and Plants under Domestication*. Darwin's statement, quite understandably, gave rise to the theory that Pastrana was not entirely human, that she may have been part-human and part-gorilla. It's an outlandish claim, to be sure. But is it true? Let's see what we know about this intriguing woman and her unusual life.

Born in Sinaloa, northwestern Mexico, in 1834, Pastrana became famous as a result of time spent touring in what were insultingly known back then as "freak shows." Typically, the "freaks" were people with tragic deformities and genetic conditions that radically altered their physical appearances. Pastrana, however, was somewhat different, in the sense that dark rumors floated around that she was the product of a human and an ape.

Pastrana was reportedly found, by a man named Retes, working as a servant girl for the governor of Sinaloa. Author J. Tithonus Pednaud said of her:

While in New York, Julia attracted the attention of many scientific minds and media moguls. One newspaper described her as "terrifically hideous" and possessing a "harmonious voice"—which gives evidence that she sang during her exhibition. One of the members of Medical society to examine her was Dr. Alexander Mott who declared her "the most extraordinary beings of the present day" and "a hybrid between human and orangutan."

Jerry Bergman, who has studied the life of Pastrana, stated:

Some alleged that she was an Afro-American, implying that she was not an ape-women but a fraud. Obviously this allegation was not good for business, so her manager had her examined by a physician named Alexander B. Mott, who concluded that she was indeed a woman but a "hybrid." ...

To further bolster their claims for Julia, she also was examined by Cleveland physician S. Brainerd. It was not uncommon in the 1800s for physicians to be poorly trained, especially about genetic problems. The doctor compared Julia's hair to that of an African under a microscope, and concluded from this "test" that Julia contained "no trace of Negro blood." It was also concluded that she was part of a "distinct species."

The legend that Pastrana was half-human and half-ape was developing quickly. The man who really made Pastrana famous, however, was Lewis B. Lent, a showman who began his career when, at the age of nineteen, he was given a financial interest in Brown & Fogg's Circus, which later became known as the Zoological Institute. Lent then went on to establish Sands & Lent, a traveling show that had at its forefront those afflicted by a variety of distressing conditions. One of those who travelled with Lent was Pastrana, who performed song and dance routines for audiences who were amazed, shocked, and frightened.

Despite her undeniably savage appearance—ape-like jaws, protruding teeth, and a hair-covered body—Pastrana was highly intelligent and learned three languages. She was an excellent cook and liked to sew. She and Lent married and had a baby, who inherited Pastrana's genetic anomalies and unfortunately died only days after birth, in Moscow, Russia. Tragically, Pastrana died just a few more days later, as a result of complications brought on by her pregnancy.

That was not the end of the story. Displaying what might rightly be perceived as a decidedly cold-hearted response to the deaths of his wife and child, Lent had their corpses mummified and placed on display. Even more outrageous, Lent quickly found a replacement for Pastrana—dubbed Zenora Pastrana—and quickly made her wife number two. The story of the mummified mother and child is a curious one. The bodies of both were regularly displayed for decades in Lent's tours of the world. They subsequently surfaced in Norway, where they were stolen, but, fortunately, recovered by the police.

From 1976 onwards, the preserved corpses were held at the University of Oslo. They might very well have stayed there indefinitely, had it not been for the enterprising work of one woman. Artist Laura Anderson Barbata spent a great deal of time arguing that the bodies of mother and child should be returned to Mexico, and the pair should be given respectable burials. Eventually, Norwegian authorities agreed. The result was that, in 2013, the remains were transferred to Mexico.

On February 13, 2013, the BBC reported:

People flocked to the town of Sinaloa de Leyva on Tuesday where Julia Pastrana was laid to rest in a white coffin adorned with white roses.

"Imagine the aggression and cruelty of humankind she had to face, and how she overcame it. It's a very dignified story," said Sinaloa Governor Mario Lopez.

"A human being should not be the object of anyone," Father Jaime Reyes Retana told mourners.

Important questions remain: Was Julia Pastrana really the product of a human mother and an ape? Was she the offspring of a female ape and a human father? The answer—despite all of the rumors—is neither. It's likely that Pastrana suffered from at least two afflictions: gingival hyperplasia and hypertrichosis. The former causes deformity in the teeth, gums, and jaws, while the latter causes the body to develop excessive amounts of hair. The combined result was a woman who

> Displaying what might rightly be perceived as a decidedly cold-hearted response to the deaths of his wife and child, Lent had their corpses mummified and placed on display.

looked startlingly ape-like, which was further emphasized by her height of just four-and-a-half feet.

Patterson, Roger, Film of Bigfoot

Depending on one's personal perspective, it's either the best evidence that Bigfoot exists or it's one of the world's most enduring, outrageous hoaxes. It's a fascinating and controversy-filled piece of film footage, shot by Roger Patterson at Bluff Creek, California, in <u>October 1967.</u> It's also a piece of film upon which the Bigfoot research community cannot agree, since the entire matter is steeped in debate, claims, and counter-claims. Of only a couple of things can we be 100 percent certain: the film exists and it shows a large, humanoid figure in a forested setting. Beyond that, all bets are off. There's only one place to start: the beginning.

Roger Patterson was not merely someone who chanced upon a Bigfoot and who had no previous knowledge of the subject; actually, quite the opposite. His fascination for the creature began years earlier, evidenced by the book he published in 1966 titled *Do Abominable Snowmen of America Really Exist?* It did not change the world of Bigfoot research, but it did spur Patterson on to even greater levels.

It's important to understand what it was that brought Patterson and a friend, Bob Gimlin, to Bluff Creek on October 20, 1967. As someone who was deeply interested in the Bigfoot phenomenon, Patterson kept abreast of breaking news and sightings within the Sasquatch-seeking community. When Patterson heard of reports of creature sightings in and around the million-acre Six Rivers National Forest in northwest California, he and Gimlin hit the trail in search of Bigfoot. According to both men, that's exactly what they found, at a tributary of the Klamath River, one of the six rivers from which the forest takes its name.

There is some controversy surrounding the precise time at which the legendary film was taken, but there's little doubt that the footage was shot in the afternoon. According to both men's accounts, when they first saw the Bigfoot they were on horseback and passing a large, uprooted tree. They couldn't fail to see a big, dark-haired, humanoid creature semi-sitting, or crouching, adjacent to the creek. The presence of the beast caused Patterson's terrified horse to react in violent fashion, which made it difficult for him to extract his camera from a bag and start filming the creature.

The footage lasts for less than a minute, is significantly shaky in parts—due to Patterson being forced to follow the beast on foot—but, nevertheless, clearly shows what most people would assume to be a Bigfoot. That much is obvious, since Patterson was able to get fairly close to the animal as he filmed it. At one point, the crea-<u>ture glances back,</u> and we see that it is evidently <u>female,</u> since its breasts can clearly be seen. It also appears to be of a significant height. The footage comes to an end when the Bigfoot vanishes into the surrounding woods. In total, the whole encounter lasted less than two minutes. Patterson filmed, while Gimlin, armed with a rifle, kept a care-

A still from what is probably the most famous film footage of Bigfoot. Taken in 1967 by Roger Patterson, the film convinced many people this is an actual Sasquatch.

ful watch on the situation—at first on horseback and then on foot. The men did not give up that easily, however. Reportedly, Patterson and Gimlin tried to pursue the creature, eventually tracking it for around three miles, but never again seeing it. Of course, they did have the film as evidence of their astonishing encounter. But is it the real deal?

On the plus side, Bigfoot authority Loren Coleman notes that a number of respected Bigfoot authorities, including the late Grover Krantz, Jeff Meldrum, and John Green, "hold that the film is valid footage of an unknown primate." Coleman also rightly states that an examination of the film by the North American Science Institute—an examination that cost in excess of $70,000—concluded the footage was genuine. It was an examination that, in Coleman's words, "suggested that the creature's skin and musculature are what one would expect to find in a living animal, not in a hairy suit, however innovatively it was constructed."

Krantz noted that of the many people who commented positively on the film, two were Dmitri Donskoy and D. W. Grieve. Krantz said that both were "highly respected experts in the biomechanics of human locomotion at prestigious institutions." Krantz added that "Donskoy found the creature to be a very massive animal that is definitely not a human being." Grieve, said Krantz, remarked that if the footage was taken at a speed of 18 frames per second, as Patterson claimed, the figure in the film "exhibits a totally different pattern of gait and cannot be human."

On the other hand, a number of people have come forward, on the record, to claim either knowledge that the Patterson film was faked or actual participation in its making. First, there is the location, Bluff Creek, which is where an infamous Bigfoot hoaxer named Ray Wallace operated from. That Wallace and Patterson met is not in doubt.

In October 1997, the late Mark Chorvinsky, of *Strange Magazine*, wrote: "Ray Wallace has claimed that he knows who was in the Patterson suit. He will not give a name, but says that the person in the suit was a Yakima Indian."

More damning, Chorvinsky added:

Wallace also says that he told Roger Patterson where to film his Bigfoot. "Roger Patterson came [over] dozens of times pumping me on this Bigfoot," Ray Wallace explained to researcher Dennis Pilichis in 1982. I felt sorry for Roger Patterson. He told me that he had cancer of the lymph glands and he was desperately broke and he wanted to try to get something where he could have a little income. Well, he went down there just exactly where I told him. I told him, "You go down there and hang around on that bank. Stay up there and watch that spot." I told him where the trail was that went down to where that big rock was. I told him where he could get those pictures down there. Bluff Creek.

Of course, the fact that Wallace, who died in 2002, was a self-admitted hoaxer, means that anything he said on the subject of Bigfoot has to be treated with significant degrees of caution.

Certainly, the most controversial, and extensive, claim came from Bob Heironimus, whose story is told in Greg Long's 2004 book, *The Making of Bigfoot*. According to Heironimus, he was the man in the suit, a secret that he kept to himself for years, fearful of the possibility of legal ramifications, including the potential threat of fraud charges.

Certainly, at six foot, two inches, Heironimus is a tall man, but is he big enough to have pulled off a hoax and portrayed a creature that most pro-Patterson observers maintain is closer to seven feet in height? That is one of the major questions that surrounds Heironimus's assertions. Heironimus is not without his supporters: family members have backed up his account. He described, in detail, the nature of the alleged costume, how it was constructed, and the circumstances under which the filming allegedly took place. The Bigfoot believers roll their eyes at such claims.

Given the long passage of time that has gone by since October 1967, it seems unlikely that the matter will ever be resolved to the satisfaction of everyone. Of only one thing can the believers and the skeptics agree upon when it comes to the Patterson film: real or not, it has become perhaps the biggest piece of Bigfoot lore of all.

> ... a number of people have come forward, on the record, to claim either knowledge that the Patterson film was faked or actual participation in its making.

Peak District Primitive Creature

During the course of undertaking research for a book dealing with landscape-based mysteries, one informant told Andy Roberts, a well-known English authority on paranormal phenomena, of a terrifying mountain-based experience that occurred during the early 1960s. The source was a boy at the time, out with a friend to investigate one of the many aircraft wrecks from the Second World War that still, today even, litter the 2,000-foot-high Bleaklow plateau in the Derbyshire Peak District, England. While visiting the crash site, the man suddenly heard his friend shout. But the reason for his cry had nothing to do with the remains of old, wrecked aircraft.

The man told Roberts:

I looked and saw, all in one instant, grouse exploding out of the heather towards us, sheep and hares stampeding towards us and behind them,

Bleaklow plateau in the Derbyshire Peak District, England, is a barren, uninhabited area, but one without much tree cover. Nevertheless, paranormal authority Andy Roberts reported a Bigfoot-like creature there.

rolling at a rapid rate towards us from the direction of Hern Clough, a low bank of cloud or fog … but what was truly terrifying was that in the leading edge of the cloud bank—in it and striding purposefully towards us—was a huge shadow-figure, a man-like silhouette, but far bigger than a man, as high as the cloudbank, as high as a house. And the terror that hit me and was driving the birds and the animals and my friend was utterly overwhelming—like a physical blow—and I have never felt the like since!

The two boys had never heard of the very similar phenomenon of a sudden outbreak of all-encompassing fear that the Big Grey Man of Ben Macdhui provokes. Instead, the man's friend attributed the terrifying incident to "Th' owd Lad," a Pennine-based term for the Devil. The man continued his story with Roberts:

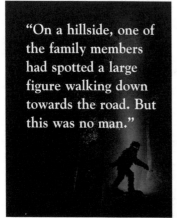

"On a hillside, one of the family members had spotted a large figure walking down towards the road. But this was no man."

We fled. We plunged over the crags above Gathering Hill—and every time I go back and look at those crags, I wonder why we didn't break our necks. We fled in mindless terror down that mountainside towards the Shelf Brook and Doctors Gate—and all the sheep and wildlife that could run or fly went careering down with us in utter panic. And then, about half way down, we seemed to run out into the sunlight—and it was all over! All of the panic was gone. The sheep stopped, put their heads down, and started to graze. Everything returned at once to normal. But back up there, on Higher Shelf Stones, wisps of mist were still coiling round.

The man did, however, have his own opinions about what might have been the cause of this particular form of what has become known as "mountain panic." These were the only additional words he could offer to Roberts:

Don't ask me to rationalize. Or rationalize it away—which is what it amounts to. I've come to the conclusion that sort of thing amounts to no more than a cop-out, a late twentieth century defensive mechanism—it's safe if it can be explained. As if "explaining away" were like defusing a bomb. I do think that every now and then, some of us—maybe all of us—stumble into an encounter with elements deeper and older than we are, and they are not, by their nature, benevolent, though they may be. This certainly wasn't.

Also on matters of a Peak District nature, Jonathan Downes reminisced on another case from this particular area:

One of the most credible reports brought to my attention … came from a family that had a daylight encounter with a large and hairy beast in the Peak District in 1991. This all occurred as they were driving near Ladybower Reservoir on the Manchester to Sheffield road. On a hillside, one of the family members had spotted a large figure walking down towards the road. But this was no man.

Well, they brought the car to a screeching halt and came face to face with an enormous creature about eight feet tall, that was covered in long brown hair with eyes just like a man's. Its walk was different, too, almost crouching. But just as the man-beast reached the road, another car pulled up behind the family and blasted their horn—apparently wondering why they had stopped in the middle of the road. Suddenly, the creature—which I presume was startled by the noise—ran across the road, jumped over a wall that had a ten-foot drop on the other side, and ran off, disappearing into the woods. Now, I know that the family has returned to the area but has seen nothing since.

The case to which Downes referred was also studied deeply by paranormal investigator Martin Jeffrey, who was able to speak in person with the family in question—who he described as being "one of the most sincerest families I have ever met"—and was able to determine that the incident occurred on a Sunday afternoon in November 1991. Jeffrey, too, got confirmation from the family of the "crouching" nature and gait of the mighty beast, and who additionally told Jeffrey of the monster: "We don't think he's dangerous ... just a creature left behind by evolution."

Of possible relevance to this "crouching" aspect of the story, Downes recalled another series of events that occurred in decades past that sound noticeably similar: "Hangley Cleeve, in Somerset, has been the scene of very similar sightings. They occurred in a local quarry, and another on the nearby barrows, where what was described as a large, crouching man-like form, covered in dark, matted hair and with pale, flat eyes was seen."

Pennsylvanian Bigfoot of the Nineteenth Century

The heading above was the title of a 1830s-era newspaper article that described strange, monstrous events in Pennsylvania that may very well have centered around the antics of a juvenile Bigfoot, rather than a fully-grown, hair-covered giant.

The article stated:

Something like a year ago, there was considerable talk about a strange animal, said to have been seen in the southwestern part of Bridgewater. Although the individual who described the animal persisted in declaring that he had seen it, and was at first considerably frightened by it, the story was heard and looked upon more as food for the marvelous, than as having any foundation in fact.

The newspaper said that the witness to the animal described it as being about the same height as a slim seven- or eight-year-old child and coated from head to toe in hair. The man encountered the beast as he picked and ate berries. As the creature came into view, it walked upright and made a curious, whistling noise.

For a moment, man and beast—both clearly astonished to run into each other—stared in awe, after which the creature quickly fled the scene, still whistling loudly.

Newspaper staff reported that the man "said it ran like the 'devil,' and continued to call it after that name."

It appears that this was not a solitary encounter, as the newspaper reported:

The same or similar looking animal was seen in Silver Lake township about two weeks since, by a boy some sixteen years old. We had the story from the father of the boy, in his absence, and afterward from the boy himself. The boy himself was sent to work in the backwoods near the New York state line. He took with him a gun, and was told by his father to shoot anything he might see except persons or cattle.

As the boy worked, his attention was drawn to something curious. As with the previously described case, it was a high-pitched whistling that distracted the boy. He assumed it was his little brother, but it was not. What it was, however, was a child-sized thing that "looked like a human being, covered with black hair."

The trembling boy raced for his gun and shot at the boy-beast. Fortunately for the creature, the boy's shaking hands ensured that none of the bullets reached their target. The hairy thing hid behind a tree, waited for a respite in the shooting, and raced off into the thick woods, whistling loudly.

The newspaper concluded: "The father said the boy came home very much frightened, and that a number of times during the afternoon, when thinking about the animal he had seen he would, to use the man's own words, 'burst out crying.'"

Whatever it was, it evidently left deep and traumatic effects upon those who encountered the possibly young Sasquatch of the Pennsylvania woods.

Philippines' Hairy Dwarfs

That one location should have in its midst two cryptid apes may sound unlikely. That is, until one realizes that the Philippines are actually comprised of more than 7,000 islands, many of them rarely visited. On various islands in the area, reports come of the Kibaan. Child-sized, covered in hair, and sporting gold-colored fangs, they like to relax in trees and strum guitar-like instruments that they fashion out of local trees. Like so many hair-covered apes of unknown kinds, the Kibaan are reputed to have backwards-facing feet.

Of course, all of this collectively sounds like a creature borne out of folklore and mythology, rather than history and reality. However, there is usually a nugget of truth to be found when one goes looking for it. And that applies to the Kibaan, too.

It's very possible that the folkloric Kibaan may have been something known as the Amomongo. Whereas the physical appearance and actions of the Kibaan sound most unlikely (and particularly so in terms of its musical prowess), the Amomongo sounds much more tangible and plausible.

Stories of a fast-running, hairy, but dwarfish beast at the base of the Kanlaon Volcano in the Philippines have been reported as recently as 2008.

By most accounts, it's a monkey that walks upright and stands around five feet tall. Unlike some of its more placid cousins around the world, the Amomongo is violent and even murderous. As an example, in June 2008, controversial reports surfaced out of La Castellana, in the Philippines province of Negros Occidental. Both farm animals and people were reportedly attacked by the fast-running, muscular beast, which spent most of its time lurking around the base of the 8,000-foot-high, still active, Kanlaon Volcano.

Over the course of June 9 to 10, a number of people were attacked by a marauding, hair-covered hominid that tore into the flesh of its victims with razor-sharp claws. Elias Galvez and Salvador Aguilar were two of the fortunate ones: they managed to escape from the clutches of the beast, but not before suffering deep lacerations. As is so often the case in such incidents, the wave of Amomongo attacks ended as mysteriously, and as quickly, as it began.

Pirate Testimony on Unclassified Apes

It's not often that one gets to read an account of Bigfoot from a full-fledged pirate! But that's exactly what happened in 1678, when a sword-wielding buccaneer named

A page from Alexander O. Exquemelin's 1678 book about buccaneers in which he also tells of wild ape-like men who attacked the Spaniards in the New World.

Alexander O. Exquemelin penned a book on his Jack Sparrow-like exploits, many of which occurred in South America. Its title was *The Buccaneers of America*. Maracaibo, Venezuela, was the location of the mysterious creatures chronicled by Exquemelin. He described Maracaibo as "a very handsome city with fine-looking houses along the waterfront. The population is considerable: counting the slaves, it is reckoned that three or four thousand souls live there, and among them 800 men capable of bearing arms, all Spaniards."

Exquemelin continued: "Beautiful rivers flow through all the surrounding countryside.... The fertile land stretches some twenty leagues, being bounded on the lake side by swamps and on the other by high mountains, always covered with snow."

One could make a sound argument that this was prime territory in which one might find a colony of creatures resembling Bigfoot. Exquemelin's next words suggest that was exactly the case:

A Spaniard told me of a sort of people who live in these mountains, of the same stature as the Indians, but with short curly hair and with long claws on their feet like apes. Their skin resists arrows, and all sharp instruments, and they are very agile climbers, having tremendous strength. The Spaniards attempted to kill some of the tribe with their lances, but the iron could not pierce their tough skin. These wild men managed to seize some of the Spaniards, carrying them up to the tree-tops and hurling them to the ground. These people have never been heard to speak. Sometimes they come down to the plantations at the foot of the mountains and carry off any women slaves they can capture.

Exquemelin concluded:

I have read various descriptions of America, but never found any mention of such people, so I believe they must be a sort of Barbary ape living in those parts, for I have seen many apes in the forest. Nevertheless, several Spaniards have assured me that these creatures are human, and that they have seen them frequently: I give it here for what it's worth. Truly, God's works are great, and these things may well be.

This particular case presents us with a bit of a conundrum: on the one hand, the animals appear to have had definitive human traits. Yet, on the other hand, they apparently lacked a language. Plus, their superior agility while climbing trees places them far more into an apish category. Maybe, they were both: nothing less than true ape-men.

Polish Bigfoot Film Footage

In August 2009, the *Austrian Times* newspaper reported on the sighting, and attendant filming, of an apparent Bigfoot in the Tatra Mountains, which are located on Poland's border with Slovakia. The newspaper noted:

Yeti experts are heading to Poland after a local man filmed a "monstrous, hairy creature" while on holiday in the Tatra Mountains. There have been rumors of a Polish Yeti in the area for centuries but this is the first time one of the strange creatures has been captured on film.

The man who took the controversial footage was twenty-seven-year-old Piotr Kowalski, of Warsaw, Poland, whose attention was drawn to the hairy thing while filming a goat on one of the mountain slopes. In Kowalski's own words: "I saw this huge ape-like form hiding behind the rocks. When I saw it, it was like being struck by a thunderbolt. Coming from Warsaw, I never really believed the local stories of a wild mountain ape-man roaming the slopes. But, now I do."

The footage was shared with the Nautilus Foundation for study and analysis. The foundation's president, Robert Bernatowicz, said: "The film clearly shows "something" that moves on two legs and is bigger than a normal man. But because the camera shakes so much it is difficult to say what it is exactly. We need to go to the site and see what traces, if any, were left."

Author David Hatcher-Childress said of this affair: "One can view the video on YouTube by doing a search such as 'Polish Yeti video.'" He describes the film as being surprisingly clear, and showing "something unusual." He adds: "I have watched it several times with great interest, and to me it appears to be genuine."

Raksaska

See: "Mysterious Jungle Races of Sumatra"

Researchers of Bigfoot

Countless books have been written about Bigfoot, the Yeti, the Yowie, and the Yeren. A significant number of words have been written about the massive, presumed-extinct, ancient ape known as *Gigantopithecus blacki* (*see* "*Gigantopithecus blacki*") And, more than a few of those words suggest that the many and varied unknown man-beasts that are said to roam among us are examples of surviving, relic populations of that very same *Gigantopithecus*.

But what if something else, something even more fantastic in its implications than the idea that Bigfoot is *Gigantopithecus*, is actually afoot? That's the scenario we are treated to in Mark A. Hall and Loren Coleman's book, *True Giants: Is Gigantopithecus Still Alive?*

This is a book that, if you're interested in Sasquatch and its hairy ilk, you'll definitely want to read. It may not, however, be the book you're anticipating or expecting. But, as I'll demonstrate, that's a very good thing.

The theory that Bigfoot, the Yeti, the Yowie (the list goes on) are indeed surviving pockets of *Gigantopithecus* is an attractive one. After all, at least some of the old stomping grounds of *Gigantopithecus* do, broadly, correspond to locales from where, today, we get reports of unknown, large apes. So, the theory does seem to make sense—at first glance.

The problem is that, for the most part, while Bigfoot and most of the rest of the hairy man-beasts are big compared to the human race, they're not that big. Creatures of seven, eight, or maybe nine feet in height are typically what we hear of from those who are fortunate enough to encounter such animals. But occasionally a rare, rogue case will come along where the witness is certain that the creature he or she saw is *far* larger—maybe, rather astonishingly, in the range of twelve to fifteen feet in height.

I've heard people suggest that since humans can reach seven or eight feet, why shouldn't there be a few oversized Bigfoot? Fair enough. But there's another explana-

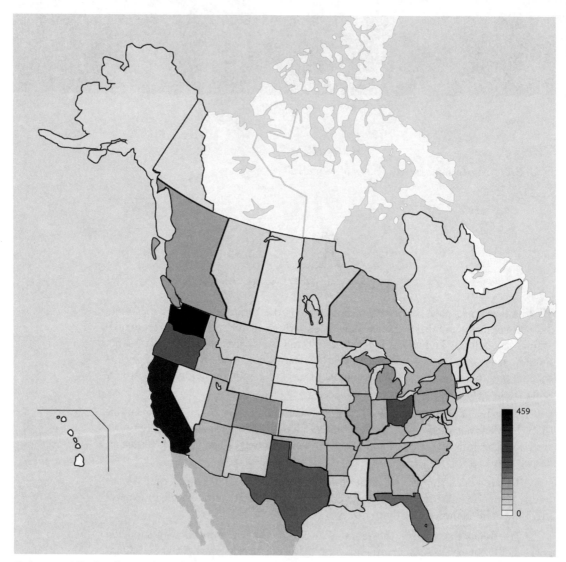

Sightings of Bigfoot have occurred all through North America, but the West Coast has had more than its share, especially Washington State, with nearly 500 sightings.

tion, too: we may be looking at different animals, rather than simply enormous versions of just one type. And maybe those rogue cases are not so rare after all. Cue *True Giants*.

So that there can be no misunderstanding of where they are coming from, Hall and Coleman note their position carefully, and early on, in their book: "These True Giants are not 'Bigfoot,' despite some efforts to make simple comparisons with creatures such as the one seen in the famous Roger Patterson-Robert Gimlin motion film of a Neo-Giant in California in 1967.... They are of a different genus of primate."

And it's with respect to this different genus of primate that we get to learn so much about the truly massive *Gigantopithecus* in the pages of *True Giants*. The reader is treated to an excellent account of how *Gigantopithecus* came to be discovered and classified; its place in both zoology and cryptozoology; how and why the assumption has been made that *Gigantopithecus*, Bigfoot, and the Yeti are one and the same; and most importantly, why that assumption suffers from some major flaws.

The authors detail extensively and authoritatively in their book that a significant number of worldwide cultures tell of huge giants that once lived among us—twelve- to fifteen-foot-tall entities, and maybe a few taller ones, too. They were a marauding, violent breed, with cannibalistic tendencies, but who also seemed possessed of a certain degree of intelligence that allowed them to fashion a degree of clothing, crude tools, weapons, homes and dens (very often in caves or underground), and perhaps even primitive rafts and boats.

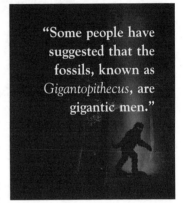

"Some people have suggested that the fossils, known as *Gigantopithecus*, are gigantic men."

Of course, much of this flies in the face of accepted wisdom that *Gigantopithecus*, a true giant, was just a huge ape. The theory that it could have been something much more is controversial. But it's a theory that Hall and Coleman back up with a wealth of fascinating accounts from the past that encompass Asia, North America, Europe, South America, and elsewhere. And, in doing so, the authors make a very good, thought-provoking case.

In fact, they are clear on the issue that dismissing *Gigantopithecus* as a gigantic ape is way off-track: "... the fossils that have been found for this particular giant primate have been attributed not to a giant man but, erroneously, to a giant ape.... Some people have suggested that the fossils, known as *Gigantopithecus*, are gigantic men. We believe that view will one day be proven correct."

And it's with this viewpoint that the pair provide us with some truly fascinating accounts that mesh with such a scenario. And it's a point of view that provokes a lot of graphic imagery. Indeed, one of the things that really hit home upon digesting *True Giants* is how much of our own history we appear to have lost and forgotten—or that we have simply chosen to relegate to the realm of fantasy. Priceless tales of times long-past when gigantic beast-men roamed the world, perhaps competing with us for food, water, and a place to call home fill the pages of this book.

But numerous cases from the last couple centuries to the present day suggest that these huge, lumbering beast-men have not gone the way of the Dodo bird, but may still be found deep in the ancient forests and the hard-to-access, huge mountain peaks that continue to dominate the wilder parts of our world.

In conclusion, *True Giants* is a book that is as groundbreaking as it is thought-provoking and paradigm-challenging. Hall and Coleman detail a remarkable theory and a rich history that serve to explain the many varied accounts of huge, hairy giants in our midst. They weave a complex and fascinating story of something gigantic, something definitively monstrous but equally man-like too, something that has lived alongside us for so long, carefully shaping and sculpting our legends and folklore.

And, it's very difficult to read *True Giants* and not come away with a deep sense of regret and loss, borne out of the probability that the full, fantastic history of these Goliath-like man-apes—and their ancient connections to, and interactions with, the human race—will likely never be known to us. However, unless or until we do learn more about not just the true nature of *Gigantopithecus*, but about our fog-shrouded history too, *True Giants* represents without a doubt the best treatment we have thus far on this fascinating and engaging subject.

Rising Sun Bigfoot

See: Bullets and Bigfoot

Rock-throwing Bigfoot

A particularly fascinating story of an encounter with a Bigfoot surfaced in the 1950s. The witness was a Native American medicine man named Frank Dan, who told his story to Bigfoot researcher and data collector J. W. Burns. The location was Morris Creek, a tributary of the Harrison River at Chehalis, British Columbia, Canada, and the date was July 1936. Burns carefully chronicled Dan's every word and prepared the following summary:

> It was a lovely day, the clear waters of the creek shimmered in the bright sunshine and reflected the wild surroundings of cliff, trees, and vagrant cloud. A languid breeze wafted across the rocky gullies. Frank's canoe was gliding like a happy vision along the mountain stream. The Indian was busy hooking one fish after another; hungry fish that had been liberated only a few days before from some hatchery. But the Indian was happy as he pulled them in and sang his medicine song. Then, without warning, a rock was hurled from the shelving slope above, falling with a fearful splash within a few feet of his canoe, almost swamping the frail craft.
>
> Startled out of his skin, Frank glanced upward, and to his amazement beheld a weird looking creature, covered with hair, leaping from rock to rock down the wild declivity with the agility of a mountain goat. Frank recognized the hairy creature instantly. It was a Sasquatch. He knew it was one of the giants—he had met them on several occasions in past years,

once on his own doorstep. But those were a timid sort and not unruly like the gent he was now facing.

Frank called upon his medicine powers, sula, and similar spirits to protect him. There was an immediate response to his appeal. The air throbbed and some huge boulders slid down the rocky mountain side, making a noise like the crack of doom. This was to frighten away the Sasquatch. But the giant was not to be frightened by falling rocks. Instead he hurried down the declivity carrying a great stone, probably weighing a ton or more, under his great hairy arm, which Frank guessed—just a rough guess—was at least 2 yards in length.

Reaching a point of vantage—a jutting ledge that hung far out over the water—he hurled it with all his might, this time missing the canoe by a narrow margin, filling it with water and drenching the poor frightened occupant with a cloud of spray. Some idea of the size of the boulder may be gained from the fact that its huge bulk blocked the channel. Later it was dredged out by Jack Penny on the authority of the department of hinterland navigation. It may now be seen on the 10th floor of the Vancouver Public Museum in the department of "Curious Rocks." When you're in Vancouver drop in to the museum and T. P. O. Menzies, curator, will gladly show it to you.

> "The giant now posed upon the other ledge in an attitude of wild majesty as if he were monarch of these foreboding haunts...."

The giant now posed upon the other ledge in an attitude of wild majesty as if he were monarch of these foreboding haunts, shaking a colossal fist at the "great medicine man" who sat awestruck and shuddering in the canoe, which he was trying to bail out with his shoe. The Indian saw the Sasquatch was in a towering rage, a passion that caused the great man to exude a repugnant odor, which was carried down to the canoe by a wisp of wind. The smell made Frank dizzy and his eyes began to smart and pop. Frank never smelt anything in his whole medicine career like it. It was more repelling than the stench of moccasin oil gone rotten.

Indeed, it was so nasty that the fish quitted the pools and nooks and headed in schools for the Harrison River. The Indian, believing the giant was about to dive into the water and attack him, cast off his fishing lines and paddled away as fast as he was able.

As a final word, it's worth noting that the teller of the story, the late J. W. Burns, has a prominent place in Bigfoot lore and history. On this specific issue, Loren Coleman said:

> According to researchers John Green and Ivan T. Sanderson, this Indian-sounding word was coined in the 1920s by J. W. Burns, a teacher who for years collected stories of wild, hairy giants from his Chehalis Indian friends. Burns combined several similar Native Canadians' names for these creatures and created the word "Sasquatch."

Rocky Mountain Footprints

In the cold, harsh winter of 1833, a man named David Thompson crossed the Rocky Mountains, specifically in the vicinity of Jasper, Alberta, Canada. It was as he did so that Thompson came across a line of very strange footprints in the snow. Thompson rationalized that they were from a "grizzled bear," while his Native American contacts believed the tracks were made by a still-living mammoth! However, a careful study of Thompson's own words, recorded in his personal journal, suggest that the culprit may have been a fully-grown Bigfoot. If that was the case, it demonstrated that discoveries of large, unidentified prints in the United States are not exclusive to relatively recent years.

Thompson recorded in his journal, on January 5, 1833:

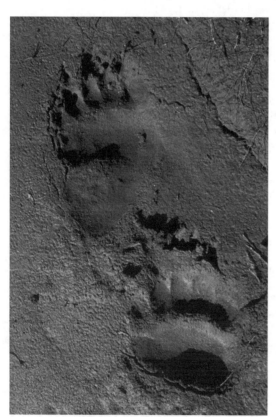

David Thompson first assumed the tracks he came across in the Canadian Rockies belonged to a grizzly bear, such as these footprints. On closer inspection, he saw he was wrong.

We are now entering the defiles of the Rocky Mountains by the Athabasca River. Strange to say, here is a strong belief that the haunt of the Mammoth is about this defile. I questioned several Indians, none could positively say they have seen him, but their belief I found firm and not to be shaken. I remarked to them, that such an enormous heavy animal must leave indelible marks of his feet, and his feeding. This they all acknowledged, and that they had never seen any marks of him, and therefore could show me none. All I could say did not shake their belief in his existence.

Thompson said that, two days later:

Continuing our journey in the afternoon we came on the track of a large animal, the snow about six inches deep on the ice; I measured it; four large toes each of four inches in length to each a short claw; the ball of the foot sunk three inches lower than the toes, the hinder part of the foot did not mark well, the length fourteen inches, by eight inches in breadth, walking from north to south, and having passed about six hours. We were in no humor to follow him; the men and Indians would have it to be a young Mammoth and I held it to be the track of a large old grizzled bear; yet the shortness of the nails, the ball of the foot, and its great size was not that of a bear, otherwise that of a very large, old bear, his claws worn away; this the Indians would not allow.

This was not the only time in the nineteenth century that a traveler chronicled such a strange experience in his journal. On March 26, 1847, an artist named Paul Kane did the same thing. He wrote:

> When we arrived at the mouth of the Kattle-poutal River, twenty-six miles from Vancouver, Washington, I stopped to make a sketch of the volcano, Mt. St. Helens, distant, I suppose, about thirty or forty miles. This mountain has never been visited by either whites or Indians; the latter assert that it is inhabited by a race of beings of a different species, who are cannibals, and whom they hold in great dread.
>
> These superstitions are taken from the statement of a man who, they say, went into the mountain with another, and escaped the fate of his companion, who was eaten by the "skoocooms," or "evil genii." I offered a considerable bribe to any Indian who would accompany me in its exploration but could not find one hardy enough to venture there.

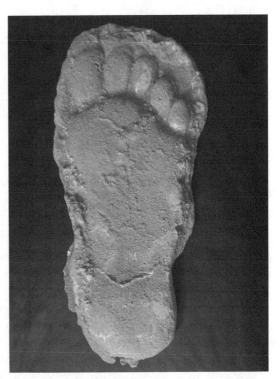

A cast made of a Bigfoot footprint. As you can see, it is clearly different from a grizzly bear's footprint.

Although Kane did not allude to the "race of beings" as being huge, hairy apes, it's important to note that Mount St. Helens has a long and fascinating history of Bigfoot encounters (*see* "Ape Canyon"; "Mount St. Helens Eruption and Bigfoot"). In that sense, a very good argument can be made that the mountain-dwelling cannibals that the Native Americans so greatly feared were, indeed, a colony of Bigfoot. And, if they were cannibalistic, this may help explain another major conundrum: the large numbers of people who vanish without a trace, every year, in the vast forests of the United States.

In 2012, Las Vegas, Nevada-based investigative journalist George Knapp wrote:

> Each year, hundreds of people are reported missing in national parks and forests. Most are eventually found, but there's a smaller category of cases that are never solved, including a few close to home. A former cop has put together hundreds of case files regarding clusters of missing persons in national parks where the circumstances are strange.
>
> "I was staying in a hotel off park service land and there was a knock at the door," said David Paulides. The person who came to confide in law enforcement veteran Dave Paulides was a government employee who told one heck of a story about people who vanish in national parks, places like Yosemite, but also national forests, including the Toiyabe west of Las Vegas.
>
> In the years since the knock at the door, Paulides has scoured small town newspaper archives and pestered federal agencies for records. He found so

many cases of missing people that one planned book became two, filled with more than 400 cases of people who went into national parks but never came out.

Food for thought ... and, just maybe, food for Bigfoot, too.

Roosevelt, President Theodore, and Sasquatch

It's not every day that a U.S. president makes comments and observations about Bigfoot. But President Theodore Roosevelt may have done exactly that in the pages of his 1890 book, *The Wilderness Hunter*. The president, who was also a keen hunter and an avid outdoorsman, told a story that sounds eerily like a close encounter with a murderous, homicidal Bigfoot. His amazing story follows, uninterrupted:

> Frontiersmen are not, as a rule, apt to be very superstitious. They lead lives too hard and practical, and have too little imagination in things spiritual and supernatural. I have heard but few ghost stories while living on the frontier, and those few were of a perfectly commonplace and conventional type. But I once listened to a goblin story, which rather impressed me.
>
> A grizzled, weather beaten old mountain hunter, named Bauman who, born and had passed all of his life on the Frontier, told the story to me. He must have believed what he said, for he could hardly repress a shudder at certain points of the tale; but he was of German ancestry, and in childhood had doubtless been saturated with all kinds of ghost and goblin lore. So that many fearsome superstitions were latent in his mind; besides, he knew well the stories told by the Indian medicine men in their winter camps, of the snow-walkers, and the specters, [spirits, ghosts, and apparitions] the formless evil beings that haunt the forest depths, and dog and waylay the lonely wanderer who after nightfall passes through the regions where they lurk. It may be that when overcome by the horror of the fate that befell his friend, and when oppressed by the awful dread of the unknown, he grew to attribute, both at the time and still more in remembrance, weird and elfin traits to what was merely some abnormally wicked and cunning wild beast; but whether this was so or not, no man can say.

President Theodore Roosevelt experienced many adventures in his life, but none so incredible as the time he ran into what may have been a Bigfoot.

When the event occurred, Bauman was still a young man, and was trapping with a partner among the mountains dividing the forks of the Salmon from the head of Wisdom River. Not having had much luck, he and his partner determined to go up into a particularly wild and lonely pass through which ran a small stream said to contain many beavers. The pass had an evil reputation because the year before a solitary hunter who had wandered into it was slain, seemingly by a wild beast, the half eaten remains being afterwards found by some mining prospectors who had passed his camp only the night before.

The memory of this event, however, weighted very lightly with the two trappers, who were as adventurous and hardy as others of their kind. They took their two lean mountain ponies to the foot of the pass where they left them in an open beaver meadow, the rocky timber-clad ground being from there onward impracticable for horses. They then struck out on foot through the vast, gloomy forest, and in about four hours reached a little open glade where they concluded to camp, as signs of game were plenty.

> "Coming back to the fire, he stood by it a minute or two, peering out into the darkness, and suddenly remarked, 'Bauman, that bear has been walking on two legs.'"

There was still an hour or two of daylight left, and after building a brush lean-to and throwing down and opening their packs, they started upstream. The country was very dense and hard to travel through, as there was much down[ed] timber, although here and there the somber woodland was broken by small glades of mountain grass. At dusk they again reached camp. The glade in which it was pitched was not many yards wide, the tall, close-set pines and firs rising round it like a wall. On one side was a little stream, beyond which rose the steep mountains slope, covered with the unbroken growth of evergreen forest.

They were surprised to find that during their absence something, apparently a bear, had visited camp, and had rummaged about among their things, scattering the contents of their packs, and in sheer wantonness destroying their lean-to. The footprints of the beast were quite plain, but at first they paid no particular heed to them, busying themselves with rebuilding the lean-to, laying out their beds and stores and lighting the fire.

While Bauman was making ready supper, it being already dark, his companion began to examine the tracks more closely, and soon took a brand from the fire to follow them up, where the intruder had walked along a game trail after leaving the camp. When the brand flickered out, he returned and took another, repeating his inspection of the footprints very closely. Coming back to the fire, he stood by it a minute or two, peering out into the darkness, and suddenly remarked, "Bauman, that bear has been walking on two legs."

Bauman laughed at this, but his partner insisted that he was right, and upon again examining the tracks with a torch, they certainly did seem to be made by but two paws or feet. However, it was too dark to make sure. After discussing whether the footprints could possibly be those of a human being, and coming to the conclusion that they could not be, the two men rolled up in their blankets, and went to sleep under the lean-to. At midnight Bauman was awakened by some noise, and sat up in his blankets. As he did so his nostrils were struck by a strong, wild-beast odor, and he caught the loom of a great body in the darkness at the mouth of the lean-to. Grasping his rifle, he fired at the vague, threatening shadow, but must have missed, for immediately afterwards he heard the smashing of the under wood as the thing, whatever it was, rushed off into the impenetrable blackness of the forest and the night.

After this the two men slept but little, sitting up by the rekindled fire, but they heard nothing more. In the morning they started out to look at the few traps they had set the previous evening and put out new ones. By an unspoken agreement they kept together all day, and returned to camp towards evening. On nearing it they saw, hardly to their astonishment that the lean-to had again been torn down. The visitor of the preceding day had returned, and in wanton malice had tossed about their camp kit and bedding, and destroyed the shanty. The ground was marked up by its tracks, and on leaving the camp it had gone along the soft earth by the brook. The footprints were as plain as if on snow, and, after a careful scrutiny of the trail, it certainly did seem as if, whatever the thing was, it had walked off on but two legs.

The men, thoroughly uneasy, gathered a great heap of dead logs and kept up a roaring fire throughout the night, one or the other sitting on guard most of the time. About midnight the thing came down through the forest opposite, across the brook, and stayed there on the hillside for nearly an hour. They could hear the branches crackle as it moved about, and several times it uttered a harsh, grating, long-drawn moan, a peculiarly sinister sound. Yet it did not venture near the fire. In the morning the two trappers, after discussing the strange events of the last 36 hours, decided that they would shoulder their packs and leave the valley that afternoon. They were the more ready to do this because in spite of seeing a good deal of game sign they had caught very little fur. However it was necessary first to go along the line of their traps and gather them, and this they started out to do. All the morning they kept together, picking up trap after trap, each one empty. On first leaving camp they had the disagreeable sensation of being followed. In the dense spruce thickets they occasionally heard a branch snap after they had passed; and now and then there were slight rustling noises among the small pines to one side of them.

At noon they were back within a couple of miles of camp. In the high, bright sunlight their fears seemed absurd to the two armed men, accustomed as they were, through long years of lonely wandering in the wilderness, to face every kind of danger from man, brute or element. There were still three beaver traps to collect from a little pond in a wide ravine nearby. Bauman volunteered to gather these and bring them in, while his companion went ahead to camp and made ready the packs.

On reaching the pond Bauman found three beavers in the traps, one of which had been pulled loose and carried into a beaver house. He took several hours in securing and preparing the beaver, and when he started homewards he marked, with some uneasiness, how low the sun was getting. As he hurried toward camp, under the tall trees, the silence and desolation of the forest weighted on him. His feet made no sound on the pine needles and the slanting sunrays, striking through among the straight trunks, made a gray twilight in which objects at a distance glimmered indistinctly. There was nothing to break the gloomy stillness which, when there is no breeze, always broods over these somber primeval forests. At last he came to the edge of the little glade where the camp lay and shouted as he approached it, but got no answer. The campfire had gone out, though the thin blue smoke was still curling upwards.

Near it lay the packs wrapped and arranged. At first Bauman could see nobody; nor did he receive an answer to his call. Stepping forward he again shouted, and as he did so his eye fell on the body of his friend, stretched beside the trunk of a great fallen spruce. Rushing towards it the horrified trapper found that the body was still warm, but that the neck was broken, while there were four great fang marks in the throat. The footprints of the unknown beast-creature, printed deep in the soft soil, told the whole story. The unfortunate man, having finished his packing, had sat down on the spruce log with his face to the fire, and his back to the dense woods, to wait for his companion. While thus waiting, his monstrous assailant, which must have been lurking in the woods, waiting for a chance to catch one of the adventurers unprepared, came silently up from behind, walking with long noiseless steps and seemingly still on two legs. Evidently unheard, it reached the man, and broke his neck by wrenching his head back with its fore paws, while it buried its teeth in his throat. It had not eaten the body, but apparently had romped and gamboled around it in uncouth, ferocious glee, occasionally rolling over and over it; and had then fled back into the soundless depths of the woods.

Bauman, utterly unnerved and believing that the creature with which he had to deal was something either half human or half devil, some great goblin-beast, abandoned everything but his rifle and struck off at speed down the pass, not halting until he reached the beaver meadows where the hobbled ponies were still grazing. Mounting, he rode onwards through the night, until beyond reach of pursuit.

Russian Ape-Man Investigations

In 2011, mystery ape investigator Richard Freeman issued the following press release, on behalf of the Centre for Fortean Zoology:

"Unlike most western scientists, he thought the creature might be a relic hominid ... rather than a great ape."

Russia, or the one-time Soviet Union, always seemed to be a step ahead of the west scientifically. They did, after all, get the first satellite into orbit, and the first man in space. They seemed to be forward thinkers and less hidebound and arrogant.

In the 1950s, when the interest in the Himalayan Yeti was at its peak, most (though certainly not all) had more or less written off the creature. Not so the Soviets. Russian polymath Dr. Boris Porshnev seriously considered the existence of such a creature. Unlike most western scientists, he thought the creature might be a relic hominid—a relative of the ancestors of man—rather than a great ape.

Here I must personally disagree with him on the nature of the Yeti, but that is beside the point. He was a scientist with an active interest in the subject.

Porshnev also found out that there were sightings of superficially similar creatures in the Soviet Union. In the Caucasus, the Pamirs, the Tien Chen and other areas were reports of hairy man-like creatures variously known as almasty, almas, dev, gul and many other names. There were records of encounters with such creatures. These seem smaller and more man-like than the classic "giant Yeti" of Tibet and the Himalayas. These could, indeed be relic hominids. "In 1958, the USSR Academy of Sciences, on Porshnev's initiative, set up a special Commission on the "snowman" question and launched an expedition to the Pamirs. Although it did not find a Yeti or almasty, the Snowman Commission was in existence for three years. It is hard to imagine any other government being so forward looking as to back a cryptozoological organization.

During its three years, the Commission amassed a huge amount of information on sightings both modern and historical. As far back as the time of Carl Linnaeus [1707–1778; the father of modern taxonomy] the creature had been given the scientific name *Homo troglodytes*.

During the three years, Porshnev compiled and published yearbooks of information on the "snowman." After the Commission was abolished he continued to compile information. Sadly, none of his books have been translated into English and even in Russia his books are rare, one having a print run of only 180. I have tried to get an inter-library loan of this book from Moscow Library with a view to photocopying it for translation, but I never did receive an answer.

In 1960, Pyotr Smolin began a seminar on the subject at the Darwin Museum in Moscow. This encouraged a second generation of researchers including Dmitri Bayanov, Igor Bourtsev, Alexandra Bourtseva, V. Pushkarev, Maya Bykova, V. Makarov, M. Trachtengerts and Gregory Panchenko.

Fifty-one years after the Snowman Commission was disbanded, the Siberian Government set up a research institute based at Kemerovo University dedicated to the study of relic hominids.

Officials of the Kemerovo administration in western Siberia have said that organizing an institute or a scientific centre would be a logical continuation of research into the Yeti.

Dr. Igor Burtsev, director of The International Center of Hominology, will join the brand new research unit. He said: "In Russia there are about 30 authoritative scientists who are engaged in studying the phenomenon of the Abominable Snowman."

"All of them will be integrated into this institute. The primary goal is to establish contact with one of the creatures." Recently 15 local people in the Kemerovo region have reported encounters with a 7-foot, man-like beast with black or reddish hair. Most reports come from the Mount Shoria wilderness.

Scottish Bigfoot

A ndy Roberts, a researcher and author of paranormal subjects such as strange creatures and UFOs, wrote about a huge, Bigfoot-like creature known as "Big Gray
Man" that lives in Scotland. It dwells on a mountain called Ben Madhui in the Cairngorms range. Roberts relates:

> When considering any physical evidence connected to the BGM [Big
> Grey Man of Ben Macdhui], it is worth noting that some accounts refer to
> photographs of unknown footprints taken in the Spey Valley [Scotland].
> Although the location of the photographs is some fifteen miles from the
> summit of Ben Macdhui, it has been claimed or inferred by some writers
> that they may of the BGM. Indeed, [author J. A.] Rennie cites a ghillie
> [attendant] as saying (upon seeing the footprints) they were "Bodach
> tracks." This comment, made by a local man may indicate the survival of
> a tradition connecting unexplained phenomena to the legendary
> "Bodach" or old man, of wider Scottish legend. As these tracks have been
> proffered as physical evidence for the BGM in the literature, they and
> their possible origins need addressing.

The actual source of the photographs to which Roberts refers is Rennie's book
Romantic Speyside, which describes how on December 2, 1952, about a mile outside of
the village of Cromdale, Rennie came across mysterious tracks which "were running
across a stretch of snow covered moorland, each print 19 inches long by about 14 inches wide and there must have been all of seven feet between each 'stride.' There was no

differentiation between a left and a right foot, and they preceded in an approximately single line."

Roberts highlighted that Rennie likened the prints—perhaps quite unsurprisingly and very understandably—to the controversial, so-called "Devil's Hoofprints" found across Devon, England, during the winter of 1855, which have been a supernatural staple and favorite for decades. His interest decidedly piqued, Rennie followed the tracks for about half a mile, until they "terminated at the foot of a pine tree, for all the world as though the strange creature making them had leapt up into the foliage of the tree."

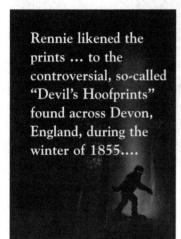

Rennie likened the prints ... to the controversial, so-called "Devil's Hoofprints" found across Devon, England, during the winter of 1855....

Twenty yards further on, Rennie picked the tracks up again. He followed them across a field and down to the river's edge, where they terminated opposite the village churchyard. Rennie rushed home for his camera and showed the resulting photographs to baffled locals.

"Writers often cite Rennie's photographs as evidence for the BGM case," offered Roberts, "but fail to quote further from his account at this point, which is regrettable as he goes on to give highly useful information," as Roberts makes clear:

Whilst working in Northern Canada in the 1920s Rennie came across similar tracks whilst crossing a frozen lake. These tracks reduced his French/Canadian companion to a state of gibbering terror as he believed them to belong to the Wendygo [also variously spelled as Wendigo, Windigo, Weendigo, and Wihtikow], a Bigfoot-like creature. Rennie was baffled by the tracks until later that winter when he saw the mysterious tracks for the second time. But on this occasion he saw them being made (*see* "Wendigo").

We now refer to Rennie's own words on the startling occurrence:

There on the flawless, smooth white of the snow, a whole succession of tracks in "line-astern" were appearing miraculously before my eyes. No sign of life anywhere, no movement even, other than the drifting clouds overhead and those tracks springing suddenly into being as they came inexorably towards me. I stood stock-still, filled with reasonless panic. The tracks were being made within 50 yards of me—20—10—then, smack! I swung round brushing the water from my eyes, and saw the tracks continuing across the lake. In that moment I knew that the Wendygo, Abominable Snowman, Bodach Mor, or what have you, was forever explained so far as I was concerned.

Rennie went on to give his explanation for the cause of both of those tracks and the ones he had seen many years later in Speyside: "Some freakish current of warm air, coming in contact with the low temperature, had set up condensation which was projected earthwards in the form of water blobs. When these landed in the snow they left tracks like those of some fabulous animal."

Commenting on Rennie's words and theory, Roberts suggested that: "Given that Rennie saw these tracks being made and felt water falling from the air, it is reasonable to assume that both the Canadian tracks and the tracks seen near the Cairngorms were the result of a rare meteorological condition."

Sedapa

See: Van Heerwarden's Ape

Senegal's Savage Ape

A West African country, Senegal is home to two distinct types of unknown ape with somewhat human-style qualities, one of which exhibits extreme hostility towards people. Its name is the Gnena. At around two to three feet in size, it lacks the bulk of Bigfoot. This does not, however, prevent it from being a potentially formidable opponent. The Gnena are very strong creatures, muscular, and possessing fierce tempers. As for their physical description, they are noted for their coats of extremely long, dark hair that hang in lank fashion from their bodies. Somewhat strangely, they have large heads that are significantly out of proportion to their bodies and have piercing, yellow eyes. When confronted by people, the Gnena will invariably intimidate them with dog-like barks, and will, if it's deemed necessary, launch an all-out attack. The Gnena are not exclusive to Senegal, however: reportedly, they live deep in the forests of numerous other countries, including the Cameroons, the Ivory Coast, Guinea, and Mali.

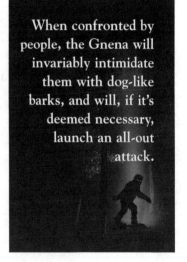

When confronted by people, the Gnena will invariably intimidate them with dog-like barks, and will, if it's deemed necessary, launch an all-out attack.

Within Senegal, the Gnena has a rival in the man-beast stakes; or, at least, it did until around the turn of the twentieth century, when reports of the creature began to tail off. It is called the Sansandryi. Although the fairly placid Sansandryi were said to have been far more ape-like than human, they apparently enjoyed wearing human clothes, whether stolen from villagers or found discarded. They reportedly had a sizeable colony in the forests surrounding the Casamance River, until around 1900 when something put an end to their presence and they were never seen again.

Sex and Bigfoot

L oren Coleman, an authority on America's most famous monster, Sasquatch, and the author of *Bigfoot! The True Story of Apes in America*, has boldly dared to go where very few other monster-hunters fear to tread: in search of Bigfoot's sex life.

> "Bigfoot researchers have been so embarrassed by the sexuality of Bigfoot that they have unfortunately been leaving out a major piece of data...."

Coleman, a firm believer in Bigfoot, and the owner of the Portland, Maine-based International Cryptozoology Museum, stated: "Too many American researchers were prudishly ignoring the sex angle of Bigfoot. A few years ago, I started challenging Bigfooters that if you're going to talk about this as a biological species, we have to take seriously that these things are having sex."

And, maybe, Bigfoot is not just having sex with others of its own kind. Coleman explains further:

I give a lecture called *Sex and the Single Sasquatch*. People laugh at first; but then, after laughing, they have to start thinking. What I've found in the sexual realm is that, as opposed to the fantasy that most people assume—of a well-endowed Bigfoot having sex with Indian native girls—the reality of the sexual aspects is mostly with regard to human men being kidnapped to have sex with younger, female Bigfoot.

Coleman states that those who have been up-close-and-personal enough to take a look at the Bigfoot male-member have described it as being "very small." Says Coleman, "This connects up very favorably with the fact that gorillas and orangutans have small penises, too. This suggests that Bigfoot is also some type of ape."

He expands further: "Bigfoot researchers have been so embarrassed by the sexuality of Bigfoot that they have unfortunately been leaving out a major piece of data that, as serious researchers, we should be looking at, because it actually enhances our case that these are real animals."

Coleman concludes: "Humans should lighten up about sex. The Bigfoot creatures are having lots of fun with it. We should be, too."

Shipton, Eric

Born in 1907, Eric Earle Shipton was an expert mountaineer who, on November 8, 1951, may have secured photographic evidence of the existence of the Abominable Snowman of the Himalayas. It was Shipton's fifth trek to the Himalayas, and specifically to Mount Everest. The group was a large one: with Shipman were Earle Riddiford, Edmund Hillary, Bill Murray, Michael Ward, and a variety of Sherpas. As the expedition came close to its end, Shipman, Sherpa Sen Tensing, and Ward stumbled upon something extraordinary southwest of Everest, specifically on the Gauri Shankar, a 23,406-foot-high mountain that stands roughly sixty miles from Kathmandu.

A summary of what was found appeared in the pages of *Eric Shipton: Everest & Beyond*, by Peter Steele:

Shipton took photographs of Ward standing beside the tracks. Lower down they were more distinct with sharply defined edges, twelve inches long by five wide; a big rounded toe projected slightly to one side, the second toe was separate, and the lateral three toes were smaller and grouped together. To give an idea of the scale, Shipton photographed his ice axe and Ward's boot beside one of the prints, which appeared to have been made with a day or so. Ward, even now, says the footprints were absolutely as Shipton described them. Ward thinks that several footprints might have been superimposed on each other, as might be made by men walking in single file.

When word got out as to what had been found, the media was eager for answers. The *Times* newspaper of London, England, printed Shipton's own words:

> The tracks were mostly distorted by melting into oval impressions, slightly longer and a good deal broader than those made by our mountain boots. But here and there, where the snow covering the ice was thin, we came upon preserved impression of the creature's foot. It showed three "toes" and a broad "thumb" to the side. What was particularly interesting was that where the tracks crossed a crevasse one could see quite clearly where the creature had jumped and used its toes to secure purchase on the other side. We followed the tracks for more than a mile down the glacier before we got on to moraine-covered ice.

In later years, Shipton elaborated upon the discovery:

> It was on one of the glaciers of the Menlung basin, at a height of about 19,000 feet, that, late one afternoon, we came across those curious footprints in the snow, the report of which has caused a certain amount of public interest in Britain. We did not follow them further than was convenient, a mile or so, for we were carrying heavy loads at the time, and besides we had reached a particularly interesting stage in the exploration of the basin.

> I have in the past found many sets of these curious footprints and have tried to follow them, but have always lost them on the moraine or rocks at the side of the glacier. These particular ones seemed to be very fresh, probably not more than 24 hours old.

> When Murray and Bourdillon followed us a few days later the tracks had been almost obliterated by melting. Sen Tensing, who had no doubt whatever that the creatures (for there had been at least two) that had made the tracks were "Yetis" or wild men, told me that two years before, he and a number of other Sherpas had seen one of them at a distance of about 25 yards at Thyangboche.

> He described it as half man and half beast, standing about five feet six inches, with a tall

Eric Shipton took this photograph in 1951 during an expedition in the Himalayas. An ice axe was placed next to the footprint to compare lengths.

A Yeti mask made by the people of Kathmandu.

pointed head, its body covered with reddish brown hair, but with a hairless face. When we reached Kathmandu at the end of November, I had him cross-examined in Nepali (I conversed with him in Hindustani). He left no doubt as to his sincerity. Whatever it was that he had seen, he was convinced that it was neither a bear nor a monkey, with both of which animals he was, of course, very familiar.

The final words go to cryptid ape authority John Napier, who said of this undeniably important historic development in the quest for the truth about the Abominable Snowman:

Shipton selected what he considered was the sharpest and clearest footprint of the series and took two photographs, one with Ward's booted foot as a scale and another with Ward's ice-axe serving the same function. The photographs were spectacular, and so were the results of their publication. Shipton's photographs, sharply in focus and perfectly exposed, are taken directly above the footprint. The photograph is unique, for it is the only item of evidence of the Yeti saga that offers the opportunity for critical analysis; ironically, however, it is also quite the most enigmatic.

Shiru

See: Ecuador's Hairy Horror

Shug Monkey of Rendlesham Forest, England

Any mention of the mysterious locale that is Rendlesham Forest, Suffolk, England, inevitably conjures up strange and surreal images of the famous, alleged UFO landing within the forest in the latter part of December 1980—a startling event witnessed by numerous U.S. Air Force personnel stationed at a nearby military base, Royal Air Force Bentwaters.

The bizarre affair has been the subject of a considerable number of books, numerous televisions shows, several investigations by military and governmental bodies, and unrelenting deep debate. Reports of strange lights, small alien-like creatures seen deep within the heart of the woods, and high-level cover-ups and sinister conspiracies are all key ingredients of the case that has, for many, become known as the "British Roswell."

More than three decades on, the events in question continue to provoke intense debate and controversy, with some believing that extraterrestrials really did land on British soil on that fateful night, or as some believe, across the course of several nights. Others hold the view that everything can be attributed to mistaken identity (of a nearby lighthouse, no less!), while some prefer the theory that a dark and dubious military experiment, and subsequent disastrous mishaps, may have been to blame for all of the fuss.

The forest covers an area that is around 1,500 hectares in size and is located in Suffolk's coastal belt known as the Sandlings. It is comprised of large, coniferous trees, as well as heathland and wetland areas, and is home to the badger, the fox, the red deer, the roe deer and the fallow deer. According to some people, however, Rendlesham Forest is home to far weirder things, too. Maybe, even, a strange form of British Bigfoot. Rendlesham Forest, as well as the Suffolk locales of West Wratting and Balsham, is the domain of a beast that, locally, has come to be known as the Shug Monkey.

Described as a bizarre combination of large ape, giant dog, and muscular bear, the creature is said to take its name from either (a) an old English word, *scucca*, meaning "demon," or an old east-coast term, *shucky*, which translates, in modern day terminology, as "hairy" or "shaggy." Maybe, and perhaps more likely, the name is even borne out of a curious melding of both terms. But, whatever the true nature of the name applied to the foul, hairy entity, its presence in the woods of Suffolk is enough to strike deep terror into the hearts of those unfortunate enough to have crossed its path—which is something to which Sam Holland can most definitely attest.

Shortly after New Year's Day in 1956, Holland was walking through the Suffolk countryside with his spaniel dog, Harry, when he was horrified to see a bizarre-looking creature come looming out of the trees some forty feet in front of him. It walked upon four huge, muscular legs—"like a lion's"—and its thick fur coat was both black and glossy.

Incredibly, said Holland, the animal was easily ten feet in length, and so could not be considered anything even remotely resembling a domestic animal, or a known wild beast of the British Isles. Holland, in a panicked state, thought for a moment that perhaps the animal was an exotic big cat that had escaped from a zoo or private estate, until it turned in his direction and he was able to see its terrible, frowning face.

Likening it to that of a silverback gorilla, Holland said that the monstrous creature possessed a

Holland compared the creature he saw to a silverback gorilla such as this one.

huge neck, intelligent-looking eyes, widely flaring nostrils, and immense, powerful jaws of a bone-crushing nature. For a moment or two, the animal looked intently at Holland and his whimpering little dog. Then, seemingly having lost interest in the pair, the gorilla-faced nightmare simply continued on its way and into the depths of the surrounding undergrowth.

Holland would later explain that the creature looked like a strange combination of ape, dog, bear, lion, and rhinoceros—an absolute chimera of the highest order, one might be inclined to say. Needless to say, the British Isles are not home to any such animal that even remotely resembles the beast that Holland says he stumbled upon all those years ago. In fact, it's fair to say that nowhere on the entire planet does such a creature dwell.

Yet, Holland is adamant that his description of the monstrous entity and his recollections of the day in question are utterly accurate in each and every respect. Today, now well into his eighties and still sprightly and fit, Holland believes that whatever the true nature of the beast he had the misfortune to run into more than half a century earlier, it was unquestionably paranormal rather than physical in origin. But from where, precisely, he admittedly has no idea.

Jonathan Downes, director of the British-based Centrer for Fortean Zoology, had a tantalizing tale to tell, too, of Rendlesham Forest's most monstrous inhabitant, the Shug Monkey:

> An ex-girlfriend of mine—an East Anglian paranormal researcher—was in possession of some video-tape which showed the paw print of some huge animal like that of a cat or a dog, but far bigger and with strange flattened finger nails rather than claws.
>
> She thought that it was a print from an alien big cat of some description, but my immediate thought was of the semi-mystical Shug Monkey. When I later found that my friend and colleague, Jan Scarff, who was brought up in the vicinity of the air bases, also knew about the so-called Shug Monkey I became even more interested, and I have been collecting reports for some years.

In view of all the above, perhaps we have not heard the last of the sinister Shug Monkey.

Shugborough Hall's Hairy Humanoids

Milford is the name of a small, centuries-old village situated in the heart of Staffordshire, England. It's also surrounded by miles and miles of what are known as the Cannock Chase woods. Those same shadowy, winding woods have a long and rich history of encounters with creatures that closely resemble the Bigfoot of the United States. Most of the encounters, which began in the 1960s and continue to this day, have occurred in the vicinity of a nearby, old, historic abode called Shugborough Hall.

Shugborough Hall in Great Haywood, Staffordshire, England, has been the home of bishops and earls for centuries. Since the 1960s, there have been several reports of a "big monkey" and other strange occurrences.

It's a huge, sprawling place, the origins of which date back to the 1700s. The hall most resembles a combination of a royal palace and the mysterious setting for a series of unexplained murders in an old Agatha Christie-style "whodunit."

It is, perhaps, highly appropriate for such an atmospheric and even eerie location that Bigfoot should make one or more appearances. Although there is just one, solitary encounter from the 1960s—a scant report that involved sightings of a "big monkey running around"—the situation was very different by the 1980s. It was in the late spring/early summer of 1981 that a number of ducks and geese in the waters surrounding Shugborough Hall were found dead. They did not appear to have been slaughtered by a wild animal, however. Instead, there were deep and foreboding suspicions that the culprits were occultists who sacrificed the unfortunate animals in an infernal rite.

When, shortly afterwards, sightings of a massive ape were reported in the same area, it provoked fears that those same occultists had, quite literally, conjured up the great ape from a supernatural realm. On two occasions, both late at night, the terrifying sounds of crazed, wild howling and growling from the darkened lawns and woods alerted hall staff. Rapid searches of the area resulted in some staff members encountering a red-eyed, hulking thing, as it charged around wildly, before vanishing into the depths of the trees.

At the time, a near-unanimous decision was taken not to discuss the events, for fear that the media, monster-hunters, and others would descend upon the hall in droves, provoking chaos and unwanted publicity. That overwhelming silence didn't prevent the beasts themselves from continuing to terrorize the neighborhood, however.

While most of the subsequent encounters were fleeting, a highly substantial and credible sighting occurred on a cold, dark night in late 2004. The witnesses were a pair

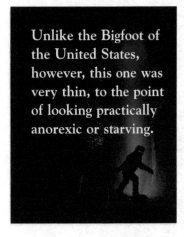

Unlike the Bigfoot of the United States, however, this one was very thin, to the point of looking practically anorexic or starving.

of police officers, patrolling the winding, tree-shrouded roads of the Cannock Chase—which included the roads around the village of Milford and Shugborough Hall. According to one of the officers—the other preferring not to comment on the matter at all—it was as they neared the entrance to the land that leads to the hall that both saw in front of them, at a distance of around eighty feet, a large, hair-covered animal of human shape. It clearly was not a human, however. The creature stood around eight-and-a-half feet tall. Unlike the Bigfoot of the United States, however, this one was very thin, to the point of looking practically anorexic or starving.

The officer driving the car slammed on the brakes and the pair could only sit and stare—in both shock and amazement—as the animal made its way onto the grounds of Shugborough Hall and was lost to the darkness. The officers decided not to pursue the animal.

It was not difficult to argue with their reasoning: Who would believe them? What would their colleagues at the police station say? Probably, the two thought, there would be endless jokes. On top of that, what kind of report could be filed? After all, it was hardly as if the British Police Force had a unit dedicated to the search for Bigfoot. So, silence was the only option—until 2006, when one of the officers confided in me the amazing facts of that late-night encounter with a British Bigfoot.

Sierra Sounds and the Voice of Bigfoot

In their efforts to seek out the truth of Bigfoot, investigators have secured a wealth of material that goes a long way towards doing proving the existence of the creatures. Footprints, film-footage, photographs, and witness testimony have all added greatly to what we know about these elusive beasts. And then there is the matter of the voice of Bigfoot.

A number of recordings have been made of what are purported to be the vocalizations of Bigfoot. While some have been explained away as known animals, there is one set of recordings that, more than any other, have stood the test of time. They have become known as the Sierra Sounds. The story of the Sierra Sounds dates back to the 1970s and is focused around two Bigfoot investigators, Ron Morehead and Alan Berry. On a number of occasions, from the early to mid-1970s, the two men captured astonishing audio recordings of what many believe to have been Bigfoot creatures—in the Sierra Nevada Mountains of California.

In Berry's own words:

A number of years ago, I was a newspaper reporter and a freelance journalist, and had the questionably good fortune to encounter Bigfoot, as the phenomenon is called. At a remote deer hunters' camp in the Sierras, I and several other men were witness to a "presence," if you like, of several creatures who were crafty enough to avoid observation, but freely vocalized and whistled, several times, without doubt, to us, and left big prints of bare feet around in the snow and pine mat. Things like this happened not once in my presence, but several times, from late September through the first week on November when a heavy snowfall drove us out of the 9,000-foot-high wilderness area.

Berry and Morehead very wisely, it transpired, decided to hang a microphone in a tree and then hooked it up to a reel to reel recorder in their camp—which was about forty feet away—in the event that they might pick up something of interest. Eventually, they did. It was the beginning of a fascinating series of investigations—and attendant recordings—that offered the Bigfoot research community new and alternative evidence.

Morehead stated:

The Bigfoot Recordings were the focus of a yearlong study at the University of Wyoming. An expert paper was written detailing their examination and analysis. The paper was presented at an academic seminar at the University of British Columbia in 1978, and subsequently published by the University Press in a 1980 anthology, "Manlike Monsters on Trial."

This was expanded on by Bigfoot authority Christopher L. Murphy:

The unusual growl-like sounds and whistles were studied by Dr. R. Lynn Kirlin, a professor of Electrical Engineering at the University of Wyoming.

While in the Sierra Nevada Mountains in California, Bigfoot investigators Ron Morehead and Alan Berry recorded the eerie cries of Bigfoot.

It was his opinion that the format frequencies found were clearly lower than for human data and their distribution does not indicate they were the product of human vocalizations and tape speed alteration. Further, Nancy Logan, a linguist in California also studied the tapes. In her opinion the vocalizations have a pitch range that is considerably more flexible than that of humans.

In an excellent and soundly argued paper titled "Characteristics of Human Language Evident in the Berry/Morehead Tapes,", retired U.S. Navy crypto-linguist R. Scott Nelson said:

> Intimidation, as a function of human language, is heard throughout the recordings, specifically on the Berry Tape in what has previously been dubbed "samurai chatter" and which I have come to refer to as "Hostility Assertion." These are vocalized by a drawn out stream of morphemes, often repeated, which are articulated at high volume in a highly hostile tone.... Several of these Hostility Assertions are articulated as forceful ululations in which the streamed morphemes may not have specific meaning in the sense of being semantically discrete. These ululations have an extremely intimidating effect on the listener and may be utilized solely for this purpose.

Nelson added: "Vocally, there are numerous 'whistles' and 'whoops' expressed on the tapes. I do not presume these have semantic meaning but are ritualistic in nature and could serve any purpose from a mating call to an assertion of dominance over his clan."

Today, the Sierra Sounds remain the most credible evidence of the voice of Bigfoot.

Silent Invasion (2010 book)

Stan Gordon is a well-known researcher, writer, and authority on many things of a Sasquatch nature—as is clearly evidenced by his 2010 book, *Silent Invasion: The Pennsylvania UFO-Bigfoot Casebook*. I know that any book suggesting that Bigfoot may somehow be inextricably linked with the UFO phenomenon is bound to raise hackles in certain quarters. However, there is surely not a Bigfoot researcher out there who has not been exposed to (at the very least) a few strange creature cases that place the hairy man-beasts into definitively supernatural—rather than zoological or cryptozoological—realms.

Whether those same Bigfoot researchers are willing to admit they have come across such cases—or are willing to give such reports some degree of credence—is a different matter, however. Fortunately, a number of researchers recognize that as preferable as it would be to place Bigfoot in a purely flesh-and-blood category, there is a significant body of data and testimony that point in a different direction, one that,

Stan Gordon is the author of *Silent Invasion,* which links UFOs to Bigfoot sightings.

to his credit, Gordon does not shy away from. Indeed, Gordon's book is a first-class study of a truly weird wave of Bigfoot-UFO activity that swamped the good folk of Pennsylvania in the period from 1972 to 1974.

In many ways, *Silent Invasion* is reminiscent of John Keel's classic *The Mothman Prophecies*, in that it focuses on the in-depth research of a dedicated, investigative author who duly finds himself up to his neck in monstrous bizarreness, ufological weirdness, and supernatural menace. *Silent Invasion* is a swirling cauldron filled with dark and ominous woods; glowing-eyed beast-men prowling the countryside by night; strange lights in the sky; UFO landings; neighborhoods gripped by terror and fear; and more. Gordon' research has enabled us to appreciate the curious chaos and calamity that collectively hit the unsuspecting folk of Pennsylvania all those years ago.

But, that's not all: macabre Men in Black, paranormal activity, psychic possession, secret government interest in Bigfoot, and prophetic visions of a dark and foreboding future all come to the fore in a book that is guaranteed to make you think twice about the true nature of Bigfoot. Gordon does not take the simplistic approach that Bigfoot is some sort of "pet of the aliens," as some might assume. Instead, he presents data that makes it clear that—even if we don't have all the answers—addressing the Bigfoot controversy from a purely zoological perspective does not work.

He notes the problematic lack of a body, the meager evidence of Bigfoot's eating habits, and its uncanny ability to always avoid capture—not to mention that the beast appears to be bullet-proof. Gordon hammers home that where Bigfoot turns up, a host of other supernatural favorites often do too.

Something strange and diabolical was afoot in Pennsylvania between 1972 and 1974. Bigfoot, UFOs, and a plethora of paranormal activity were all in evidence. There is a connection—even if it's one we're not fully able to understand yet. Until we do, however, *Silent Invasion* will provide you with much to think about and may make you totally revise your views on North America's most famous ape-man.

Singapore Sasquatch

Singapore, a 277-square-mile island with a population nearing six million, seems like an unlikely place to encounter a creature that is part-ape and part-human. There would be no place for such a creature to hide, frankly. But, apparently not: for centuries, reports have circulated of anomalous apes roaming around Singapore, a sovereign-city state of around five and a half million people, which is situated on the southern tip of the Malay Peninsula. While the details are scant, in 1805 just such a creature was encountered by a Malayan elder in the Bukit Timah region, who described the animal as an upright monkey, one with somewhat human characteristics. Today, the area is home to the Bukit Timah Nature Reserve, where, reportedly, sightings of such creatures are still made.

Sixty-five-year-old Bukit Panjang said of his knowledge of the creature: "We were always told as children when in the Kampung not to go near the forest at night due to the Monkey Man. Of course, we never saw it ourselves but it was always some uncle or friend of the family had seen it."

Although that particular comment suggests that the stories may have been the concoctions of parents, concerned that their children might get lost—or worse—in the forests, what Panjang said next suggests otherwise: "Once we were shown these footprints near the forest road, and I remem-

The Bukit Timah Nature Reserve in Singapore is home to a diverse range of animals, including primates such as this Long-tailed Macaque.

ber the strong urine smell. Whenever we heard shrieks coming from the jungle we would tell each other—don't disturb the Monkey Man.

Panjang may not have seen the creature, but others most certainly did. Singapore's *The New Paper* reached out to its readers for any information on the subject, which brought in a number of significant accounts. One read:

> I was going to the bus stop early one morning to catch the 171 bus. It was very foggy and cold. I thought I saw a tramp going through the rubbish bin, however when I approached, it called out with a loud animal sound and ran back into the forest. It was grey, hairy and ran on two legs, but had a monkey's face. I was shivering with fear and called the police but to no avail.

A second witness said: "When driving my taxi past the fire station on Upper Bukit Timah road in the middle of the night, I hit what I thought was a child that ran out in the middle of the road. It was on the car bonnet and then snarled at me—it was like a monkey but so big! It ran off injured, covered in blood, and holding its arm, which was broken."

Sisemite

See: Women Kidnapped by Unknown Animals

The Six Million Dollar Man (TV series)

In terms of Bigfoot, the 1970s was the one period, more than any other, in which there was a significant focus by the monster-hunting community on the Sasquatch-flying saucer connection and controversy. Today, the vast majority of Bigfoot investigators are intolerant of the idea that there might be a link between cryptid apes and aliens. Back then, however, things were different. And that seventies-era fascination for the UFO-Bigfoot link also spilled over into fiction.

The Six Million Dollar Man was one of the most popular television series of the 1970s. It starred Lee Majors as former astronaut Colonel Steve Austin, who, while test-flying a new, prototype aircraft, suffers a terrible accident in which he loses both of his legs, his right arm, and his left eye. It could have spelled the end of any kind of meaningful life for Austin. Except for one thing: thanks to the work of a secret government agency—the Office of Scientific Intelligence (OSI)—Austin is rebuilt, using sophisticated robotic technology called Bionics. In short, he becomes a cyborg: a half-human, half-machine, long before *Robocop* was on anyone's radar.

The long-running series (which followed in the wake of three, successful made-for-television movies) was an immediate hit with viewers. It ran for 100 episodes, inspired six movies, and provoked a spin-off show, in 1976, *The Bionic Woman* (starring Lindsay Wagner). At the time of writing, a big-screen version of *The Six Million Dollar*

Lee Majors starred in the 1970s TV series *The Six Million Dollar Man*. In one episode, the hero he plays, Steve Austin, must battle with a Bigfoot that turns out to be a robot.

Man is being planned for a 2016 release. It will star Mark Wahlberg and is slated to be retitled *The Six Billion Dollar Man*. All of which brings us to Bigfoot.

"The Secret of Bigfoot" was a two-part adventure that aired in February 1976. It was one of the most popular episodes on *The Six Million Dollar Man*. The story is set in the heavily forested mountains of California—from where a great deal of real-life sightings of Bigfoot have been made. From the outset, the tale is shrouded in intrigue: a pair of geologists, monitoring earthquake activity in the area, have vanished. The OSI, under Steve Austin's boss, Oscar Goldman (actor Richard Anderson), has been working with the geologists, Ivan and Marlene Bekey, leading to Austin playing a role in the quest to find the pair. Soon, huge, humanlike footprints are found in the area.

While Marlene remains missing, Ivan turns up, in a condition of near-hysteria. He is not the only one who turns up: a huge Bigfoot (played by wrestling legend Andre the Giant) is soon on the scene, too, and launches a violent assault on Austin and Goldman's encampment. It's during the attack that Austin wrenches off one of the arms of the hairy monster, which reveals it to be not a flesh-and-blood animal, but a highly sophisticated robot. We also learn that the Bigfoot is controlled by a group of aliens, who have a secret installation built inside one of the huge mountains.

Austin soon becomes a victim of alien abduction, in which he discovers that Marlene and Ivan were attacked because they had inadvertently uncovered evidence of the alien base. Even worse, OSI's studies in the area show that the entire West Coast is about to be hit by a devastating earthquake, one that could potentially kill millions. The only available option is to detonate, underground, a small atomic device on the fault line, thus preventing the quake from occurring. Unknown to Austin, the aliens try and prevent the nuclear explosion from taking place, since they believe—correctly—that it may also destroy their mountainous, secret abode.

Austin is determined that the earthquake must be stopped and he succeeds in thwarting the plans of the aliens to prevent it—as well as finding Marlene, much to the relief of Ivan. In the final scenes, we see that the atomic explosion has indeed prevented the catastrophic earthquake from occurring, but, as suspected, it has also caused major damage to the extraterrestrial facility. As a result, Austin—with help from Bigfoot—gives the aliens assistance in repairing the damaged parts and systems of their base.

Careful to ensure that the truth of the alien presence, and of the real nature of Bigfoot, remains hidden, the visitors from beyond wipe out Austin's memories of the bizarre and near-catastrophic events. Bigfoot is once again the enigma that it always has been.

Such was the success of this particular story that Bigfoot was brought back, in September 1976, for another two-part story: "The Return of Bigfoot." Again, the focus was on aliens and underground bases. To help boost ratings for *The Bionic Woman*, part two of the story became the opening episode for that particular show, in which Austin and the bionic woman, Jaime Summers, clash with both ETs and Sasquatch. In this episode, Bigfoot was replaced by Ted Cassidy (Lurch, in *The Addams Family*), who reprised the role a year later, in 1977, in a one-off episode titled "Bigfoot V."

For fans of *The Six Million Dollar Man*, "The Secret of Bigfoot" remains a firm favorite.

Skunk Ape of Florida

When the subject of Bigfoot comes up in conversation, for most people it prompts imagery of gigantic, bulky, eight-to-nine-feet-tall man-monsters roaming the frozen mountains and massive forests of the Pacific Northwest. Certainly, there's no shortage of such reports. But Bigfoot might not be the only cryptid ape that calls the United States its home. In Florida, particularly in swampy, wooded areas, there lives a beast known as the Skunk Ape. It also lives in Arkansas and North Carolina, but the wilds of Florida are where the beast really dominates.

There are good reasons for suggesting that the Skunk Ape is different from the creature reported to exist on the west coast. The difference in height and bulk suggests that the Skunk Ape and Bigfoot may not be one and the same. Some argue, however, that the radical differences in the terrain, temperatures, and food supplies in both locations have led to the development of a smaller form of Bigfoot in the Florida region, but, that, essentially, both animals are the same.

Confounding the matter even more, however, are reports of the creature being described as a mammoth Bigfoot. Although there is no firm consensus on what the Skunk Ape is—Bigfoot or something else—there is no denying the varied reports that exist on the creature. It's important to note that sightings of the Skunk Ape can't be blamed on the craze for Bigfoot that exists today. In fact, reports of the hairy, upright animal go back decades.

A spate of Skunk Ape encounters occurred in Florida from the late 1970s to 1980. One sighting occurred when a twenty-two-year-old man was hitchhiking on U.S. 441, around a half-mile from the town of Belleview. It was an area noted for its light forestland, which would have offered perfect cover for a Skunk Ape. It was the creature's nauseating smell that first alerted the hitchhiker to the fact that a wild animal was in the area. He real-

It was the creature's nauseating smell that first alerted the hitchhiker to the fact that a wild animal was in the area.

ized just how wild it was when the hairy, dark and upright beast briefly appeared, then vanished into the woods.

A couple days later, a security guard at a nursery in Apopka reported to the local police that something resembling Bigfoot—with fur or hair of a grey-red color—attacked him violently and tore off his shirt. Donnie Hall said he shot the creature, but it had no effect. Another story was reported by a Belleview welder who saw the man-beast, saying: "I'm six feet tall and it was bigger than me. It smelled horrible, like garbage."

> ... in 1980, in nearby Altoona, Skunk Ape enthusiasts became interested in the discovery of gigantic, size eighteen footprints.

As a result of all the local attention given to the sightings—by the public, the press, and even the police—the Florida Game and Fresh Water Commission got involved. It sent out a staff member to look at a line of tracks found at the Apopka nursery. The commission official determined that the tracks appeared to be man-made. Of course that deduction didn't settle anything, since if the Skunk Ape is a five-toed, bipedal animal, then their footprints *would* resemble human prints!

One month later, the Ocala National Forest was the site of a startling encounter with a Skunk Ape. The forest is the perfect terrain for cryptid apes to live and hide in: it is more than 600 square miles in size, is heavily and densely forested, and is filled with springs and swamps. And, for a large, aggressive, ape, there's no shortage of potential food supplies: it is home to red foxes, raccoons, boar, deer, squirrels, opossums, and gophers.

The November 1977 case was reported by sixty-seven-year-old S. L. Whatley, pastor of the Fort McCoy Baptist Church. While chopping wood on the fringes of the forest, Whatley caught sight of the creature. He said: "It was standing upright, in the middle of some palmetto bushes, and that sapsucker was at least seven and a half, maybe eight feet tall."

The Skunk Ape "had dark, lighter-than-black hair on its head and chest, not much on its arms, and none on its face. Its face and nose were rather flat, and its eyes were sunk in its sockets."

Whatley raced to his truck to grab his axe, anticipating that "me and that creature was going to mix it up." By the time he returned from his truck, however, the monster was gone. His last words on the matter to the press: alcohol hadn't touched his lips since the 1930s.

Three years later, in 1980, in nearby Altoona, Skunk Ape enthusiasts became interested in the discovery of gigantic, size eighteen footprints. Opinion was significantly divided on what the tracks showed.

Doug Sewell was the chief investigator for the Lake County sheriff's department. He came straight to the point: "I think it's a hoax. There was no indication that something that big enough to make those prints went back through the woods."

Less sure of that explanation was Lake County sergeant Dee Kirby, who made casts of a number of the massive tracks. Not only did he say that they showed a definitive arching of the step and five toes, but he added that there was some wrinkling in the instep, all of which suggested the tracks were not made by carefully carved "wooden feet."

Kirby also said, "The prints had a full four feet of distance between each one." He concluded that the creature must have weighed about 1,000 pounds and stood somewhere between ten and twelve feet tall, suggesting the beast was not the Skunk Ape and was far bigger than the average Bigfoot.

It is important to note that if the tracks were made by hoaxers, then the perpetrators chose the wrong place to make them. The site of the tracks was a remote area of the forest, and the only reason they were found was because U.S. Forestry Service contractors were in the area and stumbled on them. The affair was never resolved.

Sleeping Soviet Sasquatch

Professor Boris Porshnev wrote of a curious Russian beast and the man who encountered it:

In 1934 [geologist B. M.] Zdorick accompanied by his guide was making his way through a narrow path among a growth of wild oats on a little alpine plateau at about 8,000 feet altitude between the Darwaz Ridge and the eastern reaches of the Peter the First Range.

Unexpectedly the path leveled off and one could see how the grass was trampled on, the ground giving evidence that someone was digging around. There were splotches of blood on the path and remains of a gopher's skin. Just a little way from Zdorick and his guide, on a mound of freshly upturned earth, was a creature, asleep on his belly, fully stretched out.

He was about a meter and a half in length (approximately 4 feet 10 inches). The head and the forward limbs could not be seen because they were hidden by a growth of wild oats. The legs, however, could be seen. They had black naked soles, and were too long and graceful to have belonged to a bear; his back was also too flat to be a bear's.

The whole body of this animal was covered with fur, more like the fur of a yak, than the rich fur of a bear. The color of the fur was a grayish-brown, somewhat more prominent brown than a bear's. One could see the sides of the creature moving rhythmically in his sleep. The fear that took possession of the guide transmitted itself to Zdorick and they both turned around and ran for their life, scrambling and falling in the tall, wild grass.

On the following day Zdorick learned from the local residents, who were much alarmed by the news, that he came across a sleeping *dev*. The local residents used another word in naming the creature, and Zdorick had the impression that they were

"One could see the sides of the creature moving rhythmically in his sleep."

using the word *dev* just for him, so that he could understand better. The local residents ventured the information that in valleys of Talbar and Saffedar there were a few families of these *devs*—men, women and children. They were considered like beasts, and no supernatural power was ascribed to them. They cause no harm to the people, or their stock, but meeting them is considered a bad omen.

The geologist was very much surprised to hear that the *dev* was listed as an animal, and not a supernatural creature. He was told that the *dev* looked like a short stocky man, walking on two hind legs, and that his head and body were covered with short grayish fur. In the Sanglakh region the *devs* [are] seen very rarely, but they do roam about, either singly, or in pairs—male and female."

Slick Jr., Tom, and the Yeti

Quite possibly the closest real-life equivalent of Indiana Jones, Tom Slick was an explorer, adventurer, and seeker of strange creatures who travelled the world in hot pursuit of his passions—many of which were hairy, giant-sized, and monstrous. Born and bred in San Antonio, Texas, Slick had the good fortune to be the son of a multi-millionaire oil baron, Thomas Baker Slick Sr. Slick's nicknames were Lucky Tom and the King of the Wildcatters. Despite his vast wealth, Slick Sr. died in his forties. As a result, Tom Slick Jr. suddenly found himself swimming in dollars, enabling him to pursue his dreams.

In the 1950s, Slick searched for near-priceless diamonds in Guyana and chased down violent and marauding boar in New Zealand. Monsters, however, were his biggest passion. When Slick took note of the huge amount of publicity that the Yeti, of the Himalayas, was attracting throughout the 1950s, he knew that he had to look for the creature himself. By 1956, he was already planning ambitious treks to Nepal. Those plans hardly impressed the government of Tibet, chiefly because it was Slick's plan to zoom around the Himalayas in a helicopter, doing his utmost to find the huge, hairy, creatures. He also planned a ground excusion, with a team of dogs. Slick was denied access to the region until 1957.

The Arun River runs through the Arun Valley in Nepal, where adventurer Tom Slick traveled in search of the elusive Yeti.

In March of that year, Slick travelled to Nepal's Arun Valley. Tibetan authorities likely had not seen anything like this before: Slick turned up with metal cages and traps, with which he intended to trap Yetis. Rifles were in abundance, too—just in case. Sadly, things came to a crashing halt for Slick when, during one of his investigations, he was badly injured in a bus accident. Although he no longer participated in excursions himself, he did fund them.

There was another side to Slick, a particularly secretive and intriguing one. During the 1950s, the U.S. government was deeply concerned that the Chinese military would roll into Tibet and assume control. The CIA quietly approached Slick, essentially asking him to use his monster-hunting excursions as a cover for doing some localized spying on what was afoot on the Tibet-China border. By all accounts, Slick proved to be the perfect 007, skillfully combining his Yeti hunts with a quest to secure the latest information on the plans of the Chinese government.

Perhaps appropriately for someone who moved effortlessly within the world of espionage, Slick had a mysterious end: on October 6, 1962, his Beechcraft aircraft mysteriously exploded in mid-air, over Montana, as he flew to Canada for a few days of hunting.

The Snow Creature (1954 movie)

The Snow Creature is a 1954 movie that begins with the following voice-over:

> Cradled within the arms of the Rivers Ganges and Brahmaputra to the south and the mysterious plateau of Tibet to the north majestically stands the mightiest mountain range on the face of the Earth—The Himalaya. This is the story of an expedition to this ruggedest [sic] barrier. Not to assault on its wind swept towering heights, but to find and study plant life which had heretofore been unknown or inaccessible. This is the story of that mission, of how a small group of people found themselves in pursuit of a crude and primitive civilization, which once only existed as a figment of the imagination.

The Snow Creature was obviously made in hasty response to the early 1950s media and public fascination with the legendary Abominable Snowman of the Himalayas. The movie lacked originality, mirroring—to a shameless degree—the plot-line of the classic 1933 movie *King Kong*.

We are first treated to a map of India, which focuses on the Himalayas, the home of the famous Yeti. We are quickly introduced to the cast of characters, which is led by Dr. Frank Parrish (actor Paul Langton), an alcoholic photographer named Peter Wells, Subra (who is a Sherpa guide), and Subra's wife, Tara. Parrish is not there to seek out the Abominable Snowman, however. Rather, he is a botanist, in the Himalayas for scientific reasons. He is skeptical of the idea that the vast mountain

Actor Paul Langton played Dr. Frank Parrrish in the 1954 film about the Yeti, *The Snow Creature.*

range could be the home of a race of giant apes. His mind soon changes, however.

As the team takes a break at around 10,000 feet and sets up camp, Tara collects wood to make a welcome, warm fire. Suddenly, things change dramatically when a huge, hairy creature looms into view, and proceeds to kidnap the hysterical, screaming woman. It's all very reminiscent of the scene in *King Kong*, in which the captivated, giant ape takes possession of Ann Darrow, played famously by Fay Wray.

When a near-hysterical Subra tells Parrish what has happened, the doctor is deeply skeptical of the story, but he eventually realizes that his colleague is being all too serious. A search party is quickly launched to try and save Tara from the icy clutches of the immense beast. Parrish is still unsure what to make of it all, until the group stumbles upon a line of gigantic footprints in the snow. The reality of the situation soon hits home. Things get progressively worse: during the night, one of the guides is violently killed and the Yeti causes a huge avalanche, in an effort to wipe out the rest of the team.

The group finally finds a large, dark cave system high on the mountains, where they hide out from a huge, brewing snowstorm. It is while in the cave that Subra finds a charm that he had previously given to his wife, something that suggests that this series of caves might be the lair of the Yeti to which Tara was taken. It turns out that this is exactly the case. And there's not just one Yeti, but an entire family of them. Confronted by the giant monsters, an enraged Subra tries to shoot them. Unfortunately, his actions do nothing but provoke a cave-in, killing all of the Yetis, except for the massive, adult male that kidnapped Subra, who is knocked unconscious during the rock-fall.

Recognizing that snaring an Abominable Snowman is far more significant than discovering anything of a botanical nature, Parrish quickly takes steps to have the now-sedated creature dispatched to the United States for study and display—again, shades of *King Kong*, in which the mighty ape is captured and shipped across the oceans and paraded for all to see in New York, before everything goes inevitably awry, of course.

After a lengthy flight from the Himalayas, Parrish arrives on U.S. soil, where he must clear immigration. The immigration staff want to know if the goliath-sized, hairy thing—which is now semi-drugged in a huge crate—is human or animal. It's a moot question, since (also paralleling *King Kong*) the Yeti soon breaks out of the crate and goes on to wreak havoc.

The creature roams the city streets by night, slaughtering all who are unfortunate enough to cross its path, as Parrish and police officer Lt. Dunbar pursue it. There is something strange about the actions of the beast, however. It seems to have the ability to surface out of nowhere and vanish again just as quickly. There is nothing supernatural afoot, however. Parrish figures out that the lumbering animal is using the below-ground storm-drains to cross the city, carefully staying out of view until it surfaces and goes on its rampaging killing spree.

In a final confrontation, the Yeti is cornered in one particular drain and lunges wildly at Parrish and seizes him by the throat. It's only thanks to the actions of Lt. Dunbar that the beast is killed, by three well-placed bullets. The ending is similar enough to King Kong being hit with hundreds of bullets while atop the Empire State Building for the viewer to see where the writers got their inspiration.

Snowbeast (1977 movie)

Within the domain of Bigfoot-themed movies, there are some that are very good and more than a few that are downright terrible. Situated somewhere between are some Sasquatch films that have developed cult-like followings. One of those is a made for television movie titled *Snowbeast*.

The 1977 movie is about a killer Sasquatch on the loose near a Colorado ski resort. Gar Seberg (actor Bo Svenson) is a retired Olympic skier who, with his wife, Ellen, heads to the resort, where Seberg is seeking work. Interestingly, Ellen is played by actress Yvette Mimieux, who is not only a qualified anthropologist but also co-starred in the 1960 movie version of H. G. Wells's novel, *The Time Machine*, in which she was forced to flee from primitive, ape-like monsters living deep underground in a future Earth decimated by nuclear war. Of equal interest, *Snowbeast* was directed by Herb Wallerstein, who also worked on the popular 1970s television series, *The Six Million Dollar Man*, which featured a Sasquatch in a two-part, 1976 story, "The Secret of Bigfoot,", as well as a couple of sequels (*see* "The Six Million Dollar Man [TV series]").

No sooner have Gar and Ellen arrived at the Colorado Rockies resort when several skiers go missing. The disappearances are not due to accidents on the slopes, however. They are traced to Bigfoot, who appears to want to slaughter everyone who crosses its path. Unfortunately for the skiers, the owner of the Rill Ski Resort, Carrie Rill (actress Sylvia Sidney, whose final movie was 1996's *Mars Attacks!*), realizes that a deadly Bigfoot would be very bad for business, and so she elects to bury the

Actor Bo Svenson played the hapless retired skier who must fend off a killer Sasquatch in the 1977 movie *Snowbeast*.

facts. Sheriff Paraday, the local law-enforcement officer (played by Clint Walker, whose movies included a monster-themed 1974 production, *Scream of the Wolf*), goes along with the plan to play the matter down, by saying there's nothing stranger than a wild bear in the area, and that people should keep well away from it.

Rill's son, Tony, is a good friend of Seberg's and offers him a job at the resort. In doing so, he reveals the truth of the mysterious disappearances in the area: that they're due to a deadly Bigfoot. This fascinates Seberg, since Ellen works in the media and, coincidentally, previously was employed on a documentary show about Bigfoot.

Snowbeast takes an interesting turn by suggesting that killing such a creature might be considered murder, and particularly so if the beasts are related to humans. We see this when both Seberg and Ellen argue that taking the life of the Bigfoot is plain wrong—until the monster goes on a violent killing spree. Realizing that there is no choice but to end the reign of terror in decisive fashion, Seberg, Ellen, Sheriff Paraday, and Tony corner the creature on the edge of a mountain where a combination of bullets and a ski pole—used as a spear—end its life, and it plunges off the edge of a snowy precipice.

Snowbeast is far from being the greatest Bigfoot movie ever made, but it is an undeniably entertaining eighty-six minutes of Sasquatch mayhem.

Snowdonia, Wales

The following, admittedly controversial, story comes from a man who describes himself as "a forester in North Wales, living for much of my time in a remote mountain bothy in Snowdonia. A bothy is a small mountain hut, and there's nothing I like more than to spend some quality time on my own, amongst the hills and nature."

In March 2002, the anonymous source described his encounter at Snowdonia (an 823-square-mile national park):

> Over the years, I have received many reports of sightings of an extremely unusual creature, a "monstrous beast," as one visitor called it. This has puzzled me for a long time, and I became determined to seek out this beast for myself. It was while searching on the internet that I came across the British Beast on your website, and the thought occurred to me that maybe there is a population of these beasts spread across Britain.

> I have spent the last month or two preparing for an expedition base from my mountain bothy. The authorities refuse to give us any support, thinking that we are all crackpots. However, me and a group of colleagues managed to pull together enough resources to mount the expedition, which has just finished. I am afraid our success was limited, and there is much still to do but we did see the creature for ourselves. It attacked our camp one night, and much of our equipment was damaged. It was at least ten feet high, and stood on two legs. It seemed to be more bear-like than ape-like, it seemed

Strikingly beautiful, Snowdonia in North Wales is a national park that offers over 800 square miles of room for a "British Beast" to hide.

to be investigating our camp when a dog we had with us tried to attack it. There followed a few minutes of absolute terror, as the beast was clearly quite distressed by our invasion, and sought an escape from what must have been a confusing situation. It was fortunate that no one was injured, and we are fairly sure that the beast is not inherently dangerous to people.

A second email, received a couple of weeks later, also in anonymous fashion, reads as follows:

We have returned to the campsite twice since the incident, to try and salvage what we could. One important point is that the beast could definitely not have been a bear, from a behavioural point of view; the only time a bear stands on two legs is to sniff the air, but this animal was rampaging about on two legs. We feel it is also vital to point out that the beast was in no way aggressive, but merely felt threatened by our presence. All of our camera equipment had been damaged beyond repair, and the terrain there is mostly rock, scree and heather, so there were no tracks etc. We have spent many hours trying to piece together what we would consider to be a fairly accurate description of the beast's appearance, bearing in mind we have been unable to rely on photographic evidence.

The beast was roughly ten feet tall, when standing on two legs and gave off a strong, musky type of smell. It had dark brown hair, probably fur, and massive hands. Its eyes appeared to be red in color, and we could really sense the fear which the poor beast was enduring. For most of the time we were ducked down behind some rocks, and the campfire smoke was making it keep a fair distance away. It did attack our tent though, tearing through the sides. It was a dull and gloomy day, so when we began to take photos, the flash naturally went off. This really frightened it, and it began to head for us. So we ran off and were forced to leave the camera on its tripod. Alas, the beast picked it up and threw it against the rocks.

We feel that this bizarre animal is indeed very intelligent, and eagerly await some finer weather before embarking on another expedition. This disaster has not deterred us, and preparations are being made for next time. People are calling it the "Brecon Beacon Beast," despite it being nowhere near there. The local press seems to go for any excuse for a good alliteration!

Each and every attempt to locate and identify the witness has ended unsuccessfully. True, false, or somewhere in between? The jury remains steadfastly out on the matter of the Snowdonia Sasquatch.

Solomon Islands

The Solomon Islands are located near Papua New Guinea. They were named by Spanish adventurer Álvaro de Mendaña de Neira, who was the first known European to visit the islands, in 1568. There are more than 900 islands of widely varying size. Although no European visited the islands prior to the sixteenth century, archaeological digging has turned up evidence that primitive man inhabited at least some of them as far back as 29,000 B.C.E. There are also indications that before the Europeans were there, people regularly practiced cannibalism and exhibited violence. The islands are also noted for the presence of beasts that resemble Bigfoot.

Marius Boirayon uncovered most of the currently available data on the Solomon Island creatures. A skilled engineer and helicopter pilot, Boirayon has unearthed witness accounts that describe creatures very much like Bigfoot: the majority of them are around ten feet tall, have flaming red eyes, have hair that is a cross between brown and a deep red, and have ape-like faces.

Boirayon has made another parallel between the beasts of the Solomon Islands and the U.S. Bigfoot: in the same, precise way that there appears to be more than one kind of man-beast in the United States—the monster of the Pacific Northwest is manifestly different than the Skunk Ape of Florida, for instance (*see* "Skunk Ape of Florida")—the same can be said about the Solomon Islands.

Boirayon's findings suggest that there could be as many as three varieties of hairy hominids on the Solomon Islands. One of them is a smallish creature that is far more like a hairy, wild man of old English lore than it is a cryptid ape. The second resembles the traditional Bigfoot. The third is akin to the gigantic Nyalmo of the Himalayas (*see* "Nyalmo"), based on its description as a massive creature that typically reaches heights of fifteen to twenty feet, though it's possible that the descriptions of the creatures' massive sizes are exaggerated.

The Bigfoot of the Solomon Islands are hostile creatures. Kidnapping and eating the locals seem to be among their favorite activities. Boirayon uncovered the traumatic and terrifying story of Mango, a woman who was abducted from her village home by one of the creatures and held prisoner for around a quarter of a century, before she was finally able to escape. To the horror of her family and old friends, when Mango returned she was not the person she once was: living with the hideous beast for so long had driven her utterly insane and wild-like.

While held by the wild thing, Mango allegedly gave birth to its equally hideous-looking child after the creature forced itself upon her. Because is genetically impossible for humans and apes to inter-breed, the likelihood is that the monsters of the Solomon Islands are in reality, a type of human being.

The first European to discover the Solomon Islands was Álvaro de Mendaña de Neira in 1568, but archeologists have found that primitive people have lived there as far back as 29,000 B.C.E.

That the tropical jungles of the Solomon Islands could accommodate or hide creatures up to around nine or ten feet tall is not at all unlikely. It's difficult, however, to imagine that towering monsters of fifteen to twenty feet high could do likewise. One intriguing theory, however, explains why such immense things can't be tracked down, caught, or killed. The theory is centered around the island of Guadalcanal, the location of the 1942–1943 Battle of Guadalcanal, in which Allied forces fought the Japanese during the Second World War.

The people of Guadalcanal talk of longstanding legends of a vast underground world, far below their island, one that is only accessible if one knows where the secret entrance points can be found. So extensive are these massive caves, caverns, and underground realms, that thousands of the violent and giant beasts are rumored to inhabit their darkest corners. Much of the lore points in the direction of Guadalcanal's mountains, where, it is said, the tunnels and caves begin and run deep.

Another report of the Solomon Islands creature comes from Ezekiel Alebua, prime minister of the Solomon Islands from December 1986 to March 1989. When he was a child, Alebua was taken by his father to a large cavern on the east side of Guadalcanal, where his father pointed out huge fifteen-foot-long humanoid skeletons that lay scattered on the cave floor. How, exactly, Alebua's father knew of the cave and its eerie, long-dead inhabitants remains a mystery. Similar tales of massive, ape-like animals, and deep, labyrinthine tunnels can be found on a number of other islands that comprise the Solomon Islands, including Malaita, Choiseul, and Santa Isabel.

Southern Fried Bigfoot (2007 movie)

Southern Fried Bigfoot is a highly entertaining, thought-provoking, and suitably atmospheric documentary of Bigfoot of the Deep South. Packed with notable testimony and expert commentary from the South's leading Bigfoot-hunters and cryptozoologists, *Southern Fried Bigfoot* is required viewing for those who wish to learn more about this elusive creature, those who have been fortunate to see it, and those who have made it their life's work to uncover the truth.

This independently produced presentation explores the legends, tales, and possible reality of the hairy monsters that are purported to live in the wild areas of the South. While many have heard the legends of Bigfoot in the Pacific Northwest, the stories of "boogers," "swamp devils," and "bush apes" lurking in the South aren't as well known. With commentary from believers, skeptics, and the open-minded, *Southern Fried Bigfoot* shares a slice of Southern folklore that many people aren't aware of.

The film profiles some of the people and groups who have made efforts to study and pursue the southern Sasquatch. And while it covers the subject of strange creatures in the South, a few key legends are highlighted. They include:

- The Fouke Monster—The hairy creature that has been sighted around Fouke, Arkansas, for decades and was the inspiration for the cult classic film *The Legend of Boggy Creek*.
- The Honey Island Swamp Monster—The beast that is rumored to prowl the swamplands northeast of New Orleans, Louisiana.
- The Lake Worth Monster—A white shaggy creature that was sighted repeatedly near Fort Worth, Texas, in the late 1960s.
- The Skunk Ape—The foul-smelling creature that is said to haunt the Everglades in Florida.

Are these just legends or reality? Could there really be some type of unknown primate living in the backwoods of the South? Watch *Southern Fried Bigfoot*, listen to the legends, and judge for yourself.

Sprite of the Cemetery

Jason Hill related the details to me in 2008:

> It all started in the late 1950s. My dad was visiting a friend in Heath Hayes [a town near Cannock Chase, Staffordshire, England, the site of numerous

Bigfoot-type encounters]. This friend sadly died in the early 1990s; so I am afraid the details are secondhand. Even so, my dad is not the sort of person for tall tales; and the details he repeated to me last Sunday were the same as he told me thirty plus years ago.

It was back in 1959 and dad was at his mate's house talking when his friend's mother pipes up: "Look! In the newspaper: your little green man!" The newspaper story—dad thinks it was the *Express & Star* or the *Cannock Advertiser*—told of a little girl from Pye Green [an area of Cannock] running back home to her mother in tears.

When questioned, she said a little green man had run from the undergrowth and frightened her. Dad waited his chance and raised the question. His friend, who was very embarrassed, said that in the summer of 1958 he played cricket for GEC [the General Electric Corporation] at Stafford, his place of work, and cycled back home, later than normal across the Cannock Chase. On a weaving part of the road he saw something in the headlight of his cycle.

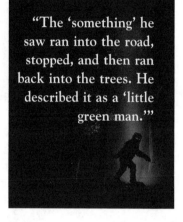

"The 'something' he saw ran into the road, stopped, and then ran back into the trees. He described it as a 'little green man.'"

The "something" he saw ran into the road, stopped, and then ran back into the trees. He described it as a "little green man."

When I first heard it, at the age of nine or ten, I thought it was great; but I grew up and thought it was a pile of rubbish—until a conversation with a friend about strange creatures on the Chase revealed he had a story to tell. Driving past the German Cemetery he felt something fall on the back of the car, like a big branch from an overhanging tree. He looked in the mirror and for a split second saw what he described as a "gremlin or sprite," little and hairy.

The more I think about it, the less it makes sense and seems logical. In fact, if I had thought it through, I probably would not have contacted you. But somewhere in a fifty year old story that has stood the test of time, and a twenty year old version, lies something. But what?

Sri Lanka

In the latter part of the nineteenth century, British adventurer and explorer Hugh Nevill was told of a race of creatures that were part-human and part-ape but which were, by the time Nevill heard the story, dead and gone—somewhere in the vicinity of five human generations earlier.

They resided in the southeast corner of Sri Lanka and, before their assumed extinction, were constantly at war with another race of hairy humanoids known as the Nittaewo. Both types of creature were fairly small—around four to five feet in height. They also shared a liking for living in deep, natural caves and caverns, and had a love of fresh, raw meat. They were not totally savage, however, as is evidenced by their apparent use of primitive stone tools.

It was not their constant warring with each other that wiped out the Nittaewo and their unnamed furry foes, however: it was man. Reportedly, the last of the Nittaewos were killed in a violent confrontation at a cave in the Kataragama Hills.

A similar story was told to explorer Frederick Lewis, a story that also suggested the Nittaewos were long gone. In this case, the account came from Dissan Hamy, whose grandfather reportedly helped build a huge bonfire at the mouth of the cave, as a means to kill the creatures by smoke inhalation.

Stig of the Dump (TV series)

Author and Kent, England-based cryptozoologist Neil Arnold said:

> When I were a lad, I watched and collected some of the weirdest examples of children's television; from eerie documentaries, to low-budget dramas, from supernatural series to psychedelic cartoons. One of the most intriguing and certainly most influential things I watched was *Stig of the Dump*, adapted from the Clive King classic novel which was originally published in the '60s.

Arnold noted:

> For those of you who are not familiar with this delightful tale, it concerns a young boy named Barney who, whilst staying with his nan, somewhere in Kent, discovers an old chalk quarry which just happens to be inhabited by a Neanderthal-type humanoid who Barney calls Stig. When we are first introduced to Stig, one could almost visualize a completely hair covered humanoid, something akin to a small Sasquatch.

> Despite being a huge fan of both series and book, I never realized that such a work may well have been based on an area close to my heart, and my house—Blue Bell Hill in Kent. In the book there is mention of Sevenoaks, but only recently I re-read the book and to my amazement found some odd cases of synchronicity which often pepper local folklore.

Did Clive King secretly know something of real hairy wild men dwelling deep in the heart of the Kent countryside?

> Could truth be stranger than fiction? Did Clive King secretly know something of real hairy wild men dwelling deep in the heart of the Kent countryside? And, if so, did he then weave some of that reality into his engaging page-turner? According to what Arnold had to say, very possibly, yes:

> Over the course of the fascinating book Barney and Stig become great friends, but like so many great kids' programs and books of that era, from the '60s to the '80s, we are often left to wonder as to whether Stig was a real creature or all part of Barney's strange imagination.

Either way, upon re-reading the book, I was amazed at how the author had mentioned several "fictional" items which I would eventually uncover as fact many decades later.

Arnold continued with the curious parallels between the fiction of *Stig of the Dump* and the reality of what has taken place in certain parts of mysterious Kent:

On a less cryptozoological note, we are introduced to the "Standing Stones" in Chapter Nine [of King's novel], which could be a reference to Kit's Coty House, a set of Neolithic stones said to be older than Stonehenge, which jut from a field at Blue Bell Hill. These stones have a lot of folklore attached to them. Some suggest that the stones are used as a calendar, or could be a mark of where a great and bloody battle once took place. Others believe the stones to have once been used for sacrificial means, and there are those who opt for the more fanciful rumour that they were constructed by witches on a dark and stormy night.

When we are first introduced to Stig, Barney, with a bump on the head along the way, falls into a steep chalk quarry (there are such quarries at the base of Blue Bell Hill) and accidentally stumbles upon the den of the creature called Stig. Oddly, for almost a century there have been reports from the quarries around Blue Bell Hill of a "Wildman" of sorts.

There have, indeed, as Arnold revealed:

A woman many years ago, growing up in the neighboring village of Wouldham often spoke about how in the 1960s her grandmother would tell her bedtime stories of the local "hairy man" seen near the standing stones. The woman mentioned that her grandmother had grown up with these stories and had seen the man-beast herself. In the 1970s a woman named Maureen saw a hair-covered, hulking great creature with glowing eyes one night whilst tending to a campfire with her boyfriend.

In 1992, a similar beast was seen at Burham, a neighboring village of Blue Bell Hill, by several men on their way to the pub. The men were all members of the Territorial Army and not prone to flights of fancy, but they were all spooked by the massive humanoid which appeared near the chalk quarry. In 2008 a man-beast was seen by a female motorist in Kent. She was so terrified by the creature she almost crashed her vehicle.

And, also in relation to Arnold's research concerning Clive King's much-cherished story, there are still further aspects of cryptozoology that seem to pop up within the pages of the engaging novel:

Kit's Coty House is a Neolithic burial site near Blue Bell Hill, Kent, England. The ancient stones are mentioned in *Stig of the Dump.*

Stig of the Dump also makes a couple of references to leopards, and in particular one specimen which Stig captures and skins in the local quarry. Barney finds the skin of the exotic cat in Stig's den and one begins to wonder whether Barney has stepped into some ancient period or Stig has killed an animal that has escaped from a private collection.

As anyone with an appreciation of British history and mystery will be acutely aware, sightings of large and exotic cats in the British Isles absolutely proliferate. They even date back centuries, and in precisely the same area that has so fascinated Arnold, as he shared with us:

"The "beast" was also recorded by a local Reverend as being the size of a calf. Some believe the animal was a hellhound...."

Interestingly there are several reports of large cats on the loose around Blue Bell Hill dating back to the 1500s. I saw a black leopard three times (twice in 2000 and once in 2008) near Blue Bell Hill, but interestingly the area where Stig would have killed his prey is the same area which once housed a local zoo. During the early part of the 1900s several children playing on the Downs reported seeing a black leopard. Some people believe it escaped from the zoo, then owned by Sir Tyrwhitt-Drake, although this was never proven. The children reported that the authorities came out, flushed the animal from the undergrowth and shot it dead.

During the 1700s, a large animal was said to have killed a rambler on the Pilgrim's Way, an ancient track-way which runs through Blue Bell Hill. The "beast" was also recorded by a local Reverend as being the size of a calf. Some believe the animal was a hellhound but I'm of the belief it was a large cat, misunderstood at the time and confined to superstition.

On this particular aspect of the story, Arnold closed thus, and in thought-provoking fashion:

A number of children's programs and books a few decades ago always hinted at some bizarre, psychedelic landscape of imagination, dream and eerie drama. I just wonder if Clive King knew of such local folklore and built the story around it, or by accident manifested some of the forms which have become embedded into local lore. Either way, *Stig* ... is a magical story and a great place to start for any would-be adventurer and explorer, like I was all those years ago.

Suicide, Sasquatch, and the Restless Dead

There can be very little doubt that one of the most controversial theories to explain the presence of cryptid apes is that some of them (but most certainly not the majority of them) are the human dead returned in spectral, animal form. To be sure, it's a scenario that most seekers of unknown apes have absolutely no time for. However, it must be noted that in centuries past, there was a widely held belief that restless spirits could travel from their ethereal plane of existence back to our world, albeit in monstrous forms—including those of large, ape-like beasts.

Dr. David Clarke, an expert on folklore and mythology, said:

One enduring folk belief is that human beings, as well as devils, witches and fairies could shape-shift and appear in animal form. The type of story appears in trial records, pamphlets and folklore throughout the middle ages where animal familiars are identified with the devil. Earlier accounts lack the preoccupation with demonic creatures. An early list of shape-shifting apparitions was prepared by a Cistercian monk in North Yorkshire [England] around 1400. It contains accounts of ghosts changing forms from human to crow, dog, goat, horse and even a haystack. These are described as human souls trapped in purgatory, appealing for help from the living to escape their predicament.

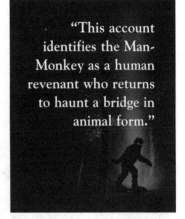

"This account identifies the Man-Monkey as a human revenant who returns to haunt a bridge in animal form."

In relation to the January 1879 affair of the Man-Monkey, which terrified the villagers of Ranton, England (*see* "Man-Monkey of the Shropshire Union Canal"), Clarke said:

This account identifies the Man-Monkey as a human revenant who returns to haunt a bridge in animal form. The manner of its appearance, in the form of "a strange black creature with great white eyes" and the fear created by its actions leaping on the back of the horse, resonates with contemporary accounts of ghostly activity elsewhere.

Was the soul of the man who, according to local police knowledge, apparently "drowned in the cut," really running wild around Ranton in the guise of the semi-spectral Man-Monkey? Many might disagree. One who gave a great deal of thought to this theory, and who finally came to embrace it, was Charlotte Burne—the author of an 1883 book, *Shropshire Folklore*, and the first person to write about and investigate the saga of the Man-Monkey.

Burne said of the sightings in and around Ranton:

I believe this to have originated in the classical and medieval notion of werewolves, living men who could assume the shape of a wolf at pleasure. Sometimes also a corpse would arise from its grave in the form of a wolf, and might do incalculable damage if it were not at once beheaded and cast into the nearest stream. This is a Prussian fancy, and the English King John too is said to have gone about as a werewolf after his death. Wolves have been extinct in England long enough to have disappeared from popular tales though not so many centuries as most people suppose, but the Man-Monkey seems very like the old fable in a new guise.

Elliott O'Donnell, who, in 1912, penned a classic study on lycanthropy called *Werewolves*, wrote:

It is an old belief that the souls of cataleptic and epileptic people, during the body's unconsciousness, adjourned temporarily to animals, and it is therefore only in keeping with such a view to suggest that on the deaths of such people their spirits take permanently the form of animals. This would account for the fact that places where cataleptics and idiots have died are often haunted by semi and by wholly animal types of phantasms.

Researcher Andrew Gable has noted an eerie parallel to the saga of the Man-Monkey—and its connection to death. It's a story that originates in Pennsylvania. Gable said:

On November 3 [2009], Mindi and I took a trip to Reading to do a bit of early Christmas shopping. While there, we decided to stop at the old Union Canal, so we could check out Lock 49. On August 17, 1875, Louise Bissinger, distraught over her husband's infidelities, took her three children on an outing along the Tulpehocken Creek. She had a basket tied around her waist, and when she reached the area of Lock 49, she grabbed her children tightly and plunged in. The children were still alive when witnesses arrived at the scene, but they drowned before the bodies could be pulled from the canal. The bodies were taken to Gring's Mill nearby. Later reports had it that while Mr. Bissinger mourned the deaths of his children, he callously was unmoved by the death of his wife. The stories have it that the ghostly forms of the Bissinger children are seen walking along the canal's towpath.

Gable said that the Man-Monkey

… is about the traditions of a shambling humanoid—what could be called a Bigfoot, though it is likely that it, like other British sightings, are something else—along the Union Canal in Shropsphire, England. One aspect mentioned was the humanoid as the ghost of s suicide whose body was found in the canal. I had mentioned … the coincidence of another Union Canal with a suicide in its history, as well. This possible presence of some sort of humanoid furthers the coincidence.

From British cryptozoologist Neil Arnold comes the following, which is also of deep relevance to this subject:

At Wallasea Island [England] there was once a place called the Devil's House which sat on the bleak marshlands flanking the River Crouch. During one particular harvest a local laborer experienced a terrible creature whilst working in one of the barns. He had heard his name being called on several occasions and

The Greek philosopher Paracelsus believed that all people had two spirits in them—one human (or divine) and one animal—and that one or the other dominates the spirit after death.

the sudden drop in temperature told him that something wasn't right. Although spooked, the man continued his work when suddenly he felt as though he was possessed and had a sudden urge to commit suicide.

The laborer found a piece of old rope, fastened it around his neck as a noose and climbed a ladder to tie the rope around a beam. A voice rasped "Do it, do it," in his ear, but then something even more bizarre happened. Looking upward the man saw a terrible ape-like creature swinging from the timbers. The phantom ape had bright yellow eyes that glowed in the gloom. It appeared rather slim in form and was completely black in color. This hideous apparition seemed to jolt him out of his suicidal trance and scrambled down the ladder and fled the barn.

The final words on this controversy go to the aforementioned Elliott O'Donnell:

According to Paracelus, man has two spirits—an animal spirit and a human spirit—and that in after life he appears in the shape of whichever of these two spirits he has allowed to dominate him. If, for example, he has obeyed the spirit that prompts him to be sober and temperate, then his phantasm resembles a man; but on the other hand, if he has given way to his carnal and bestial cravings, then his phantasm is earthbound, in the guise of some terrifying and repellent animal.

Sykes, Bryan, and the Abominable Snowman

On October 17, 2013, Britain's Channel 4 reported:

New DNA research on hair samples by Professor Bryan Sykes, a leading British geneticist, may reveal the answer to the centuries-old mystery of the Yeti: it is a genetic match to an ancient polar bear. The results feature in a new Channel 4 documentary series, *Bigfoot Files* presented by Mark Evans, who sets off on a global quest to unlock the real story of Bigfoot.

Yetis, also known as the "Abominable Snowman," have been recorded for centuries in the Himalayas, with local people and even eminent mountaineers, claiming to have come face-to-face with hairy, ape-like creatures. A photograph of a "Yeti" footprint, taken by British climber Eric Shipton at the base of Everest in 1951, sparked global Yeti mania.

As Channel 4 noted, there was a major, new development in the matter of the Abominable Snowman and the matter of what, precisely, the creature might be:

Bryan Sykes, Professor of Human Genetics at the University of Oxford, set out to collect and test "Yeti" hair samples to find out which species they came from. In particular he analyzed hairs from two unknown animals, one found in the Western Himalayan region of Ladakh and the other from Bhutan, 800 miles east.

After subjecting the hairs to the most sophisticated DNA tests available, and comparing the results to other animals' genomes stored on the GenBank database, said Channel 4, Professor Sykes "found that he had a 100% match with a sample from an ancient polar bear jawbone found in Svalbard, Norway, that dates back at least 40,000 years—and probably around 120,000 years ago—a time when the polar bear and closely related brown bear were separating as different species."

This led Channel 4 to add: "Of the various explanations, Professor Sykes believes that the most likely is that the animals are hybrids—crosses between polar bears and brown bears; the species are closely related and are known to interbreed where their territories overlap."

Professor Sykes, himself, said of his discoveries:

This is an exciting and completely unexpected result that gave us all a surprise. There's more work to be done on interpreting the results. I don't think it means there are ancient polar bears wandering around the Himalayas. But we can speculate on what the possible explanation might be. It could mean there is a sub species of brown bear in the High Himalayas descended from the bear that was the ancestor of the Polar Bear. Or it could mean there has been more recent hybridization between the Brown Bear and the descendent of the ancient Polar Bear.

As climate change causes brown bears and polar bears to interact more, scientists are discovering natural hybrids. This specimen is kept at the Rothschild Museum, Tring, England.

Channel 4 continued that Professor Sykes's theory was

… backed up in the Channel 4 series by legendary mountaineer Reinhold Messner, the first man to climb Everest without oxygen, who has studied Yetis since he had a terrifying encounter with a mysterious creature in Tibet in 1986. During his research he uncovered an image in a 300-year-old Tibetan manuscript of a "Chemo"—another local name for the "Yeti." The translation of the Tibetan text is clear: "The Yeti is a variety of bear living in inhospitable mountainous areas."

Channel 4 expanded that results had been submitted for publication in a peer-reviewed science journal, adding that Professor Sykes was undertaking additional work to try and resolve the matter, once and for all. "Bear DNA," they explained, "is complex and the exact timing of the split between polar bears and brown bears is controversial. It also begs the question of whether these bears are still in the region now."

The channel was not wrong when it stated:

The Yeti DNA result is part of the most ambitious "Bigfoot" DNA analysis the world has ever seen, the Oxford Lausanne Collateral Hominid Project, which is led by Professor Sykes and has looked at the genetic relationship between our own species of *Homo sapiens* and other hominids.

In 2012, Channel 4 said:

Professor Sykes put out a worldwide call for samples from formally undescribed species, such as the Yeti in the Himalayas, Sasquatch in America's Pacific North West and the Almasty in the mountains and tundra of Russia. All are mysterious creatures that have fascinated cryptozoologists and confounded scientists for decades. The study set out to discover whether "Bigfoot" is an ancient hominid, a member of the human family like Neanderthals, giant apes or some other species—or whether they are simply hoaxes. It's a controversial subject, beset with scandals that have destroyed the careers of respected scientists in the past. But Professor Sykes is undeterred.

Sykes commented:

Bigfootologists and other enthusiasts seem to think that they've been rejected by science. Now, I think that's a complete distortion of what science is about. Science doesn't accept or reject anything. All it does is examine the evidence and that is what I'm doing.

Teepees and Tree Structures

On numerous occasions, Bigfoot seekers have reported finding curious creations in areas where Bigfoot has been seen. Essentially, they are teepee-like structures that appear to have been created by something with intelligence—and a great deal of strength, too. The latter is made abundantly evident by the fact that in many cases the branches of the trees used to create these sometimes huge structures appear to have been wrenched off. In other cases, the branches appear to have been carefully bent over and intertwined.

As for why Bigfoot might engage in such curious behavior, there are several theories. At first glance, one might assume they have been constructed to offer the beasts a degree of shelter, particularly during the winter. In many cases, however, there does not appear to have been any attempt made to create a canopy or walls. In other words, the structures are open to the environment and all of its attendant harshness.

Other theories are more intriguing: it has been speculated that perhaps the teepees represent territorial markers, created by Bigfoot creatures to alert others of their kind that they are present in the area. They may also be a warning to man, to stay firmly away—although, of course, the obscure nature of the formations effectively means that very few humans would likely understand such a warning, never mind act upon it.

Whatever the purpose of the Bigfoot teepees, they are often found in areas where Bigfoot has been seen. Personally, I have seen them on several occasions. One was in 2005 when, along with fellow creature seeker Ken Gerhard, I traveled to Lake Worth,

The author discovered this teepee-like structure formed from bent-over trees in Ray Roberts Lake, Texas.

Texas, to investigate the legend of the Goat Man, which may well have been a white Bigfoot. On a small island on the lake—Greer Island—Gerhard and I found such a formation, along with the remains of a devoured fish and a large depression in the ground that indicated that something large and heavy sat there for a period of time.

I made a similar discovery in 2008, when I traveled to Ray Roberts Lake, Texas, with Lance Oliver, of the Denton Area Paranormal Society (DAPS). In one particular, heavily wooded part of the lake, we found numerous such creations, all of which appeared to have been fashioned with a high degree of intelligence, strength, and dexterity.

All of the above notwithstanding, it's important to acknowledge that at least some Bigfoot teepees are the work of Mother Nature. Jonathan Downes, of the Centre for Fortean Zoology, addressed this point in 2012:

> I've always found the whole "Bigfoot teepee" thing dodgy as hell. I'll give you an example. Just recently, we bought a chainsaw, as there are places in the garden—the trees—that haven't been pruned in years. And there are bits and places where the branches have grown together in what look like quite a complicated way. This is in my little garden in Woolsery [England]. You've got trees and branches doing odd things. And, it is things like this that mean I've never been impressed by the Bigfoot teepees. I think they are purely natural phenomena and nothing to do with Bigfoot—in Britain or anywhere.

Given that many Bigfoot investigators would likely disagree with Downes, it would be wise to keep an open mind, but always err on the side of caution, when it comes to the controversy of the Bigfoot tree structure phenomenon.

Telepathy

One of the most controversial claims within the field of Bigfoot study is one that suggests the creatures are able to converse with us via mind-to-mind communication, or telepathy. Many Bigfoot investigators who believe that Bigfoot is simply an unidentified ape scoff at such theories about telepathy. Some investigators, however, are not sure the matter can be relegated solely to the world of fantasy.

The *Real Psychic Power* website notes:

> Connie Willis writing for Huffpost tells of her psychic bigfoot encounter while on what I believe was an expedition deep into the woods to try and find Bigfoot. She notes that after falling asleep in the popup tent she was sleeping in, she was awoken when it began to rock. The other person in

the tent was out cold and Willis then reported her psychic Bigfoot encounter.

And it was quite an encounter, as Willis, herself, admitted:

My body was frozen solid and then I realized something was standing at the end of where my feet were on the other side of this tent-smelling-skinny-winny-keep-you-from-rain canvas, but no keeping-you-from-big-hairy-creatures canvas. I felt what I believe were two big beings standing right outside where I was. I then heard what I later learned was called Mind-speak, "Well, here you go. This is what you came to see." Yes, I heard that. I now knew what was inches away from me, my chance to see the legendary Bigfoot, and not just one but two. All I had to do was unzip the window and I would see them. I could feel them actually waiting for me to make my decision to do it. Then I did, I made my decision. I didn't want to see them.

Bigfoot investigator Linda Jo Martin offers the following: "My goal as a Bigfoot researcher has always been to learn to communicate with them. I want to create friendships with these forest people, to learn how they think, and what they think. For me, psychic ability, ESP [extrasensory perception], is a valuable tool for Bigfoot research. Even if the forest people have a different language, I can clearly understand them through ESP."

Texas Sasquatch

While the theory that Bigfoot might inhabit the massive forests of the Pacific Northwest is perceived as being entirely possible, some researchers find it unlikely that such creatures might be found deep in the heart of Texas. Nevertheless, there is a rich body of data from the Lone Star State that strongly suggests Bigfoot does indeed dwell in the huge state.

Ken Gerhard is a dedicated seeker of Bigfoot and numerous other unknown animals. As a resident San Antonio, Gerhard knows a great deal about Bigfoot in his home state. He says:

A letter that the late anthropologist and Bigfoot researcher Dr. Grover Krantz received during 1975 described a sighting which took place about thirty miles north of San Antonio at a private lake. The letter-writer explained how the eyewitness had been fishing at the small, secluded body of water on a twenty-thousand-acre property when he heard a loud splash. Gazing across the water, the man observed a large, grey figure standing on top of a hundred-and-fifty-foot-high, limestone cliff opposite him.

Since he could not make out much in the way of details, the man relied on the scope of a rifle he was carrying, in order to observe the creature more clearly. As he did so, the witness was

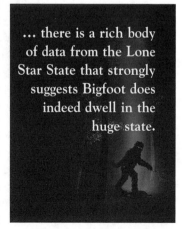

... there is a rich body of data from the Lone Star State that strongly suggests Bigfoot does indeed dwell in the huge state.

able to estimate that the animal stood eight- or nine-feet tall and he could tell it had long, gray fur and a round, catlike head. He watched the thing evidently manhandling some large branches for about five minutes or so. The following morning, the curious man made his way over to the spot where the huge figure had been standing and observed trampled brush, broken branches and a massive, overturned boulder.

Gerhard shares the details of another case:

A military base in a major city is probably the very last place from where you would ever expect to hear Bigfoot reports emanating; but, nonetheless, there was an intriguing spate of such sightings near San Antonio's now defunct Kelly Air Force Base, during the summer of 1976. It all began when twenty-eight-year-old Ed Olivarri, a telephone-worker living near the corner of West Fenfield and Quintana Roads, noticed that his small, black dog, Lick-em, was barking at something in the yard at around seven in the morning.

Ed went outside to try and see what the commotion was all about. Because his view was obstructed by a neighbor's tool shed, Olivarri proceeded cautiously and carefully to the picket fence that ran along an alley behind his house. From there, he could make out the figure of a large animal lying on the ground with its back to him, and at a distance of about forty yards. When a train whistle sounded from nearby railroad tracks, he watched in disbelief as a seven-foot-tall, brown, hairy creature stood up on two legs and ran off like a man into the nearby woods. Ed was unsurprisingly hesitant to tell anyone about what he had seen, for fear of frightening his elderly mother, Guadalupe, but eventually confided in his brother about the strange visitor.

Moving on to East Texas, Gerhard has even more to reveal:

In Florida's swamps, sightings of similar creatures, known amongst the populace as Skunk Apes, have been documented for absolute decades. As we might expect, stories of these so-called swamp apes, wooly boogers and wild-men extend throughout the bottomlands of the southeastern United States. Like other indigenous peoples in the Americas, the Caddo tribe of east Texas have ancient legends which tell of tall, hairy beings that live deep in the heart of the woods. And, with literally millions of acres of dense forestland in east Texas, it isn't totally beyond the realm of possibility that these elusive giants could remain hidden from us ... lurking just beyond the shadows, and largely surfacing by night to both prowl and feed.

One of the earliest accounts to be published in Texas involves the so-called Cypress Swamp Monster, also referred to as the Caddo Critter. The monster has been making the news around Marion and Harrison Counties in the far northeast corner of the state since 1965. It was on August 20 of that year that thirteen-year-old Johnny Maples was walking home from a friend's house. It was a normal day; for a while, at least. Johnny was on FM 1784, between Prospect and Lodi, when he began to hear noises emanating from the adjacent bushes. He called out twice, thinking that perhaps it was someone he knew from the area. When there was no reply, Johnny became concerned, and picked up a couple of rocks and hurled them into the brush.

"That's when this large, hairy man or beast appeared near the fence," he recalled. As the frightened boy began running away down the road—even removing his shoes to run ever-faster—the creature climbed over the fence and began to give chase.

"I ran as hard and fast as I could, but he kept up with me and he wasn't running, either, just sort of walking along behind me," Maples remarked. "The last time I turned around, the beast had gone off the road and disappeared into the woods." When young Johnny finally made it home, his mother found him in a distinct state of shock, with a pair of very badly blistered feet. His description of the monster was as follows: "About seven feet tall with thick, long black hair all over its body, except for the face, stomach and palms of its hands."

Caddo Lake on the border of Louisiana has a rich history of encounters with the so-called Caddo Critter. The lake was, in fact, both the location of, and the inspiration for, a B-horror movie titled *The Creature from Black Lake*, about a violent, killer-Bigfoot. A swampy, sinister, and foreboding place indeed, the lake seems like the perfect address where one might find a reclusive monster. It is connected to the system of waterways that leads to Boggy Creek and Fouke, Arkansas, home of the Fouke monster, and the subject of the cult classic, and near-legendary, film, *The Legend of Boggy Creek*.

Just a bit south of Caddo Lake, in Harrison County, lies the town of Hallsville, near Longview. During the summer of 1976, a report from there told of two Bigfoot creatures that were apparently traveling together. One was described as having white hair and standing an unbelievable twelve feet tall. Its partner appeared to be female and was shorter, with reddish hair. The beings were apparently observed standing in a cornfield happily shucking corn!

Thloh-Mung

See: Nyalmo

Tornit

See: Eskimo Legends of Mighty Man-Beasts

Traverspine, Canada, "Gorilla"

In 1933, writer Elliott Merrick told of a Bigfoot-style monster roaming around Happy Valley-Goose Bay, Labrador, Canada, around two decades earlier. The specific location was the small town of Traverspine. Merrick said:

Ghost stories are very real in this land of scattered lonely homes and primitive fears. The Traverspine "Gorilla" is one of the creepiest. About twenty years ago one of the little girls was playing in an open grassy clearing one autumn afternoon when she saw coming out of the woods a huge hairy thing with low-hanging arms. It was about seven feet tall when it stood erect, but sometimes it dropped to all fours. Across the top of its head was a white mane.

Merrick continued that the beast gave the girl an eerie grin, which allowed the girl to see its large, white teeth.

Merrick continued that the beast gave the girl an eerie grin, which allowed the girl to see its large, white teeth. It was when the animal reportedly "beckoned" the girl towards it that the girl, hardly surprisingly, fled for her life, and for the safety of the family home. The family quickly responded but the creature was gone. It had most definitely left its mark, however, as Merrick noted:

Its tracks were everywhere in the mud and sand, and later in the snow. They measured the tracks and cut out paper patterns of them which they still keep. It is a strange-looking foot, about twelve inches long, narrow at the heel, and forking at the front into two broad, round-ended toes. Sometimes its print was so deep it looked to weigh 500 pounds. At other times the beast's mark looked no deeper than a man's track.

According to Merrick, hunts for the creature were quickly organized, which involved local lumbermen, armed with rifles, scouring the woods, fields, and the nearby Mud Lake, by day and night. The beast remained oddly elusive. Even bear traps proved to be utterly useless.

Such was Merrick's interest in this story, he pursued it with vigor:

A dozen people have told me they saw its track with their own eyes and it was unlike anything ever seen or heard of. One afternoon one of the children saw it peeping in the window. She yelled and old Mrs. Michelin grabbed a gun and ran for the door. She just saw the top of its head disappearing into a clump of trees. She fired where she saw the bushes moving and thinks she wounded it. She says too that it had a ruff of white across the top of its head. At night they used to bar the door with a stout birch beam and all sleep upstairs, taking guns and axes with them.

The presence of the creature also provoked a significant reaction in the dogs of Traverspine, too, a matter that Merrick was careful to document:

The dogs knew it was there too, for the family would hear them growl and snarl when it approached. Often it must have driven them into the river for they would be soaking wet in the morning. One night the dogs faced the thing, and it lashed at them with a stick or club, which hit a corner of the house with such force it made the beams tremble. The old man and boys carried guns wherever they went, but never got a shot at it. For the two winters it was there.

Tunnit

See: Eskimo Legends of Mighty Man-Beasts

Twenty-first-century Sasquatch

There's no doubt that many of the sightings of, and encounters with, Bigfoot occurred in decades past. Certainly, there's no lack of old cases to capture people's attention: the 1924 "kidnapping" of Albert Ostman, the close encounter of William Roe in 1955, and the "Patterson Film" of 1967 make that abundantly obvious. But, Bigfoot has not gone away. Quite the opposite.

Arizona might not be the first place people think of when they give thought to where Bigfoot creatures might live. But, in late 2006, reports began to surface out of the eastern and central parts of Arizona, with many of them coming from the people of the White Mountain Apache Tribe. Tucson's Channel 3 covered the story.

Scott Davis, the producer of 3TV in Tucson, said:

Footprints in the mud. Tufts of hair on a fence. Ear-piercing screeches in the night. These are only fragments of the stories now coming from the White Mountains in Eastern Arizona.

For years the White Mountain Apache Nation has kept the secret within tribal boundaries. "We're not prone to easily talk to outsiders" said spokeswoman Collette Altaha. "But there have been more sightings than ever before. It cannot be ignored any longer."

It is a creature the world knows as "Bigfoot."

"No one's had a negative encounter with it," said Marjorie Grimes, who lives in Whitewater, the primary town on the reservation. Grimes is one of many who claim to have seen the creature over the last 25 years. Her first sighting was in 1982. Her most recent was in the summer of 2004, driving home from the town of Cibecue. She becomes more animated as the memory comes forth. "It was all black and it was tall! The way it walked; it was taking big strides. I put on the brakes and raced back and looked between the two trees where it was, and it was gone!" Grimes' son Francis has a story. Their neighbor Cecil Hendricks has a story. Even police officers have had strange encounters. Officer Katherine Montoya has seen it twice. On a recent Monday night dozens of people called into the tribe's radio station, KNNB, to talk about what they'd seen.

Also in Arizona, in 2008, the story of a woman named Donna surfaced. She said of her Bigfoot encounter, in the vicinity of Springville:

We spotted it on the old Bigelow homestead. It was walking down the treeline along the Little Colorado River on the south side of the creek. It was huge—about 8 feet tall. It didn't seem too worried about us either. We were on the road a good 100 yards from the creature, and we were in our truck. We had just dropped down off the plain on the South Fork access road. We wanted to look at the old abandoned house. Then we spotted it.

According to Tucson television producer Scott Davis, frightening screetches in the night have been heard in the White Mountains of eastern Arizona, and hair tuft evidence has been gathered, as well.

> It was large, looked black. There was no clothing, so it was not a man. We watched it until it moved back into the tree line.

Colorado was the site of a memorable encounter in 2000. It was a case investigated by Theo Stein of the *Denver Post* newspaper. The witness was a woman named Julie Davis, described as being an "experienced backcountry camper from rural Boulder County and a former volunteer with the Great Bear Foundation." It was on the afternoon of August 5, 2000, in the San Juan National Forest, that Davis had her Sasquatch sighting.

She said:

> It was gigantic—it must have been 8 feet tall. My first thought was, "I'm looking at something I've never seen before." I didn't even think Bigfoot. The notion that these animals were out there in Colorado never crossed my mind. It had very, very broad shoulders—huge shoulders. Its face was almost completely covered in fur but human-like, on the human side of halfway between a human and gorilla. I've had a lot of time to get to know what bears look like up close. This animal was bigger than any bear.

Rather fascinatingly, at one point the creature uttered a "low rumble" and a second, somewhat smaller, creature came out of the woods, peering intently at Davis—after which, both Bigfoot suddenly turned and ran into the depths of the forest. Davis decided to stay another day, but the creatures did not return.

In 2004, author Whitley Strieber reported at his website: "In the Yukon village of Teslin, Bigfoot has been seen at a construction site near the airport. Conservation Officer Dave Bakica says the two people who saw it 'claim they thought it was a person standing beside the road, but couldn't tell from all the dust. By the time they turned around to look back they said this person was completely covered in hair and took just two strides to get across the whole Alaska highway."

Underground Wild Man
See: London Underground Yetis

Van Heerwarden's Ape

The late Ivan T. Sanderson told of a fascinating encounter with a cryptid ape that occurred in Indonesia in 1918, the final year of the First World War. According to Sanderson, the witness, Mr. van Heerwarden was

> timber-cruising from the other side (the northeast) of the Barisans in Palembang province, but down in the swamp forests by the coast near the Banjoe-Asin River. In 1918 he spotted two series of tracks on the banks of a small creek in the Musi River district; one larger than the other, as if of a mother and child, as he remarks. These were perfectly human but exceedingly small. Later he discovered that a Mr. Breikers had also found such tracks in the same area.

Sanderson noted that, fascinated by what he had discovered, van Heerwarden began to dig deep into the heart of the puzzle and uncovered additional accounts of the creatures. Of these reports, Sanderson said:

> Their descriptions agreed perfectly in that they were about 5 feet tall, walked erect, were clothed in black hair that formed a mane, and had prominent teeth. Van Heerwarden later heard that a hunter had found a dead one and tried to carry it back to his village but its body was much

decomposed and the hunter himself died shortly afterward. Another, he learned, was said to have been spotted in a river and surrounded by locals in canoes but it dived adroitly and escaped.

Fortunately for van Heerwarden, he had yet another encounter, this one in October 1923, in the Pulu-Rimau forest, while he was engaged in a hunt for pigs. Since the pigs eluded him, van Heerwarden decided find a place where pigs would not see him. It was not a pig that passed by, however, but something else, something absolutely unanticipated.

Van Heerwarden recorded the facts himself:

I happened by chance to look round to the left and spotted a slight movement in a small tree that stood alone. By now it was time for me to be going home, for it was not advisable to journey through such country after sundown. But all the same I was tempted out of curiosity to go and see what had caused the movement I had noticed. What sort of animal could be in that tree?

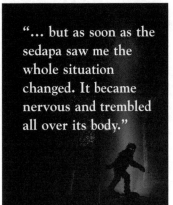

"... but as soon as the sedapa saw me the whole situation changed. It became nervous and trembled all over its body."

My first quick look revealed nothing. But after walking round the tree again, I discovered a dark and hairy creature on a branch, the front of its body pressed tightly against the tree. It looked as if it were trying to make itself inconspicuous and felt that it was about to be discovered. It must be a sedapa. Hunters will understand the excitement that possessed me.

At first I merely watched and examined the beast which still clung motionless to the tree. While I kept my gun ready to fire, I tried to attract the sedapa's attention, by calling to it, but it would not budge. What was I to do? I could not get help to capture the beast. And as time was running short I was obliged to tackle it myself. I tried kicking the trunk of the tree, without the least result. I laid my gun on the ground and tried to get nearer the animal.

I had hardly climbed 3 or 4 feet into the tree when the body above me began to move. The creature lifted itself a little from the branch and leant over the side so that I could then see its hair, its forehead and a pair of eyes which stared at me. Its movements had at first been slow and cautious, but as soon as the sedapa saw me the whole situation changed. It became nervous and trembled all over its body. In order to see it better I slid down on to the ground again.

The sedapa was also hairy on the front of its body; the color there was a little lighter than on the back. The very dark hair on its head fell to just below the shoulder-blades or even almost to the waist. It was fairly thick and very shaggy. The lower part of its face seemed to end in more of a point than a man's; this brown face was almost hairless, whilst its forehead seemed to be high rather than low. Its eyebrows were the same color as its hair and were very bushy. The eyes were frankly moving; they were of the darkest color, very lively, and like human eyes. The nose was broad with fairly large nostrils, but in no way clumsy; it reminded me a little of a Kaffir's. Its lips were quite ordinary, but the width of its mouth was strikingly wide when open.

Its canines showed clearly from time to time as its mouth twitched nervously. They seemed fairly large to me, at all events they were more developed than a man's. The incisors were regular. The color of the teeth was yellowish white. Its chin was somewhat receding. For a moment, during a quick movement, I was able to see its right ear which was exactly like a little human ear. Its hands were slightly hairy on the back. Had it been standing, its arms would have reached to a little above its knees; they were therefore long, but its legs seemed to me rather short. I did not see its feet, but I did see some toes which were shaped in a very normal manner.

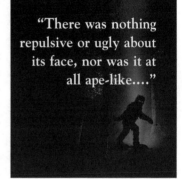

"There was nothing repulsive or ugly about its face, nor was it at all ape-like...."

This specimen was of the female sex and about 5 feet high. There was nothing repulsive or ugly about its face, nor was it at all ape-like, although the quick nervous movements of its eyes and mouth were very like those of a monkey in distress. I began to walk in a calm and friendly way to the sedapa, as if I were soothing a frightened dog or horse; but it did not make much difference.

When I raised my gun to the little female I heard a plaintive "hu-hu," which was at once answered by similar echoes in the forest nearby. I laid down my gun and climbed into the tree again. I had almost reached the foot of the bough when the sedapa ran very fast out along the branch, which bent heavily, hung on to the end and then dropped a good 10 feet to the ground. I slid hastily back to the ground, but before I could reach my gun again, the beast was almost 30 yards away.

It went on running and gave a sort of whistle. Many people may think me childish if I say that when I saw its flying hair in the sights I did not pull the trigger. I suddenly felt that I was going to commit murder. I lifted my gun to my shoulder again, but once more my courage failed me. As far as I could see, its feet were broad and short, but that the sedapa runs with its heels foremost is quite untrue.

Varmint of Mine Hill

On January 8, 1894, the Dover, New Jersey, press reported on the presence of a beast that didn't sound like a Bigfoot, but also didn't sound like a normal man living in the wild, either. In many respects, it seemed to curiously straddle both camps:

> There is a wild man in the woods near Mine Hill, and though the parties that have been hunting for him for several days have often felt cold in

their heavy coats the object of the search seems to get along comfortably with no more protection from the winter chill than an abundant set of whiskers.

Though this place is in a ferment of excitement over the affair, there are some persons who cast doubt upon the genuineness of the wild man; but that there is such a person and that he is in a condition that invites a speedy death from cold is blushingly told by Bertha Hestig, Lizzie Guscott, and Katie Griffin.

They saw the wild man for a brief moment Saturday afternoon, and they shrieked so loud and long that the business of the mill and nearly the whole town came to a standstill. The wild man didn't, however. He gave an answering shriek of terror and took to the woods.

"The Deans endeavored to seize him, but he picked up a club and brandished it."

"He didn't have no shoes on," ingenuously said Bertha, in telling the story to-day, "and mutton suet on his chest wouldn't ha' done him a bit of harm." The existence of the wild man doesn't rest on the testimony of the girls alone, and although many persons who claim to have seen the uncanny stranger differ in their descriptions of him, "Mike" and "Bill" Dean tell a straight story.

They are woodchoppers, and they first saw him. They were cutting wood on Friday last near the Indian Falls clearing, in one of the most lonely parts of the mountain. Suddenly their hounds began a violent barking at the base of a large rock. "It's a bear or some varmint," said "Bill," seizing his axe more firmly and running over to the dogs. He was closely followed by "Mike." As they reached the spot a savage looking figure sprang from behind the rock. "Mike" Dean, who was almost upon him, sprang backward as though indeed faced by a bear. The stranger was apparently middle aged, nearly six feet tall, and about a hundred and eighty pounds in weight.

His face was thickly covered with a dark, unkempt beard. He looked savagely at the woodchoppers for an instant and then sprang to the rocks and began talking to an imaginary object. As he was approached he darted from the rocks and began running up and down the clearing and at intervals yelling frantically, all the time working his arms as though rowing a boat. This leads to the belief that he is probably a crazy sailor.

The Deans endeavored to seize him, but he picked up a club and brandished it. One of the dogs sprang at him and received a blow that nearly killed it. The woodchoppers then fled and telephoned from the company store to this city for help.

A scouting party was at once organized, and under the direction of City Marshal James Hagen and Policeman Tredenick started for the scene. The wild man had disappeared into the dense underbrush. The searchers found the imprint of his bare feet in the middle ground. The party separated and kept up the search until late that night. Parties have left this city every day since. Fifty men scoured the mountains in every direction on Saturday, but without success. Sunday the woods were searched all day by numerous bands.

The man appeared on Saturday evening at the home of the Russels, about a half-mile from the scene of Friday's encounter. He tried to gain an entrance, but finding he was unable to do so began searching the premises as though looking for food. The family was greatly frightened. The man disappeared as mysteriously as he came.

William Mullen was returning from a walk on Sunday morning when the wild man suddenly made his appearance in the road in front of him. Both stopped and gazed at each other intently. Then the wild man gave a shriek and darted towards the woods in the direction of the Dickerson mine.

One of the searchers that went out on the mountain Saturday said the party found numerous imprints of the man's bare feet, and in one instance they had found a small sapling which had been gnawed, as though by a human being. It was on Saturday afternoon that the three girls who are employed at the Dover Silk Mill at the foot of the Dover Mountains saw the man. They were standing at their looms and looking out the windows.

They noticed the underbrush part and the next instant the man stepped into view. Their screams brought the other employees to the windows. The girls said the man's body was a mass of scratches and bruises. The scouting party that has been out at various times will leave this place tomorrow morning under the leadership of Marshal James Hagen and prosecute a more rigorous search. Inquiry has been made at the Morris Plains Asylum, but none of the inmates are missing.

It's worth noting that this case tells of a creature that is seen near old mines—giving weight to the idea that Bigfoot may be largely subterranean in nature.

Venezuela's Hairy Dwarfs

The overwhelming majority of the Bigfoot-like creatures cited in this book have terrestrial origins. There are, however, a number of reports that at least a small percentage of them come from other worlds and galaxies: aliens of the hairy kind, but seen right here, on our planet. Perhaps the best examples of this phenomenon surfaced in Venezuela in late 1954.

This event began sometime after midnight on November 28. All was normal for awhile for Jose Ponce and Gustavo Gonzalez, as they traveled along a small road on the fringes of Caracas, Venezuela. The dark road was suddenly lit up by what the astonished pair could only describe as a bright ball of light, with a circumference of around three feet. It swayed slightly in the air, not unlike a small boat bobbing along on the water.

The two slowed down their vehicle as they approached it, eventually coming to a complete halt. It was then that astonishment was replaced by outright terror. While Ponce stayed inside the van, Gonzalez cautiously exited the vehicle; he began to slowly and tentatively walk towards the hovering globe. Suddenly, Gonzalez found himself thrown to the ground by an unseen force. The reason why the attacker was initially unseen was because of its small size. Gonzalez, to his shock and fear, was finally able to see what had assaulted him: a hair-covered creature, about three feet tall, that was built like a man. Acting on impulse and adrenalin, Gonzalez attempted to plunge his knife into the body of the creature, but the knife bounced off it.

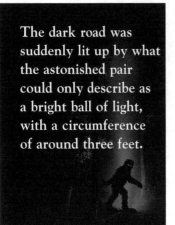

The dark road was suddenly lit up by what the astonished pair could only describe as a bright ball of light, with a circumference of around three feet.

In mere seconds, another hairy dwarf was on the scene and temporarily blinded Gonzalez with a bright light that emitted from a powerful, flashlight-type device. Shocked to the core, Ponce gathered his wits and jumped out of the van to help his friend, who was stumbling around, his eyesight still affected by the powerful beam that hit him with full force. To Ponce's growing concern, two more of the hairy creatures surfaced out of the shadows, and both made their way towards the men armed with large rocks.

Although the presence of the rocks suggested to the men that the hairy things were ready to kill them, with hindsight it seems they were only a defensive measure. Fortunately the creatures did not use the rocks. The small things raced to the ball of light and, somehow, launched themselves inside it, despite its equally small size and vanished in the blink of an eye!

Ponce drove wildly to the nearest police station where the two men reported the incident. A police doctor (who, as fortune would have it, also witnessed part of the confrontation) examined both men and found a deep gash on Gonzalez's torso, a likely result of the creature knocking him to the ground.

Twelve days later, on December 12, Jesus Gomez and Lorenzo Flores were out hunting when they became prey for something wild. They were hunting in thick woods and overgrown fields, the type of places where anything could have lurked. And did! As with Gonzales and Ponce two weeks previously, Gomez and Flores first encountered some form of small UFO, described as being like two wash basins on top of one another.

Despite the small size of the vehicle, four hairy creatures leaped out and immediately tried to drag the near-hysterical Gomez to the craft. Flores lashed out at one of the beasts with his unfortunately unloaded shotgun, only to see it shatter into pieces when it hit the near-armor-plated-like body of the animal. A brief fight for life followed, as the pair did their utmost not to fall victim to the freakish foursome. Finally, the hairy aliens retreated to their vehicle, jumped aboard, and soared into the night sky. Like Gonzalez back in November, Gomez and Flores bore the marks of the attack: deep scratches and violently torn clothing.

Six days later, the San Carlos del Zulia area of Venezuela was hit by the marauding mini-foots. Jesus Paz was a passenger in a vehicle when he alerted the driver that he needed to urinate in the nearby woods. He did not know it at the time, but there

Gomez and Flores were hunting deep in the forests of Venezuela when they witnessed a small UFO, and four hairy creatures leaped out of it.

was something waiting there ready to pounce. Paz headed for the privacy of some bushes, while his friends waited in the vehicle.

Suddenly, the air was filled with the sounds of terrible screams. Paz's friends wasted no time in exiting the car and racing to the bushes. To their horror, Paz was lying on the grass, unconscious and covered in cuts and gashes. As they focused their attention on Paz, a small hairy humanoid raced out of the bushes, headed towards a small compact UFO—similar to that described by previous witnesses—and soared away into the heavens.

Fortunately, there were no lasting effects on any of the witnesses of the three attacks. It was a unique series of events, the likes of which have seldom been seen before or since. The matter of the hairy dwarves of Venezuela remains the conundrum it was back in 1954. Whether highly advanced creatures from our own planet—but living in stealth amongst us—or vicious, primitive-looking creatures from the stars, we will likely never know.

We will also likely never know whether the near-deadly, predatory dwarves were successful in kidnapping, or possibly killing, others in Venezuela during that time.

Wakki

See: Australia's Beast-Men

Waladherahra

See: Australia's Beast-Men

Wales's Hidden Village

In 1993, Julian and Emma Orbach purchased a 180-acre piece of land in west Wales's Preseli Mountains. Ultimately, the hillside compound, which was surrounded and camouflaged by trees and bushes, became home to more than twenty like-minded souls, all of who wished to live outside the regular confines of what passes for society.

They constructed grass-covered, wooden buildings, became very much self-sufficient and, for all intents and purposes, created a self-enclosed community, the existence of which very few people knew. That the secret village resembled something straight out of the Middle Ages or—as the media noted, when the story broke—Tolkien's *Lord of the Rings* only added to the curious and near-magical nature of the area.

Astonishingly, the Orbachs, as well as their friends and colleagues, lived in blissful peace and stealth for five years before anyone in authority even realized what was going on. In fact, the only reason why the story ever surfaced at all was because, in 1998, a survey aircraft in the area happened to take aerial photographs of the area and caught sight of their hidden hamlet—which, most unfortunately for the Orbach family and their friends, finally blew their cover. It didn't take any time at all before the humorless wrath of local government reared its ugly head.

With no planning permission having ever been obtained for the village, the government was adamant that the buildings had to be destroyed. Thus began a years-long campaign in which the unsmiling men in black suits sought to "just follow orders," while those who called the Narnia-like area their home, fought to remain there, untouched and unspoiled by officialdom and the Nanny State. At one point, bulldozers arrived at the scene, waiting for the command to flatten the eight buildings that comprised their secret village.

Fortunately, it did not come to that. In 2008, a decade after the existence of the village first became public knowledge, and fifteen years after the first steps to create it had been taken, the government caved in. By then, far more mindful of so-called "green" issues than it had been in earlier years, officialdom agreed that as long as the villagers followed certain governmental rules and regulations and could demonstrate that they were improving the biodiversity of the area and conserving the surrounding woodland, they could stay where were they were, and their *Lord of the Rings*-type dwellings could remain intact and forever free of bureaucracy.

The above does not have a direct relevance to the matter of Bigfoot. But, what it does serve to demonstrate is that people can live, and have lived, in the wild for years, in situations where they remain outside of society, unknown to others, including the ever-watching eyes of government. And, if they can do exactly that, maybe others have too. The wild places and wilder people of our planet, perhaps, are not quite as extinct as many might well assume.

Wallace, Ray

Within the domain of Bigfoot research, there are hundreds, possibly thousands, of credible sightings of Sasquatch and similar creatures. Unfortunately, some of the cases that have gone down in monster-hunting circles are those born not out of credibility, but out of hoaxing and infamy. There is no better example of this than the controversial life and career of Ray Wallace.

Born in Missouri in 1918, Wallace is an integral part of Bigfoot lore, although much of it from a negative perspective. Wallace's story goes like this: In the early months of 1957, Wallace was appointed contractor on a new road construction project based at Bluff Creek, California. The foreman was Wallace's brother, Wilbur. Dozens of workers were brought in to complete the project. As the work progressed, a number of strange events reportedly occurred, such as huge oil drums being thrown around the area, with no real culprit in sight.

One year later, in early 1958, enormous footprints were stumbled upon at the Korbel, California-based Mad River on a construction site run by Ray Wallace. At the same time, work continued at Bluff Creek. One of those brought on board was Gerald Crew. In August, something strange and unsettling occurred at Bluff Creek: after a weekend spent back at home in Salyer, Crew returned to work, only to find huge footprints all around his bulldozer. Although he first thought it was a hoax, he felt it was wise to tell both Wallace brothers of his discovery. It wasn't long before the press learned of the footprints that were found. Andrew Genzoli of the *Humboldt Times* soon used the term "Bigfoot."

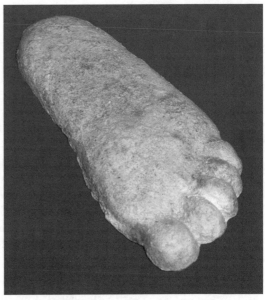

Although the story was big news, some of the leading figures within Bigfoot research, such as Ivan T. Sanderson, found the whole thing fascinating— due the history of hairy, man-beasts in the area— but troubling just the same. He had deep worries that Ray Wallace was engaged in some trickery. Wallace was a controversial character. Bigfoot authority Loren Coleman sayid: "Wallace said he had seen UFOs two thousand times, Bigfoot hundreds of times, and had, since the early days,

A plaster cast of the footprint discovered by Gerald Crew in 1958.

claimed … he had film footage of Bigfoot a year before the Crew footprint finds." His purported footage never surfaced.

On November 22, 2002, and at the age of 84, Wallace died of heart failure. Upon his death, Wallace's family claimed that he had engaged in widespread fakery, which included case reports and footprints. However, the media extended the hoax angle beyond just Wallace. The press presented Wallace as the man who practically gave birth to Bigfoot, implying that Bigfoot itself was a hoax.

As an example, the *Seattle Times* ran a story titled "Lovable Trickster Created a Monster with Bigfoot Hoax." The newspaper ignored the fact that Bigfoot accounts have existed since the early 1800s.

Wa-mbilikimo

See: Kenya's Collection of Unknown Apes

Warner's Ranch Wild Man

One of the most compelling early encounters with Bigfoot occurred in February 1876, a few miles east of Warner's Ranch, California, which is located near San Diego County and that was, and still is, home to the Cupeño, a Native American tribe. A man identified only as L. T. H. sent the details of the astounding event to the press. He wrote:

> About ten days ago Mr. Turner Helm and myself were in the mountains about ten miles east of Warner's Ranch, on a prospecting tour, looking for the extension of a quartz lode which had been found by some parties sometime before. When we were separated, about half a mile apart—the wind blowing very hard at the time—Mr. Helm, who was walking along looking down at the ground, suddenly heard someone whistle.

> Looking up he saw "something" sitting on a large boulder, about fifteen or twenty paces from him. He supposed it to be some kind of an animal, and immediately came down on it with his needle gun. The object instantly rose to its feet and proved to be a man. This man appeared to be covered all over with coarse black hair, seemingly two or three inches long, like the hair of a bear; his beard and the hair of his head were long and thick; he was a man of about medium size, and rather fine features—not at all like those of an Indian, but more like an American or Spaniard.

> They stood gazing at each other for a few moments, when Mr. Helm spoke to the singular creature, first in English and then Spanish and then Indi-

Warner's Ranch in California was the setting for a Bigfoot report back in 1876.

an, but the man remained silent. He then advanced towards Mr. Helm, who not knowing what his intentions might be, again came down on him with the gun to keep him at a distance. The man at once stopped, as though he knew there was danger. Mr. Helm called to me, but the wind was blowing so hard that I did not hear him.

The wild man then turned and went over the hill and was soon out of sight; before Mr. Helm could come to me he had made good his escape. We had frequently before seen this man's tracks in that part of the mountains, but had supposed them to be the tracks of an Indian. I did not see this strange inhabitant of the mountains myself; but Mr. Helm is known to be a man of unquestioned veracity, and I have no doubt of the entire truth of his statement. L. T. H.

Water and Swimming Bigfoot

Max Westenhofer was a German pathologist who, in the early 1940s, made a controversial and thought-provoking comment: "The postulation of an aquatic mode of life during an early stage of human evolutions is a tenable hypothesis, for which further inquiry may produce additional supporting evidence."

Almost two decades later, marine biologist Alister Hardy added that very ancient "primitive ape stock" may have been forced—by competing predators and circumstances—"to feed on the sea shores and to hunt for food, shell fish, sea urchins, etc., in the shallows of the coast. I suppose that they were forced into the water just as we have seen happen in so many other groups of terrestrial animals."

While it is obvious that lakes, oceans, and rivers are not the natural habitats of Bigfoot, there's a large body of data available that shows that, unlike many apes and monkeys, Bigfoot is quite an adept swimmer and is comfortable in water.

The North American Wood Ape Conservancy said:

Swimming must be examined alongside the terrestrial gait of the wood ape since it appears to be an important means of locomotion throughout the range of this species in North America, especially on the west coast. Circumstantial evidence, such as reports of the presence of wood apes on small islands off the coast of British Columbia, has suggested they swim. Observations of wood apes actually swimming have confirmed this.

Lisa Shiel, who has had personal interactions with Bigfoot, uncovered an example of Bigfoot in the water from the nineteenth century. She outlined the story: "In the 1830s, reports emerged from the area around Fish Lake, Indiana, of a four-foot-tall 'wild child' loitering in the vicinity—and swimming in the lake."

[A] large body of data available that shows that, unlike many apes and monkeys, Bigfoot is quite an adept swimmer and is comfortable in water.

Shiel continued: "In another incident that took place in September 1967, a fisherman casting his net on the delta of the Nooksack River in Washington State felt something tug on his net. A moment later something began dragging his net upstream. When he shined his flashlight at the thief, he saw a hairy hominid in the river hauling in the net."

A third case came from the people who run the website *Today in Bigfoot History!* They stated:

William Drexler's campsite overlooked Phantom Ship Island. He had just finished his sausage and egg breakfast and was smoking his morning pipe, just looking out over Crater Lake. That is when he noticed something moving on Phantom Ship Island.

Phantom Ship Island is a small, craggy island on Crater Lake that takes its name from its "ghost-ship"-like appearance, which is particularly noticeable when the mist hovers low and thick. The story continues:

Drexler got out his binoculars. It took him a minute or two before he was able to get a good bead on the moving figure. What Drexler saw was a brownish grey Bigfoot, obviously soaking wet, stretching out on some rocks near the water's edge. The creature was luxuriated. Drexler watched the creature for awhile lounge in the sun. Then after a bit the Bigfoot climbed to the other side of the island and Drexler lost sight of it.

One of the most fascinating examples originated near Ketchikan, Alaska, at some point around the turn of the 1960s. The story, provided by longtime Bigfoot

Phantom Ship Island in Crater Lake, Oregon, indeed looks like a sailing vessel. Strange that a Bigfoot would be spotted on it, but apparently it had gone for a swim and then decided to sunbathe on the small island.

authority and investigator John Green, had a bit of a "friend of a friend" aspect to it, but that makes it no less fascinating. It revolved around a young boy named Errol, who, one particular night, was fishing with his father, when his flashlight illuminated something terrifying standing in the water: a large, humanoid creature, but one that was clearly not human, staring intently at him.

"Standing on the high bank in the moonlight he watched dumb-struck as what looked like a huge ape-like animal swam to the other side of the river...."

The boy screamed, and a posse of men came running, just in time to illuminate the dark waters with their flashlights. They saw the huge beast dive into the water and start swimming "like a frog," before vanishing from view, as it plunged ever deeper into the depths. In moments, it was gone—demonstrating its skills as a powerful, fast swimmer.

Rupert Matthews, the author of *Bigfoot*, reported:

In July 1965 a Sasquatch was seen swimming some distance away from the shore of Princess Royal Island, British Columbia. The fisherman who saw it realized with little apprehension that it was actually swimming for his boat, so he started up his outboard motor and sped off. At this point four more Sasquatch appeared on a nearby beach and watched him.

There have been sightings of swimming Bigfoot in Texas, too. Rob Riggs, who has deeply studied reports of the creatures in and around the Big Thicket area of the Lone Star State (*see* "Big Thicket Sasquatch"), told of one particularly notable case of a watery Sasquatch:

John's family home is on the edge of the Trinity River swamps near Dayton. One night he heard a disturbance on the porch where he kept a pen of rabbits. He investigated just in time to see a large, dark form make off with rabbit in hand. John impulsively followed in hot pursuit, staying close enough to hear the rabbit squeal continuously.

John was able to close in on the creature, to a point where he witnessed something amazing occur, as Riggs revealed: "Standing on the high bank in the moonlight he watched dumb-struck as what looked like a huge ape-like animal swam to the other side of the river, easily negotiating the strong current, and never letting go of the rabbit."

In March 2007, the "Goldie E." family told of swimming Bigfoot around Trinidad, California. Rather bizarrely, the creatures were reportedly seen swimming alongside sea lions, as they negotiated the waters from Trinidad Head Rock to Flat Iron Rock! The biting, cold waters apparently affected the Bigfoot not a bit.

Welsh Sasquatch of the Caves

Oliver Lewis, a key and integral player within the Centre for Fortean Zoology, has investigated a fascinating old legend pertaining to the definitive Welsh Bigfoot.

He revealed that villagers in Nant Gwynant—a picturesque valley situated in Snow-donia, Gwynedd, North Wales—have for many a century told, in hushed tones, a tur-bulent and nightmarish story of how the dark and mysterious Cave of Owen Lawgoch in the old valley came to be known as the abode of "the hairy man."

Lewis's word has shown that long ago, villagers and shepherds in the area of Nant Gwynant were plagued by a silent and stealthy thief who would break into their homesteads under the protective covers of shadow and darkness on a disturbingly reg-ular basis. Those same villagers and shepherds would awaken to find that their goats and cows had been inexplicably milked, much-needed food was stolen, and a number of sheep were taken during the night, never to be seen again, their unfortunate fates surely sealed. The carnage and thievery, said Lewis, "went on for some years and every time anyone laid a trap for the thief it never took the bait and the finger of popular suspicion passed from ne'er-d'-well to ne'er-d'-well, with each suspect's guilt eventual-ly being disproved."

So, what was allegedly the true nature of the nightmarish beast said to have been roaming the densely-treed, ancient valley? According to North Wales-based legend it

Picturesque Nant Gwynant in Wales is home to the definitive legend about the Welsh Bigfoot that broke into homes and farms, stealing food and milking cows and goats.

was a creature of undeniably primitive proportions and terrifying appearance, one that seemed intent on tormenting the people of the picturesque area whenever, and however, possible, as Lewis noted:

One day a shepherd was returning from the mountains later than usual and spotted something strange; a huge, burly naked man covered from head to toe in thick red fur was resting on a neighboring hill. The shepherd suspected that this out of place and strangely hirsute giant might be the thief that was plaguing the village, so the shepherd snuck past the man without being detected and ran back to the village as soon as he was out of sight.

The story continued that when the shepherd in question breathlessly reached the heart of Nant Gwynant, he persuaded all of the available men of the village to join him in a quest to, once and for all, rid the area of the creature that had descended upon the village. Evidently, and unfortunately, not much thought went into this particular exercise.

It basically involved little more than the hysterical posse charging up the green hill towards the wild man with crude, homemade weapons in hand, while simultaneously screaming at him at the top of their lungs. Not surprisingly, alerting the hairy man-thing to their presence was hardly the cleverest of moves that the group could have made. The mighty beast shot away on all fours and, as Lewis noted, in a fashion that suggested "the skill and precision of a deer."

> As soon as it caught wind of the scent of the hounds, the hairy thing was gone, once again bounding away in almost graceful fashion....

A close and careful watch of the hill and its immediate surroundings was made from that day onwards, in the event that the man-beast might return to once again wreak diabolical havoc upon Nant Gwynant. It was a wise decision. Barely a few days passed before the menacing entity returned, to both feed voraciously and spread fear and chaos across the immediate land.

This time, however, the villagers took a new approach to tackling their quarry. The plan was to let loose a pack of vicious hounds upon the British Bigfoot-type animal, in the hope that the dogs would succeed where the men had overwhelmingly failed. Unfortunately, this action proved fruitless, too. As soon as it caught wind of the scent of the hounds, the hairy thing was gone, once again bounding away in almost graceful fashion as it made its successful escape, easily leaving the snarling dogs far behind.

Lewis revealed that an alternative plan of action was then put into place:

One man came up with the idea of consulting a magician. The magician told the villagers to find a red haired greyhound without a single hair of a different color and this would be able to catch the man. After much searching and bartering with local towns and villages the people of Nant Gwynant found a dog that fitted the bill and proudly took him home. When the villagers next saw the hairy man they were ready with the red greyhound and it was set loose to catch the hairy man. The hairy man escaped again by leaping down a small cliff.

Were the people of Nant Gwynant cursed to forever have the marauding thing in their very midst? No. If the men, the dogs, and even the supernatural powers of a renowned and mysterious purveyor of ancient magic had failed to terminate the monster-man and its terrible actions, then, quite clearly, another approach was sorely needed. It fell upon one of the women of the village to come up with a plan of attack to rid the area of the terrifying beast. Lewis explained what happened next:

> One woman was so angered by her frequent losses she decided to stay up every night and hide herself in the front room of her farmhouse to wait for when the hairy man decided to pay a visit. Sure enough after a few weeks the hairy man went to the wrong house and the lady was waiting with a hatchet. She remained hidden, until the man had squeezed his bulky frame halfway through the window, before she struck him with her hatchet. The unexpected blow cleaved off the hairy man's hand in one blow and he recoiled back out of the window before the woman could smite him with a further whack. The brave woman dashed out of her door, hatchet in hand ready to finish the man off but by the time she had gotten outside he had fled.

The wretched terror that had descended upon Nant Gwynant had finally reached its end, much to the overwhelming relief of the entire neighborhood, as Lewis revealed:

> When the village awoke the next day and the men learned what had happened they followed the trail of blood the hairy man had left behind to a cave beneath a local waterfall. As the big hairy man was never seen again it was assumed by the villagers that he had died in the cave, so the cave was named "the cave of the hairy man."

Wendigo

The vast majority of reports on record suggest that the Bigfoot creatures are largely solitary and prefer to stay away from humankind as much as possible. Even when Bigfoot and people do cross paths, the beasts generally use intimidation to ward off their unwelcome visitors—and perhaps even stranger methods, too, such as infrasound (*see* "Infrasound and Bigfoot").

There are, however, rare and not entirely verified accounts of Bigfoot mutilating, killing, and even eating people (*see* "Roosevelt, President Theodore, and Sasquatch"). Thankfully, such reports are in the minority—unless one believes that many of the thousands of people who go missing in the United States every year are helping, in a most unfortunate way, to feed and fuel Bigfoot. All of which brings us to a creature that has, for centuries, been greatly feared by Native Americans: the Wendigo.

A terrifying thing that appears prominently within the lore of the Algonquin people—the most widespread and populated of the Native American groups, with tribes originally numbering in the hundreds—the Wendigo is an evil, cannibalistic, and rampaging creature with the ability to possess human souls and minds, forcing them to do its dark bidding.

Humans have the ability to transform into a Wendigo, especially if they have engaged in cannibalism. Notably, in centuries past, those who were suspected by the Algonquin of being Wendigos were decapitated after death, to prevent them from rising from the grave and going on slaughtering, people-eating rampages.

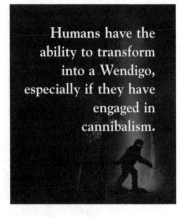

Humans have the ability to transform into a Wendigo, especially if they have engaged in cannibalism.

Many of the reports of the Wendigo are focused around large forests, freezing cold and wintery environments, and dark woods. In light of that, there is a theory that the stories of the Wendigo are the result of a distortion of real events, involving Native Americans who were forced to resort to cannibalism when food was scarce in the winter months; and tales told to try and dissuade people from cannibalism, by making them think that eating human flesh would turn them into Wendigos. That the Wendigo is often described as a large, marauding, humanoid beast that dwells deep in the forest, however, suggests we should leave the door open to a highly disturbing possibility: that Bigfoot has viewed the human race as its prey.

White Bigfoot

The overwhelming majority of reports about Bigfoot and similar creatures describe them as having brown or black hair. On occasion, the witnesses talk of red or reddish hair. On even rarer occasions, people claim to encounter white Bigfoot—possibly indicating the existence of albinism in the species.

In my personal files, I have just one report of a White Bigfoot. Rather curiously, it came from Lubbock, Texas—an area of the United States hardly noted for vast forests or woodland in which to hide. The witness, driving between Lubbock and Levelland in 2001, said she saw the large animal race across the highway sometime after 10:00 P.M. on a chilly winter's night.

In 2010, highly controversial footage surfaced anonymously that alleged to show a white Bigfoot in woods in Carbondale, Pennsylvania. In no time at all, it appeared on YouTube, along with the following statement:

> The owner's story is that he knew of sightings of a white Bigfoot type creature in the area. When he heard a disturbance in his backyard of his wooded property, be brought a video camera and a flashlight out in hopes of catching the something on tape. When he heard the rustling of leaves in the distance he pointed his flashlight and camera at the spot, thus catching the creature on film. He claims he was 10 to 15 feet away from the creature. He says, "I never really expected to catch anything like that on video." The town has been confirmed as Carbondale, Pennsylvania.

When the footage surfaced, it provoked major debate within the Bigfoot-seeking community. Most people believed it was a hoax. Others, however, weren't quite so sure.

Researcher Joe Black said: "[Bigfoot researcher] MK Davis posted a stabilized version of the "Pennsylvania White Bigfoot Video." Thanks to MK you can now see detail that was difficult to see in the original. I have watched this video over and over. Part of me wants to say this is real, but upon closer inspection I found many suspicious items that have led me to believe this video is a hoax.

The person put on white makeup, then put on some sort of white jacket. On the head a white mesh material was used that fit very tight. Using a flashlight with a video camera was the perfect way to cover any flaws and only showing the subject from the waist up. Since no mask was used, facial expressions and reaction to the light would look very natural. Jerking the flashlight also made the subject appear like it moved very fast.

At the *Weird Animal Report* website, "Erika" offered her thoughts and observations on the controversy:

The first thing I noticed about this video is, who grabs a camera and starts filming in the dark like that? Doesn't it seem more plausible that some kids got bored over their summer vacation, and decided to fake a Sasquatch video? (I know I did something very similar over one particularly dull summer vacation when I was a teenager, myself. And that was the 1980s, when

This is a carving of a Bigfoot made in DuBois, Pennsylvania. The state has had many Bigfoot sightings, including the famous 2010 white Bigfoot witnessed near Carbondale.

we didn't have the great digital technology that we do today!) The video has been edited such that a definite mood is created. You get about 30 seconds of "dude walking through the woods and I can't see anything." It's very Blair Witch. The first time I watched it, I half suspected this was going to be one of those "screamer" videos. I turned down the volume and leaned back in my chair, just in case. It's hardly definitive evidence: just a gut-level impression that it has all been tidily packaged to provide a specific experience.

Despite the highly controversial nature of the 2010 footage, the reports don't end there, as investigator Paul Seaburn demonstrated in October 2014:

Recently in Eddington, Maine, a boy (name not given) told Bill Brock and AJ Marston, members of the cryptid research organization Team Rogue, that he saw a big white creature running into the woods near his family's home. "I was walking and then … I hear something run over there. I look up and then there is something big, white and it runs right into the woods … and it's just gone." The boy's family didn't see the creature but reported finding a deer leg that "had just been ripped off, and was just sitting there." Brock and Marston say they found footprints and used a tree the boy saw it standing near to estimate the unpigmented cryptid was about eight feet tall. This is at least the second white Bigfoot sighting in Maine in a year. A man walking his dog on Christmas reported seeing one in Litchfield. Another white Bigfoot was reported in nearby Shaftsbury, Vermont, in January 2014.

If white Bigfoot do exist, then they are clearly in the minority. This strongly suggests we are dealing with albinos, rather than a specific offshoot of Bigfoot that is always white in color. On the issue of albinism, the National Organization for Albinism and Hypopigmentation stated:

The word "albinism" refers to a group of inherited conditions. People with albinism have little or no pigment in their eyes, skin, or hair. They have inherited altered genes that do not make the usual amounts of a pigment called melanin. One person in 17,000 in the U.S.A. has some type of albinism. Albinism affects people from all races. Most children with albinism are born to parents who have normal hair and eye color for their ethnic backgrounds. Sometimes people do not recognize that they have albinism. A common myth is that people with albinism have red eyes. In fact there are different types of albinism and the amount of pigment in the eyes varies. Although some individuals with albinism have reddish or violet eyes, most have blue eyes. Some have hazel or brown eyes. However, all forms of albinism are associated with vision problems.

It's important to note that albinism is not something exclusive to people. Susan L. Nasr said:

The occurrence of albinism runs the gamut across the animal kingdom. According to the *Missouri Conservationist*, published by the Missouri Department of Conservation, at least 300 species in North America have had at least one reported instance of albinism. Researchers observe albinism occurs once out of every 10,000 mammal births. Albinism is much more common in birds, occurring once in every 1,764 births. Diluting or spreading out a species' gene pool greatly reduces the chance of albinism.

Perhaps the idea of a white Bigfoot is not as unlikely as it seems at first glance.

White Pongo (1945 movie)

White Pongo is the title of a 1945 movie that co-stars Maris Wrixon and Ray "Crash" Corrigan, both also of the 1940 movie *The Ape* (see "The Ape [1940 movie]"). It tells the story of a quest to find the truth of a legendary—some say folkloric—white gorilla said to live deep in the heart of Belgian Congo and which is reputed to be the missing link between man and the apes.

Evidently, albino apes running amok in jungle environments were all the rage in 1945....

The movie begins as a local tribe prepares to sacrifice a man named Gunderson. Fortunately, Gunderson is saved from the clutches of the Grim Reaper by the sudden appearance of a huge albino ape, which proceeds to attack the tribespeople. During the mayhem, Professor Gerig, who lives with the tribe, quickly gives Gunderson a journal that tells of the findings of a now-deceased colleague of the scientist, a man named Dierdorf, who was obsessed with finding the truth of the white monster.

After an arduous and feverish trek through the jungle, Gunderson finally makes his way to a settlement on the Congo River. Just before dying from fever, he hands over the priceless journal to a group of European colonists. They decide to launch an expedition that they hope will finally figure out the truth of the legendary creature. They succeed in doing exactly that, but not before we see the immense beast doing battle with a regular gorilla and kidnapping Pamela Bragdon, played by Wrixon. Echoing *King Kong* of 1933, Pamela is freed from the clutches of the White Pongo, the beast is captured, and plans are made to load it aboard a boat and send it to London, England, for study.

Rather oddly, an almost identical movie, one that also starred Corrigan, *The White Gorilla*, was made the same year. Evidently, albino apes running amok in jungle environments were all the rage in 1945 (*see* "White Bigfoot").

And, finally, there is one notable, and rather intriguing, tie-in between the White Pongo of the movie's title and the real-life Bigfoot: in the movie, the beast is described as having flaming eyes, just like so many of the world's genuine cryptid apes.

Wild Man of the Navidad

Back in the 1830s, a wave of terror gripped the people of Sublime, Texas, which is situated between the cities of Houston and San Antonio. On numerous occasions, fearful locals reported seeing a wild, hair-covered creature that looked distinctly humanoid in appearance. It became known as the Wild Man of the Navidad. Typically, the encounters occurred in fields and woodland, and ended with the beast making good its escape. The theories for what the creatures might have been were wide and varied. Some locals believed it was a monkey of some kind, while more than a few Sublime folks were inclined to think that some kind of deviltry was afoot. Whatever the true answer, the wave of sightings came to an abrupt end—although, over the decades, a few, further, sporadic reports surfaced from Sublime.

The story of Sublime's Wild Man surfaced occasionally in books and periodicals—and most prominently within the pages of J. Frank Dobie's 1938 book *Tales of Old-Time Texas*, which was published by the Texas Folklore Society. More than seventy years after Dobie's book first surfaced, the Wild Man of the Navidad made a bold and dramatic return in a movie, courtesy of an Austin, Texas-based film company called Greeks Productions, and Kim Henkel, the writer of one of the most notorious and revered horror films of all time, *The Texas Chainsaw Massacre*.

Greeks Productions is the brainchild of filmmakers Justin Meeks and Duane Graves. Meeks grew up in Corpus Christi, Texas, and received degrees in psychology and film at Texas A&M University in 2001, before moving to Austin and landing a role on the television show *Prison Break*. Graves was born and raised in San Antonio and, like Meeks, also secured a degree in film at Texas A&M, and went on to direct the critically acclaimed documentary *Up Syndrome*: an intimate portrait of a childhood friend born with Down Syndrome.

Henkel had been the pair's professor of screenwriting and film production at Texas A&M, which provided both Meeks and Graves with the perfect background and opportunity to immerse themselves in the world of on-screen terror. After they set up Greeks Productions, in the spring of 2002 the duo quickly began work on a trilogy of short, black-and-white, 16mm horror films: *Headcheese*, *Voltagen* and *The Hypostatic Union*, all of which were released internationally by Shock-O-Rama Cinema.

But what was it that prompted the pair to develop the strange story of the Wild Man of the Navidad for the big screen? Graves told me:

> We knew we wanted to do a horror movie set in Texas, but we didn't really have a story. I had heard of the Wild Man—kind of like a handed-down story from my grandfather. But I didn't know too much about it. So, we started reading up on old Texas legends, got a copy of J. Frank Dobie's *Tales of Old-Time Texas* and read about the Wild Man of the Navidad. Then we went to Sublime to check the place out.

Graves continued:

> We went there on a kind of production-scouting trip. The idea was to stick to the conventional story that everyone had written about. While we were there, we would go in this little place called Red's Tavern, which is really the only place in town, and talk to the old folks about the Wild Man; and it was through them that we got hooked up with a guy named Dale S. Rogers.

It transpired that Rogers was related to Reverend Samuel C. A. Rogers, on whose land many of the original Wild Man of the Navidad encounters had occurred back in the 1800s. Over the years, the reverend had carefully collected numerous jaw-dropping stories pertaining to sightings of the beast and its beastly activities, many of which were published in Dobie's *Tales of Old-Time Texas*.

Until the mid-1970s, Graves and Meeks learned as they delved further into the mystery, Dale S. Rogers and his invalid wife had lived in a quaint

J. Frank Dobie (1888–1964) penned the 1938 book *Tales of Old-Time Texas,* in which he mentions the Wild Man of the Navidad.

ranch-house that was situated on the same Texas acreage that the long-dead reverend had previously owned, a great deal of which is heavily wooded and reputedly still unexplored to this very day.

Presently, a Texas historical marker detailing the legend of the Wild Man of the Navidad can be found on the perimeter of Rogers's land, which sits alongside Highway 90, west of Sublime. Even now, travelers visiting the marker report hearing unusual "bellowing sounds" from deep within the woods that surround the Navidad River and that extend beyond the lonely stretch of highway.

Graves said to me: "All of these ideas of the Wild Man being some sort of slave [are] a bunch of fabricated baloney. Those things were out there for years and they still might be. I saw one many times. My daddy saw it. My granddaddy saw it. It was more animal than anything else. And if anyone crossed it, it sure wouldn't hesitate to let you know that.

> "All of these ideas of the Wild Man being some sort of slave [are] a bunch of fabricated baloney...."

Gaining Rogers's trust, Graves and Meeks were provided with his detailed and absolutely indispensable journals that carefully chronicled and described the many and varied historic Wild Man encounters in the vicinity, as well as old Super-8 films of the area, and illustrations of the creature—all of which, collectively, became the inspiration for the movie.

Graves added:

We then hooked up with Ken, as he'd been our professor in college and had written *Chainsaw*. He came on-board; and Justin and me started developing it: as co-writers and directors. Everyone kept telling us we should make it into a slasher movie: killing teenagers. We didn't want that. We wanted to keep it as close to the original legend and [to] Dale's journals as we could.

The movie will not disappoint those with a deep passion for Bigfoot: it is darkly rich in atmosphere and conjures up graphic and unsettling imagery of a sinister little town that is sitting atop a wealth of eerie and ominous secrets. And to describe the locale as a little town is not an exaggeration: by 2000, the population of Sublime had only reached seventy-five. Try and imagine the best parts of *Twin Peaks*, *The X-Files*, and *The Legend of Boggy Creek* thrown into the mix, and then given a strong shot of independent film-making of a distinctly cool kind, and you have *The Wild Man of the Navidad*.

"Wild Man" of the Sixes

See: Hairy Men of the Old Mines

Wild Men of Britain

In 2012, I interviewed Jonathan Downes—the director of the British-based Centre for Fortean Zoology—on the nature of British, hairy, wild man reports. He told me:

One of the things that interest me—and I'm going out on a limb with this; it's not something most cryptozoologists agree with—is that the veneer of civilization of man is very, very thin. Just look at the ways in which otherwise perfectly normal men will behave when they go to war. Look at the way mobs behave.

I believe that all over the world, at various times—including Britain—there have been people that have regressed back through the layers of society and civilization. In some cases of so-called "feral children," they have been found with a fine down of hair all over their bodies. This is something that is quite well known, and is something that can appear in conditions like anorexia, or where, for whatever reason, a person is very malnourished. They start to develop fine hair on their bodies, under certain circumstances.

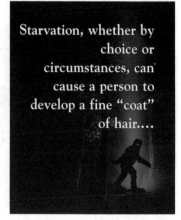

Starvation, whether by choice or circumstances, can cause a person to develop a fine "coat" of hair....

The hair to which Downes refers is called lanugo hair. Starvation, whether by choice or circumstances, can cause a person to develop a fine "coat" of hair, one that is particularly noticeable on the legs, face, back, and chest. On occasion, the hair can take on a rather significant furry appearance. It is a direct by-product of the loss of fat. As starvation overwhelms the body, fat levels decrease. Since, in part, fat helps to insulate us from the harshness of cold weather, the body over-compensates for its loss of fat by creating a new form of insulation: lanugo hair.

Downes also told me:

I think it is quite possible that you may have had situations where individuals—in earlier centuries and in Britain and elsewhere—may have been cast out of their village. Maybe they were just mentally ill, but the people of their village were in fear of them, so they were banished to the woods or whatever. They may have lived in the wild from then on, eking out primitive existences, and who being malnourished, may have developed fine hair over their bodies that then gets coated and matted with mud and leaves, and suddenly you have legends of wild men. They may have even bred if there were groups of them. And it wouldn't surprise me at all if, maybe, this led to at least some of the legends of wild men in Britain, but not all of them. They may well have been people who *went* wild, but who were not primitive people, as such.

Mark North and Robert Newland have studied reports of wild men in their home county of Dorset, England. They have uncovered centuries-old reports of wild men dwelling deep within the woods of Yellowham Hill, which is situated near the town of Dorchester. Of particular note, the hairy wild men had a particular liking for females of the area—to the extent that, on more than a few occasions they would abduct them and even impregnate them. Such stories may have been exaggerated or fabricated, to prevent irate fathers and husbands from finding out what their daughters or wives had been up to with the village locals!

On the other hand, perhaps the wild men of Dorset were something much different, far more ancient, and deeply mysterious. Even so, that the wild men could

Yellowham Hill is in the Puddletown Forest near Dorchester, England, where there have been reports of wild men over the centuries.

reputedly successfully mate with human females suggests some form of ancestral connection between us and them, maybe even a common ancestor.

It should be noted, too, that right next to Dorset is the English county of Somerset, also known for its wild man-type reports. Back to Downes:

Many years ago, the area around what is now an abandoned mine at Smitham Hill, in Somerset, was linked to tales of strange beasts seen watching the miners. Sometimes on returning to work in the morning, the men would find that carts and equipment had been pushed over and thrown around during the night.

These things, whatever they were, are still seen in that area today; or, at least, as late as November 1993. This is an exact quote taken from a witness whose case is in my files: "I was on a walk through the woods, when I heard a twig snap. I thought nothing of it and continued on. Suddenly the dogs became very agitated and ran off home. At this point I became aware of a foul smell, like a wet dog and a soft breathing sound. I started to run, but after only a few feet, I tripped and fell. I decided to turn and meet my pursuer only to see a large, about seven feet tall, dark brown, hairy, ape-like man. It just stood, about ten feet away, staring at me. It had intelligent looking eyes and occasionally tilted its head as if to find out what I was. After about twenty seconds it moved off into the forest."

Perhaps somewhere deep within the wilder parts of southern England, the ancient wild men still live on, totally oblivious to what such an extraordinary revelation, if proved, would provoke in the scientific and zoological communities.

Willow Creek (2013 movie)

Craig Woolheater, the owner of *Cryptomundo*, an immensely popular website that focuses on unknown creatures, called *Willow Creek* (2013) one of the best Bigfoot-themed movies ever made. The movie was both written and directed by comedian Bobcat Goldthwait, probably best known for his recurring roles as Zed in the *Police Academy* movies. As one might expect with Goldthwait at the helm, the film has its funny and lighthearted moments. It would be wrong, however, to describe

Willow Creek as a comedy, however. *Harry and the Hendersons* this most definitely is not.

Willow Creek demonstrates one thing from the outset: Goldthwait has a keen knowledge of Bigfoot history and the Bigfoot-seeking community. This is obvious from the fact that the film takes much of its inspiration from real-life Bigfoot-based incidents and cases.

The movie tells the story of Jim and Kelly (actors Bryce Johnson and Alexie Gilmour) who head off to Humboldt County, California, in search of the site of the legendary and controversial Bigfoot encounter of Roger Patterson and Bob Gimlin in 1967 (*see* "Patterson, Roger, Film of Bigfoot"). It's clear that, of the two, Jim is the Bigfoot enthusiast. Kelly is his girlfriend who does her best to put up with what she sees as Jim's growing, tedious, monster obsession.

For Jim, the whole thing is very much an adventurous road trip. With that in mind, the pair takes with them a camcorder to record every aspect of the trip—and, hopefully, to film Bigfoot, too. The first sign we get of the disturbing activity that soon follows comes when the duo turn up in the town of Willow Creek and are cryptically warned to keep out of the woods—something that, rather inevitably, only spurs Jim on even more.

The lighthearted banter between Kelly and Jim comes to an end when, after trekking miles into the woods, in search of the hallowed ground on which Bigfoot (or a man in a suit) trod back in 1967, the pair becomes lost. Concern and worry turn to fear when something large and violent stalks their camp as they sit terrified out of their wits, in their tent. I will not give the conclusion of the movie away, except to say that it is nerve-jangling, and Bigfoot fans will not be disappointed. Nor were those who reviewed it.

At the website of acclaimed reviewer Roger Ebert, fellow reviewer Brian Tallerico wrote:

> The centerpiece of "Willow Creek" is an extended sequence that everyone making a found footage film should be forced to watch. And take notes. The camera doesn't move. There are no quick cuts. There are no asides to the camera/audience to break the tension. We are merely in the tent with Jim and Kelly, watching their faces and, most of all, listening. What is scarier than an unexplainable, unidentifiable sound in the pitch-black woods, miles from civilization? "Willow Creek" makes the case that the answer is nothing.

In June 2014, Eric Kohn, of *Indiewire*, stated of Goldthwait's production:

> "Willow Creek" has been quietly screening at regional festivals over the summer and may have a hard time getting noticed in a sea of

Bobcat Goldthwait wrote and directed the 2013 Bigfoot movie, *Willow Creek.*

similar projects: Last year saw the release of the poorly received "Bigfoot: The Lost Coast Tapes," while "Blair Witch" co-director Eduardo Sánchez has been developing his own spooky found footage Bigfoot movie, "Exists." However, "Willow Creek" stands alone because it aims to engage with several genres at once. While it eventually devolves into exploring the terrifying prospects of something hairy lurking about in the shadows, Goldthwait uses that thrill factor to validate the commitment of Bigfoot believers. "Willow Creek" never feels like an attempt to proselytize, but it's a smart recognition of the dangers involved in doubt.

Women Kidnapped by Unknown Animals

In 1915, the now long defunct *Museum Journal*, published quarterly by the University Museum of the University of Pennsylvania, Philadelphia, ran a fascinating article on what, in hindsight, sounds like an anomalous ape, one said to live in the deep woods and forests of Guatemala. Its name was El Sisemite.

It read:

There is a monster that lives in the forest. He is taller than the tallest man and in appearance he is between a man and a monkey. His body is so well protected by a mass of matted hair that a bullet cannot harm him. His tracks have been seen on the mountains, but it is impossible to follow his trail because he can reverse his feet and thus baffle the most successful hunter.

As has been previously noted, there is a longstanding, worldwide tradition of crytid apes being able to "reverse" their feet.

The *Museum Journal* continued that the "great ambition" of the creature,

... which he has never been able to achieve, is to make fire. When the hunters have left their camp fires he comes and sits by the embers until they are cold, when he greedily devours the charcoal and ashes. Occasionally the hunters see in the forest little piles of twigs which have been brought together by El Sisemite in an unsuccessful effort to make fire in imitation of men.

[T]here is a longstanding, worldwide tradition of crytid apes being able to "reverse" their feet.

We also see, as the *Museum Journal*'s article revealed, two other staples of man-beast lore: a quasi-supernatural aspect to the creature and its obsession with kidnapping people, very often women:

His strength is so great that he can break down the biggest trees in the forest. If a woman sees a Sisemite, her life is infinitely prolonged, but a man never lives more than a month after he has looked into the eyes of the monster. If a Sisemite captures a man he rends the body and crushes the bones between his teeth in great enjoyment of the flesh and blood. If he captures a woman, she is carried to his cave, where she is kept a prisoner.

Besides his wish to make fire the Sisemite has another ambition. He sometimes steals children in the belief that from these he may acquire the gift of human speech. When a person is captured by a Sisemite the fact becomes known to his near relations and friends, who at the moment are seized with a fit of shivering. Numerous tales are told of people who have been captured by the Sisemite.

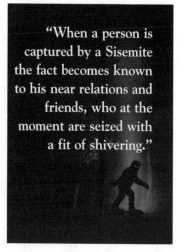

"When a person is captured by a Sisemite the fact becomes known to his near relations and friends, who at the moment are seized with a fit of shivering."

One such case of kidnapping was specifically detailed by the journal. The article also has a somewhat supernatural aspect to it, in that one of the key individuals in the story suffered from what are termed "Sisemite shivers," the sense of the creature in a person's midst, even if it can't be seen. The saga began:

A young couple, recently married, went to live in a hut in the woods on the edge of their milpa in order that they might harvest the maize. On the road Rosalia stepped on a thorn and next morning her foot was so sore that she was unable to help Felipe with the harvesting, so he went out alone, leaving one of their two dogs with her.

He had not been working long when the dreaded feeling, which he recognized as Sisemite shivers, took hold of him and he hastily returned to the hut to find his wife gone and the dog in a great fright. He immediately set out for the village, but met on the road the girl's parents, who exclaimed, "You have let the Sisemite steal our child, our feelings have told us so." He answered, "It is as you say."

In no time at all, the local police were on the case, suspecting that the story of the Sisemite was nothing but an ingenious ruse, one created to hide the fact that the young man had killed his wife.

The boy was cross-examined, but always answered, "The Sisemite took her, no more than that I know." He was, in spite of the girl's parents' protests, suspected of having murdered his young wife, and was thrown into jail, where he remained many years.

We may never know if the police's suspicions about Felipe were correct or if a grave miscarriage of justice took place. Either way, the mystery only added to the mythos surrounding the Sisemite and its obsession with kidnapping women.

The *Museum Journal* was not yet done with this controversial story, however. There was far more to tell.

At last a party of hunters reported having seen on Mount Kacharul a curious being with a hairy body and flowing locks that fled at the sight of them. A party was organized that sought the capture of this creature at any cost. Some days later, this party returned with what seemed to be a wild woman, of whom the leader reported as follows:

On Mount Kacharul we hid in the bushes. For 2 days we saw nothing, but on the third day about noon this creature came to the brook to drink and we captured her, though she struggled violently. As we were crossing the brook with her, a Sisemite appeared on the hillside, waving his arms and

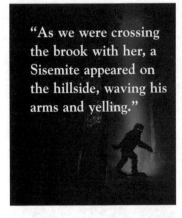

"As we were crossing the brook with her, a Sisemite appeared on the hillside, waving his arms and yelling."

yelling. On his back was a child or monkey child which he took in his hands and held aloft as if to show it to the woman, who renewed her struggle to be free. The Sisemite came far down the hill almost to the brook; he dropped the child and tore off great branches from big trees which he threw at us.

The young man was brought from his cell into the presence of this wild creature and asked if he recognized her. He replied, "My wife was young and beautiful; the woman I see is old and ugly." The woman never spoke a word and from that time on made no sound. She refused to eat and a few days after her capture she died. Felipe lived to be an old man, and the grandmother of the woman who told this story remembered him as the man whose wife had been carried away by the Sisemite.

One final point: the so-called "Sisemite shivers," reported by so many, sound very much like the sense of dread that is often found in Bigfoot cases, which may be attributable to the creatures' use of directed infrasound (*see* "Infrasound and Bigfoot").

Woodwose and Ancient Encounters

The word "Woodwose" has its origins in ancient England. It's also a word steeped in mystery and legend. Although there is no solid consensus on its origins, the likelihood is that it's derived from *wudu*, an old word meaning "forest" and *wasa* or, in today's terminology, "being." In that sense, the Woodwose is a being of the forest, a hairy, wild humanoid of the woods—a creature similar to Bigfoot.

Tabitca Cope, author of a number of books, including the Loch Ness Monster-themed *Dark Ness*, has carefully and extensively studied the mystery of the Woodwose. Her research has shown that the Woodwose was predominantly reported across England from the fourteenth to the sixteenth century. It was most often described as a large, man-like beast, covered in a coat of tight, curly hair, heavily bearded, and almost invariably carrying a large, wooden club. At times, the wild Woodwose would cover its body in ivy, moss, and leaves—possibly as a form of camouflage.

On this same topic, English author and researcher Elizabeth Randall said that the Woodwose is:

> usually shown as a complete, part human, figure carrying a club with the limbs being leafy. It also often shows a thick beard and wears a cap. The Woodwose may also be shown holding the club in different positions. Sometimes this is on its side and sometimes it is raised. There is a theory that a raised club depicts the figure before it was converted to Christianity, but it's probably more correct to believe that it was raised to ward off evil spirits.

Cope noted that reports of what sound like Woodwose date back thousands of years and can be found in the pages of notable manuscripts:

The first "Wild Man" appearing in the worlds' literature was Enkidu in the ancient Sumerian *Epic of Gilgamesh*. Created by the goddess Aruru (also known as Anu) to appease the prayers of the subjects of Gilgamesh who tired of his ironhanded rule, Enkidu was made to match the strength of Gilgamesh and to do battle with him, although he actually became Gilgamesh's closest ally. Historian Fred Gladstone Skinner wrote that Enkidu was "a valiant god of battle, whose entire body was covered with hair, shaggy as a woman's head. His clothes were of animal skins and, like an animal, he grazed in the fields and fought with the wild beasts for a place at the water holes."

The Woodwose legend has been a part of English folklore for centuries. In this photo, two Woodwoses are depicted on a coat of arms on a ledger slab in St. Peter's Church in Brighton, England.

Bigfoot and the Woodwose share one common factor: both are hair-covered, bipedal hominids. There is, however, one major difference between them: whereas Bigfoot is very ape-like, the Woodwose is far more akin to a primitive human. This has led to the development of a number of intriguing and thought-provoking theories. First, there is the idea that the story of the Woodwose may have had its origins with feral people—individuals who shunned society, and all its trappings and conventions, and elected to live their lives in the wild, far away from humanity. Over time, they descended into a state of near-animal-like savagery, accentuated by their predilection for covering their bodies in leaves, moss, and bark.

An equally notable theory suggests the Woodwose may actually have been the last, straggling, surviving remnants of Neanderthals. The general consensus is that Neanderthals surfaced around 600,000 years ago and died out around 40,000 B.C.E. Could, however, isolated pockets have survived for longer—as in for much longer? Perhaps we should not rule out such a possibility, no matter how unlikely and unpalatable such a scenario might be for the scientific community.

Perhaps of relevance to all this is a belief among the old Europeans that if a person chose to live in the wild, he or she would descend into a state of savagery—to the extent that they would grow excessive coats of hair and lose their ability to talk and instead grunt and growl like a wild animal. Perhaps those beliefs were borne out of occasional sightings of relic Neanderthals.

An interesting report of a Woodwose appears in a thirteenth-century Norwegian text titled *Konungs skuggsjá* (in English, *The King's Mirror*). One might be inclined to take the view that what *The King's Mirror* describes is an encounter with a Neanderthal. The relevant, translated part reads as follows:

It once happened in that country (and this seems indeed strange) that a living creature was caught in the forest as to which no one could say definitely whether it was a man or some other animal; for no one could get a word from it or be sure that it understood human speech. It had the human

The thirteenth-century Norwegian text *Konungs skuggsjá* describes an encounter with a Neanderthal not unlike this recreation of one.

shape, however, in every detail, both as to hands and face and feet; but the entire body was covered with hair as the beasts are, and down the back it had a long coarse mane like that of a horse, which fell to both sides and trailed along the ground when the creature stooped in walking.

Another, distinctly different, theory suggests the Woodwose may have been a magical entity, one possessed of strange powers. Elizabeth Randall's research into this particular area led her to say:

Celtic tales attribute poetic, or prophetic, powers to wild men. In Welsh tradition, especially, such powers are given to Myrddi, (aka Merlin), who at one point becomes mad and goes into a forest where he finds himself able to write prophetic poetry. Mediaeval literature and art are full of wild men stories and icons, and while most are portrayed as being mainly human, they are sometimes shown as crawling on all fours and attacking dogs. Rather than being the true "wild man of the woods," who lives a feral life, it is possible that the Woodwose is a strange being that manifests itself into reality from time to time. If that is true, then it may account for the occasional reports that still surface today.

Whether the Woodwose are people living wild, the last remnants of the Neanderthals, or something strangely supernatural, they still provoke chills and fears in those parts of England where the myths and legends of old continue to hold solid sway.

World War II Wild Men

The Second World War brought forth death on a massive scale, worldwide carnage, and the atomic bomb. It also brought forth a number of reports of savage man-beasts. Two prominent cases came from the former Soviet Union, one in 1941 and the other in 1944. The source of the first account was a respected figure in the Medical Service arm of the Soviet Army: Lt. Col. V. S. Karapetyan. The location was, rather notably, not far from the Caucasus Mountains, from where numerous reports have surfaced of the Bigfoot-like Almasty (*see* "Almasty Expedition").

For around twelve weeks, Karapetyan and his unit were stationed at Buynaksk, in the Republic of Dagestan, doing their utmost to lessen the alarming expansions across Europe by the Nazis. One particular morning, and quite out of the blue, a Buynaksk-based police officer visited Karapetyan's camp and shared with him some astonishing news.

High in the surrounding cold peaks, a man had been captured by local villagers. This was not a normal man, however. Rather intriguingly, he was described as an espionage agent in "disguise." It was a description that puzzled Karapetyan—at least, until he saw the man up close, in an old barn where he was being held, and then realized it was actually a very apt description. Karapetyan said:

> I can still see the creature as it stood before me, a male, naked and bare-footed. And it was doubtlessly a man, because its entire shape was human. The chest, back, and shoulders, however, were covered with shaggy hair of a dark brown color (it is noteworthy that all the local inhabitants had black hair). This fur of his was much like that of a bear, and 2 to 3 centimeters long. The fur was thinner and softer below the chest. His wrists were crude and sparsely covered with hair. The palms of his hands and soles of his feet were free of hair. But the hair on his head reached to his shoulders partly covering his forehead. The hair on his head, moreover, felt very rough to the hand. He had no beard or moustache, though his face was completely covered with a light growth of hair. The hair around his mouth was also short and sparse.

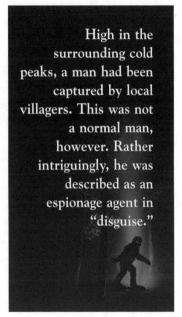

High in the surrounding cold peaks, a man had been captured by local villagers. This was not a normal man, however. Rather intriguingly, he was described as an espionage agent in "disguise."

> The man stood absolutely straight with his arms hanging, and his height was above the average—about 180 cm. He stood before me like a giant, his mighty chest thrust forward. His fingers were thick, strong, and exceptionally large. On the whole, he was considerably bigger than any of the local inhabitants.

> His eyes told me nothing. They were dull and empty—the eyes of an animal. And he seemed to me like an animal and nothing more.

> As I learned, he had accepted no food or drink since he was caught. He had asked for nothing and said nothing. When kept in a warm room he sweated profusely. While I was there, some water and then some food (bread) was brought up to his mouth; and someone offered him a hand, but there was no reaction. I gave the verbal conclusion that this was no disguised person, but a wild man of some kind. Then I returned to my unit and never heard of him again.

Only three years later, and as the Second World War continued to rage, yet another encounter with a Russian wild man occurred, also in the Caucasus Mountains. In this case, the source of the story was a police officer, Erjib Koshokoyev. As the resident of a small town in the mountainous area, it was Koshokoyev's responsibility to ensure that there was no Nazi incursions in the area—which he did a very good job of thwarting, by all accounts.

As part of his job, Koshokoyev led regular horseback sorties into the mountains: the last thing anyone needed were hordes of German troops overrunning the area. On a dark, autumn night in 1944, the unit of men was conducting its regular search of the area when, suddenly, one of the horses reared up—seemingly in terror—and threw its rider to the ground. Exactly why became immediately obvious. Standing in the shadows, and at a distance of around seventeen or eighteen feet, was a tall, human-like figure coated in reddish hair. For a few seconds, no one moved, such was the terrifying nature of the situation. That is, until the creature suddenly broke into an astonishingly fast run and the band of men raced after it.

As the beast charged across the cold, dark landscape, it noticed an old shepherd's hut and threw open the door and slammed it shut—an action that suggested a fair degree of intelligence on its part. To his credit, Koshokoyev quickly deduced that whatever the beast was, it should be taken alive. Koshokoyev was already thinking about having it transferred to a military-scientific detachment at Nalchik, which was the capital of the republic of Kabardino-Balkaria.

The operation to snare the primitive man was not going to be an easy one, so Koshokoyev whispered to the group that they should approach slowly and carefully to surround the hut, ensuring that the thing had no way to escape. Unfortunately, the plan didn't go as Koshokoyev had hoped.

In some fashion, it appears the hairy man realized what was afoot and burst out of the hut, racing around it in wild and frantic fashion. Although terrified by the monstrous appearance and horrific nature of the beast, the men did their best to keep calm. That worked—at least, until the monster charged at them, which resulted in the group scattering. The man-monster vanished as it headed into a large, wooded ravine.

One final, strange thing: according to Koshokoyev, the animal was partially dressed in what resembled a torn and tattered kaftan. It was never seen again.

"Yellow Top" of Canada

On July 27, 1923, the North Bay, Ontario, Canada-based newspaper, the *Nugget*, told a strange, albeit brief, story that dealt with an unusual animal that was linked to the presence of old mines in the area. The article reads like this:

> Mr. J. A. MacAuley and Mr. Lorne Wilson claim they have seen the Precambrian Shield Man while working on their mining claims North and East of the Wettlaufer Mine near Cobalt. This is the second time in seventeen years that a hairy apelike creature nicknamed "Yellow Top" because of a light-colored "mane" has been seen in the district.

According to MacAuley and Wilson, as they took test samples from the land, they saw what, on first inspection, looked like a bear "picking at a blueberry patch." They were right about the blueberries, but not about the "bear."

Wilson told a *Nugget* reporter: "It kind of stood up and growled at us. Then it ran away. It sure was like no bear that I have ever seen. Its head was kind of yellow and the rest of it was black like a bear, all covered with hair."

The newspaper concluded: "The first report of the creature was made in September, 1906, by a group of men building the head-frame at the Violet Mine, east of Cobalt. It has not been seen since that time."

Yeren of China

Next to the legendary fire-breathing dragon, it's China's most famous monster: the Yeren, a huge, unidentified ape that almost certainly—in terms of its close proximity—has connections to the Abominable Snowman of the Himalayas and the various large and similar animals said to roam the huge mountains, such as the Nyalmo. While Yeren have been seen in a number of areas of China, certainly the one area most prominently known for sightings is Hubei, a province in central China. It's dominated by numerous mountains—including the Daba Mountains and the Wudang Mountains—and the Jianghang Plain. The massive, near-4,000-mile-long Yangtze River also flows through Hubei.

It's specifically the western portion of Hubei in which the Yeren has been spotted—an area noted for its dense forest and treacherous mountains. One theory of what

In Western Hubei Province, China, the entrance to a Yeren cave is marked with with large, painted letters saying "Ye Ren Dong" ("Wild Man Cave").

the Yerens is that they are *Gigantopithecus* (*see* "*Gigantopithecus blacki*"), a massive, presumed extinct, ape that dwelled in China hundreds of thousands of years ago. A second theory is that the animal represents some form of huge, and unacknowledged, orangutan.

Interestingly, just like Bigfoot in the United States, the Yeren comes in a variety of colors. Its hair has been described as red, brown, and black. As for its height, while most reports describe creatures the average height of an adult human male to about eight feet, there are a number of cases involving colossal mountain monsters in excess of ten feet. Despite their imposing appearances, however, the Yeren are said to be relatively placid, quiet creatures that shun humankind.

Sightings of the Yeren cannot be blamed upon hype borne out of the fascination for Bigfoot. That is made clear by the fact that news of these immense animals has been reported for centuries. A translated, seventeenth-century document from Hubei noted: "In the remote mountains of Fangxian County, there are rock caves, in which live hairy men as tall as three meters. They often come down to hunt dogs and chickens in the villages. They fight with whoever resists."

Of course, the final comment contradicts reports about the creature's placid nature. Also, the reference to the Yeren's hunting dogs adds weight to the notion that dogs and Bigfoot are not on friendly terms with each other.

The evidence for the existence of the Yeren in more recent years is equally impressive. In 1940, it's said that the body of a dead Yeren turned up in Gansu. Female and over six feet in height, it was examined by Chicago biologist Wang Tselin. Interestingly, Tselin was unable to figure out if the beast was a form of ape, a primitive human, or an odd combination of both.

In Tselin's own words:

Around September or October, we were travelling from Baoji to Tianshui via Jiangluo City; our car was between Jiangluo City and Niangniang Plain when we suddenly heard gunshots ahead of us. When the car reached the crowd that surrounded the gunman, all of us got down to satisfy our curiosity. We could see that the "wildman" was already shot dead and laid on the roadside.

The body was still supple and the stature very tall, approximately 2 metres. The whole body was covered with a coat of thick greyish-red hair which was very dense. Since it was lying face-down, the more inquisitive of the passengers turned the body over to have a better look. It turned out to be a mother with a large pair of breasts, the nipples being very red as if it had recently given birth. The hair on the face was shorter. The face was narrow with deep-set eyes, while the cheek bones and lips jutted out. The scalp hair was roughly one chi long and untidy. The appearance was very similar to the plaster model of a female Peking Man. However, its hair seemed to be longer and thicker than that of the ape-man model. It was ugly because of the protruding lips.

According to the locals, there were two of them, probably one male and the other female. They had been in that area for over a month. The "wild-

This artifact at the Khumjung monastery in Nepal is purported to be the scalp of a Yeti.

men" had great strength, frequently stood erect and were very tall. They were brisk in walking and could move as rapidly uphill as on the plain. As such, ordinary folks could not catch up with them. They did not have a language and could only howl.

Moving onto the 1970s, and specifically May 1976, there is a fascinating story of a number of government personnel—all based at Hubei—who, as they drove along a stretch of road dominated by thick woods in the early, pre-dawn hours, came face to face with a Yeren.

In its haste to escape from the approaching jeep, the red-haired creature raced up a slope, but lost its footing and tumbled onto the road, landing right in front of the shocked group. Reportedly, the animal did not rear up onto its legs, but took a crouching stance—perhaps intended to intimidate the group by provoking fear it was about to lunge at them. Fortunately, that did not happen. What did happen is that the beast raced off, yet again—after one of the men hurled a stone in its direction. Although the creature had undeniable physical traits of an ape, its eyes were described as being eerily human-like, displaying intelligence and inquisitiveness.

As sightings of the creatures continued to be reported in the 1970s, and then into the 1980s, the Chinese Academy of Sciences got involved and established an ambitious program to try and resolve the mystery of the Yeren. It was no easy task, and no hard, undeniable evidence ever surfaced. But many credible witnesses provided testimony.

One such witness gave a report on an encounter with a Yeren:

He was about seven feet tall, with shoulders wider than a man's, a sloping forehead, deep-set eyes and a bulbous nose with slightly upturned nostrils. He had sunken cheeks, ears like a man's but bigger, and round eyes, and also bigger than a man's. His jaw jutted out and he had protruding lips. His front teeth were as broad as a horse's. His eyes were black. His hair was dark brown, more than a foot long and hung loosely over his shoulders. His whole face, except for the nose and ears, was covered with short hairs. His arms hung below his knees. He had big hands with fingers about six inches long and thumbs only slightly separated from the fingers. He didn't have a tail, and the hair on his body was short. He had thick thighs, shorter than the lower part of his leg. He walked upright with his legs apart. His feet were each about 12 inches long and half that broad in front and narrow behind, with splayed toes. He was a male. That much I saw clearly.

Monster authority Brad Steiger reported on a sighting in the 1990s:

In October 1994, the Chinese government established the Committee for the Search for Strange and Rare Creatures, including among its members specialists in vertebrate paleontology and paleoanthropology. A loose consensus among interested members from the Chinese Academy of Sciences maintains that the Yeren are some species of unknown primates.

Today, the search for the Yeren continues in China, in much the same way that Bigfoot is sought in the United States and the Yowie in Australia.

Yeti of the Himalayas

Bigfoot is certainly the most famous of the world's many hairy man-beasts. Running a close second, however, is the Yeti, also known as the Abominable Snowman. The specific region in which the legendary beast is said to roam is the Himalayas, a vast, mountainous expanse that dominates Nepal and Tibet.

In the same way that the United States appears to be the home of several different creatures—such as the huge, lumbering apes of the Pacific Northwest and the smaller skunk-apes of Florida—there also appears to be more than one kind of Yeti. Reportedly they range from man-sized creatures to enormous giants, close to twenty feet in height. Of course, claims of such extreme and extraordinary heights must be treated cautiously. They may well be distorted accounts of encounters with animals of smaller stature, but no less impressive, perhaps around twelve to thirteen feet tall (see "Nyalmo").

There is another Bigfoot parallel, too. Native American tradition tells of ancient awareness of the hairy beasts of the United States. Likewise, tales of hair-covered giants roaming the Himalayas also extend back into the fog of time. Take, for example, the stories of the Lepcha people. They are among the oldest of the various tribes that inhabit Sikkim, situated in northeast India. Their presence, however, extends to Tibet—and specifically to the heart of Nepal. It's not surprising, then, that they may have encountered Yetis during the course of their travels and expansions. Indeed, Lepcha lore tells of Goliath-sized, hairy humanoids that lived high in the Himalayas and used rocks to kill their prey, such as goats.

In the modern era, it was in the 1800s that matters became particularly intriguing. In the early 1830s an expedition was launched to the Himalayas by a skilled mountain-climber, Brian Houghton Hodgson. According to Hodgson: "My shooters were once alarmed in the Kachár by the apparition of a 'wild man,' possibly an ourang, but I doubt their accuracy. They mistook the creature for a càcodemon or rakshas (demons), and fled from it instead of shooting it. It moved, they said, erectly: was covered with long dark hair, and had no tail." None of the team expected to encounter giant, hair-covered hominids on the Himalayas, but that was exactly what they encountered. Particularly baffling to the team, the creatures they saw—typically at a distance—walked solely on its hind limbs.

Just one year before the turn of the twentieth century, Laurence Waddell's book, *Among the Himalayas*, was published. In the book, Waddell described how a number of Tibetans had told him of huge, hairy, ape-like animals that moved like people and which

An illustration of a Yeti by Philippe Semeria.

lived in the mountains. Waddell put little faith in the accounts, despite having personally come across some intriguing, large footprints in the snow. The reports from Hodgson's team, coupled with that of Waddell, provoked short waves of interest; it wasn't, however, until the 1920s that matters heated up.

The Everest Reconnaissance Expedition was launched in 1921, under the leadership of Lieutenant-Colonel Charles Howard-Bury of the British military (*see* "Howard-Bury, Lt. Col. C. K., Yeti Encounter"). No one on the expedition anticipated coming across anything unusual, but that was exactly what they found, in the form of huge, human-like footprints, thousands of feet up in the snow-covered mountains. When word of the strange discoveries began to spread, a newspaper reporter, Henry Newman, decided to look into the matter for himself. It didn't take long before Newman had collated a respectably sized body of material on the legendary mountain roamer, which he famously dubbed the Abominable Snowman—a somewhat mistaken distortion of the term used by the locals, *metoh*, meaning "filthy."

Without doubt, it was the decade of the 1950s that really caught the imagination of the media and the scientific community. Britain's media was hot on the trail of the creature, as were respected mountaineers, including Sir Edmund Hillary and Eric Shipton. Although interest in, and reports of, the Yeti dipped in subsequent years, the controversy was revived in 2014, when a professor of genetics at Oxford University, England, revealed his findings, which suggested the Yeti was actually a bear, possibly one that was part-polar bear and part-brown bear (*see* "Sykes, Bryan, and the Abominable Snowman").

Within the field of cryptozoology, the most likely candidate for the Yeti is *Gigantopithecus*, a truly gigantic ape that science tells us has been extinct for tens of thousands of years. That the immense beast dwelled in the very areas where Yetis are seen to this day suggests a distinct, but astounding, possibility that *Gigantopithecus* may still be with us (*see* "*Gigantopithecus blacki*").

Yowie Sightings in Australia

Creatures of a Bigfoot-like appearance are not exclusive to the United States, the Himalayas, and the wilds of South America, Russia, and China. Australia is the domain of the huge, apish Yowie. In the same way that Native Americans have a long history of reports of Sasquatch—and particularly so in the Pacific Northwest—Australia's aboriginal people have long told of the existence of the towering Yowie. There is another parallel between the North American Bigfoot and the Yowie of Australia: a careful perusal of old newspapers shows that the Yowie, just like Bigfoot, was known long before the term "Bigfoot" was created, back in the 1950s.

Many of the sightings of Yowies occur in and around the vast Blue Mountains that dominate the city of Sydney and what is termed the Sydney Basin. A firsthand report, from February 1842, offers a graphic description of the beasts. It was published, as a letter, in the pages of the *Australian and New Zealand Monthly Magazine*:

> This being they describe as resembling a man of nearly the same height, with long white hair hanging down from the head over the features, the arms as extraordinarily long, furnished at the extremities with great talons, and the feet turned backwards, so that, on flying from man, the imprint of the foot appears as if the being had traveled in the opposite direction. Altogether, they describe it as a hideous monster of an unearthly character and ape-like appearance.

Then, on December 9, 1882, a firsthand account surfaced from Mr. H. J. McHooey, who told the *Australian Town and Country Journal* newspaper the following:

> A few days ago I saw one of these strange creatures. I should think that if it were standing upright it would be nearly five feet high. It was tailless and covered with very long black hair, which was of a dirty red or snuff-color about the throat and breast. Its eyes, which were small and restless, were partly hidden by matted hair that covered its head. I threw a stone at the animal, whereupon it immediately rushed off.

Sightings of the Australian Yowie are not limited to the past. In early 1993, Neil Frost, who lived in the Blue Mountains area, encountered in the shadows of his backyard an animal that he estimated weighed close to 300 pounds, walked on two legs, and had a thick coat of hair and bright red eyes. When the beast realized it had been spotted, it shot away at high speed and into the shadows. Despite attempts on the part of Frost and a friend, Ian Price, to track down the beast on several occasions, the Yowie skillfully eluded them—just like its American cousin, Bigfoot, so very often does, too.

Midway through June 2013, Australia's *Northern Star* newspaper reported on a recent encounter. Journalist Jamie Brown wrote: "The latest sighting took place recently just north of Bexhill when a Lis-

A statue of a Yowie in—appropriately—Yowie Park, Kilcoy, Queensland, Australia.

more resident and music videographer spied the classic creature crossing a moonlit Bangalow Road. The witness, who has asked not to be named for fear of reprisal, said he was driving back home from a night of filming at Eltham and had just turned onto the Bangalow Road heading for Lismore when he spied a creature jumping a barbed wire paddock fence before briefly pausing at the edge of the road. Suddenly the beast moved across the two lanes of bitumen, raising his arm to apparently shield its eyes from the bright high beam glare of the approaching car.

The anonymous witness commented: "I would have seen it for between 20 and 30 seconds. It was really moving at the time. It leapt the fence no problem. All I can remember was seeing this large black object with a solid build, lanky legs and long lanky arms. It wasn't clothed ... it wasn't wearing clothes like a human."

The Yowie, it seems, lives on.

Zana and the Half-Human Controversy

It was in 1964 that Professor Boris Porshenev uncovered, in Russia's Caucasus Mountains, what was described to him by the villagers of Tkhina as the bones of a female Almasty (*see* "Almasty Expedition"), Russia's very own Bigfoot. Brad Steiger said that according to Porshenev, a "preliminary investigation of the skeleton determined that its skeletal structure was different to that of a female member of *Homo sapiens.*"

It was a discovery that became inextricably linked to a story that dated back to the mid-1860s. A nobleman named Edgi Genaba, who had an estate in Tkhina, returned to the village one day with something remarkable in tow. It was a strange, savage-looking thing of primitive proportions. Clearly, in some respects, at least, it was human. But it was unclear whether it was actually *Homo sapiens.* Reportedly, the creature—a female—was given to Genaba by a vassal of Prince D. M. Achba, an expert hunter and the ruler of the Zaadan region, who took the wild woman alive while out in the woods.

Genaba wasted no time in building a secure enclosure, one in which the creature, soon named Zana, could be housed. Initially, there were understandable concerns that Zana might prove to be hostile and murderous, hence the reason why she was kept confined. For a while, at least, Genaba's actions made sense: Zana was definitely unstable, lived in a hole she dug in the enclosure, and ate like a wild animal. Over the course of a couple of years, however, things began to change.

Eventually, the people of Tkhana came to accept that Zana was no longer the threat they had feared she might originally have been, and as a result, she was given a

> The most controversial claim made about Zana is that she gave birth to five children. The fathers, however, were reportedly not male Almasty, but the men of Tkhana.

significant amount of freedom to wander around the village and interact with the people of the area. Zana was, by all accounts, a quick learner and quite intelligent: she helped around the village, hauling sacks of grain and preparing firewood, and seemingly enjoying her daily tasks, too.

It's clear from the descriptions that Zana was no normal woman: her immense body was covered in dark hair, she shunned clothing—even in the freezing temperatures of the Caucasus Mountains—and she could not speak a word. Of her physical appearance, Igor Bourtsev said:

Her face was terrifying; broad, with high cheekbones, flat nose, turned out nostrils, muzzle like jaws, wide mouth with large teeth, low forehead and eyes of a reddish tinge. But the most frightening feature was her expression which was purely animal, not human. Sometimes, she would give a spontaneous laugh, baring those big white teeth of hers. The latter were so strong that she easily cracked the hardest walnuts.

Despite repeated attempts to try and have Zana learn to speak the local Russian dialect, it came to nothing: mumble and squeal was just about all that Zana could manage, depending on her mood and demeanor. She was, however, a creature obsessed with cleanliness, never missing a day of bathing in the cold waters of a local spring. Zana also had an obsession with rocks. She enjoyed chipping away at them and placing them into various designs and piles, as if doing so held some form of significance for her.

The most controversial claim made about Zana is that she gave birth to five children. The fathers, however, were reportedly not male Almasty, but the men of Tkhana. Brad Steiger has made a valuable observation on this claim: "If true, the implications of Zana's having bred with men of the village are really quite staggering. If the wild woman truly did conceive with human males, then she was not an ape."

Related to this aspect of the story is the rumor that four of the children died, while the sole survivor fled for the vast mountains from which its mother reportedly originated. Zana supposedly lived until the 1880s, when she passed away, and her life was celebrated by the people of Tkhana, who had come to embrace her as one of their very own.

Of course, it's a fascinating and undeniably engaging story, but is it true? Or, rather, how much of it is true and how much is folkloric distortion? Read on....

Zana's DNA under the Microscope

On November 1, 2013, Britain's Channel 4 put out a press release that outlined the facts concerning a new documentary it was about to air on Zana. It read, in part:

Bryan Sykes, Professor of Human Genetics at the University of Oxford, has carried out DNA tests on saliva samples taken from descendants of Zana—a so-called "wild woman" captured in the late 19th century in southern Russia, who local people believe was an "Almasty."

Professor Sykes' research (part of a worldwide analysis of alleged Bigfoot samples), has yielded a remarkable result: that Zana's ancestry was 100% Sub-Saharan African and that she was most probably a slave brought to the region by the ruling Ottomans.

His findings feature in a new Channel 4 documentary series, *Bigfoot Files* …, presented by Mark Evans, who is on a global quest to unlock the real story of Bigfoot. Zana's story is extraordinary. She is said to have been captured in the forests of Abkhazia, a remote part of Russia's Caucasus region, in the 1870s. Imprisoned, it's said, for two decades by a local landowner, she was described by eyewitnesses as being "very big, strong, her whole body covered with hair." Chillingly, Zana had four children with local men.

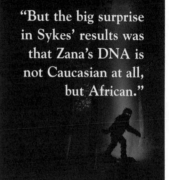

"But the big surprise in Sykes' results was that Zana's DNA is not Caucasian at all, but African."

Russia's "Almasty Hunters" have been obsessed with her story for over half a century and have always believed that Zana could be a surviving Neanderthal, the human-like species that is thought to have died out tens of thousands of years ago.

Channel 4 continued, and explained the background to Professor Sykes's work and conclusions:

To answer the riddle and establish what species she belonged to, Professor Sykes has tested samples from six of Zana's living descendants. He has also recovered DNA from a tooth taken from the skull of one of her sons, Khwit. Such work is highly specialized and Sykes was the first geneticist *ever* to extract DNA from ancient bone.

The results are complex and fascinating. First, they show that Zana was, in fact, no more Neanderthal than many of the rest of modern humans. When the Neanderthal genome was sequenced in 2010 it became clear that Europeans and Asians contain around 2 to 4% of Neanderthal DNA; almost certainly the result of interbreeding.

But the big surprise in Sykes' results was that Zana's DNA is not Caucasian at all, but African. Khwit's tooth sample confirms her maternal African ancestry and the saliva tests on the six living descendants show that they all contain African DNA in the right proportions for Zana to have been genetically 100% sub-Saharan African.

"The most obvious solution that springs to mind is that Zana or her ancestors were brought from Africa to Abkhazia as slaves, when it was part of the slave trading Ottoman Empire, to work as servants or laborers," says Professor Sykes. "While the Russians ended slavery when they took over the region in the late 1850s, some Africans remained behind. Was Zana one of them, who was living wild in the forest when she was captured?"

> "... Zana could be evidence of a hitherto unknown human 'tribe,' dating from a distant time when the human species was still evolving...."

It was an entirely valid question. As Channel 4 rightly noted, however: "That theory would not explain her extraordinary features, described by reliable eyewitnesses."

The amazing story, and the attendant, astounding discoveries of Professor Sykes were far from over. An even more sensational discovery was made, as Channel 4 highlighted:

Having carefully studied the skull of Zana's son, Khwit, Professor Sykes believes there are some unusual morphological skull features—such as very wide eye sockets, an elevated brow ridge and what appears to be an additional bone at the back of the skull—that could suggest ancient, as opposed to modern, human origins.

And Sykes has raised the bold theoretical possibility that Zana could be a remnant of an earlier human migration out of Africa, perhaps tens of thousands, of years ago. If correct, Zana could be evidence of a hitherto unknown human "tribe," dating from a distant time when the human species was still evolving and whose ancestors were forced into remote regions, like the Caucasus Mountains, by later waves of modern humans coming out of Africa.

Zana may not have been an Almasty or a surviving Neanderthal, but the astonishing conclusion that she may well have originated with "a hitherto unknown human 'tribe'" most assuredly leaves the door open for the possibility of other, "hitherto unknown" humans inhabiting the wilder parts of the planet—and, maybe, some of them are more ape-like than human.

Zemu Glacier Unknown Ape

It is a fact that sightings of the mammoth Yetis of the Himalayas are far less prevalent than they were in prior decades. The 1920s, for example, saw a number of intriguing encounters. A perfect example is the story of N. A. Tombazi, a British photographer who also was a Fellow of the Royal Geographic Society. It was while at a height of around 15,000 feet on the Zemu Glacier, and at a distance of around 600 to 900 feet, that Tombazi spied something profoundly weird on the slopes. He later recorded his thoughts on this 1925 affair, which make for fascinating reading:

The intense glare and brightness of the snow prevented me from seeing anything for the first few seconds, but I soon spotted the "object" referred to, about two to three hundred yards away down the valley to the east of our camp. Unquestionably, the figure in outline was exactly like a human being, walking upright and stopping occasionally to uproot or pull at some dwarf rhododendron bushes. It showed up dark against the snow and, as far as I could make out, wore no clothes. Within the next minute or so it had moved into some thick scrub and was lost to view.

Unfortunately, as Tombazi admitted, the brief sighting of the beast did not give him the opportunity to focus his "telephoto camera" on it, which would surely have offered a far more detailed study of the creature, had he been able to do so. Nevertheless, the encounter was not entirely over. A few hours later, and as Tombazi began his descent, he made a detour to where the creature was seen. Although he did not see the thing again, he did find its footrpints. Back to Tombazi:

> I examined the footprints which were clearly visible on the surface of the snow. They were similar in shape to those of a man, but only six to seven inches long by four inches wide at the broadest part of the foot. The marks of five distinct toes and of the instep were perfectly clear, but the trace of the heel was indistinct, and the little that could be seen of it appeared to narrow down to a point.

Tombazi continued with his description of the prints:

> I counted fifteen such footprints at regular intervals ranging from one-and-a-half to two feet. The prints were undoubtedly of a biped, the order of the spoor having no characteristics whatever of any imaginable quadruped. Dense rhododendron scrub prevented any further investigations as to the direction of the footprints, and threatening weather compelled me to resume the march. From enquiries I made a few days later at Yoksun, on my return journey, I gathered that no man had gone in the direction of Jongri since the beginning of the year.

John Napier, a noted authority on unknown apes, suggested that what Tombazi saw may have been a bear.

John Napier, a noted authority on unknown apes, suggested that what Tombazi saw may have been a bear. Napier said of the tracks: "The dimensions and the indistinct narrow heel-print suggest as much."

On the other hand, we need to keep in mind Tombazi's very own words. Yes, bears can walk on their hind legs. Tombazi's comments on what he saw, however, describe something very much unlike a bear: "… the figure in outline was exactly like a human being, walking upright … the prints were undoubtedly of a biped, the order of the spoor having no characteristics whatever of any imaginable quadruped."

Whatever N. A. Tombazi really encountered all those years ago remains the enigma to us as it did to the man himself.

Zoo Escapees

One of the most enduring explanations put forth to explain sightings of anomalous apes is that they are not unknown animals, but actually escapees from zoos and menageries. If there were just one or two cases on record, one might be inclined to suggest the stories possess a degree of merit. That there are, however, dozens of such stories, is a good indication they are a relatively modern-day myth that has taken hold and perpetuated.

In 2009, paranormal expert and author Mike Dash was leafing through a copy of the December 8, 1878, edition of England's *Sheldrake's Aldershot & Sandhurst Military Gazette* and came across a fascinating story that sat below the eye-opening headline "Capturing a Gorilla in Shropshire." The article began in an appropriately controversial fashion:

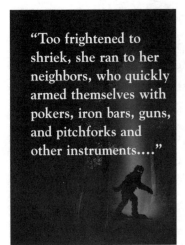

"Too frightened to shriek, she ran to her neighbors, who quickly armed themselves with pokers, iron bars, guns, and pitchforks and other instruments...."

For a fortnight past the district around Madeley Wood, Salop has been in a state of intense excitement, by the alleged depredations committed by a gorilla, which is said to have escaped from a wild beast menagerie travelling to Bridgnorth. The animal was stated to have first made his appearance in the neighborhood of that town, where in the darkness of the night it was severally seen by a clergyman and a policeman, both of whom fled. It is also said to have appeared at several places in the immediate neighborhood.

If the story was true, then it seems to have led to a spectacular case of mistaken identity, and near-tragedy, too, as the *Gazette's* writer noted:

A few evenings since the occupier of a house in Madeley Wood went to bed at a reasonable hour, with the greater portion of his family, leaving his "gude wife" up, who took the opportunity to visit a neighbor, leaving the door open and a candle burning.

Returning in a short time, she was horrified at seeing a bent form, with a goodly array of gray hair around its face, crouching over the expiring embers of the fire, apparently warming itself, the light having gone out. Too frightened to shriek, she ran to her neighbors, who quickly armed themselves with pokers, iron bars, guns, and pitchforks and other instruments of a similar character, and marched in a body to capture the gorilla.

The "gorilla"—on this occasion, anyway—turned out to be nothing of the sort, as the article made clear:

The form was seen sitting at the fire, but evidently aroused by the approaching body, rose to its full height and revealed the figure of an eccentric character well known in the neighborhood as "Old Johnny," who seeing the door open had quietly walked in to light his pipe, accidentally "puffed" the candle out, and was very near being captured, if not exterminated, in mistake for an escaped gorilla.

The on-the-loose animal, reported the *Gazette*, "has not been heard of since."

The reason I mention all of the above, is because the location is only a stone's throw from Bridge 39, on the Shropshire Union Canal, where the Man-Monkey was seen, just a few weeks after the article was published (*see* "Man-Monkey of the Shropshire Union Canal").

While I don't personally think that the following case is a provable example of the escape of some form of ape from a British zoo, the fact that it occurred in the vicinity of just such a place, and one that happens to house the second largest collection of primates in the entire world, is admittedly, somewhat intriguing, and not a matter that can be ignored.

The story comes from James Culwick, who told me that, back in 1992, when he was fifteen, he and several of his friends had a curious experience at Norton Juxta Twycross, Leicestershire. A very little village indeed, Norton (the *Juxta* part of the name comes from the Latin for "next to") is bounded on its east side by the Ashby Canal and is situated only a very brief distance from England's famous Twycross Zoo—an eighty-acre facility, which was founded in 1963 by Molly Badham and Nathalie Evans.

Culwick recalls the distinctly strange affair: "There was a church in this village [a twelfth-century structure, the Holy Trinity Church], and behind the church was a small wooded area and fields, where we used to generally mess about and have a sneaky beer or two. One sunny day though myself and two friends (no beers involved) were messing about having a laugh as teenagers do when one of my friends shouted that he had suddenly seen something move through the undergrowth.

He was genuinely shocked by what he saw as he claimed it was very tall, moving on two legs and covered in thick hair. On hearing my friend shout,

I spun round as I had my back to him, I recall, and I too caught sight of something truly strange. It was only a glimpse, however, but I do remember seeing something through the leaves which was tall with scraggy brown fur. All I can remember is that immediately after the sighting I was shocked and so was my friend. We were quite scared and also perplexed because whatever we saw vanished after making its appearance. What is also worth noting is that my other friend saw nothing at all, very odd.

That the beast was described by Culwick as being of significant height effectively rules out a wandering, escaped little monkey from Twycross Zoo as being the cause of the commotion. Surely something of much bigger proportions would not have gone unnoticed by the zoo's personnel. Nevertheless, it is worth noting the words of the staff of the zoo itself:

We have the largest collection of primate species of any zoo in the world, outside Japan. Twycross is the only U.K. zoo to hold all four species of great ape, including bonobos [also called pygmy chimpanzees]. We also have a very successful breeding record and many of our primates can be observed in breeding groups with individuals of various ages and stages of development.

An orangutan enjoys a drink at the Twycross Zoo in Leicester, England. It was speculated that the animals seen in the area could have been zoo escapees. However, such an escape would have been detected by the zoo staff.

> That gorillas don't grow anywhere near twelve feet in height did not stop the legend from developing, suggesting they do exactly that!

Did one of the zoo's many primates briefly escape into the small woods around Norton, only to be quickly captured and the whole event covered up? Or was the beast seen by Culwick and his friends something far stranger? Two decades later, I suspect neither we nor Culwick will ever have solid answers for those questions.

Taking a trip across the Atlantic, there is the Beaman Monster of Kansas City, Missouri. Close to Beaman is the city of Sedalia, where, allegedly, in 1904, a train crashed in the vicinity, and which was carrying a large number of circus animals, including a gorilla that stood twelve feet tall! That gorillas don't grow anywhere near twelve feet in height did not stop the legend from developing, suggesting they do exactly that! The descendants of this Goliath-like animal (and, presumably, a similar escapee of the opposite sex and size) are, locals conclude, today's man-monsters of Beaman.

Then, on January 28, 1921, an article, titled "Chase Gorilla to Mountains," appeared in the pages of the Gettysburg, Pennsylvania, *Times*. In part, it stated:

> "Gorilla" warfare which was started last week in the vicinity of Idaville, when Adams County residents, well armed, pursued what is believed to be an animal that escaped from a circus car when it was wrecked, not long ago, was renewed by citizens of Rouzerville Wednesday night when an armed posse scoured the Blue Ridge slopes in the hope of getting a shot at the beast.

No one, by now, should be surprised to learn that the beast of Idaville—like so many other cryptid apes—seemed to be impervious to bullets, skillfully evading each pursuer on every occasion, and finally made good its escape, forever.

Said to lurk deep in the swamps of Louisiana, the Honey Island Swamp Monster, as it has become infamously known, has been reported roaming the area since the early 1960s. Local folklore tells of the crash of a train in the area during the early years of the twentieth century. The train was supposedly transporting a variety of animals on behalf of a travelling circus, which included a number of chimpanzees that made a quick and spectacular bid for freedom in the wake of the crash. The result: The now free chimps supposedly bred with the local alligator population and spawned the nightmarish monster of the swamps.

These stories of apes having escaped from circuses—and, in the process, provoking monster legends—are just a handful of dozens. The unlikely list goes on and on.

Zoological Society Revelations of an Unidentified Ape in India

In 1915, respected explorer and botanist Henry J. Elwes read a fascinating piece of correspondence at a meeting of the Zoological Society of London, England. Elwes received it from forestry officer J. R. O. Gent, who was stationed at the time in Darjeeling, in the Indian state of West Bengal. In his letter to Elwes, Gent said:

> I have discovered the existence of another animal but cannot make out what it is, a big monkey or ape perhaps—if there were any apes in India. It is a beast of very high elevations and only goes down to Phalut in the cold weather. It is covered with longish hair, face also hairy, the ordinary yellowish-brown color of the Bengal monkey. Stands about 4 feet high and goes about on the ground chiefly, though I think it can also climb. The peculiar feature is that its tracks are about 18 inches or 2 feet long and toes point in the opposite direction to that in which the animal is moving. The breadth of the track is about 6 inches. I take it he walks on his knees and shins instead of on the sole of his foot.

> He is known as the Jungli Admi or Sogpa. One was worrying a lot of coolies working in the forest below Phalut in December; they were very frightened and would not go into work. I set off as soon as I could to try and bag the beast, but before I arrived the Forester had been letting off a gun and frightened it away, so I saw nothing.

> An old choukidar of Phalut told me he had frequently seen them in the snow there, and confirmed the description of the tracks. It is a thing that practically no Englishman has ever heard of, but all the natives of the higher villages know about it. All I can say is that it is not the Nepal Langur, but I've impressed upon people up there that I want information the next time one is about.

FURTHER READING

(All websites were last checked in December 2014.)

"1925—Russia's Caucasus Pamir Range, the Vanch Mountains." http://www.bigfoot encounters.com/sbs/vanch.htm. 2014.

"1980 Cataclysmic Eruption." http://volcanoes.usgs.gov/volcanoes/st_helens/st_helens_geo_hist_99.html. February 7, 2013.

"The Abominable Snowman." http://homepages.bw.edu/~jcurtis/Scripts/Abominable/intro.html. 2014.

"About Tom Slick." http://www.mindscience.org/about/about-tom-slick. 2013.

Adair, Melissa. "Infrasound: The Bigfoot ZAP??" http://bigfootchicks.blogspot.com/2012/06/infrasound-bigfoot-zap.html. June 26, 2012.

Alaskan-Yukon Magazine. August 1908.

"Alberni Has a Wild Man Vancouver Island Mowgli Said to Be No Myth—Seen by a Prospector Recently." *Yukon World*. August 1906.

Alexander, Heather. "Kemah Man Moves to Big Thicket in Search of Bigfoot." http://www.chron.com/news/houston-texas/texas/article/Kemah-man-moves-to-Big-Thicket-in- search-of-5516732.php. May 13, 2014.

Allen, Betty. "Story of Century Old Big Foot in Idaho Adds Color to Legend." *Humboldt Times*. January 3, 1959.

Alley, J. Robert. *Raincoast Sasquatch*. Surrey, British Columbia: Hancock House Publishers, 2003.

American Monsters. "Beast of Brassknocker Hill: (England)." http://www.americanmonsters.com/site/2010/11/beast-of-brassknocker-hill-england/. November 28, 2010.

"Animal Magic as Warlock Reveals Mystery behind Plaits Found in Horses' Manes." http://www.theguardian.com/world/2009/dec/07/horse-mane-plaits-magic-ritual. December 7, 2009.

"Animals: Primates." http://twycrosszoo.org/animals/primates/. 2014.

"Anonymous Former National Guardsman Claims Mount St. Helens Burnt Bigfoot Story Happened." http://bigfootevidence.blogspot.com/2012/09/anonymous-former-national-guardsman.html. September 15, 2012.

"The Ape Man of Dartmoor." http://www.legendarydartmoor.co.uk/big_foot.htm. December 17, 2012.

"Aquatic Ape Hypothesis." https://www.princeton.edu/~achaney/tmve/wiki100k/docs/Aquatic_ape_hypothesis.html. 2014.

"Are They Dangerous?" http://www.bfro.net/gdb/show_FAQ.asp?id=659. 2014.

Arnold, Neil, "Stig of the Dump and Its Crypto-Connections." http://forteanzoology.blogspot.com/2010/12/neil-arnold-stig-of-dump-and-its-crypto.html. December 21, 2010.

———. "The Phantom Ape-Man." http://forteanzoology.blogspot.com/2010/01/neil-arnold-phantom-ape-man.html. January 4, 2010.

———. "The Satanic Ape." http://forteanzoology.blogspot.com/2012/03/neil-arnold-satanic-ape.html. March 27, 2012.

———. "The Whatsit of Wanstead Woods." http://londonist.com/2008/11/the_saturday_strangeness_22.php. November 15, 2008.

Ashlin, Scott. "The Snow Creature (1954)." http://www.1000misspenthours.com/reviews/reviewsn-z/snowcreature.htm. 2014.

Associated Press. "Charles B. Pierce, Director of 'Boggy Creek,' Dies at 71." http://www.nytimes.com/2010/03/10/arts/10pierce.html?_r=0. March 10, 2010.

———. "Infrasound linked to spooky effects." http://www.nbcnews.com/id/3077192/ns/technology_and_science-science/t/infrasound-linked-spooky-effects/#.VFlFZO-PKM8. September 7, 2003.

Australian and New Zealand Monthly Magazine, Vol. 1, no. 2. February 1842.

"Australian Apes." *Australian Town and County Journal.* December 9, 1882.

Bartholomew, Paul, Bob Bartholomew, William Brann, and Bruce Hallenbeck. *Monsters of the Northwoods.* New York, NY: privately printed, 1992.

Bayanov, Dmitri. *In the Footsteps of the Russian Snowman.* Surrey, British Columbia: Hancock House Publishers, 2004.

Bergman, Jerry. "Darwin's Apemen and the Exploitation of Deformed Humans." http://creation.mobi/deformed-humans-exploited-as-apemen. *Journal of Creation.* December 2002.

———. "Human-Ape Hybridization: A Failed Attempt to Prove Darwinism." http://www.icr.org/article/4593/. 2002.

"'Bigfoot' DNA Sequenced in Upcoming Genetics Study—Five-Year Genome Study at DNA Diagnostics Yields Evidence of Homo Sapiens/Unknown Hominin Hybrid Species in North America." http://www.prweb.com/releases/2012/11/prweb10166775.htm. November 28, 2012.

"Bigfoot Powers." http://cryptozoo.monstrous.com/bigfoot_powers.htm. December 8, 2014.

"Bigfoot Sighting on Cannock Chase." http://www.birminghammail.co.uk/news/local-news/bigfoot-sighting-on-cannock-chase-234257. September 2, 2008.

Bigfoot: Tales of Unexplained Creatures: UFOs and Psychic Connections. Rome, OH: Page Research, 1978.

Binns, Daniel. "WANSTEAD: Is 'Bigfoot' on the Loose in Woods?" http://www.guardian-series.co.uk/news/3836299.WANSTEAD__Is__Bigfoot__on_the_loose_in_woods_/. November 11, 2008.

Black, Joe. "Pennsylvania White Bigfoot Video—Real or Hoax?" http://bf-field-journal.blogspot.com/2012/08/pennsylvania-white-bigfoot-video-real.html. August 13, 2012.

Black, Tom. "The Rising Sun Bigfoot." http://strangedigest.com/the-rising-sun-bigfoot/. May 21, 2014.

Blackburn, Lyle. *Lizard Man: The True Story of the Bishopville Monster*. San Antonio, TX: Anomalist Books, 2013.

———. *The Beast of Boggy Creek: The True Story of the Fouke Monster*. San Antonio, TX: Anomalist Books, 2012.

Boirayon, Marius. *Solomon Island Mysteries*. Kempton, IL: Adventures Unlimited Press, 2010.

———. "The Giants of the Solomon Islands and Their Hidden UFO Bases." http://www.thewatcherfiles.com/giants/solomon-giants.htm. 2012.

Bord, Janet, and Colin Bord. *Bigfoot Casebook*. Enumclaw, WA: Pine Winds Press, 2006.

Bould, Sarah. "Editor in Plea to Missing "Wolfman" of Wales." http://www.holdthefrontpage.co.uk/2012/news/editor-in-plea-to-missing-wolfman-of-wales/. February 17, 2012.

Bourtsev, Igor. "A Skeleton Still Buried and a Skull Unearthed: The Story of Zana." http://www.bigfootencounters.com/creatures/zana2.htm. 2014.

Bravo, Damian. "The Mande Burung (Jungle Man) of India." http://bigfootevidence.blogspot.com/2012/07/the-mande-burung-jungle-man-of-india.html. July 18, 2012

Brett, G. "Snowbeast (1977)." http://www.oh-the-horror.com/page.php?id=748. December 6, 2010.

Brewer, Ebenezer Cobham. *Dictionary of Phrase and Fable, Giving the Derivation Source, or Origin of Common Phrases, Allusions, and Words That Have a Tale to Tell*. London, UK: Cassell, 1905.

"A Brief History of Shugborough." http://www.shugborough.org.uk/theshugborough estate/EstateHistory.aspx. 2014.

"British Columbia Mowglis: Tribe of Wild Men Roaming Woods and Frightening People." *Van Wert Daily Bulletin*. October 28, 1905.

Brown, Jamie. "Yowie Sighted at Bexhill—Witness Asks to Stay Anonymous." http://www.northernstar.com.au/news/call-it-what-you-will-a-yeren-a-yeti-or-a-yowie-bu/1908497/. June 15, 2013.

Brown, Theo. *Devon Ghosts*. Norwich, UK: Jarrold, 1982.

"Capturing a Gorilla in Shropshire." *Sheldrake's Aldershot & Sandhurst Military Gazette*. December 8, 1878.

Carpenter, Scott. "Bigfoot and Infrasound." http://bf-field-journal.blogspot.com/p/theory-bigfoot-cancreate-and-use.html. 2014.

Casady, Michelle. "Oliver, Famed Chimp, Dies." http://www.mysanantonio.com/news/local_news/article/Oliver-famed-chimpanzee-found-dead-3605135.php. June 2, 2012.

Chapman, Douglas. "Chaos in Delhi: Monkey Man Madness." http://www.strangemag.com/monkeyman.html. 2014.

"Chase Gorilla to Mountains." *Gettysburg Times*. January 28, 1921.

Childress, David Hatcher. *Yetis, Sasquatch & Hairy Giants*. Kempton, IL: Adventures Unlimited Press, 2010.

Chorvinsky, Mark. "Some Thoughts about the Patterson Bigfoot Film on Its 30th Anniversary." http://www.strangemag.com/pattersonfilm30th.html. 2014.

Ciochon, Russell L. "The Ape That Was." http://www.uiowa.edu/~bioanth/giganto.html. 2014.

Coleman, Loren. *Bigfoot! The True Story of Apes in America*. New York: Paraview-Pocket Books, 2003.

———. "East London Bigfoot?" http://www.cryptozoonews.com/uk-bf/. November 22, 2008.

———. "The Myakka Skunk Ape Photographs." *Fate*. May 2001.

———. "Oil, Slick, Yeti, CIA … and Libya?" http://www.cryptomundo.com/cryptozoonews/ slick-317/, March 17, 2011.

———. "Random Reports of Bigfoot Wearing Clothes." http://cryptomundo.com/cryptozoo-news/bushman/. May 4, 2009.

———. "Sierra Sound'Al Berry Has Died (Updated)." http://cryptomundo.com/ cryptozoo-news/berry-obit/. January 31, 2012.

———. "Tom Slick and JFK?" http://copycateffect.blogspot.com/2012/03/tom-slick-jfk.html. March 16, 2012.

———. *Tom Slick and the Search for the Yeti*. London, UK: Faber & Faber, 1989.

———. "Yeti Hunter Sir Edmund Hillary Dies." http://www.cryptozoonews.com/hillary-obit/. January 10, 2008.

——— and Jerome Clark. *Cryptozoology A to Z*. New York: Simon & Schuster, 1999.

——— and Patrick Huyghe. *The Field Guide to Bigfoot and Other Mystery Primates*. San Antonio, TX: Anomalist Books, 2006.

Colvin, Andrew B., and Jeffrey Pritchett. *Praise for the Hairy Man: The Secret Life of Bigfoot*. Seattle, WA: Metadisc Books, 2013.

Compton, James R. "Slick, Thomas Baker, Jr." http://www.tshaonline.org/handbook/online/articles/fsl07. 2013.

Cope, Tabitca. "The Woodwose, the Origin of Bigfoot?" http://cryptozoo-oscity.blogspot.com/2012/02/wodewose-origin-of-bigfoot.html February 27, 2012.

Cornet, Sharon Eby. "Vanishing Bigfoot and Anecdotal Accounts: Implications and Challenges for Researchers." http://www.sunstar-solutions.com/BFvanishing.htm. May 22, 2005.

Courtney, Roger. *A Greenhorn in Africa*. London, UK: Herbert Jenkins, Ltd., 1940. "Cowlitz County Washington." http://www.bigfootencounters.com/sbs/mtsthelens_bodies.htm. 2014.

Cunningham, Gary & Coghlan, Ronan. *The Mystery Animas of Ireland*. Woolsery, UK: CFZ Press, 2010.

Crypto Journal, The. "Strange Encounters with the Nyalmo." http://bfsearcher.blogspot.com/2012/08/strange-encounters-with-nyalmo.html. August 13, 2012.

Cuba24h. "The Guije Living on Rivers." http://www.cuba24horas.com/en/historia/110-tradiciones/382-the-gueije-living-on-rivers. 2014.

Darwin, Charles. *The Variation of Animals and Plants under Domestication*. New York: D. Appleton & Co., 1883.

Dash, Mike. "A British Bigfoot?" http://blogs.forteana.org/node/65. February 11, 2009.

Davis, Scott. "Apaches Go Public with Bigfoot Sightings." http://www.fvza.org/prbigfoot.html. September 2, 2006.

"Do Bigfoot Really Have the Ability to Turn Invisible?" http://bigfootevidence.blogspot.com/2014/05/do-bigfoot-really-have-ability-to-turn.html. May 3, 2014.

Dobie, Frank. *Tales of Old-Time Texas*. Austin, TX: University of Texas Press, 1984.

"Does Bigfoot Kill Dogs?" http://pararational.com/does-bigfoot-kill-dogs/. August 1, 2014.

Downes, Jonathan. *Monster Hunter*. Woolsery, UK: CFZ Press, 2004.

———. "The Hunt for the Bolam 'Beast.'" http://www.cfz.org.uk/expeditions/03bolam/. January 23, 2003.

Downes, Jonathan, and Richard Freeman. "Surviving Neanderthals?" *Expedition Report 2008: Russia*. Woolsery, UK: CFZ Press, 2007.

"DREADED WILD MEN Strike Fear into Indian Children." *Lethbridge Herald*, March 3, 1934.

Eberhart, George, M. *Mysterious Creatures: A Guide to Cryptozoology*. Santa Barbara, CA: ABC-CLIO, 2002.

Erika. "Albino Bigfoot Filmed in PA?" http://weirdanimalreport.com/article/albino-bigfoot-filmed-pa. July 24, 2011.

Exeter Watchman. "Another Wonder." September 22, 1818.

Exquemelin, Alexander O. *The Buccaneers of America.* Mineola, NY: Dover Publications, 2000.

"Face of 'the Wolfman' of Pantyffynnon tips." http://www.southwalesguardian.co.uk/news/9516464.Face_of__the_Wolfman__of_Pantyffynnon_tips/. February 7, 2012.

Faraci, Devin. "Schlock Corridor: Raw Meat (1972)." http://badassdigest.com/2012/01/16/schlock-corridor-raw-meat-1972/. January 16, 2012.

Ferrell, Ed. *Strange Stories of Alaska and the Yukon.* Kenmore, WA: Epicenter Press, Inc., 1996.

"Folklore of Bhutan—Migoi, the Yeti." http://bhutancanada.org/folklore-of-bhutan-migoi-the-yeti/. March 1, 2013.

Fountain, Bill. *Hecate Hill.* http://www.playscripts.com/play/1144. 2006.

Freeman, Richard. "Debbie Martyr." *Fortean Times,* April 2004.

———. "On the Trail of the Orang Pendek, Sumatra's Mystery Ape." http://www.theguardian.com/science/blog/2011/sep/08/orang-pendek-sumatra-mystery-ape. September 8, 2011.

———. *Orang-Pendek: Sumatra's Forgotten Ape.* Woolsery, UK: CFZ Press, 2011.

Gable, Andrew. "A Trip to Lock 49." http://masksofmesingw.blogspot.com/2009/11/trip-to-lock-49.html. November 13, 2009.

Gerhard, Ken. *Encounters with Flying Humanoids.* Woodbury, MN: Llewellyn Worldwide, Ltd, 2013.

———, and Nick Redfern. *Monsters of Texas.* Woolsery, UK: CFZ Press, 2010.

Germann, Kyle. "The Hairy Hands of Dartmoor." http://demonhunterscompendium.blogspot.com/2013/07/the-hairy-hands-of-dartmoor.html. July 15, 2013.

"Glamis Castle." http://www.mysteriousbritain.co.uk/scotland/angus/hauntings/glamis-castle.html. 2014.

Gooch, Stan. *The Paranormal.* New York: Harper & Row, 1978.

Gordon, Stan. *Really Mysterious Pennsylvania: UFOs, Bigfoot & Other Weird Encounters Casebook One.* Greensburg, PA: Bulldog Design, 2010.

———. *Silent Invasion: The Pennsylvania UFO-Bigfoot Casebook.* Greensburg, PA: privately printed, 2010.

"A Gorilla in Idaho." *Minnesota Weekly Record.* January 23, 1869.

Green, John. *On the Track of the Sasquatch.* New York: Ballantine Books, 1973.

———. *Sasquatch: The Apes among Us.* Victoria, BC: Cheam Publishing, 1978.

GreyWolf. "Woodwose aka Sasquatch." http://sasquatchievoice.ning.com/profiles/blogs/woodwose-aka-sasquatch. 2014.

"Guije, a Different Cuban Figure." http://www.cubaheadlines.com/2007/06/22/guije_a_different_cuban_figure.html. June 22, 2007.

Guttilla, Peter. *The Bigfoot Files*. Santa Barbara, CA: Timeless Voyager Press, 2003.

"The Hairy Hands." http://www.bbc.co.uk/devon/discovering/legends/hairy_hands .shtml. September 24, 2014.

"The Hairy Hands." http://www.legendarydartmoor.co.uk/hairy_hands.htm. October 8, 2012.

"The Hairy Hands—Legendary Dartmoor." http://www.legendarydartmoor.co.uk/hairy_ hands.htm. October 21, 2014.

"Hairy Wild Man Sought in Swamp." *Oshkosh Northwestern*. April 15, 1938.

Hall, Mark A., and Loren Coleman. *True Giants: Is Gigantopithecus Still Alive?* San Antonio, TX: Anomalist Books, 2010.

Hallowell, Mike. "Cleadon BHM." http://forteanzoology.blogspot.com/2009/12/mike-hallowell-cleadon-bhm.html. December 10, 2009.

Hansen, Frank. "I Killed the Ape-Man Creature of Whiteface." *Saga*, July 1970.

Hardy, Michael. "Bigfoot Is Hiding in the Big Thicket." http://www.houstoniamag .com/news-and-profiles/people-and-profiles/articles/bigfoot-hiding-big-thicket-east-texas-may-2014. April 30, 2014.

Harpur, Merrily. *Mystery Big Cats*. Loughborough, UK: Heart of Albion Press, 2006.

"Has a British Scientist Finally Unlocked the Mystery of the Yeti?" http://www.channel 4.com/info/press/news/has-a-british-scientist-finally-unlocked-the-mystery-of-the-yeti. October 17, 2013.

Hawkes, Ernest William. *The Labrador Eskimo*. Charleston, SC: Nabu Press, 2010.

Henderson, Eric. "Harry and the Hendersons." http://www.slantmagazine.com/film/ review/harry-and-the-hendersons. April 29, 2007.

Heuvelmans, Bernard. *On the Track of Unknown Animals*. London, UK: Routledge, 1995.

Holm-Olsen, Ludvig, editor. *The King's Mirror: AM 243 a fol*. Early Icelandic Manuscripts in Facsimile, XVII. Copenhagen, Denmark: Rosenkilde and Bagger, 1987.

Holyfield, Dana. "Honey Island Swamp Monster Official Site." http://swampmonster .weebly.com/. 2014.

"*Homo neanderthalensis*." http://humanorigins.si.edu/evidence/human-fossils/species/ homo-neanderthalensis. October 8, 2014.

Hoosier Folklore, Vol. 5. March 1946: 19.

Howard-Bury, Charles K. *Mount Everest: The Reconnaissance, 1921 (1922)*. Whitefish, MT: Kessinger Publishing, LLC, 2010.

"Humboldt County, Trinidad, California Sasquatches Swimming Offshore—Winter 2007." http://www.bigfootencounters.com/stories/trinidadCA07.htm. 2014.

Hunt, Brigadier Sir John. *The Ascent of Everest*. London, UK: Hodder & Stoughton, 1953.

Hunter, Don, and Rene Dahinden. *Sasquatch: The Search for North America's Incredible Creature*. Toronto, ON: The Canadian Publishers, 1993.

Hynek, Dr. J. Allen. *The Hynek UFO Report*. New York: Sphere Books, 1978.

Jeffrey, Martin. "The Big Hairy Encounter." http://homepage.ntlworld.com/chris .mullins/DERBYSHIRE%20BHM.htm. February, 1998.

Jenkins, David. "Quatermass and the Pit Review." http://www.littlewhitelies.co.uk/ theatrical-reviews/quatermass-and-the-pit-21030. 2014.

Johnson, Donald A. "Encounters with Aliens on this Day: November 28." http:// www.ufoinfo.com/onthisday/November28.html. 2014.

Jolin, Dan. "The Descent: Caving Terror for a Group of Wide-Girls." http://www.empire online.com/reviews/reviewcomplete.asp?FID=11243. 2014.

"Kevin Peter Hall Biography." http://www.imdb.com/name/nm0001310/bio?ref_=nm_ ov_bio_sm. 2014.

Kipling, Rudyard. *The Jungle Book*. Mineola, NY: Dover Publications, 2000.

Knapp, George. "I-Team: Strange Circumstances Surround Park Disappearances." http://www.8newsnow.com/story/18150329/i-team. May 4, 2012.

Kohn, Eric. "Review: Forget 'Godzilla,' Bobcat Goldthwait's 'Willow Creek' Is the Monster Movie of the Summer." http://www.indiewire.com/article/review-forget- godzilla-bobcat-goldthwaits-willow-creek-is-the-monster-movie-of-the-summer. June 3, 2014.

Krantz, Dr. Grover. *Bigfoot Sasquatch Evidence*. Boulder, CO: Johnson Books, 1992.

Lapseritis, Jack. *The Psychic Sasquatch: And Their UFO Connection*. Blue Water Pub- lishing, 1998.

Lee, Janet. "Bigfoot Almost Made Me Lose My Baby." http://www.freerepublic.com/ focus/f-chat/1602122/posts. March 23, 2006.

"Lepcha—Religion." http://www.everyculture.com/South-Asia/Lepcha-Religion.html. 2014.

Lewis, Oll. "The Big Hairy Man of Nant Gwynant." http://forteanzoology.blogspot .com/2009/05/oll-lewis-big-hairy-man-of-nant-gwynant.html. May 16, 2009.

Lindsay, Robert. "Bigfoot News July 12, 2014." http://robertlindsay.wordpress.com /2014/07/12/bigfoot-news-july-12-2014/. July 12, 2014.

Long, Greg. *The Making of Bigfoot: The Inside Story*. Amherst, NY: Prometheus Books, 2004.

Lowe. Keith. *Tunnel Vision*. New York: MTV Books, 2001.

"Lurking Bigfoot: Trick or Treat?" *Sentinel Star*. October 5, 1977.

MacKinnon, John Ramsey. *In Search of the Red Ape*. San Diego, CA: Holt, Rinehart & Winston, 1974.

Mai-Li. "The Habits and Whereabouts of the 'Sasquatch' aka 'Bigfoot.'" http:// con- sciouslifenews.com/habits-whereabouts-sasquatch-aka-bigfoot/. April 5, 2012.

Marsden, William. *The History of Sumatra.* London, UK: Thomas Payne & Son, 1874.

Martin, Linda Jo. "It Has Been Proven That We're All Psychic, and This Can Be Applied to Bigfoot Research." http://bigfootsightings.org/proven-psychic/. May 7, 2012.

———. "Telepathic Bigfoot Research." http://friendsofsasquatch.com/telepathic-big-foot-research/. May 25, 2012.

Matthews, Rupert. *Bigfoot: True-Life Encounters with Legendary Ape Men.* London, UK: Arcturus Publishing, 2008.

"Mayor's Worries for 'Wolfman' in Bitter Weather." http://www.southwales-evening-post.co.uk/Mayor-s-worries-Wolfman-bitter-weather/story-15175566-detail/story.html. February 9, 2012.

"McCaskill's Myths." http://news.bbc.co.uk/2/shared/spl/hi/programmes/morning_show/html/myths.stm. 2013.

McClanahan, Jim R. "Bigfoot Horse Hair Braiding." http://apeimmortal.wordpress.com/2013/03/14/bigfoot-hair-braiding/. March 14, 2013.

McNally, S.A. "Beast of Brassknocker Hill (UK)." http://visitcryptoville.com/2013/11/21/beast-of-brassknocker-hill-uk/. November 21, 2013.

Merrick, Elliott. *True North: A Journey into Unexplored Wilderness.* Berkeley, CA: North Atlantic Books, 2010.

Merrill, Randy. "Mapinguari: Legendary Man-Eating Cryptid of the Amazon Rainforest." http://demonhunterscompendium.blogspot.com/2013/06/mapinguari-legendary-man-eating-cryptid.html. June 29, 2013.

Millar, John. "Millar's Movie: Shauna Loved Working in the Dark." *Sunday Mail,* July 3, 2005.

Miss Squatcher. "The Infrasonic Effects of Bigfoot." Berkeley, CA: North Atlantic Books, 2010. http://misssquatcher.blogspot.com/2013/10/the-infrasonic-effects-of-bigfoots.html. October 10, 2013.

"Mogollon Monster." http://www.mogollonmonster.com/. 2014.

Moore, Jim. "Alister Hardy's Original 'Aquatic Ape Theory.'" http://www.aquaticape.org/hardy.html. 2014.

"More Proof That Bigfoot Does Not Like Dogs." http://bigfootevidence.blogspot.com/2012/07/more-proof-that-bigfoot-does-not-like.html. July 17, 2012.

Morehead, Ron. "The Bigfoot Recordings (Bigfoot Sounds)." http://ronmorehead.com/the-bigfoot-recordings-bigfoot-sounds/. April 1, 2013.

Morrissey, Beth. "Lanugo and Eating Disorders." http://www.eatingdisorderexpert.co.uk/lanugoandeatingdisorders.html. September 20, 2012.

Murphy, Christopher L. "A Tragic Victim of Circumstances." http://www.hancockhouse.com/article.php/20050920121057844. September 20, 2005.

———. *Bigfoot Encounters in Ohio.* Blaine, WA: Hancock House Publishers, 2006.

———, with John Green and Thomas Steenburg. *Meet the Sasquatch*. Surrey, BC: Hancock House Publishers, 2004.

Murray, Noel. "Pre-Star Wars, *Six Million Dollar Man* and *Bionic Woman* Were Beacons for Young Nerds." http://www.avclub.com/article/pre-istar-warsii-six-million-dollar-mani-and-ibion-92782. February 21, 2013.

Museum Journal, Vol. VI, no. 3. September 1915.

"Mysterious Jungle Races of Sumatra." *Singapore Free Press and Mercantile Advertiser*. July 19, 1932.

Naish, Darren. "De Loys' Ape and What to Do with It." http://blogs.scientificamerican.com/tetrapod-zoology/2014/07/17/de-loys-ape-and-what-to-do-with-it/. July 17, 2014.

Napier, John. *Bigfoot: The Yeti and Sasquatch in Myth and Reality*. New York: E.P. Dutton, 1973.

Nasr, Susan L. "How Albinism Works." http://health.howstuffworks.com/skin-care/problems/medical/albinism6.htm. 2014.

"Native American Bigfoot Figures of Myth and Legend." http://www.native-languages.org/legends-bigfoot.htm. 2012.

Nelson, R. Scott. "Characteristics of Human Language Evident in the Berry/Morehead Tapes." http://www.nabigfootsearch.com/Bigfootlanguage.html. 2011.

"The New Daughter." http://www.metacritic.com/movie/the-new-daughter. 2014.

Newkirk, Greg. "Has the Ape Canyon Cabin, Site of the Most Famous Bigfoot Attack in History, Been Discovered?" http://whofortedblog.com/2013/07/10/has-the-ape-canyon-cabin-site-of-the-most-famous-bigfoot-attack-in-history-been-rediscovered/. July 10, 2013.

Newland, Robert J., and Mark J. North. *Dark Dorset: Tales of Mystery, Wonder and Terror*. Woolsery, UK: CFZ Press, 2007.

"Nittaewo." http://www.unknownexplorers.com/nittaewo.php. 2006.

"Non-Human Intelligent Beings on This Earth in Past and Present." http://www.soul-guidance.com/houseofthesun/dp09.htm. 2014.

O'Donnell, Elliott, *Animal Ghosts: Or Animal Hauntings and the Hereafter*. Whitefish, MT: Kessinger Publishing, 2003.

———. *Scottish Ghost Stories*. Charleston, SC: Nabu Press, 2010.

———. *Werewolves*. Royston, UK: Oracle Publishing Ltd. 1996.

"Ouachita National Forest." http://www.fs.usda.gov/ouachita. 2014.

Pain, Stephanie. "Blasts from the Past: The Soviet Ape-Man Scandal." http://www.newscientist.com/article/mg19926701.000-blasts-from-the-past-the-soviet-apeman-scandal.html#.VEVB5RaEeSo. August 23, 2008.

Patterson, Roger, and Chris Murphy. *The Bigfoot Film Controversy*. Blaine, WA: Hancock House Publishers, 2005.

Pednaud, J. Tithonus. "Julia Pastrana—The Nondescript." http://www.thehumanmar vels.com/julia-pastrana-the-nondescript/. 2014.

"Pennsylvanian's Encounter Mysterious Creatures, and UFOs During 2010." http://www.stangordon.info/rep_2010.htm. 2011.

"Police Get Caught Up in Spot of Monkey Business." http://www.herald scot-land.com/sport/spl/aberdeen/police-get-caught-up-in-spot-of-monkey-business-1.309867, *The Herald*, January 18, 1999.

"Police Seek 'Wolfman' Living in Woods." http://www.telegraph.co.uk/news/newstopics/howaboutthat/9071013/Police-seek-Wolfman-living-in-woods.html. February 9, 2012.

"Police Think Mystery Footprints Are Fakes." *Houston Chronicle*. July 2, 1980.

"Polish Yeti Caught on Film." http://www.austriantimes.at/image/8623/news/Around_the_World/2009-08-28/16003/Polish_Yeti_caught_on_film. August 28, 2009.

Powell, Thom. *The Locals: A Contemporary Investigation of the Bigfoot/Sasquatch Phenomenon*. Blaine, WA: Hancock House Publishers, 2003.

"Pre-1832: B.H. Hodgson's Yeti Report." http://www.anomalyinfo.com/?q=Stories/1832-b-h-hodsons-yeti-description. 2014.

"The Psychic Powers of Bigfoot?" http://realpsychicpower.com/the-psychic-powers-of-bigfoot. 2013.

Puckett, Newbell Niles. *Folk Beliefs of the Southern Negro*. Chapel Hill, NC: University of North Carolina Press, 1926.

Randall, Elizabeth. *From Lyonesse to Alien Big Cats and Back Again*. CreateSpace, 2014.

Rawicz, Slavomir. *The Long Walk: The True Story of a Trek to Freedom*. Guilford, CT: Lyons Press, 2010.

Redfern, Nick. Interview with Adam Davies, July 28, 2008.

———. Interview with Bill Fountain, November 6, 2007.

———. Interview with Duane Graves, September 1, 2008.

———. Interview with Jonathan Downes, March 26, 2012.

———. Interview with Jonathan Downes, June 2, 2005.

———. Interview with Neil Arnold. April 4, 2012.

———. Interview with Ronan Coghlan, March 18, 2012.

———. *Man Monkey: In Search of the British Bigfoot*. Woolsery, UK: CFZ Press, 2007.

———. "Sex and the Supernatural." *Penthouse*, October 2010.

———. "The Wildest Man of All." http://mysteriousuniverse.org/2013/08/the-wildest-man-of-all/. August 29, 2013.

Rennie, J.A. *Romantic Strathspey*. London, UK: Robert Hale, Ltd., 1956.

Rhodes, Peter. "Night Terror with a British Bigfoot." *Express & Star*. January 11, 2003.

Rife, Philip. *Bigfoot across America*. Bloomington, IN: iUniverse, 2000.

Riggs, Rob. *In the Big Thicket*. New York: Paraview Press, 2001.

Roberts, Andy. "The Big Grey Man of Ben Macdhui and Other Mountain Panics." *Strangely Strange but Oddly Normal*. Woolsery, UK: CFZ Press, 2010.

Robson, E. Iliff. *Arrian, with an English Translation by E. Iliff Robson. Anabasis Alexandri (Books I–IV). Vol. I.* Cambridge, MA: Harvard University Press, 1967.

Roe, William. *Affidavit*. August 26, 1957.

Roosevelt, Theodore. *The Wilderness Hunter*. New York: G.B. Putnam, 1906.

"Russian Scientists Use Google Maps to Find Yeti." http://english.pravda.ru/society/anomal/25-03-2009/107296-google_yeti-0/. March 25, 2009.

Russell, Davy. "Invisible Sasquatch." http://www.bigfootencounters.com/articles/invisible.htm. February 29, 2000.

Salkeld, Luke. "Lost Middle-class Tribe's 'Secret' Eco-village in Wales Spotted in Aerial Photograph Taken by Plane." http://www.dailymail.co.uk/news/article-1056637/Lost-middle-class-tribes-secret-eco-village-Wales-spotted-aerial-photograph-taken-plane.html. September 17, 2008.

Salter, Jim. "40 Years On, 'Momo' Debate Lingers." http://www.semissourian.com/story/1870690.html. July 15, 2012.

Sanderson, Ivan T. *Abominable Snowmen: Legend Come to Life*. Kempton, IL: Adventures Unlimited Press, 2006.

———. "The Missing Link." *Argosy*, May 1969.

Seaburn, Paul. "Another White Bigfoot Sighting Reported in Maine." http://mysteriousuniverse.org/2014/10/another-white-bigfoot-sighting-reported-in-maine/. October 13, 2014.

Shiel, Lisa A. *Backyard Bigfoot*. Lake Linden, MI: Slipdown Mountain Publications LLC, 2006.

———. "Bigfoot Infrasound: Likely or Long Shot?" http://cryptomundo.com/bigfoot-report/bigfoot-infrasound-likely-or-long-shot/. March 10, 2014.

———. *Forbidden Bigfoot*. Lake Linden, MI: Jacobsville Books, 2013.

———. "The Uncomfortable Truth about Telepathy and Bigfoot." http://lisashiel.jacobsvillebooks.com/blog/the-uncomfortable-truth-about-telepathy-and-bigfoot/. December 6, 2013.

Shipton, Eric. *The Six Mountains-Travel Books*. Seattle, WA: Mountaineers Books, 1985.

Shuker, Dr. Karl. "'Ape-Man' Oliver—The Chimp That Made a Chump Out of Science." http://karlshuker.blogspot.com/2013/01/ape-man-oliver-chimp-that-made-chump.html. January 26, 2013.

———. "A Devil of a Mystery from Smethwick." http://karlshuker.blogspot.com/2010/09/devil-of-mystery-from-smethwick.html. September 4 2010.

———. "Where the Wild Things Are? In Search of the Woodwose, Europe's Elusive Man-Beast." http://karlshuker.blogspot.com/2012/12/where-wild-things-are-in-search-of.html. December 14, 2012.

"Sightings of Florida's Myakka Skunk Ape." https://www.youtube.com/watch?v=jqoFf XNx4hc. March 14, 2014.

"Some Thing in the Woods." http://www.bigfootencounters.com/articles/something.htm. November 28, 2002.

"Southern Fried Bigfoot." http://www.southernfriedbigfoot.com/. 2014.

Steele, Peter. *Eric Shipton: Everest & Beyond*. Seattle, WA: Mountaineers Books, 1998.

Steenburg, Thomas N. *Sasquatch: Bigfoot—The Continuing Mystery*. Blaine, WA: Hancock House Publishers, 2004.

Steiger, Brad. *Real Monsters, Gruesome Critters, and Beasts from the Darkside*. Canton, MI: Visible Ink Press, 2011.

Stein, Theo. "Camper Says She Was 12 Feet from Curious Giant." http://www.free republic.com/focus/f-news/820483/posts. January 10, 2003.

Strieber, Whitley. "Bigfoot Spotted in the Yukon, Hiding in Sumatra." http://www .unknowncountry.com/news/bigfoot-spotted-yukon-hiding-sumatra. June 21, 2004.

Strickler, Lon. "Bigfoot Recovery: Mt. St. Helens / Battle Mountain Complex." http:// www.phantomsandmonsters.com/2012/09/bigfoot-recovery-mt-st-helens-eruption.html. September 17, 2012.

———. "The Bigfoot Paradox." http://www.phantomsandmonsters.com/p/near-end-of-overnight-appearance-of.html. 2014.

"Swimming Bigfoot 1948, Upper Crater Lake, Wyoming: Bigfoot Sunning on Phantom Ship Island." https://bigfoothistory.wordpress.com/tag/swimming-bigfoot/. December 1, 2014.

"Tales of the Beaman Monster Still Linger in Pettis County, Missouri." http://www .bigfootencounters.com/articles/beaman_monster.htm. February 20, 2008.

Tallerico, Brian. "Willow Creek." http://www.rogerebert.com/reviews/willow-creek-2014. June 6, 2014.

Thorner, W. E. "The Torness Trows—An Eyewitness Account." http://www.orkneyjar .com/folklore/trows/hoytrow.htm. 2014.

Tombazi, N.A. *Account of a Photographic Expedition to the Southern Glaciers of Kangchenjunga in the Sikkim Himalaya*. privately printed, 1925.

"Torphins: The Belti Beast." http://www.torphins.org/hominid.asp. 2010.

Townshend, Marchioness, and Maude Ffoulkes. *True Ghost Stories*. Old Saybrook, CT: Konecky & Konecky, 2009.

Trismegistus, Pete. "Alabama Man Admits He's Local 'Forest Monster.'" http://hoaxes .livejournal.com/81989.html. July 25, 2003.

Turolla, Pino. *Beyond the Andes: My Search for the Origins of Pre-Inca Civilization*. New York: HarperCollins, 1980.

"UFOs and Bigfoot/Open Lines." http://www.coasttocoastam.com/show/2014/11/28. November 28, 2014.

United Press International. "Creature Sighted." November 15, 1977.

U.S. Department of the Interior, U.S. Fish and Wildlife Service. "Are We Ready for 'Bigfoot' or the Loch Ness Monster?" http://www.bfro.net/gdb/show_article.asp?id =304. December 21, 1977.

Waddell, L.A. *Among the Himalayas*. Philadelphia, PA: J.B. Lippincott, 1899.

Waller, Dennis. *In Search of the Kushtaka: Alaska's Other Bigfoot*. Bedford, TX: Dennis Waller, 2014.

Wargan, Pawel. "A Dream of Soviet Ape-Men." http://roadsandkingdoms.com/2013/ a-dream-of-soviet-ape-men/. 2014.

"Was Russian 'Bigfoot' Actually an African Slave?" http://www.channel4.com/info/ press/news/was-russian-bigfoot-actually-an-african-slave. November 1, 2013.

Wayman, Erin. "Did Bigfoot Really Exist? How Gigantopithecus Became Exitinct." http://www.smithsonianmag.com/science-nature/did-bigfoot-really-exist-how-gigantopithecus-became-extinct-16649201/. January 9, 2012.

"The Web of Fear." http://www.bbc.co.uk/doctorwho/classic/episodeguide/weboffear/. 2014.

Weidenreich, Franz. *Apes, Giants, and Man*. Chicago, IL: University of Chicago Press, 1946.

Wells, H.G. *The Time Machine*. New York: New York Review Books, 2005.

"The Wendigo Legend." http://www.gods-and-monsters.com/wendigo-legend.html. 2014.

"What is Albinism?" http://www.albinism.org/publications/what_is_albinism.html. 2014.

"White Pongo (1945)." http://bmoviemadness.com/white-pongo-1945/. November 15, 2012.

"Who Is Sasquatch/Bigfoot?" http://www.soul-guidance.com/houseofthesun/bigfoot.html. 2014.

"Wild Man Hunt in New Jersey." *New York Herald*. January 9, 1894.

"Wild Man of the Navidad, The." http://www.wildmanofthenavidad.com/. 2014.

Williams, Michael. *Supernatural Dartmoor*. Ilkley, UK: Bossiney Books, 2003.

Winnert, Derek. *The Abominable Snowman*. http://derekwinnert.com/the-abominable-snowman-1957-peter-cushing-forrest-tucker-classic-movie-review-1267/. May 31, 2014.

"Wood Ape Description." http://woodape.org/index.php/about-bigfoot/bigfoot-descrip-tion. 2014.

Woolheater, Craig. "Beasts in the Midst—The Mapinguari." http://cryptomundo.com/ bigfoot-report/beasts-in-the-mist-the-mapinguari/. October 24, 2005.

———. "Bio of Craig Woolheater." http://cryptomundo.com/craigwoolheater/. 2014.

"World's 'Ugliest Woman' Julia Pastrana Buried 150 Years On." http://www.bbc.com/news/world-latin-america-21440400. February 13, 2013.

Yapp, Nate. "The Ape (1940)." http://classic-horror.com/reviews/ape_1940. October 30, 2006.

Young, Bob. "Lovable Trickster Created a Monster with Bigfoot Hoax." http://community.seattletimes.nwsource.com/archive/?date=2002 1205&slug=raywallaceobit 05m. December 5, 2002.

INDEX

Note: (ill.) indicates photos and illustrations.

A

Aberdeen, Scotland, 49
Abkhazia, Russia, 343
The Abominable Snowman, 1–4, 2 (ill.), 160
Abominable Snowman. See also Yeti
  The Abominable Snowman, 2–3
  Bryan Sykes and the, 285–87
  Eric Shipton, 254, 256
  India's cryptid apes, 119
  invisibility, 127
  London Underground Yetis, 160
  The Long Walk, 163
  loping ape-man of Tenboche Monastery, 163
  Lt. Col. C. K. Howard-Bury Yeti encounter, 114
  orange-red-colored Sasquatch, 208
  Orang-pendek of Sumatra, 209
  Russian ape-man investigations, 249
  Scottish Bigfoot, 252
  The Snow Creature, 271–72
  Yeren of China, 334
  Yeti of the Himalayas, 337–38
Academy of Sciences, 131
Achba, Prince D. M., 341
Adair, Melissa, 122
The Addams Family, 267
Afghanistan, 219, 270
Africa, 147, 165, 343–44
Africa, East, 15, 141, 191
Africa, West, 253
Agassiz, Canada, 57
Agatha Christie, 259
Agogwes, 191
Aguilar, Salvador, 233
Air Force, 76, 140–41, 155, 256

Alabama, 4–5, 43
Alaska
  canal creature of, 46–48
  Cougar Lake wild men, 57
  eskimo legends of mighty man-beasts, 72
  Kushtaka of, 148–49, 150 (ill.)
  Malaspina Glacier Monster, 166 (ill.), 166–67
  twenty-first-century Sasquatch, 297
  water and swimming Bigfoot, 312
Alaska-Yukon Magazine, 166
Albert, Maj. John E., 140
Alberta, Canada, 67, 123, 178, 242
Alebua, Ezekiel, 277
Alexander the Great, 5 (ill.), 5–7
Alexander the Great (Robson), 5
Algonquin people, 316–17
aliens
  bridge-based encounters, 40
  flying saucers and Bigfoot, 80
  Kelly-Hopkinsville gunfight in the woods, 139–141
  London Underground Yetis, 160
  Native Americans, Bigfoot, and, 195–97
  shug monkey of Rendlesham Forest, 256, 258
  Silent Invasion, 263
  The Six Million Dollar Man, 265–67
  Venezuela's hairy dwarves, 303–4
Allen, Benedict, 210
Allen, Betty, 174
Alley, J. Robert, 167
Alligator Lake, 57
Almas, 248
Almasty

Bryan Sykes and the Abominable Snowman, 287
Canada's cryptid ape-men, 45
eskimo legends of mighty man-beasts, 74
expedition, 7–9
Gigantopithecus blacki, 87
horse-braiding and Bigfoot, 112
Orang-Cooboo and Orang-Googoo, 206
of Russia, 10–13
Russian ape-man investigations, 248
World War II wild men, 330
Zana and the half-human controversy, 341–42
Zana's DNA under the microscope, 343–44
Altaha, Collette, 295
Altered States [movie], 13–14
Altered States (Chayefsky), 13
Altoona, Florida, 268
Amazon, the, 172–73
American Psycho, 198
An American Werewolf in London, 161
Amman Valley, 222
Ammanford, Wales, 221
Amomongo, 232–33
Among the Himalayas (Waddell), 337
The Anabis of Alexander (Arrian), 5
ancestral memories of giant apes, 14–16
ancient encounters, Woodwose and, 328–330, 329 (ill.)
Anderson, Alvin, 42
Anderson, Richard, 266
Andes, the, 71, 112
Andre the Giant, 266
Anfalov, Anton A., 11
Animal Ghosts (O'Donnell), 28

ALSO FROM VISIBLE INK PRESS

Alien Mysteries, Conspiracies, and Cover-Ups
by Kevin D. Randle
ISBN: 978-1-57859-418-4

Angels A to Z, 2nd edition by Evelyn Dorothy Oliver and James R Lewis
ISBN: 978-1-57859-212-8

Armageddon Now: The End of the World A to Z
by Jim Willis and Barbara Willis
ISBN: 978-1-57859-168-8

The Astrology Book: The Encyclopedia of Heavenly Influences, 2nd edition by James R Lewis
ISBN: 978-1-57859-144-2

Conspiracies and Secret Societies: The Complete Dossier, 2nd edition
by Brad Steiger and Sherry Hansen Steiger
ISBN: 978-1-57859-368-2

The Dream Encyclopedia, 2nd edition
by James R Lewis and Evelyn Dorothy Oliver
ISBN: 978-1-57859-216-6

The Encyclopedia of Religious Phenomena
by J. Gordon Melton
ISBN: 978-1-57859-209-8

The Fortune-Telling Book: The Encyclopedia of Divination and Soothsaying
by Raymond Buckland
ISBN: 978-1-57859-147-3

Hidden Realms, Lost Civilizations, and Beings from Other Worlds
by Jerome Clark
ISBN: 978-1-57859-175-6

Real Aliens, Space Beings, and Creatures from Other Worlds,
by Brad Steiger and Sherry Hansen Steiger
ISBN: 978-1-57859-333-0

Real Encounters, Different Dimensions, and Otherworldly Beings
by Brad Steiger with Sherry Hansen Steiger
ISBN: 978-1-57859-455-9

Real Ghosts, Restless Spirits, and Haunted Places, 2nd edition
by Brad Steiger
ISBN: 978-1-57859-401-6

Real Miracles, Divine Intervention, and Feats of Incredible Survival
by Brad Steiger and Sherry Hansen Steiger
ISBN: 978-1-57859-214-2

Real Monsters, Gruesome Critters, and Beasts from the Darkside
by Brad Steiger and Sherry Hansen Steiger
ISBN: 978-1-57859-220-3

Real Vampires, Night Stalkers, and Creatures from the Darkside
by Brad Steiger
ISBN: 978-1-57859-255-5

Real Zombies, the Living Dead, and Creatures of the Apocalypse,
by Brad Steiger
ISBN: 978-1-57859-296-8

The Religion Book: Places, Prophets, Saints, and Seers
by Jim Willis
ISBN: 978-1-57859-151-0

The Spirit Book: The Encyclopedia of Clairvoyance, Channeling, and Spirit Communication
by Raymond Buckland
ISBN: 978-1-57859-172-5

Unexplained! Strange Sightings, Incredible Occurrences, and Puzzling Physical Phenomena, 3rd edition
by Jerome Clark
ISBN: 978-1-57859-344-6

The Vampire Book: The Encyclopedia of the Undead, 3rd edition
by J. Gordon Melton
ISBN: 978-1-57859-281-4

The Werewolf Book: The Encyclopedia of Shape-Shifting Beings, 2nd edition
by Brad Steiger
ISBN: 978-1-57859-367-5

The Witch Book: The Encyclopedia of Witchcraft, Wicca, and Neo-paganism
by Raymond Buckland
ISBN: 978-1-57859-114-5

"Real Nightmares" E-Books by Brad Steiger

Book 1: True and Truly Scary Unexplained Phenomenon

Book 2: The Unexplained Phenomena and Tales of the Unknown

Book 3: Things That Go Bump in the Night

Book 4: Things That Prowl and Growl in the Night

Book 5: Fiends That Want Your Blood

Book 6: Unexpected Visitors and Unwanted Guests

Book 7: Dark and Deadly Demons

Book 8: Phantoms, Apparitions, and Ghosts

Please visit us at visibleinkpress.com.